Pickett's Charge: Eyewitness Accounts

Pickett's Charge:

Eyewitness Accounts

Edited by Richard Rollins

Rank and File Publications
1994

ISBN #0-9638993-0-9 (Softcover)
ISBN #0-9638993-1-7 (Hardcover)

Library of Congress Catalog Card Number
93-87643

First printing: 1994
Revised: 1996

Printed in the United States on recycled, acid-free paper

Cover design by Kenneth Hammond

No one man can tell the story of Pickett's charge

The author being in the ranks in this charge situated so as to see and know what occurred and how, and because none of my regimental comrades have written of it, because as Historian and commissioned to tell something of the thrilling scenes connected with this unparalleled and world renown charge are my reasons for recounting some of the incidents seen and realized in the last act of that bloody drama on the fields of Gettysburg, July 3rd, 1863.

--Private Ralph O. Sturtevant, 13th Vermont

You know Sir, how little an officer with a small command, devoted to the work at hand, will trouble himself with general operations, and really knows nothing but what takes place around him. We were in a hot place for shot came from all directions. . . . Those days were full of horrible sights: the night after the great charge was unearthly from the cries of the wounded who could not be cared for: the air was full of groans and prayers; we had supper with the dead all about us; yet in all these sickening scenes there was, I think no hatred; the malice and rascality engendered by the war is at the rear. There is a certain mutual respect among those who accept the wager of battle. . . . In the presence of such tremendous issues men thought in a way that affected their whole future. No man can begin to tell the whole story of such a conflict, for more than earthly powers were engaged in it.

--Captain S. C. Armstrong, 125th New York

Table of Contents

Section I. "It Was Not Ordered Without Mature Consideration": Planning The Charge

Section II. "They Would Have Made The Charge Without An Officer Of Any Description": Preparing For The Charge

Section III. "It Seemed That Death Was In Every Foot Of Space": The Cannonade

Section IV. "Everything Was A Wild Kaleidoscopic Whirl": The Charge of Pickett's Division

Section V: "Great Praise Is Due The Enlisted Men": The Federal Left

Section VI. "The Colors Were Planted On The Works": The Charge of Pettigrew's and Trimble's Divisions

Section VII. "Our Artillery . . . Saved The Day And Won The Victory": The Federal Right

Acknowledgments

I thank all the following individuals and organizations for giving permission to publish the following items. Ayer Company for *Soldier of the South: General Pickett's War Letters to His Wife*; Regional/Genealogical Publishing Company for quotations from Maud Carter Clement, *The History of Pittsylvania County Virginia*; Pennsylvania Historical and Museum Commission for Frank Haskell's "Gettysburg;" Special Collections Library, Duke University for A. N. Jones to W. Fry, July 5, 1863, Joseph Mayo to Charles Pickett, July 25, 1863, and W. W. Bentley to W. T. Fry, July 9, 1863, in the George Edward Pickett Papers; Colgate University Library and Edmonston Publishing, Inc. for quotations from Thomas Ward Osborn, *The Eleventh Corps Artillery at Gettysburg. The Papers of Major Thomas Ward Osborn*; New Hampshire Historical Society for Tully McCrea to John Bachelder, 30 March 1904 and Anthony McDermott to John Bachelder, no date, Bachelder Papers; Vermont Historical Society for Wheelock Veazey to G. G. Benedict, 11 July 1864; Mississippi State Archives for William Peel's Diary; Frank Yates of Richmond for Henry T. Owen to Col. H. A. Carrington, January 27, 1878; Mr. William Walker of Mandeville, Louisiana for David Johnston's untitled essay; Museum of the Confederacy for Report of Col. R. M. Mayo, August 14, 1863; Gettysburg National Military Park for Augustin Parsons to ?, June 2, 1889, excerpts from the Diary of Walter A. Van Rensselaer, Gulian Weir, "Recollections of the 3d day at Gettysburg with Battery C", and J. L. Kemper to W. H. Swallow, February 4, 1886; Minnesota Historical Society for Daniel Bond, "Bond Recollections"; University of Virginia for Erasmus Williams to John Daniels, no date, John Daniels Papers; North Carolina State Archives for Louis S. Young to William J. Baker, February 10, 1864, Francis Winston Papers; Virginia Historical Society for James Hodges Walker's essay; Maryland Historical Society for Isaac Trimble's diary in *Maryland Historical Magazine*.

In a sense, this book is a product of the Civil War Round Table of Long Beach, of which I have been a member for several years, and President for the last five years. It is a friendly, interesting and helpful group, and many of them have contributed to this effort in various ways. Since I might forget someone if I started naming individuals, I'll just say "thanks" to each and every member.

Steve Madden, George Otott, and Jim Stanbery read each and every word of this book in various drafts, and discussed it with me at length. Their comments ranged from conceptualization to specific details, and helped me clarify issues and avoid stupid mistakes. Harold Bernstein and Ed Franks read and criticized the introduction, and their comments were also very helpful. Every writer and editor needs readers who can criticize, stimulate, and suggest improvements. I can't thank them enough. If this book is a success in any way, it is partially due to their efforts.

Scott Hartwig at the Gettysburg National Military Park Library helped me locate several documents. Some of the research Wayne Motts did for me on the capture of Confederate flags at Gettysburg was useful in this book.

Roy Marcot and Lee Merideth, both of whom have published outstanding books of their own, gave me great guidance in the technical and business aspects of publishing.

Cliff, Peggy, Junie and Ermine Bream opened their homes to me and gave me a wonderful, unforgettable week in Gettysburg and Leesburg. Junie's fresh-water pool provided a spectacular means of cooling off after long days on the battlefield, walking Pickett's Charge from several perspectives. Cliff opened my eyes to see what the Charge looked like from the perspective of Kemper's brigade, and gave me a whole new, and historically more comprehensive, understanding of what happened there.

Much of this book is in part a result of hours of conversation with Dave Shultz. He knows more about Federal artillery on July 3rd than I ever will, and he has taught me much about it. Some day he will publish a superb book on that subject. He worked long and hard drawing the maps included here, and his talents both as an historian and artist enhance this book.

All of the mistakes and errors are my own.

Dedication

In *America Goes To War*, Bruce Catton wrote that:

We are people to whom the past is forever speaking.
We listen to it because we cannot help ourselves, for
the past speaks to us with many voices. Far out of
that dark nowhere which is the time before we were
born, men who were flesh of our flesh and bone of our
bone went through fire and storm to break a path to
the future. We are part of the future they died for;
they are part of the past that bought the future.
What they did--the lives they lived, the sacrifices
they made, the stories they told and the songs they
sang and, finally, the deaths they died--make up a
part of our own experience. We cannot cut ourselves
off from it. It is as real to us as something that
happened last week. It is a basic part of our heritage
as Americans.

The past is indeed forever speaking to us with many voices,
and some of those voices belong to my ancestors.

Nicholas Rawlins (1646-1693), born in England, came to
Massachusetts Bay around 1660 and settled in Newbury, where
successive generations lived until they moved to New Hampshire
and Maine in 1776. During King Phillip's War of 1675-1676 he
served in Col. Samuel Appleton's Regiment, Massachusetts Bay
Militia, taking part in the "swamp fight" in Rhode Island.

His grandson, John Rawlins (1717-?), marched off to fight
the British in 1776, at age 59. He served in several organizations,
including Capt. Jonathan Poor's company, Massachusetts troops,
in March 1777, with his son, David Rolins(1758-?). David also
served in several organizations, including Capt. Paul Moody's
company, Newbury, Mass., minutemen, 1776, as a Private and
musician (fifer).

John Rawlins had six sons, five of whom voluntarily found
their way into the army. My great-great-great-great-grandfather,
Stephen Rollins (1750-1842), not only served with several detachments of militia defending the coast of Maine throughout the war,
but also signed, in July of 1776, a declaration by the citizens of the
town of Bakerstown (now Poland, Maine) that they would serve in
the militia and fund all expenses of the town's defense; in effect,
their own declaration of independence. Benjamin Rollins (1752-
1835), fought with a New Hampshire regiment. John Rollins (1755-
1821) served in Capt. Noyes' company of Newbury militia and stayed

in the army through the siege of Boston. His twin brother, Moses (1755-1777), marched off to Boston with Capt. Jacob Gerrish's company of Newbury minutemen on 19 April, 1775, stayed with the army in Col. Moses Little's regiment and fought at Bunker Hill. In 1776 he moved to New Hampshire and in 1777 joined the 1st New Hampshire regiment. He was killed at Saratoga in October, 1777.

Stephen's son, Moses (1787-?), served in Capt. William B. Bray's company of Massachusetts cavalry during the War of 1812.

At least fifteen of Stephen Rollins' descendants took part in the Civil War. His nephew, John Rollins (1800-1875), volunteered at the age of 62 and served three years in the 37th Iowa, known as "the graybeard regiment" because all the men were 45 or over. John's son William (1834-1863), a member of the 113th Illinois, died of "camp fever" during the Vicksburg campaign. Another son, Thomas Edward Rollins (1843-1902), marched and fought with the 7th Iowa from Shiloh to Atlanta, where he was severely wounded.

My branch of the family moved to Michigan in 1855, and has lived there ever since, around Pentwater, Hart, and Three Rivers. My great-grandfather Albert was too young to join the Federal army, but his brother, George (1838-1904), marched and fought with the 100th Indiana from Vicksburg to the surrender of the remnants of the Army of Tennessee in 1865. George's cousin, Philip Rollins (1842-1870), signed up as a 19 year old private in the 19th Maine, and on July 3rd, 1863, took part in the repulse of Pickett's Charge. As part of Brig. Gen. William Harrow's brigade the 19th Maine helped defend the stone wall south of the Angle, then when Kemper's brigade passed by, made a right wheel and ran up to the Angle, firing as they went. Philip made it through 3 years in the Second Corps without a scratch. Another cousin, Alfred (1820-1914), was not so lucky. He served in the 1st U.S. Sharpshooters, and lost an arm at Chancellorsville.

At least one of Stephen Rollins' great-grandsons went to war in the Army of Northern Virginia. James Gage Rollins (1800-1875), signed up with the 12th Mississippi in 1862, caught a bullet in the arm at Beaver Dam Creek during the Peninsula Campaign of 1862, and went back to Port Gibson to recuperate. While there he became engaged in defending his home when Ulysses S. Grant crossed the Mississippi River there in May, 1863.

"The Theme Of The Poet, Painter And Historian Of All Ages":

Pickett's Charge in Space and Time

An Introduction

Levi Baker, an artilleryman in the 9th Massachusetts Light Artillery, had manned a gun on Cemetery Ridge that day. Years later he would recall that shortly after the charge had been defeated and the Confederates had retreated down the slope and across Emmitsburg Road, he and his comrades knew that they had participated in an event that would become legendary. They wandered down to the Angle, where men were still dying from their wounds, and stood there surrounded by the human wreckage of fierce combat. Near what remained of Lieutenant Alonzo Cushing's battery, they looked over the field and mused about the events of the day: "I recognized then and there that this battle was to be, in all probability, regarded as a great turning point in history," he wrote. "I did not believe the Confederates would ever surpass their efforts on that gory field. The ridge where Cushing went down beside his guns, where the hand to hand conflict took place, is regarded as the high water mark of the Rebellion. . . . "[1]

Baker and his friends were not alone in their realization that they had participated in something that went beyond average experience, even beyond the typical experience of combat. The feeling was widespread that Pickett's Charge had been a significant event, perhaps *the* significant event, in the war. On July 4th, Charles M. Blackford, an adjutant on Lieutenant General James Longstreet's staff, would write to his wife that "they vastly outnumbered us, and though our men made a charge which will be the theme of the poet, painter and historian of all ages, they could not maintain the enemy's lines much less capture them. . . . Our loss in men and officers exceeds anything I have ever known."[2] Three weeks later, a Southern officer who participated in the event referred to it as the "celebrated charge,"[3] and thus recorded the language the men were using in their private conversations to think about and discuss what had happened. As soon as the charge failed, the mythic quality of Pickett's Charge emerged as easily recognizable, and quickly entered a part of America's folk-lore.

The veterans themselves contributed to the legend of Pickett's Charge. For many, it was the highpoint of their time in the army, perhaps even in their lives. After the war, and especially with the rise of the veterans' organizations in the 1880s, they spent much time talking about it, and even writing about it. Much of what they wrote ended up in obscure places, or was never published, and thus is unavailable to the modern reader. This volume is in part an effort to make their accounts of their experiences more available.

Today Pickett's Charge is one of the most celebrated of all American military encounters, ranking with the actions of the minutemen at Lexington and Concord, the incident at Little Big Horn, and the invasion of Europe in 1944. As Blackford predicted, it has come down to us through poetry, painting and historical studies as a riveting moment in time. Indeed, it may well be the most mythic of all American military events: the gallant soldiers of the South, the golden-haired Pickett at their head, bravely walking through shot and shell, led over the wall by the valiant Armistead, only to be beaten back by the stalwart sons of the Union.

While Pickett's Charge has a firm place in American folk-lore, and though at times it seems that every man at Gettysburg on July 3, 1863, left an account of it, surprisingly little secondary scholarship exists. The only full-length, in-depth study of the event is George Stewart's excellent and absorbing *Pickett's Charge: A Microhistory of the Final Assault at Gettysburg, July 3, 1863*, published over thirty years ago.[4] Kathy Georg-Harrison's *Nothing But Glory: Pickett's Division At Gettysburg*, is equally impressive, but covers only that fraction of the battle experienced by the men of Pickett's division.[5] Single chapters in the works of Glenn Tucker, Edwin Coddington, and Douglas S. Freeman all concentrate on various aspects of the charge.[6] It is the nature of historical narrative to concentrate on the story, not on the individual, and thus much is left out of even the best work by any historian. Furthermore, it is often the case that, in telling the historically significant aspects of the battle, an author emphasizes the important decisions of the leaders, not the experiences of the rank and file. This compilation of individual experiences is therefore a supplement to those works, not an attempt to replace them.

As it unfolded, Pickett's Charge had virtually no chance of success. Major General George Gordon Meade and his subordinates had well prepared their defensive position. With over 150 guns lined up between Cemetery Hill and Little Round Top, and many more available in the Artillery Reserve, and elements of the 1st, 5th, 6th, 11th and 12th corps available as reinforcements, the Federal position was likely secure.

However, Pickett's Charge was certainly neither conceived nor planned to be as ineffective as it became, and therein lies a significant and somewhat overlooked story. Was General Robert E. Lee so poor a military tactician that he would send his men across that valley, amidst the shot and shell of over 150 cannon and infantry massed behind a stone wall, towards almost certain death?

That long march across the valley—a hallowed essence of the moment—is but an essence only, and not the entire story. Indeed, the larger story and the larger significance is more complicated and confusing than what we usually imagine.

To think of Pickett's Charge solely as a doomed infantry charge is to oversimplify what actually occurred. It ignores the overall conception of the operation and the elements that actually came into play. It blinds us to the important role played by Confederate artillery and cavalry, and perhaps even more importantly, the role of the Federal artillery in the repulse. It narrows our focus to a small section of the field, a few hundred square yards around the Angle. It limits our scope of understanding to a small percentage of the deeds of individuals who saw action in it, all the way from the Rail Road Cut and Oak Hill to Little Round Top, and from the cavalry battlefield to the staging areas west of Seminary Ridge. Pickett's Charge involved all elements of the two armies—infantry, artillery, cavalry—as well as all levels of soldiers, from Lee and Meade at the top to the common foot soldier and even the support elements, including cooks and teamsters.

All who were there sensed the high drama of the moment. During the morning of the 3rd a rumor swept through the Army of Northern Virginia. Lee would send the entire army, or most of it, in a frontal assault all along the line. Colonel E. P. Alexander heard it, and passed it on to Major General George Pickett.[7] Lieutenant General A. P. Hill heard it, went to Lee and "begged General Lee to let me take in my whole Army Corps. He refused, and said what remains of your corps will be my only reserve. . . ."[8]

Many Southerners went into battle thinking that this was the crucial moment of the war. The outcome of the war seemed to hang in the balance. As one participant said:

> . . . From the teamsters to the general in chief it was known that the battle was yet undecided—that the fierce combat was to be renewed. All knew that victory won or defeat suffered, was to be at a fearful cost—that the best blood of the land was to flow copiously as a priceless oblation to the god of battle. The intelligent soldiers of the South knew and profoundly felt that the hours were potential—that on them possibly hung the success of their cause—the peace and independence of the Confederacy.[9]

Pickett's Charge was an event that was shaped by, and is best understood as a result of, two basic factors. First, it is the logical result of the strategic plan of the Confederate invasion of Pennsylvania, as filtered through the specific individuals who organized that campaign: Jefferson Davis, Robert E. Lee and the political leadership of the Confederacy. Second, on the level of battlefield tactics, it was a logical extension of the events of July 1 and 2, 1863.

On the strategic level the planning of Pickett's Charge started not on July 2nd, but back in Richmond in May. After the victory at Chancellorsville the leadership of the Confederacy discussed their overall Grand Strategy. Should they concentrate on another campaign in the east, or send troops to the western theater to help defeat Grant at Vicksburg or Rosecrans in Tennessee?[10] At a meeting in Richmond with Secretary of War James Seddon on May 6, Lieutenant General James Longstreet suggested sending two of his divisions west, and Seddon and President Jefferson Davis liked the idea. Four days later Lee telegraphed his view to Seddon. He opposed the idea: it probably wouldn't help in the West and it exposed his army to an attack by a much greater force. Lee pointed out that it might in fact end up with the Confederacy losing in both theaters. He apparently convinced Longstreet of his views, for on the 13th Longstreet wrote to a Confederate Senator: "When I agreed with [Seddon] and yourself about sending troops west it was under the impression that we would be obliged to remain on the defensive here. But the prospect of an advance changes the aspect of affairs."[11] Two days later Lee met in person with Seddon and Davis and presented his idea for an alternative plan: invade Pennsylvania and inflict a crushing defeat on the Federal army on their own ground.

The campaign plans lacked a clear focus, but Davis and Lee hoped, from the beginning, that it would achieve in some way a significant military victory that would have far-ranging political effects, including the possibility of an end to the war itself. It might result in a defensive battle, like Fredericksburg, or an offensive one, like Chancellorsville. Perhaps a successful invasion, with no battle but maneuvers threatening Philadelphia, Baltimore, Washington and New York, would be enough. The invasion would coincide with a trip north by Vice President Alexander Stephens, who left Richmond on July 3rd, bound for Washington and negotiations with the Lincoln administration. Machinations were underway in France and England to secure political recognition from the European powers.[12] On the march north Lee wrote to Davis urging him not to reject any peace feelers, and to take advantage of any negotiations. With peace negotiations under way, "the war would no longer be supported" in the North, "and that after all is what we are interested in bringing about."[13]

Robert E. Lee has come down to us as a man with a singular military outlook, one who kept above politics. This is far from accurate, for Lee was involved in nearly all significant political

decisions after his rise to command of the Army of Northern Virgi
in 1862. The Gettysburg campaign would be a perfect example of
Von Clausewitz's dictum that military action is an extension of
diplomacy: Lee meant to achieve political ends by military means.
On June 27, he told Major General Isaac Trimble of his plans for the
forthcoming battle. When the Army of the Potomac followed him
into Pennsylvania, he said, "I shall throw an overwhelming force on
their advance, crush it, follow up the success, drive one corps back
on another, and by successive repulses and surprises . . . create a
panic and virtually destroy the army. . . . [Then] the war will be over
and we shall achieve the recognition of our independence."[14] Colonel Eppa Hunton of the 8th Virginia spent half an hour talking with
Lee as they rode in front of Brigadier General Richard B. Garnett's
brigade on the road into Pennsylvania. Hunton expressed doubts
about the campaign, but Lee replied that the invasion would be a
great success, and if so, "would end the war. . . ."[15]

After Second Manassas, Fredericksburg and Chancellorsville, the defeated Army of the Potomac had simply walked back to
Washington and reorganized. Thus these were hollow victories,
essentially without significant political results. At Gettysburg on
July 2nd and 3rd, Longstreet would suggest a flank movement
followed by a defensive posture. Lee firmly and repeatedly rejected
this maneuver. To his way of thinking, that could only lead to more
bloody and indecisive combat. Lee wanted none of that here in
Pennsylvania. He wanted to win, and win big. Robert E. Lee did not
march into Pennsylvania to win another useless battle.

Historian James McPherson, in his pulitzer-prize winning
book *Battle Cry of Freedom*, summed up the concept that was to
govern the campaign:

> The invasion of Pennsylvania would remove the
> enemy threat on the Rappahannock, take the armies
> out of war-ravaged Virginia, and enable Lee to feed
> his troops in the enemy's country. *It would also
> strengthen Peace Democrats, discredit Republicans,
> reopen the question of foreign recognition, and per-
> haps even conquer peace and recognition from the
> Union government itself.*[16] [emphasis added]

All of this was in Lee's mind as the battle opened. He may
not have gone into Pennsylvania to precipitate an offensively
aggressive fight, but by the end of July 2nd, all the elements were
in place. He was supremely confident of his men; he believed the
center of the Federal line to be Meade's weak point. Pickett's Charge,
coming after two days of indecisive but bloody combat reminiscent
of previous battles, would be one final attempt to break the Federal

lines and destroy the Army of the Potomac.

On the tactical level, the specific elements of Pickett's Charge began taking shape on the evening of July 2nd and continued to evolve in the minds of Lee and his subordinates until the charge took place. The military operation, as conceived on the evening of the 2nd, changed considerably on the morning of the 3rd. During its execution, several of its major components failed, were altered by the events of the moment, or never took place. The result was an attack that varied significantly from what was planned, or what Lee ordered.

Lee's official report is explicit. Every word is significant and must be carefully considered. He believed his army had done reasonably well through the first two days of the battle. The plan on the 2nd had been to attack up the Emmitsburg Road toward the town of Gettysburg. On the 3rd, he stated, *"the general plan was unchanged:"*

> The result of the day's operations induced the belief that, *with proper concert of action,* and with the increased support that the positions gained on the right would enable the artillery to render the assaulting columns, we should ultimately succeed, and it was accordingly determined *to continue the attack.* [17] [emphasis added]

Longstreet's corps, including all three divisions commanded by McLaws, Hood, and Pickett, "was ordered to attack the next morning, and General Ewell was directed to assail the enemy's right at the same time." Lee went on to say that "General Longstreet's dispositions were not completed as early as was expected . . . ."[18] Longstreet and Lee normally tented near each other, and it was Longstreet's habit to ride to Lee's tent at the end of a days' fighting and discuss matters with Lee. He did not do so on July 2nd, and one can easily imagine Lee waiting for him until he went to sleep or until he thought it was too late to talk.

Longstreet says he was not ordered on July 2nd to attack early on the 3rd.[19] The weight of historical evidence strongly suggests otherwise. Perhaps the courier did not reach him with the order. Perhaps Longstreet was so emotionally opposed to the charge that he simply denied the existence of the order. One doubts that Robert E. Lee would officially report that, on the evening of the 2nd, he had ordered Longstreet to attack early on the 3rd, if he had not actually done so. In addition, we know that Lieutenant General Richard Ewell, commander of the Second Corps on the far left of the Confederate line in front of Culp's Hill, received orders to move at dawn on the 3rd.[20]

Brigadier General William N. Pendleton, Chief of Artillery, stated he had received orders from Lee that the artillery of all three corps were to prepare for opening, "as early as possible . . . a concentrated and destructive fire, consequent upon which a general advance was to be made."[21]   Colonel E. P. Alexander, who commanded Longstreet's artillery during the charge, had received orders and was placing guns at 3 o'clock in the morning.[22]

Together these reports signify that Lee's plan on the evening of July 2nd was for an artillery barrage to precede a morning attack by Longstreet's corps, timed to coincide with Ewell's advance, which was designed to distract the Federal right and tie down reinforcements.

On the morning of the 3rd the Federals attacked the Confederates on Ewell's front just past daybreak, and thus ruined the idea of coordinating attacks. When Lee and Longstreet met in the morning it was already too late for an early attack. After a long discussion during which they rode up and down the lines and peered through glasses at the Federal position, Longstreet tried to convince Lee to flank the Federals rather than attack head-on, but Lee decided to renew the attack up the Emmitsburg Road to the center of the Federal line.

The plan as it evolved during the morning of the 3rd was not a simple infantry charge against a strong position. It was instead a complicated plan involving infantry, artillery and cavalry, a "combined operation" in modern military jargon. Unfortunately, no member of the high command of the Army of Northern Virginia chose to describe it in all its particulars. In the only significant written comment Lee would make after the war, he remarked that victory would have been gained in the Pennsylvania campaign if "one determined and united blow [could] have been delivered by our whole line."[23] That characterization, though it is cryptic and much must be read into it, is as good a definition of Pickett's Charge as any left by those who commanded it.

Since not one of the men involved in the conceptualization of the charge left a concise account of all the elements of the plan and how they were to have worked in coordination, we are left to piece it together. Adjutant James Crocker of the 9th Virginia in Armistead's brigade, who was wounded in the charge and spent the rest of his life believing that the charge had failed in execution, not in conceptualization, did describe it in nearly modern terms. Crocker spent a good deal of time after the war studying the battle, corresponding and talking with other veterans, and writing about it. He summarized it as follows:

> It was to be made in the morning—presumably in the
> early morning—with the whole of Longstreet's corps,

composed of the divisions of Pickett, McLaws and
Hood, together with Heth's division, two brigades of
Pender and Wilcox's brigade, and that the assaulting
column was to advance under the cover of the
combined artillery fire of three corps, and that the
assault was to be the combined assault of infantry
and artillery—the batteries to be pushed forward as
the infantry progressed, to protect their flanks and
support their attack closely. The attack was not
made as here ordered.[24]

Add to Crocker's outline the participation of Stuart's cavalry
and the support of the brigades of Brigadier General Ambrose
Wright and Brigadier General Carnot Posey in Major General
Richard Anderson's division of Hill's corps, and a full outline of the
plan of the charge begins to emerge.

The artillery must achieve a key objective: it must subdue
the Federal artillery all along the line, from the "rocky hill," as Little
Round Top was known, to Cemetery Hill. Some batteries would
move forward to support the advance, firing from spots just ahead
of the infantry to keep up the pressure on the Federal artillery on the
ridge. This would include not just the guns of Longstreet's corps,
but those of Hill's and Ewell's corps as well. Batteries as far east as
Benner's Hill and as far north as the ten rifled pieces near the Rail
Road Cut along the Chambersburg Road, would be involved.[25] This
was such an important goal that Lee got nearly his entire artillery
involved. Of the 51 batteries of artillery in the Army of Northern
Virginia on July 3rd, only six did not participate in the cannonade
or charge. To put it another way, 88% of Lee's batteries became
involved in the cannonade, the charge, or both.[26]

The infantry would consist of nearly two-thirds of the entire
Army. The charge would consist of an advance by Pickett, supported
by the divisions of Major Generals Henry Heth and William Pender,
of Hill's corps. The latter two were wounded on July 1st, and
replaced by Major Generals Johnston Pettigrew and Isaac Trimble.
Critical to its success would be support from Anderson's division of
Hill's corps, which was supposed to advance when the attack
succeeded. The brigades of Brigadier General Cadmus Wilcox and
Colonel David Lang would follow Pickett on the right flank. In
addition, Anderson had Brigadier General Ambrose Wright's and
Brigadier General Carnot Posey's brigades ready to support the
breakthrough.[27] Longstreet would have Major General Lafayette
McLaws' division in place ready to follow up.[28] Finally, just north of
the Bliss property and roughly half-way between Seminary Ridge
and Cemetery Ridge would be four additional brigades, under the
commands of Brigadier General Edward Thomas and Colonel Abner

Perrin of Pender's division, and Brigadier Generals George Doles and Steven Ramseur of Major General Robert Rodes' division in Ewell's corps. They would be within easy striking distance if needed.

It is a measure of Lee's determination to achieve a smashing victory that he probably ordered the infantry to utilize a specific tactic: the bayonet charge. This maneuver, which a recent military historian characterized as a "shock attack," was designed not to kill the opposing infantry (though much of that would necessarily occur), but to shock and disorganize them.[29] It would do what Lee had told Trimble he planned to do: "create a panic and virtually destroy the army."

A bayonet charge entailed several elements. The troops would be instructed to fix bayonets on their rifles and move rapidly toward the enemy. They would be told to hold their fire until very close to the enemy's lines, thus ensuring both a greater effectiveness of fire and developing a psychological element in surprising their opponents. They would be instructed to yell when they got close, thus causing more fear. Finally, they would break the enemy's lines, and, with support troops coming up behind them, clear the area and destroy the enemy's lines.

The bayonet charge was a tactic well known to military leaders on both sides. It had been taught at West Point, and used in the Mexican War. It had been used successfully by both sides in previous battles, most notably by John Bell Hood's brigade at Gaines' Mill during the Peninsula campaign in 1862. Hood had led his troops to the Federal lines, yelling "don't halt here! Forward! Forward! Charge right down on them and drive them out with the bayonet!" Indeed Hood had become famous, and won promotion to division command for his skill and leadership in this type of attack. As Paddy Griffith has said, "the aim [of the bayonet charge] was to get close, break into the defender's carefully prepared firing line and then exploit the confusion which followed."[30]

This maneuver required an inordinate amount of self-control for the Civil War soldier. The typical battle consisted largely of two relatively static opposing lines firing at each other. Later in the war, as the use of earthworks and fortifications became wide-spread, battles became even more static. Moreover, the bayonet charge required men to hold their fire while running into the face of direct fire from both musketry and cannon. They had to control their fears: "it took exceptional leadership, or exceptionally high quality soldiers, to make the system work." Lee's supreme confidence in his men is revealed in a letter he wrote to John Bell Hood in May. "I agree with you in believing that our army would be invincible if it could be properly organized and officered," said Lee. "There never were such men in an army before. They will go anywhere and do anything if properly led." Men of this calibre could carry Cemetery Ridge in a bayonet charge.[31]

Longstreet's men had used the bayonet charge before, and Lee no doubt missed Hood, who had been wounded on July 2nd. It was a calculated risk, but Lee had been successful before with unorthodox tactics, and he was determined to win a major victory on July 3rd. As Griffith said, "the essence of shock tactics was the deliberate acceptance of a higher risk in order to achieve a more decisive result."[32]   Robert E. Lee was just the man to take such a risk. In the recesses of his mind Lee may have remembered the words written to him by Secretary of War James Seddon on June 10th, words that Lee probably read somewhere in Pennsylvania. As his superior, Seddon had urged Lee to take "some risk to promote the grand results that may be attained by your successful operations."[33]

Lee's plan hinged partially on reinforcements following Pickett's men. Wilcox's and Lang's brigades did step off toward the ridge, but were too little, too late, and without clear directions of where they were supposed to go. Anderson had Wright's and Posey's brigades in motion, but upon Longstreet's order, pulled them back.[34] Longstreet himself says that the "divisions of McLaws and Hood were ordered to move to closer lines . . . to spring to the charge as soon as the breach at the centre could be made." He added that "the general order required further assistance from the Third Corps if needed. . ." and that "McLaws was ordered to press his left forward. . . ."[35] Though no exact count can be made, it is clear that plans for throwing fresh troops into the breach made by Pickett did exist.

Finally, Lee's plan included a key role for the cavalry, the heretofore missing Stuart. Reinforced by Jenkins' brigade, Stuart would circle around to the rear of the Federal position on Cemetery Hill, and either cut off a Federal retreat, or attack the vulnerable rear of the Army of the Potomac as Pickett's Charge hit the front.[36] Thus, all three elements of the Army of Northern Virginia, and all three infantry corps, would be involved.

But of course Pickett's Charge did not concern only the Army of Northern Virginia. On the evening of July 2 it was apparent to Meade and his officers that battle would resume on the next day. They were satisfied, as Longstreet knew they would be, to let Lee dictate, by and large, what would happen. But they did begin planning their defense on the evening of the second, and did not stop until after the repulse. Their plans included preparation by all the infantry corps on the field, as well as the artillery and cavalry.[37] Thus, on the Federal side as well as the Confederate side, Pickett's Charge was not a static, set-piece, but a military operation that evolved over time.

Today we stand at the Angle and look straight across the valley to the Virginia monument. We like to imagine the Confederates emerging from the woods at that point. In fact, that was an artillery and support area: no infantry emerged from there and marched straight across to the Angle. The left flank of Pickett's division came out 100 to 200 yards south, and the right flank of the Pettigrew—Trimble line was about 100 yards north of that spot. The right flank of Pickett's line was nearly a mile south, on the other side of the Spangler farm; the left of Pettigrew and Trimble, over a half mile north. In addition, these distances are measured in a straight line. The ground covered by Pickett's Charge is not flat, and thus the lengths they marched are slightly longer than the measurements given here.

The rolling nature of the land is significant and must not be overlooked. It played an important part in the memories of the eyewitnesses. If one walks from the Virginia monument to the Angle today, using the path marked out by the Park, the land appears more or less level. But if one walks from the swale south of the Spangler farm, where Brigadier General James Kemper's brigade on the right of Pickett's division stepped off, to the Emmitsburg Road and then to the Angle, one will find three swales from which neither Cemetery Ridge nor the left of the Confederate line can be seen. And if one walks from where the left of the Pettigrew-Trimble line stepped off to the Angle, the same phenomena will be observed. There are two swales, one west of the Bliss barn and one east of the Bliss barn, from which neither Cemetery Ridge nor the right of the Confederate line can be seen. This probably explains some, and perhaps most, of the numerous Confederate accounts of the charge in which an author recalls being unable to see Confederate troops to their right or left.

From one perspective, Pickett's Charge was made by two separate wings, designed to come together at the Angle. Pickett's division, the main attack force, came not across the valley from the Virginia monument area, but from the south-west, moving in a north-easterly direction. The right of Kemper's brigade brushed the Klingle house, several hundred yards south of the Codori barn, and crossed Emmitsburg Road in that vicinity. They marched almost due north, through the Plum Run valley and up the Emmitsburg Road, their line being broken by the Codori farm. They made a left oblique near Plum Run. It is possible that some of the men in Kemper's brigade may have crossed the Emmitsburg Road a second time, and then a third time as they charged up the slope to the stone wall, though no documentation of this exists. The Pettigrew-Trimble wing moved south-east from Seminary Ridge, across the Bliss property.

The area covered by the Confederate infantry during the charge formed a trapezoid. It extended along Seminary Ridge from the MacMillan house to the swale on the south side of the Spangler farm, a distance of 2,000 yards; from the swale to the stone wall, some 1500 yards; and from the stone wall to the MacMillan house, a distance of 1,333 yards. The stretch of the Federal line they hit, along the stone wall from the Brian barn south to just past the copse of trees, is about 450 yards. The total ground covered is approximately 1/2 of a square mile.[38]

When one considers the artillery action associated with the charge, the area expands dramatically. The operation demanded, and received, the attention and cooperation of Confederate artillery batteries in all three corps, including the artillery reserve of each corps. Hill's artillery reserve, north of the Chambersburg Road on Oak Hill, had two Whitworth rifles, the most accurate long-range weapons available to the South. They enfiladed the Federal artillery and infantry on Cemetery Ridge.[39] Guns in the artillery reserve of Ewell's corps, located on Benner's Hill some 2,500 yards east and north of Cemetery Ridge, fired on the Federal artillery and successfully enfiladed the line. Major Thomas Osborn, commander of the Federal 11th corps artillery on Cemetery Hill, described the initial effectiveness of the fire from their rear:

> The fire from our west front had progressed 15 to 20 minutes when several guns opened on us from the ridge beyond East Cemetery Hill. The line of fire from these last batteries, and the line of fire from the batteries on our west front, were such as to leave the town between the two lines of fire. These last guns opened directly on the right flank of my line of batteries. The gunners got our range at almost the first shot.
>
> Passing low over Wainright's guns they caught us square in flank and with the elevation perfect. It was admirable shooting. They raked the whole line of batteries, killed and wounded the men and horses, and blew up the caissons rapidly. I saw one shell go through six horses standing broadside.[40]

On the southern end of the field, Federal guns on Little Round Top, a distance of some 3 miles from the Whitworths, fired on Pickett's men.

Pickett's Charge also covered the ground from the staging and hospital areas west of Seminary Ridge to the East Cavalry Battlefield, a distance of some 3 or 4 miles. It certainly gained the attention of, and occupied the minds of, nearly all of the 150,000 men involved in the armies, their support elements, as well as citizens of Gettysburg. Thus, the space occupied by Pickett's Charge is significantly greater than the area between Seminary and

Cemetery Ridges.

The question of time in Pickett's Charge poses a fascinating and significant problem. First, standardized time was not introduced in the United States until long after the war was over. During the war each individual based his sense of time by whatever measurement he chose. For many it was the watch of a comrade; for others, the chiming of the village clock or church bells. This meant that there were often significant discrepancies among battle reports and other accounts of an activity. It has long been the common belief that the cannonade began at about 1:00 p.m., and ended two hours later. Today that would be from 2:00 until 4:00, since modern Daylight Saving Time is one hour ahead of standard time. In addition, 1:00 p. m. to one individual might be 1:30, 2:00 or even 3:00 to another. For example, Brigadier General Robert O. Tyler, commanding the Artillery Reserve of the Army of the Potomac, said the cannonade began at 12 o'clock and continued until after 3. p. m.[41] Colonel Theodore B. Gates, in charge of the 80th New York Infantry south of the copse of trees, reported the artillery beginning at 12:30.[42] Captain Emmanuel D. Roath, 107th Pennsylvania, said it began at 1:30.[43] Colonel Thomas Smyth of the 1st Delaware Infantry of Brigadier General Alexander Hays' brigade, whose troops were behind the wall north of the inner angle, reported that the cannonade began at 2:00 and "continued without intermission until 5 p.m."[44] Captain Patrick Hart, 15th New York battery in McGilvery's line near the present location of the Pennsylvania monument, remembered that the cannonade ended and the charge began at 5:00 p.m.[45]

Second, for most of the men who were there, time as we know it disappeared during Pickett's Charge. The stress of combat gave time a subjective, elastic quality. Their intellectual and psychological faculties were so focused on the task at hand that, for some of the men, time halted all together, while for others it stretched out into infinity. As one private said, "every moment was so appalling and the horrid scenes all about us so dreadful we took no thought of swift passing time."[46] Brigadier General John Gibbon, who commanded the division of the 2nd corps defending the Angle, understood this and had this to say about time and the cannonade preceding Pickett's Charge: "How long did this pandemonium last? Measured by our feelings it might have been an age. In point of fact it may have been an hour or three or five. The measurement of time under such circumstances, regular as it is by the watch, is exceedingly uncertain by the watchers."[47] Lieutenant Tully McCrea, in Woodruff's battery on Cemetery Ridge, remembered this sensation for the rest of his life. Writing in 1904, he recalled that "the Artillery fire of the enemy, which I have since learned lasted two hours, but which seemed to me to have lasted two days, suddenly ceased. . . ."[48]

This subjective quality of time must be remembered when reading eyewitness events of Pickett's Charge. Too much reliance upon a writer's statement of time can mislead the reader.

A note should be added about the documents included in this collection, and the reasons for choosing them. George Stewart culled through some 450 eyewitness accounts in writing his book. I have looked at nearly all of the items he cited, as well as of those cited by authors who have written since 1959. I have even been fortunate enough to find a few that were apparently unavailable to previous students of the Charge. During this research I looked at regimental histories, memoirs, the *Southern Historical Society Papers,* the *War of the Rebellion,* (commonly referred to as the *Official Records,* or simply the *OR*), *Confederate Veteran,* the various papers published by the state branches of the Military Order of the Loyal Legion of the United States, and many others. I have also examined collections of documents in the Gettysburg National Military Park, Queen's University in Kingston, Ontario, the University of Virginia, Duke University, Virginia Historical Society, Virginia State Library, The University of North Carolina, and the Huntington Library in San Marino, California.

The documents are presented in a certain order. Confederates are first, since they were the aggressors. With a few exceptions, the documents are presented in order of the rank of the author at the time of the battle, highest being first. On occasion I have placed an account by a lower ranking individual in advance of its natural place, usually because it is an account of the actions of a higher ranking person. I began with the intention of identifying each and every individual mentioned by name in each document, but soon gave it up. It would have taken years to complete.

This collection could easily be several times its current length. The job of choosing what to include and exclude was not an easy one. I used several criteria in selecting items. First, the ability of a text, in conjunction with the rest of the documents included herein, to tell the story of the charge as fully as possible, as we know it today. Second, a document generally must have a level of specificity of content. The more personal it is, the better, and an effort was made to include a diversity of experiences, from general officers to individual privates and newspaper reporters. Third, preference is given to those that tell the story of the common soldier. Fourth, a document that is written shortly after the battle is preferable to one written decades later, for obvious reasons. Fifth, an effort was made to assure authenticity of the text. The only items included that have any significant doubt associated with them are the letters from George Pickett. In that case I have included a short statement about the debate over their authenticity and directions on how to look into that particular question a little further. I felt that their extraordinary content demanded inclusion. Finally, I have included the relevant passages from the "classics" of Pickett's Charge: the essays written by Frank Haskell, Edwin Porter Alexander, and James Longstreet.

It may help the reader to look at an account not included. Captain George K. Griggs, Co. K, 38th Virginia, Armistead's brigade, kept a diary. It has some interesting features, but ultimately failed the six-part test:

> Friday 3rd.
> 3 AM ordered forward moved to right of Gettysburg some six miles we formed with the division line battle in front of _____ it rained little in the morning but cleared off very hot.
> 8 P.M. I have just gotten through one of the most terrible ordeals of my life. Thank God I am alive thought I have a severe flesh wound in my right thigh a minnie ball having passed
> Friday. July 3rd 1863.
> Our division charged the enemy across a field about half-mile wide they being behind a rock fence, dirt works & we had no protection had to climb two fences the enemy throwing shell grape & all kind of missiles of death at us, but we moved steadily forward, driving them from their strong position capturing all their guns but we had lost too many to hold our trophies & having no reinforcement & the enemy being on our flanks & rear had to cut our way back. our loss was heavy & do not know now what Col. Edmonds & Capt. Towns are reported killed. Al my Lieuts are wounded 20 of my Co. are wounded & 17 missing. I do not know who is living. I carried 49 muskets in fight. Kind Heavenly Father we would humbly pray Thee to Comfort those who lay wounded from to days work & soon restore them to health go to the many distressed families & enable them to bear their losses without Complaint.[49]

This might be called a "standard account." It lists the precise number of casualties in the company, which is of some importance, but adds little to our understanding of the event. It contains no information about planning, preparation, tactics, nor any specifics about individual experiences. One gets little sense of place or experience. Without the date, it could be a description of almost any engagement during the war.

Some of the authors have made obvious mistakes, such as

estimating the Confederate force at 30,000 men. Others have made less obvious errors. Not wanting to indulge in an ongoing dialog of corrections, I have generally not pointed out all the errors; the reader should beware of taking every word at face value. Some authors contradict others; I leave it to the reader to decide for himself or herself which to believe.

A word needs to be said about the structure of this collection. I considered two different organizational strategies. My original inclination was to treat these essays as literature, and present each one intact, in general order of significance or in rough chronological order. I found that this would present the reader with too much repetition of detail. Instead I have chosen to divide the event of Pickett's Charge into nine categories of experience: the planning of the charge; the preparation for battle on the morning of July 3rd; the cannonade; the Confederate and Federal left and right flanks, the Angle, and some post-battle comments. Thus, the present structure reflects chronological development, Federal and Confederate perspectives, and geographic separation. It does require that some accounts be broken into segments and presented piecemeal in more than one section. On the other hand, some accounts contain a little material that could be included in a section different from the one in which they are first introduced, but in my judgement not enough to stand alone. In such cases, such as Arthur Fremantle's descriptions of Longstreet during the battle, I have included them in the original presentation. There is some overlap, and some repetition. I could find no perfect solution to this problem.

I have generally left the documents as written. Be aware that spelling was far less standardized in the 19th century than it is today. You will see many different spellings of Emmitsburg, as well as other words. I have added [sic] only in the most obvious cases, those in which I felt that if I didn't, the reader would think it was a typographical error.

Finally, I call this action Pickett's Charge because Pickett was the field commander; his division was the spearhead of the attack, and in 1863 and after that is what the participants called it. What to call this event did not become a topic for debate until the controversy between the Virginians and North Carolinians broke out a decade after the war. No diminution of the efforts of the men in the Pettigrew-Trimble line is intended. Likewise the Army of the Potomac, for one could easily argue that the event should be called "The Meade-Hunt-Hancock Defense of Cemetery Ridge," or some variation of that phrase. Neither "The Pickett-Pettigrew-Trimble Charge," nor "Longstreet's Grand Assault" roll easily off the tongue; both fall strangely upon the ear. Any or all of these phrases may well better describe the historical reality of the event, but Pickett's Charge is what the general public knows it as, and no other title seems to work quite so well.

Notes

1. Levi W. Baker, *History of the Ninth Massachusetts Battery* (South Framingham: Lakeview Press, 1888), 261. Baker went on to say he felt the fighting of the 2nd was more historically significant, just as others have occasionally felt that another time and place was the "high water mark of the Rebellion."

2. Charles Minor Blackford, quoted in Susan Leigh Blackford, Compiler, *Letters From Lee's Army or Memoirs of Life In and Out of The Army in Virginia During the War Between the States* (New York: Charles Scribner's Sons, 1947), 188.

3. Report of Col. C. H. Cabell, August 1, 1863, United States War Department, *The War of the Rebellion: A Compilation of the Official Records of the Union and Confederate Armies* 70 Volumes in 128 parts (Washington, D. C.: Government Printing Office, 1880-1901) (hereafter cited as *OR*), 1, 27, 2, 376.

4. (Boston: Houghton-Mifflin, 1959).

5. (Hightstown, Md.: Longstreet House, 1987)

6. Glenn Tucker, *High Tide At Gettysburg* (Dayton: Morningside, 1987); Edwin Coddington, *The Gettysburg Campaign* (Dayton: Morningside, 1968); Douglas S. Freeman, *Lee's Lieutenants: A Study In Command V. III. Gettysburg to Appomattox* (New York: Charles Scribner's Sons, 1944).

7. Alexander, *Military Memoirs of a Confederate* (New York: Scribner's, 1907), 422; George Pickett, Letter to his Wife, July, 1863, in Arthur Crew Inman, ed., *General Pickett's War Letters To His Wife* (Freeport, N.Y.: Books For Libraries Press, 1971), 73.

8. Quoted in a letter from Wm. H. Palmer to T. M. R. Talcott, in T. M. R. Talcott, "The Third Day At Gettysburg," *Southern Historical Society Papers* (Richmond: Southern Historical Society, 1876-1930), (Hereafter cited as *SHSP*), 1916, 40.

9. James F. Crocker, *Gettysburg—Pickett's Charge and Other War Addresses* (Portsmouth, Va.: n. p., 1915), 37.

10. See James McPherson, *The Battle Cry of Freedom: The Civil War Era* (New York: Ballantine Books, 1988), 647-648.

11. Longstreet to Louis Wigfall, May 13, 1863, quoted in Archer Jones, *Confederate Strategy from Shiloh to Vicksburg* (Baton Rouge: Louisiana State University Press, 1961), 208.

12. McPherson, *Battle Cry of Freedom*, 649-651.

13. Lee to Davis, June 10, 1863, Clifford Dowdey and Louis Manarin, Eds., *The Wartime Papers of Robert E. Lee* (Boston: Little, Brown, 1961), 508-9.

14. Quoted in Douglas Southall Freeman, *R. E. Lee: A Biography* (New York: Charles Scribner's Sons, 1945), Vol. III, 58-

59.

15. Eppa Hunton, *Autobiography of Eppa Hunton* (Richmond: William Byrd Press, 1933), 87.

16. McPherson, *Battle Cry of Freedom*, 647.

17. Report of Robert E. Lee, __, __, [January,] 1864, *OR*, 1, 27, 2, 320.

18. *Ibid.*

19. James Longstreet, *From Manassas to Appomattox: Memoirs of the Civil War in America* (Philadelphia: J. B. Lippincott, 1896), 385.

20. Report of Lieut. Gen. Richard S. Ewell, ____, _____, 1863, *OR*, 1, 27, 2, 447.

21. Report of Brig. Gen. William N. Pendleton, Sept. 12., 1863, *OR*, 1, 27, 2, 351. (emphasis added)

22. Edward Porter Alexander, "The Great Charge and Artillery Fight at Gettysburg," *Battles and Leaders of the Civil War* Robert Underwood and Clarence Clough Buel, Eds., Vol. II (New York: Century, 1888), 361.

23. Quoted in Captain Robert E. Lee, *Recollections and Letters of General Robert E. Lee (Garden City, N.J.: Garden City Publishing, 1924)*, 106.

24. James F. Crocker, "Gettysburg—Pickett's Charge," *SHSP*, 124.

25. Report of Lieut. Col. Thomas Carter, August 5, 1863, *OR*, 1, 27, 2, 603.

26. The only batteries not involved were the 1st Richmond Howitzers, Salem Artillery, Norfolk Light Artillery, 1st Maryland, Allegheny Artillery, and Chesapeake Artillery.

27. R. H. Anderson, *SHSP*, III(1879), 52. See also Longstreet's comments in Longstreet's Report, *OR*, 1, 27, 2, 360.

28. Longstreet's Report, *OR*, 1, 27, 2, 359-360.

29. Paddy Griffith, *Battle Tactics of the Civil War* (New Haven: Yale University Press), 140-145. I qualify my statement here with the term "probably" only because no written order, nor a report of one, for a bayonet charge, exists. Lee did not use written orders at Gettysburg. Even if he did not order that this particular tactic be used, all the component elements were utilized. Thus Pickett's Charge was indeed a bayonet charge, whether or not Lee or Longstreet used the term to describe what they wanted to take place.

30. *Ibid.*, 142-143.

31. *Ibid.*

32. Lee to Hood, May 21, 1863, *Wartime Papers*, 490.

33. Seddon to Lee, June 10, 1863, *OR*, 1, 27, 3, 882.

34. Anderson's Report, *OR*, 1, 27, 2, 614-615.

35. Longstreet's Report, *OR*, 1, 27, 2, 359-360.

36. Stuart's Report, *OR*, 1, 27, 2, 697.

37. John Gibbon, *Recollections of the Civil War* (New York: G. P. Putnam, 1928), 140-152.

38. Measurements were made using the Maxon-Bachelder map of 1880.

39. Report of Major D. G. McIntosh, July 30, 1863, *OR*, 1, 27, 2, 675.

40. Osborn, quoted in Alexander, *Military Memoirs*, 427.

41. Report of Brig. Gen. Robert O. Tyler, August 30, 1863, *OR*, 1, 27, 1, 875.

42. Report of Col. Theodore B. Gates, July 4, 1863, *OR*, 1, 27, 1, 318.

43. Report of Capt. Emmanuel D. Roath, August 15, 1863, *OR*, 1, 27, 1, 305.

44. Report of Col. Thomas A. Smyth, July 17, 1863, *OR*, 1, 27, 1, 465.

45. Report of Captain Patrick Hart, 15th New York Battery, August 2, 1863, *OR*, 1, 27, 2, 889.

46. R. O. Sturtevant, *Pictorial History of the 13th Vermont Volunteers* (Burlington: The Self-Appointed Committee of Three, 1913), 305.

47. John Gibbon, *Recollections*, 148-149.

48. Tully McCrea to John Bachelder, March 30, 1904, Bachelder Papers, New Hampshire Historical Society.

49. Diary of George Griggs, *SHSP*, VI(1878), 250.

Section I

"It Was Not Ordered Without Mature Consideration":

Planning The Charge

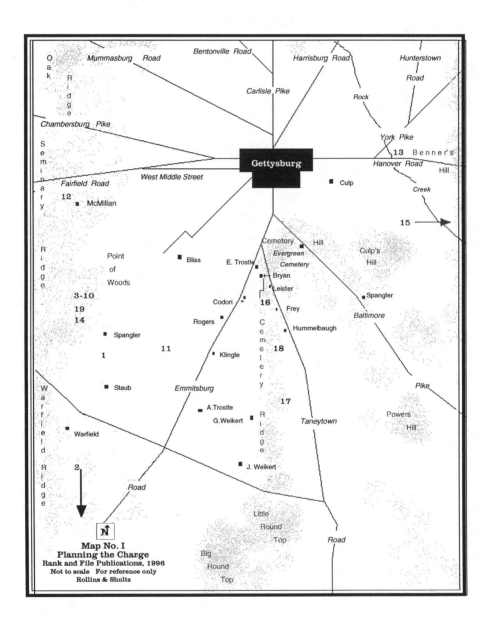

Oak Ridge

Mummasburg Road

Bentonville Road

Harrisburg Road

Hunterstown Road

Carlisle Pike

Rock

Chambersburg Pike

York Pike

Seminary Ridge

13 Benner's

Fairfield Road

West Middle Street

Gettysburg

Hanover Road

Hill

Culp

Creek

12 McMillan

15 →

Cemetery Hill

Culp's Hill

Point of Woods

Bliss

E. Trostle

Evergreen Cemetery

Bryan

Leister

3-10
19
14

Codori

16

Spangler

Rogers

Frey

Baltimore

Spangler

1

11

Klingle

Hummelbaugh

18

Staub

Emmitsburg

Cemetery Ridge

17

Pike

Warfield Ridge

A.Trostle

G.Weikert

Taneytown

Powers Hill

Warfield

Road

J. Weikert

2 ↓

Little Round Top

Road

N

Map No. I
Planning the Charge
Rank and File Publications, 1996
Not to scale For reference only
Rollins & Shultz

Big Round Top

1. James F. Crocker, Adjutant in the 9th Virginia, grown up in Virginia but gone to Pennsylvania College, Gettysburg College was then known, graduating as valedictorian and as a member of Phi Beta Kappa in 1850. He returned to Virginia and had a promising legal career when the war broke out. After the war he returned to Virginia and became a highly respected Judge and politician. He left two accounts of his experiences at Gettysburg, and both are included here. In this essay he summarizes the optimism, confidence, and sense of determination that pervaded the Army of Northern Virginia on the morning of the 3rd. He also recalls the combined operation of artillery, infantry and cavalry that Lee planned. James F. Crocker, "My Personal Experiences in Taking Up Arms. . . ," *Southern Historical Society Papers* (Richmond: Southern Historical Society, 1876-1930), [hereafter cited as *SHSP*], XXXIII(1905), 120-130.

The invasion of Pennsylvania was wise and prudent from the standpoint of both arms and statesmanship. Everything promised success. Never was the Army of Northern Virginia in better condition The troops had unbounded confidence in themselves and in their leaders They were full of the fervor of patriots, had abiding faith in their cause and in the favoring will of Heaven. There was an elation from the fact of invading the country of an enemy that had so cruelly invaded theirs. The spirit and elan of our soldiers was beyond description. They only could know it who felt it. They had the courage and dash to accomplish anything — everything but the impossible. On the contrary, the Federal army was never so dispirited, as I afterwards learned from some of its officers. And this was most natural. They marched from the bloody fields of Fredericksburg and Chancellorsville, the scenes of their humiliating and bloody defeat, to meet a foe from whom they had never won a victory. But alas, how different the result!

. . . General Lee determined to renew the attack on the morrow. He ordered Longstreet to make the attack next morning with his whole corps and sent to aid him in the attack of Heth's division under Pettigrew. Lane's and Scales' brigades of Anderson's division under General Trimble and also Wilcox's brigade and directed General Ewell to assail the enemy's right at the same time. "A careful examination" says Lee, "was made of the ground secured by Longstreet and his batteries placed in position which it was believed would enable them to silence those of the enemy. Hill's artillery and part of Ewell's was ordered to open simultaneously and the assaulting column to advance under cover of the combined fire of the three. The batteries were directed to be pushed forward as the infantry progressed, protect their flanks and support their attacks closely." Every word of this order was potentially significant. You will thus observe Lee's plan of attack. It was to be made in the morning — presumably in the early morning — with the whole of Longstreet's Corps, composed of the divisions of Pickett, McLaws and Hood, together with Heth's division, two brigades of Pender and Wilcox's brigade, and that the assaulting column was to advance under the cover of the combined fire of the artillery of the three corps, and that the assault was to be the combined assault of infantry and artillery — the batteries to be pushed forward as the infantry progressed, to protect their flanks and support their attack closely. The attack was not made as here ordered. The attacking column did not move until 3 P M, and when it did move it was without McLaws' and Hood's divisions and practically without Wilcox's brigade and without accompanying artillery. The whole attacking force did not exceed 14,000, of which Pickett's division did not exceed 4,700. General Lee afterwards claimed that if the attack had been made as he ordered, it would have been successful.

2. General Robert E. Lee's concept of the action that we know today as Pickett's Charge was a product of his long-range strategic thinking and the situation as he found it on July 2nd. We may begin with a glance into his conception of his army and its relationship to its opposition. In a letter to one of his key subordinates, division commander John Bell Hood, written just after what was perhaps his greatest victory at Chancellorsville, and the death of his most aggressive corps commander, Lt. Gen. Thomas J. "Stonewall" Jackson, Lee comments on his men and the problem of leadership. His enormous confidence in his men is underscored by his statement that his men will do whatever he asks of them. Yet Lee realizes that he has lost a key officer, one who could be counted on to press the battle whenever he could see an advantage, and that a key to the upcoming campaign would be the ability of his subordinates to display the aggressiveness and ability to get things done that Jackson had given him. These two themes would be extremely important in the planning and execution of the most important single maneuver of the campaign and possibly the entire war. R. E. Lee to General John B. Hood, May 21, 1863, *The Wartime Papers of Robert E. Lee* Clifford Dowdey, ed., (New York: Da Capo Press, 1961), 490.

My Dear General:
. . . I grieve much over the death of General Jackson. For our sakes not for his. He is happy and at peace. But his spirit lives with us. I hope it will raise up many Jacksons in our ranks. . . . I rely much upon you. You must so inspire and lead your division as that it may accomplish the work of a corps. . . . I agree with you in believing that our army would be invincible if it could be properly

organized and officered. There never were such men in an army before. They will go anywhere and do anything if properly led. But there is the difficulty — proper commanders. Where can they be obtained? . . . Wishing you every health and happiness, and commending you to the care of a kind providence,

I am, now and always your friend, R. E. Lee

3. Arthur James Lyon Fremantle, Captain of His Majesty's Coldstream Guards and Lieutenant-Colonel in the British army, wrote one of the classics in the literature of the American Civil War. Fremantle had the rare combination of being a trained military observer, charming raconteur, and insightful student of cultural nuances. He was very well-liked by the generals of the Army of Northern Virginia. He entered the Confederacy in Texas in April 1863 and left in July, along the way gaining access to most of the leading personalities of the South, including Lee, Jefferson Davis, Braxton Bragg, and Joe Johnston. In this excerpt from his book, *Three Months in the Southern States* (New York: n.p., 1864), Fremantle describes Lee and Longstreet and their relationship, thus offering a context for the discussions of tactics. He then gives his unique view of the activities of the day(248-272).

30th June (Tuesday).—This morning, before marching from Chambersburg, General Longstreet introduced me to the commander-in-chief General Lee. Lee is, almost without exception, the handsomest man of his age I ever saw. He is fifty-six years old, tall, broad-shouldered, very well made, well set up — a thorough soldier in appearance; and his manners are most courteous and full of dignity. He is a perfect gentleman in every respect. I imagine no man has so few enemies, or is so universally esteemed. Throughout the South, all agree in pronouncing him to be as near perfection as a man can be. He has none of the small vices, such as smoking, drinking, chewing, or swearing, and his bitterest enemy never accused him of any of the greater ones. He generally wears a well-worn long gray jacket, a high black felt hat, and blue trousers tucked into his Wellington boots. I never saw him carry arms; and the only mark of his military rank are the three stars on his collar. He rides a handsome horse, which is extremely well groomed. He himself is very neat in his dress and person, and in the most arduous marches he always looks smart and clean.

In the old army he was always considered one of its best officers; and at the outbreak of these troubles, he was Lieutenant-colonel of the 2d cavalry. He was a rich man, but his fine estate was one of the first to fall into the enemy's hands. I believe he has never slept in a house since he has commanded the Virginian army, and he invariably declines all offers of hospitality, for fear the person offering it may afterwards get into trouble for having sheltered the Rebel General. The relations between him and Longstreet are quite touching — they are almost always together. Longstreet's corps complain of this sometimes, as they say that they seldom get a chance of detached service, which falls to the lot of Ewell. It is impossible to please Longstreet more than by praising Lee. I believe these two Generals to be as little ambitious and as thoroughly unselfish as any men in the world. Both long for a successful termination of the war, in order that they may retire into obscurity. Jackson (until his death the third in command of their army) was just such another simple-minded servant of his country. It is understood that General Lee is a religious man, though not so demonstrative in that respect as Jackson; and, unlike his late brother in arms, he is a member of the Church of England. His only faults, so far as I can learn, arise from his excessive amiability . . .

3d July (Friday). — At 6 A. M. I rode to the field with Colonel Manning, and went over that portion of the ground which, after a fierce contest, had been won from the enemy yesterday evening. The dead were being buried, but great numbers were still lying about; also many mortally wounded, for whom nothing could be done. Amongst the latter were a number of Yankees dressed in bad imitations of the Zouave costume. They opened their glazed eyes as I rode past in a painfully imploring manner. We joined Generals Lee and Longstreet's Staff: They were reconnoitering and making preparations for renewing the attack. As we formed a pretty large party, we often drew upon ourselves the attention of the hostile sharpshooters, and were two or three times favored with a shell. One of these shells set a brick building on fire which was situated between the lines. This building was filled with wounded, principally Yankees, who, I am afraid, must have perished miserably in the flames. Colonel Sorrell had been slightly wounded yesterday, but still did duty. Major Walton's horse was killed, but there were no other casualties amongst my particular friends.

The plan of yesterday's attack seems to have been very simple — first a heavy cannonade all along the line, followed by an advance of Longstreet's two divisions and part of Hill's corps. In consequence of the enemy's having been driven back some distance, Longstreet's corps (part of it) was in a much more forward situation than yesterday. But the range of heights to be gained was still most formidable, and evidently strongly intrenched.

The distance between the Confederate guns and the Yankee position. . . i. e., between the woods crowning the opposite ridges — was at least a mile of quite open, gently undulating, and exposed to artillery the whole distance. This was the ground which had to be crossed in to-day's attack. Pickett's division, which had just come up, was to bear the brunt in Longstreet's attack, together with Heth and Pettigrew in Hill's corps. Pickett's division was a weak one (under 5,000), owing to the absence of two brigades. At noon all Longstreet's dispositions were made; his troops for attack were deployed into line, and lying down in the woods; his batteries were ready to open. The general then dismounted and went to sleep for a short time. The Austrian officer and I now rode off to get, if possible, into some commanding position from whence we could see the whole thing, without being exposed to the tremendous fire which was about to commence. After riding about for half an hour without being able to discover so desirable a situation, we determined to make for the cupola, near Gettysburg, Ewell's headquarters. Just before we reached the entrance to the town, the cannonade opened with a fury which surpassed even that of yesterday.

4. In his official report of the battle, written in January of 1864, Lee gave a brief but succinct analysis of the plan of Pickett's Charge, and of its failure. He noted that it was a continuation of the successes of the 2nd, and was to feature the coordination of the artillery of the entire army, Ewell's infantry corps on the left, and Longstreet's men, who would be the main attacking force. He noted that it was originally planned and ordered for the early morning hours, but was delayed because of Longstreet's fear of the Union troops that would be in his rear if he sent all his men forward. He recalled the destructive fire of the Federal artillery once the men had begun crossing the field, and the exhaustion of the Confederate artillery's ammunition, which allowed the Federals to direct a withering fire upon the charge virtually without fear of counterbattery fire. He notes that he was not informed of the lack of ammunition. In essence, he described the failure of his subordinates to carry out his plans. Report of General Robert E. Lee, January, 1864, *OR*, 1, 27, 2, 320-321.

The result of this day's operations induced the belief that, with proper concert of action, and with the increased support that the positions gained on the right would enable to artillery to render the assaulting columns, we should ultimately succeed, and it was accordingly determined to continue the attack. The general plan was unchanged. Longstreet, re-enforced by Pickett's three brigades, which arrived near the battlefield during the afternoon of the 2d, was ordered to attack the next morning, and General Ewell was directed to assail the enemy's right at the same time. The latter, during the night, re-enforced General Johnson with two brigades from Rodes' and one from Early's division.

General Longstreet's disposition were not completed as early as was expected, but before notice could be sent to General Ewell, General Johnson had already become engaged, and it was too late to recall him. The enemy attempted to recover the works taken the preceding evening, but was repulsed, and General Johnson attacked in turn.

After a gallant and prolonged struggle, in which the enemy was forced to abandon part of his intrenchments, General Johnson found himself unable to carry the strongly fortified crest of the hill. The projected attack on the enemy's left not having been made, he was enabled to hold his right with a force largely superior to that of General Johnson, and finally to threaten his flank and rear, rendering it necessary for him to retire to his original position about 1 p. m.

General Longstreet was delayed by a force occupying the high, rocky hills on the enemy's extreme left, from which his troops could be attacked in reverse as they advanced. His operations had been embarrassed the day previous by the same cause, and he now deemed it necessary to defend his flank and rear with the divisions of Hood and McLaws. He was, therefore, re-enforced by Heth's division and two brigades of Pender's, to the command of which Major-General Trimble was assigned. General Hill was directed to hold his line with the rest of his command, afford General Longstreet further assistance, if required, and avail himself of any success that might be gained.

A careful examination was made of the ground secured by Longstreet, and his batteries placed in positions, which, it was believed, would enable them to silence those of the enemy. Hill's artillery and part of Ewell's was ordered to open simultaneously, and the assaulting column to advance under cover of the combined fire of the three. The batteries were directed to be pushed forward as the infantry progressed, protect their flanks, and support their attacks closely.

About 1 p. m., at a given signal, a heavy cannonade was opened, and continued for about two hours with marked effect upon the enemy. His batteries replied vigorously at first, but toward the close their fire slackened perceptibly, and General Longstreet ordered forward the column of attack, consisting of Pickett's and Heth's divisions, in two lines, Pickett on the right. Wilcox's brigade marched in rear of Pickett's right, to guard that flank, and Heth's was supported by Lane's and Scales' brigades, under General Trimble.

The troops moved steadily on, under a heavy fire of musketry and artillery, the main attack being directed against the enemy's left center.

His batteries reopened as soon as they appeared. Our own

having nearly exhausted their ammunition in the protracted cannonade that preceded the advance of the infantry, were unable to reply, or render the necessary support to the attacking party. Owing to this fact, which was unknown to me when the assault took place, the enemy was enabled to throw a strong force of infantry against our left, already wavering under a concentrated fire of artillery from the ridge in front, and from Cemetery Hill, on the left. It finally gave way, and the right, after penetrating the enemy's lines, entering his advance works, and capturing some of his artillery, was attacked simultaneously in front and on both flanks, and driven back with heavy loss.

The troops were rallied and reformed, but the enemy did not pursue.

5. Lieutenant General James Longstreet, Lee's second in command, left five separate versions of his role in the planning and execution of Pickett's Charge, all with variations on the same themes. This is the first, his official report, written to Lee barely three weeks after the battle. He mentions having planned a move around the Federal flank, the plan he preferred to follow, and Lee's rejection of it, as well as his own doubts about the charge against Cemetery Hill. He does not mention Lee's order on the 2nd for action on the 3rd, and his description of the meeting with Lee is very brief, containing little of the dramatic exchange that he would describe in later essays. He notes that he found out that there was not enough artillery ammunition to support the charge, and that he would have rescinded the orders if he had felt that it was in his power to do so. Report of Lieut. Gen. James Longstreet, July 27, 1863, *OR*, 1, 27, 2, 359-60.

On the following morning our arrangements were made for renewing the attack by my right, with a view to pass around the hill occupied by the enemy on his left, and to gain it by flank and reverse attack. This would have been a slow process, probably, but I think not very difficult. A few moments after my orders for the execution of this plan were given, the commanding general joined me, and ordered a column of attack to be formed of Pickett's, Heth's, and part of Pender's divisions, the assault to be made directly at the enemy's main position, the Cemetery Hill. The distance to be passed over under the fire of the enemy's batteries, and in plain view, seemed too great to insure great results, particularly as two-thirds of the troops to be engage in the assault had been in a severe battle two days previous, Pickett's division alone being fresh.

Orders were given to Major-General Pickett to form his lines under the best cover that he could get from the enemy's batteries, and so that the center of the assaulting column would arrive at the salient of the enemy's position, General Pickett's line to be the guide and to attack the line of the enemy's defenses, and General Pettigrew, in command of Heth's division, moving on the same line as General Pickett, was to assault the salient at the same moment. Pickett's division was arranged, two brigades in the front line, supported by his third brigade, and Wilcox's brigade was ordered to move in rear of his right flank, to protect it from any force that the enemy might attempt to move against it.

Heth's division, under the command of Brigadier-General Pettigrew, was arranged in two lines, and these supported by part of Major-General Pender's division, under Major-General Trimble. All of the batteries of the First and Third Corps, and some of those of the Second, were put into the best positions for effective fire upon the point of attack and the hill occupied by the enemy's left. Colonel Walton, chief of artillery of First Corps, and Colonel Alexander had posted our batteries and agreed with the artillery officers of the other corps upon the signal for the batteries to open. About 2 p. m. General Pickett, who had been charged with the duty of arranging the lines behind our batteries, reported that the troops were in order and on the most sheltered ground. Colonel Walton was ordered to open the batteries. The signal guns were fired, and all the batteries opened very handsomely and apparently with effective fire. The guns on the hill at the enemy's left were soon silenced. Those at the Cemetery Hill combatted us, however, very obstinately. Many of them were driven off, but fresh ones were brought up to replace them. Colonel Alexander was ordered to a point where he could best observe the effect of our fire, and to give notice of the most opportune moment for our attack.

Some time after our batteries opened fire, I rode to Major [James] Dearing's batteries. It appeared that the enemy put in fresh batteries about as rapidly as others were driven off. I concluded, therefore, that we must attack very soon, if we hoped to accomplish anything before night. I gave orders for the batteries to refill their ammunition chests, and to be prepared to follow up the advance of the infantry. Upon riding over to Colonel Alexander's position, I found that he had advised General Pickett that the time had arrived for the attack, and I gave the order to General Pickett to advance to the assault. I found then that our supply of ammunition was so short that the batteries could not reopen. The order for this attack, which I could not favor under better auspices, would have been revoked had I felt that I had that privilege. The advance was made in very handsome style, all the troops keeping their lines accurately, and taking the fire of the batteries with great coolness and delibera-tion. About half way between our position and that of the enemy, a ravine partially sheltered our troops from the enemy's fire, where a short halt was made for rest. The advance was resumed after a moment's pause, all still in good order. The enemy's batteries soon opened upon our lines with canister, and the left seemed to stagger under it, but the advance was resumed, and with some degree of steadiness. Pickett's troops did not appear to be checked by the batteries, and only halted to deliver a fire when close under musket-range. Major-General Anderson's division was ordered forward to support and assist the wavering columns of Pettigrew and Trimble. Pickett's troops, after delivering fire, advanced to the charge, and entered the enemy's lines, capturing some of his batteries, and gained his works. About the same moment, the troops that had before hesitated, broke their ranks and fell back in great disorder, many more falling under the enemy's fire in retiring than while they were attacking. This gave the enemy time to throw his entire force upon Pickett, with a strong prospect of being able to break up his lines or destroy him before Anderson's division could reach him, which would, in its turn, have greatly exposed Anderson. He was, therefore, ordered to halt. In a few moments the enemy, marching against both flanks and the front of Pickett's division, overpowered it and drove it back, capturing about half of those of it who were not killed or wounded. General Wright, of Anderson's division, with all of the officers, was ordered to rally and collect the scattered troops behind Anderson's division, and many of my staff officers were sent to assist in the same service. Expecting an attack from the enemy, I rode to the front of our batteries, to reconnoiter and superintend their operations.

The enemy threw forward forces at different times and from different points, but they were only feelers, and retired as soon as our batteries opened upon them. These little advances and checks were kept up till night, when the enemy retired to his stronghold, and my line was withdrawn to the Gettysburg road on the right, the left uniting with Lieut. Gen. A. P. Hill's right. After night, I received orders to make all the needful arrangements for our retreat. The orders for preparation were given, and the work was begun before daylight on the 4th.

6. After Lee's death in 1870, former Confederate generals, most notably William Pendleton, Chief of Artillery of the Army of Northern Virginia at Gettysburg, and Jubal Early, a division commander in Ewell's Corps, began to criticize Longstreet's actions at Gettysburg. As time went on, their attacks became increasingly shrill, and Longstreet's attempts to clear his name also became increasingly strident. For an analysis of the post-war developments, see Thomas Connelly, *God and General Longstreet* (Chapel Hill: University of North Carolina Press, 1987). In 1877, the Philadelphia

Weekly Times ran a series of essays about Gettysburg, written by participants. This was Longstreet's first post-war effort at explaining what had happened, and was reprinted as "General James Longstreet's Account of the Campaign and Battle," in the *SHSP*, V(1878), 54 -86. He recounts his discussions with Lee on the morning of the 3rd and his belief that "no 15,000 men ever arrayed for battle can take that position." If true, that would have been a stunning statement, one that Lee must have found difficult to counter. Longstreet gives a brief account of the charge, then utilizes a statement of his feelings for, and relationship with Lee as an introduction to a list of eight points critical of Lee's handling of the battle. He claims that Lee had said he would follow a strategically offensive but tactically defensive plan, which would have precluded headlong assaults such as that of Pickett's men, and denies he was ordered to attack at dawn. He begins the essay by including verbatim a letter he had written after the battle.

> Camp, Culpepper Courthouse   July 24, 1863
> My Dear Uncle:
> Your letters of the 13th and 14th were received on yesterday. As to our late battle, I cannot say much. I have no right to say anything, in fact, but will venture a little for you alone. If it goes to aunt or cousins, it must be under promise that it will go no further. The battle was not made as I would have made it. My idea was to throw ourselves between the enemy and Washington, select a strong position, and force the enemy to attack us. So far as is given to man the ability to judge, we may say with confidence that we should have destroyed the Federal army, marched into Washington, and dictated our terms, or, at least, held Washington and marched over as much of Pennsylvania as we cared to, had we drawn the enemy into attack upon our carefully chosen position in his rear. General Lee chose the plans adopted; and he is the person appointed to choose and to order. I consider it a part of my duty to express my views to the Commanding-General. If he approves and adopts them it is well; if he does not, it is my duty to adopt his views, and to execute his orders as faithfully as if they were my own. I cannot help but think that great results would have been obtained had my views been thought better of; yet I am much inclined to accept the present condition as for the best. I hope and trust that it is so. Your programme would all be well enough had it been practicable; and was duly thought of, too. I fancy that no good ideas upon that campaign will be mentioned at any time that did not receive their share of consideration by General Lee. The few things that he might have overlooked himself were, I believe, suggested by myself. As we failed, I must take my share of the responsibility. In fact, I would prefer that all the blame should rest upon me. As General Lee is our

commander, he should have the support and influence we can give him. If the blame (if there is any) can be shifted from him to me, I shall help him and our cause by taking it. I desire, therefore, that all the responsibility that can be put upon me shall go there and shall remain there. The truth will be known in time, and I leave that to show how much of the responsibility of Gettysburg rests on my shoulders.

Most affectionately yours,

J. LONGSTREET.

To A. B. Longstreet, L. L. D., Columbus, Ga.

I did not see General Lee that night. On the next morning he came to see me, and fearing that he was still in his disposition to attack, I tried to anticipate him by saying: "General, I have had my scouts out all night, and I find that you still have an excellent opportunity to move around to the right of Meade's army and manoeuvre him into attacking us." He replied, pointing with his fist at Cemetery Hill: "The enemy is there, and I am going to strike him." I felt then that it was my duty to express my convictions; I said: "General, I have been soldier all my life. I have been with soldiers engaged in fights by couples, by squads, companies, regiments, divisions and armies, and should know as well as any one what soldiers can do. It is my opinion that no 15,000 men ever arrayed for battle can take that position," pointing to Cemetery Hill. General Lee in reply to this ordered me to prepare Pickett's division for the attack. I should not have been so urgent had I not foreseen the hopelessness of the proposed assault. I felt that I must say a word against the sacrifice of my men; and then I felt that my record was such that General Lee would or could not misconstrue my motives. I said no more, however, but turned away. The most of the morning was consumed in waiting for Pickett's men and getting into position. The plan of assault was as follows: Our artillery was to be massed in a wood from which Pickett was to charge, and it was to pour a continuous fire upon the cemetery. Under cover of this fire, and supported by it, Pickett was to charge.

Our artillery was in charge of General E. P. Alexander, a brave and gifted officer. Colonel Walton was my chief of artillery, but Alexander being at the head of the column, and being first in position, and being besides an officer of unusual promptness, sagacity and intelligence, was given charge of the artillery and arrangements were completed about one o'clock General Alexander had arranged that a battery of seven ll-pound howitzers, with fresh horses and full caissons, were to charge with Pickett, at the head of his line, but General Pendleton, from whom the guns had been borrowed, recalled them just before the charge was made, and thus deranged this wise plan. Never was I so depressed as upon that day.

I felt that my men were to be sacrificed, and that I should have to order them to make a hopeless charge. I had instructed General Alexander, being unwillingly to trust myself with the entire responsibility, to carefully observe the effect of the fire upon the enemy, and when it began to tell to notify Pickett to begin the assault. I was so much impressed with the hopelessness of the charge that I wrote the following note to General Alexander: "If the artillery fire does not have the effect to drive off the enemy or greatly demoralize him, so as to make our efforts pretty certain, I would prefer that you should not advise General Pickett to make the charge. I shall rely a great deal on your judgment to determine the matter, and shall expect you to let Pickett know when the moment offers." To my note the General replied as follows: "I will only be able to judge the effect of our fire upon the enemy by his return fire, for his infantry is but little exposed to view, and the smoke will obscure the whole field. If, as I infer from your note, there is an alternative to this attack, it should be carefully considered before opening our fire, for it will take all of the artillery ammunition we have left to test this one thoroughly, and if the result is unfavorable, we will have none left for another effort, and even if this is entirely successful it can only be so at a very bloody cost." I still desired to save my men and felt that if the artillery did not produce the desired effect I would be justified in holding Pickett off. I wrote this note to Colonel Walton at exactly 1:30 P. M.: "Let the batteries open. Order great precision in firing. If the batteries at the peach orchard cannot be used against the point we intend attacking, let them open on the enemy at Rocky Hill." The cannonading which opened along both lines was grand. In a few moments a courier brought a note to General Pickett (who was standing near me) from Alexander, which, after reading, he handed to me. It was as follows: "If you are coming at all you must come at once, or I cannot give you proper support; but the enemy's fire has not slackened at all; at least eighteen guns are still firing from the Cemetery itself." After I had read the note Pickett said to me: "General, shall I advance?" My feelings had so overcome me that I would not speak for fear of betraying my want of confidence to him. I bowed affirmative and turned to mount my horse. Pickett immediately said: "I shall lead my division forward, sir." I spurred my horse to the wood where Alexander was stationed with artillery. When I reached him he told me of the disappearance of the seven guns which were to have led the charge with Pickett, and that his ammunition was so low that he could not properly support the charge. I at once ordered him to stop Pickett until the ammunition had been replenished. He informed me that he had no ammunition with which to replenish. I then saw that there was no help for it, and that Pickett must advance under his orders. He swept past our artillery in splendid style, and the men marched steadily and compactly down the slope. As they started up the ridge over one hundred cannon from the breastworks of the Federals hurled a rain of cannister, grape and shell down upon them; still they pressed on until half way up the slope, when the crest of the hill was lit with a solid sheet of flame as the masses of infantry rose and fired. When the smoke cleared away Pickett's division was gone. Nearly two-thirds of his men lay dead on the field, and the survivors were sullenly retreating down the hill. Mortal man could not have stood that fire. In half an hour the contested field was cleared and the battle of Gettysburg was over.

When this charge had failed I expected that of course the enemy would throw himself against our shattered rallies and try to crush us. I sent my staff officers to the rear to assist in rallying the troops, and hurried to our line of batteries as the only support that I could give them, knowing that my presence would impress upon every one of them the necessity of holding the ground to the last extremity. I knew if the army was to be saved those batteries must check the enemy. As I rode along the line of artillery I observed my old friend Captain Miller, Washington Artillery, of Sharpsburg record, walking between his guns and smoking his pipe as quietly and contentedly as he could sit his campfire. The enemy's skirmishers were then advancing and threatening assault. For unaccountable reasons the enemy did not pursue his advantage. Our army was soon in compact shape, and its face turned once more toward Virginia. I may mention here that it has been absurdly said that General Lee ordered me to put Hood's and McLaws' divisions in support of Pickett's assault. General Lee never ordered any such thing. After our troops were all arranged for assault General Lee rode with me twice over the lines to see that everything was arranged according to his wishes. He was told that we had been more particular in giving the orders than ever before; that the commanders had been sent for and the point of attack had been carefully designated, and that the commanders had been directed to communicated to their subordinates, and through them to every soldier in the command, the work that was before them, so that they should nerve themselves for the attack and fully understand it. After leaving me he again rode over the field once, if not twice, so that there was really no room for misconstruction or misunderstanding of his wishes. He could not have thought of giving any such an order. Hood and McLaws were confronted by a largely superior force of the enemy on the right of Pickett's attack. To have moved them to Pickett's support would have disengaged treble their number of Federals, who would have swooped down from their rocky fastnesses against the flank of our attacking column and swept our army from the field. A reference to any of the maps of Gettysburg will show from the position of the troops that this would have been the inevitable result.   General Lee and myself never had any deliberate conversation about Gettysburg. The subject was never broached by either of us to the other. On one occasion it came up casually and he said to me (alluding to the charge of Pickett on the 3d), "General, why didn't you stop all that thing that day ?." I replied that I could not under the circumstances assume such a responsibility, as no discretion had been left me.

Before discussing the weak points of the campaign of Gettysburg, it is proper that I should say that I do so with the greatest affection for General Lee and the greatest reverence for his memory.   The relations existing between us were affectionate, confidential, and even tender, from first to last. There was never a harsh word between us. It is then with a reluctant spirit that I write a calm and critical review of the Gettysburg campaign, because that review will show that our Commanding-General was unfortunate at several points. There is no doubt that General Lee, during the crisis of that campaign, lost the matchless equipoise that had usually characterized him, and that whatever mistakes were made were not so much matters of deliberate judgment as the impulses of a great mind disturbed by unparalleled conditions.   General Lee was thrown from his balance (as is shown by the statement of General Fitzhugh Lee) by too great confidence in the prowess of his troops and (as is shown by General Anderson's statement) by the deplorable absence of General Stuart and the perplexity occasioned thereby.

With this preface I proceed to say that the Gettysburg campaign was weak in these points — [here he lists six points dealing with the campaign up to the morning of July 3rd.] Seventh, on the morning of the 3d it was not yet too late to move to the right and manoeuvre the Federals into attacking us. Eighth, Pickett's division should not have been ordered to assault Cemetery Ridge on the 3d, as we had already tested the strength of that position sufficiently to admonish us that we could not dislodge him. While the co-operation of Generals Ewell and Hill, on the 2d, by vigorous assault at the moment my battle was in progress, would in all probability have dislodged the Federals from their position, it does not seem that such success would have yielded the fruits anticipated at the inception of the campaign. The battle as it was fought would, in any result, have so crippled us that the Federals would have been able to make good their retreat, and we should soon have been obliged to retire to Virginia with nothing but victory to cover our waning cause. The morale of the victory might have dispirited the North and aroused the South to new exertions, but it would have been nothing in the game being played by the two armies at Gettysburg. As to the abandonment of the tactical defensive policy that we had agreed upon, there can be no doubt that General Lee deeply deplored it as a mistake. This remark, made just after the battle, "It is all my fault," meant just what it said. It adds to the nobility and magnanimity of that remark when we reflect that it was the utterance of a deep-felt truth rather than a mere sentiment. In a letter written to me by General Lee in January, 1864, he says: "had I taken your advice at Gettysburg instead of pursuing the course I did, how different all might have been." Captain T. J. Gorie, of Houston, Texas, a gentleman of high position and undoubted integrity, writes to me upon this same point as follows: "Another important circumstance which I distinctly remember was in the winter of 1864, when you sent me from East Tennessee to Orange Courthouse with dispatches for General Lee. Upon my arrival there General Lee asked me in his tent, where he was alone with two or three Northern papers on his table. He remarked that he had just been reading the Northern official report of the Battle of Gettysburg; that he had become satisfied from reading those reports that if he had permitted you to carry out your plans on the third day, instead of making the attack on Cemetery Hill, we would have been successful." I cannot see, as has been claimed, why the absence of General Lee's cavalry should have justified his attack on the enemy. On the contrary, while they may have perplexed him, I hold that it was additional reason for his not hazarding an attack. At the time the attack was ordered we were fearful that our cavalry had been destroyed. In case of a disaster, and a forced retreat, we should have had nothing to cover our retreat. When so much was at stake as at Gettysburg the absence of the cavalry should have prevented the taking of any chances.

7. By the 1890s Longstreet had endured two decades of vicious attacks on his military skills and personal character. The strain shaped his memoirs, published in Philadelphia in 1896 as *From Manassas to Appomattox: Memoirs of the Civil War in America* (Philadelphia: J.B. Lippincott, 1896). He attacked Lee and all his detractors, and strongly defended himself much more vehemently than he had in 1863 or 1877. His account of his dialogue with Lee is considerably different: he claims to have been more forceful and detailed in his opposition to the attack. He says that it would have taken 30,000 men to be successful, and that he was so opposed to the charge that Lee should have put someone else in command(385-395).

GENERAL LEE has reported of arrangements for the day,—
The General plan was unchanged. Long-
street, reinforced by Pickett's three brigades, which

arrived near the battlefield during the afternoon of the 2d, were ordered to attack the next morning, and General Ewell was ordered to attack the enemy's right at the same time. The latter during the night reinforced General Johnson with two brigades from Rodes and one from Early's division.

This is disingenuous. He did not give or send me orders for the morning of the third day, nor did he reinforce me by Pickett's brigades for a morning attack. As his head-quarters were about four miles from the command, I did not ride over, but sent, to report the work of the second day. In the absence of orders, I had scouting parties out during the night in search of a way by which we might strike the enemy's left, and push it down towards his centre. I found a way that gave some promise of results, and was about to move the command, when he rode over after sunrise and gave his orders. His plan was to assault the enemy's left centre by a column to be composed of McLaws's and Hood's divisions reinforced by Pickett's brigades. I thought that it would not do; that the point had been fully tested the day before, by more men, when all were fresh; that the enemy was there looking for us, as we heard him during the night putting up his defences; that the divisions of McLaws and Hood were holding a mile along the right of my line against twenty thousand men, who would follow their withdrawal, strike the flank of the assaulting column, crush it, and get on our rear towards the Potomac River; that thirty thousand men was the minimum of force necessary for the work; that even such force would need close cooperation on other parts of the line; that the column as he proposed to organize it would have only about thirteen thousand men (the divisions having lost a third of their numbers the day before); that the column would have to march a mile under concentrating battery fire, and a thousand yards under long-range musketry; that the conditions were different from those in the days of Napoleon when field batteries had a range of six hundred yards and musketry about sixty yards.

He said the distance was not more than fourteen hundred yards. General Meade's estimate was a mile or a mile and a half (Captain Long, the guide of the field of Gettysburg in 1888, stated that it was a trifle over a mile). He then concluded that the divisions of McLaws and Hood could remain on the defensive line; that he would reinforce by divisions of the Third Corps and Pickett's brigades, and stated the point to which the march should be directed. I asked the strength of the column. He stated fifteen thousand. Opinion was then expressed that the fifteen thousand men who could make successful assault over that field had never been arrayed for battle; but he was impatient of listening, and tired of talking, and nothing was left but to proceed. General Alexander was ordered to arrange the batteries of the front of the First and Third Corps, those of the Second were supposed to be in position; Colonel Walton was ordered to see that the batteries of the First were supplied with ammunition, and to prepare to give the signal-guns for the opening combat. The infantry of the Third Corps to be assigned were Heth's and Pettigrew's divisions and Wilcox's brigade.

. . .While this contention was in progress the troops ordered for the column of assault were marching and finding positions under the crest of the ridge, where they could be covered during the artillery combat. Alexander put a battery of nine guns under the ridge and out of the enemy's fire to be used with the assaulting column.

General Lee said that the attack of his right was not made as early as expected, — which he should not have said. He knew that I did not believe that success was possible; that care and time should be taken to give the troops the benefit of positions and the grounds; and he should have put an officer in charge who had more confidence in his plan. Two-thirds of the troops were of other commands, and there was no reason for putting the assaulting forces under my thirds. He had confidence in General Early, who advised in favor of that end of the line for battle. Knowing my want of confidence, he should have given the benefit of his presence and his assistance in getting the troops up, posting them, and arranging the batteries; but he gave no orders or suggestions after his early designation of the point for which the column should march. Fitzhugh Lee claims evidence that General Lee did not even appear on that part of the field while the troops were being assigned to position.

As the commands reported, Pickett was assigned on the right, Kemper's and Garnett's brigades to be supported by Armistead's; Wilcox's brigade of the Third Corps in echelon and guarding Pickett's right; Pettigrew's division on Pickett's left, supported by the brigades of Scales and Lane, under command of General Trimble. The brigades of Pettigrew's division were Archer's, Pettigrew's, Brockenbrough's, and Davis's (General Archer having been taken prisoner on the 1st, his brigade was under command of Colonel Fry; General Scales being wounded on the same day, his brigade was commanded by Colonel Lowrance.) The ridge upon which the commands were formed was not parallel to that upon which the enemy stood, but bending west towards our left, while the enemy's line bore northwest towards his right, so that the left of the assaulting column formed some little distance farther from the enemy's line than the right. To put the troops under the best cover during the artillery combat they were thus posted for the march, but directed to spread their steps as soon as the march opened the field, and to go in places of correct alignment.

Meanwhile, the enemy's artillery on his extreme right was in practice more or less active, but it's meaning was not known or reported, as the sharp-shooters of the command on the right had a lively fusillade about eleven o'clock, in which some of the artillery took part. The order was that the right was to make the signal of battle. General Lee reported that his left attacked before due notice to wait for the opening could be given, which was a mistake, inasmuch as the attack on his left was begun by the Federals, which caused his left to their work. General Meade was not apprehensive of that part of the field, and only used the two divisions of the Twelfth Corps, Shaler's brigade of the Sixth, and six regiments of the First and Eleventh Corps in recovering the trenches of his right, holding the other six corps for the battle of his centre and left. He knew by the Confederate troops on his right just where the strong battle was to be.

The director of artillery was asked to select a position on his line from which he could note the effect of his practice, as to advise General Pickett when the enemy's fire was so disturbed as to call for the assault. General Pickett's was the division of direction, and he was ordered to have a staff-officer or courier with the artillery director to bear notice of the moment to advance.

The little affair between the skirmish lines quieted in a short time, and also the noise on our extreme left. The quiet filing of one or two of our batteries into position emphasized the profound silence that prevailed during our wait for final orders. Strong battle was in the air, and the veterans of both sides swelled their breasts to gather nerve and strength to meet it. Division commanders were asked to go to the crest of the ridge and take a careful view of the field, and to have their officers there to tell their men of it, and to prepare them for the sight that was to burst upon them as they mounted the crest.

. . .When satisfied that the work of preparation was all that it could be with the means at hand, I wrote Colonel Walton, of the Washington Artillery, —

> HEAD-QUARTERS JULY 3, 1863.
>   COLONEL,—Let the batteries open. Order great care and precision in firing. When the batteries at the Peach Orchard cannot be used against the point we intend to attack, let them open on the enemy's on the rocky hill.
>   Most respectfully,
>   JAMES LONGSTREET,
>   Lieutenant-General, Commanding.

At the same time a note to Alexander directed that Pickett should not be called until the artillery practice indicated fair opportunity. Then I rode to a woodland hard by, to lie down and study for some new thought that might aid the assaulting column. In a few minutes report came from Alexander that he would only be able to judge of the effect of his fire by the return of that of the enemy, as his infantry was not exposed to view, and the smoke of the batteries would soon cover the field. He asked, if there was an alternative, that it be carefully considered before the batteries opened, as there was not enough artillery ammunition for this and another trial if this should not prove favorable.

He was informed that there was no alternative; that I could find no way out of it; that General Lee had considered and would listen to nothing else; that orders had gone for the guns to give signal for the batteries; that he should call the troops at the first opportunity or lull in the enemy's fire.

The signal-guns broke the silence, the blaze of the second gun mingling in the smoke of the first, and salvoes rolled to the left and repeated themselves, the enemy's fine metal spreading its fire by the converging lines, ploughing the trembling ground, plunging through the line of batteries, and clouding the heavy air. The two or three hundred guns seemed proud of their undivided honors and organized confusion. The Confederates had the benefit of converging fire into the enemy's massed position, but the superior metal of the enemy neutralized the advantage of position. The brave and steady work progressed.

Before this the Confederates of the left were driven from their captured trenches, and hope of their effective co-operation with the battle of the right was lost, but no notice of it was sent to the right of the battle. They made some further demonstrations, but they were of little effect.

Not informed of the failure of the Confederates on the left and the loss of their vantage-ground, we looked with confidence for them to follow the orders of battle.

General Pickett rode to confer with Alexander, then to the ground upon which I was resting, where he was soon handed a slip of paper. After reading it he handed it to me. It read:

> If you are coming at all, come at once, or I cannot give
> you proper support, but the enemy's fire has not
> slackened at all. At least eighteen guns are still from
> the Cemetery itself.   Alexander.

Pickett said, "General, shall I advance?"

The effort to speak the order failed, and I could only indicate it by an affirmative bow. He accepted the duty with seeming confidence of success, leaped on his horse, and rode gayly to his command.   I mounted and spurred for Alexander's post.   He reported that the batteries he had reserved for the charge with the infantry had been spirited away by General Lee's chief of artillery; that the ammunition of the batteries of position was so reduced that he could not use them in proper support of the infantry. He was ordered to stop the march at once and fill up his ammunition-chests.   But, alas! there was no more ammunition to be had.

The order was imperative. The Confederate commander had fixed his heart upon the work. Just then a number of the enemy's batteries hitched up and hauled off, which gave a glimpse of unexpected hope. Encouraging messages were sent for the columns to hurry on,—and they were then on elastic springing step. The officers saluted as they passed, their stern smiles expressing confidence. General Pickett, a graceful horseman, sat lightly in the saddle, his brown locks flowing quite over his shoulders. Pettigrew's division spread their steps and quickly rectified the alignment, and the grand march moved bravely on. As soon as the leading columns opened the way, the supports sprang to their alignments. General Trimble mounted, adjusting his seat and reins with an air and grace as if setting out on a pleasant afternoon ride. When aligned to their places solid march was made down the slope and past our batteries of position.

Confederate batteries put their fire over the heads of the men as they moved down the slope, and continued to draw the fire of the enemy until the smoke lifted and drifted to the rear, when every gun was turned upon the infantry columns. The batteries that had been drawn off were replaced by others that were fresh. Soldiers and officers began to fall, some to rise no more, others to find their way to the hospital tents. Single files were cut here and there, then the gaps increased, and an occasional shot tore wider openings, but, closing the gaps as quickly as made, the march moved on. The divisions of McLaws and Hood were ordered to move to closer lines for the enemy on their front, to spring to the charge as soon as the breach at the centre could be made. The enemy's right overreached my left and gave serious trouble. Brockenbrough's brigade went down and Davis's in impetuous charge. The general order required further assistance from the Third Corps if needed, but no support appeared. General Lee and the corps commander were there, but failed to order help.

Colonel Latrobe was sent to General Trimble to have his men fill the line of the broken brigades, and bravely they repaired the damage. The enemy moved out against the supporting brigade in Pickett's rear. Colonel Sorrel was sent to have that move guarded, and Pickett was drawn back to that contention. McLaws was ordered to press his left forward, but the direct fire of infantry and cross-fire of artillery was telling fearfully on the front. Colonel Fremantle rode up to offer congratulations on the apparent success, but the big gaps in the ranks grew until the lines were reduced to half their length. I called his attention to the broken, struggling ranks. Trimble mended the battle of the left in handsome style, but on the right the massing of the enemy grew stronger and stronger. Brigadier Garnett was killed, Kemper and Trimble were desperately wounded; Generals Hancock and Gibbon were wounded. General Lane succeeded Trimble, and with Pettigrew held the battle of the left in steady ranks.

Pickett's lines being nearer, the impact was heaviest upon them. Most of the field officers were killed or wounded. Colonel Whittle, of Armistead's brigade, who had been shot through the right leg at Williamsburg and lost his left arm at Malvern Hill, was shot through the right arm, then brought down by a shot through his left leg.

General Armistead, of the second line, spread his steps to supply the places of fallen comrades. His colors cut down, with a volley against the bristling line of bayonets, he put his cap on his sword to guide the storm. The enemy's massing, enveloping numbers held the struggle until the noble Armistead fell beside the wheels of the enemy's battery. Pettigrew was wounded, but held his command.

General Pickett, finding the battle broken, while the enemy was still reinforcing, called the troops off. There was no indication of panic. The broken lines marched back in steady step. The effort was nobly made, and failed from blows that could not be fended. Some of the files were cut off from retreat by fire that swept the field in their rear. Officers of my staff, sent forward with orders, came back with their saddles and bridles in their arms. Latrobe's horse was twice shot.

Looking confidently for advance of the enemy through our open field, I rode to the line of batteries, resolved to hold it until the last gun was lost. As I rode, the shells screaming over my head and ploughing the ground under my horse, an involuntary appeal went up that one of them might take me from scenes of such awful responsibility; but the storm to be met left no time to think of one's self. The battery officers were prepared to meet the crisis,—no move had been made for leaving the field. My old acquaintance of Sharpsburg experience, Captain Miller, was walking up and down behind his guns, smoking his pipe, directing his fire over the heads of our men as fast as they were inside of the danger-line; the other officers equally firm and ready to defend to the last. A body of skirmishers put out from the enemy's lines and advanced some distance, but the batteries opened severe fire and drove it back. Our men passed the batteries in quiet walk, and would rally, I knew, when they reached the ridge from which they started.

General Lee was soon with us, and with staff-officers and others assisted in encouraging the men and getting them together.

8. Colonel A. L. Long served Lee as a military secretary, and took part in the meeting with Longstreet on the morning of the 3rd. He notes that Lee's original plan was changed when Ewell, who was to take the Union rear at Culp's Hill, was pushed back by Federal troops. He also states that the only serious issue under discussion was Longstreet's concern over the Federal artillery on Little Round Top, and that Long's assertion that Confederate guns could suppress them assuaged Longstreet's fears. He describes Lee's plan slightly differently than Longstreet, claiming that Hood and McLaws were to actively support Pickett, but that Longstreet held them back. Col. A. L. Long, *Memoirs of Robert E. Lee* (London: Sampson Low, Marston, Searle and Rivington, 1886), 286-294.

The dawn of the 3d of July found the two armies in the position in which the battle of the preceding day had ended. Though Cemetery Ridge remained intact in the hands of the Federals, yet the engagement had resulted at every point in an advantage to the Confederates. Longstreet had cleared his front of the enemy, and occupied the ground from which they had been driven. Ewell's left held the breastworks on Culp's Hill on the extreme right of the Federal line. Meade's army was known to have sustained heavy losses. There was, in consequence, good reason to believe that a renewed assault might prove successful. Ewell's position of advantage, if held, would enable him to take the Federal line in reverse, while an advance in force from Longstreet's position offered excellent promise of success. General Lee therefore determine to renew the assault.

Longstreet, in accordance with this decision, was reinforced, and ordered to assail the heights in his front on the morning of the 3d, while Ewell was directed to make a simultaneous assault on the enemy's right. Longstreet's dispositions, however, were not complete as early as those of Ewell, and the battle opened on the left before the columns on the right were ready to move. Johnson, whose men held the captured breastworks, had been considerably reinforced during the night, and was on the point of resuming the attack when the Federals opened on him at four o'clock with a heavy fire of artillery which had been placed in position under cover of the darkness. An infantry assault in force followed, and, though Ewell's men held their ground with their usual stubbornness, and maintained their position for four hours, they were finally forced to yield the captured breastworks and retire before the superior force of the enemy.

This change in the condition of affairs rendered necessary a reconsideration of the military problem, and induced General Lee, after making a reconnaissance of the enemy's position, to change his plan of assault. Cemetery Ridge, from Round Top to Culp's Hill, was at every point strongly occupied by Federal infantry and artillery, and was evidently a very formidable position. There was, however, a weak point upon which an attack could be made with a reasonable prospect of success. This was where the ridge, sloping westward, formed the depression through which the Emmitsburg road passes. Perceiving that forcing the Federal lines at that point and turning toward Cemetery Hill the right would be taken in flank and the remainder would be neutralized, as its fire would be as destructive to friend as foe, and considering that the losses of the Federal army in the two preceding days must weaken its cohesion and consequently diminish its power of resistance, General Lee determined to attack at that point, and the execution of it was assigned to Longstreet, while instructions were given to Hill and Ewell to support him, and a hundred and forty-five guns were massed to cover the advance of the attacking column.

The decision here indicated was reached at a conference held during the morning of the field in front of and within cannon-range of Round Top, there being present Generals Lee, Longstreet, A. P. Hill, and H. Heth, Colonel A. L. Long, and Major C. S. Venable. The plan of attack was discussed, and it was decided that General Pickett should lead the assaulting column, to be supported by the divisions of McLaws and Hood and such other force as A. P. Hill could spare from his command. The only objection offered was by General Longstreet, who remarked that the guns on Round Top might be brought to bear on his right. This objection was answered by Colonel Long, who said that the guns on Round Top could be suppressed by our batteries. This point being settled, the attack was ordered, and General Longstreet was directed to carry it out.

. . . The attack of Pickett's division of the 3d has been more criticized, and is still less understood, than any other action of the Gettysburg drama. General Longstreet did not enter into the spirit of it, and consequently did not support it with his wonted vigor. It has been characterized as rash and objectless, on the order of "charge of the Light Brigade." Nevertheless, it was not ordered without mature consideration and on grounds that presented fair prospects of success. By extending his left wing west of the Emmitsburg road, Meade weakened his position by presenting a weak centre, which being penetrated, his wings would be isolated and paralyzed, so fare as regarded supporting each other. A glance at a correct sketch of the Federal position on the 3d will sufficiently corroborate this remark, and had Pickett's division been promptly supported when it burst through Meade's centre, a more positive proof would have been given, for his right wing would have been overwhelmed before the left could have disengaged itself from woods and mountains and come to its relief.

Pickett's charge has been made the subject of so much discussion, and General Lee's intentions in ordering it have been so misunderstood, that it is deemed proper to here offer, in one who was thoroughly conversant with all the facts.

. . . So far, we had succeeded in every encounter with the enemy. It was thought that a continuance of the attack as made by Longstreet offered promise of success. He was ordered to renew the fight early on the 3d; Ewell, who was to co-operate, ordered Johnson to attack at an early hour, anticipating that Longstreet would do the same. Longstreet delayed. He found that a force of the enemy occupying high ground on their left would take his troops in reverse as they advanced. Longstreet was then visited by General Lee, and they conferred as to the mode of attack. It was determined to adhere to the plan proposed, and to strengthen him for the movement he was to be reinforced by Heth's division and two brigades of Pender's of Hill's corps. With his three divisions which were to attack Longstreet made his dispositions, and General Lee went to the centre to observe movements. The attack was not made as designed: Pickett's division, Heth's division, and two brigades of Pender's division advanced. Hood and McLaws were not moved forward. There were nine divisions in the army; seven were quiet, while two assailed the fortified line of the enemy. A. P. Hill had orders to be prepared to assist Longstreet further if necessary. Anderson, who commanded one of Hill's divisions and was in readiness to respond to Longstreet's call, made his dispositions to advance, but General Longstreet told him it was of no use — the attack had failed. Had Hood and McLaws followed or supported Pickett, and Pettigrew and Anderson been advanced, the design of the commanding general would have been carried out: the world would not be so at a loss to understand what was designed by throwing forward, unsupported, against the enemy's stronghold so small a portion of our army. Had General Lee known what was to happen, doubtless he would have maneuvered to force General Meade away from his strong position by threatening his communications with the East, as suggested by ____; but he felt strong enough to carry the enemy's lines, and I believe success would have crowned his plan had it been faithfully carried out.

The author can add his testimony to that of Colonel Taylor. The original intention of General Lee was that Pickett's attack should be supported by the divisions of McLaws and Hood and General Longstreet was so ordered. This order was given verbally by General Lee in the presence of Colonel Long and Major Venable of his staff and other officers of the army.

It is to be regretted that we have no report from the gallant General Pickett in regard to this celebrated charge. It has, however, recently been developed that Pickett did make a very full report, which he forwarded to General Lee. The report severely criticized the failure to furnish him with the supporting force which had been ordered; and Lee, with his usual magnanimity, and in his great desire for harmony between that officers of his army, returned the report to Pickett, requesting him to withdraw it and to substitute in its stead a report embracing merely the casualties of his command; to which Pickett assented and destroyed his first report.

9. Brigadier General William Pendleton commanded Lee's artillery. His report of the planning shows how much he relied on Alexander to organize the right, and did little on his own to organize the guns of Hill's and Ewell's Corps. The disorganization and ineffectiveness of the Confederate artillery rests largely on his shoulders. Pendleton's inability to see to it that the guns could be and were resupplied with ammunition, the removal of the guns Alexander had counted on to go forward to provide protection for the infantry; and the tendency to overshoot the Federal positions add up to one of the major failures of the day. This report amounts to a whitewash of his own ineptitude on July 3rd. Report of Brig. Gen. William N. Pendleton, Sept. 12., 1863, *OR*, 1, 27, 2, 351-353.

By direction of the commanding general, the artillery along our entire line was to be prepared for opening, as early as possible on the morning of the 3d, a concentrated and destructive fire, consequent upon which a general advance was to be made. The right, especially, was if practicable, to sweep the enemy from his stronghold on that flank. Visiting the lines at a very early hour toward securing readiness for this great attempt, I found much (by Colonel Alexander's energy) already accomplished on the right. Henry's battalion held about its original position on the flank. Alexander's was next, in front of the peach orchard. Then came the Washington Artillery Battalion, under Major Eshleman, and Dearing's battalion on his left, these two having arrived since dusk of the day before; and beyond Dearing, Cabell's battalion had been arranged, making nearly sixty guns for that wing, all well advanced in a sweeping curve of about a mile. In the posting of these there appeared little room for improvement, so judiciously had they been adjusted. To Colonel Alexander, placed here in charge by General Longstreet, the wishes of the commanding general were repeated. The battalion and battery commanders were also cautioned how to

fire so as to waste as little ammunition as possible. To the Third
Corps artillery attention was also given. Major Poague's battalion
had been advanced to the line of the right wing, and was not far from
its left. His guns also were well posted. Proper directions were also
given to him and his officers. The other battalions of this corps, a
portion of Garnett's, under Major [Charles] Richardson, being in
reserve, held their positions of the day before, as did those of the
Second Corps, each group having specific instructions from its
chief. Care was also given to the convenient posting of ordnance
trains, especially for the right, as most distant from the main depot,
and due notice given of their position.

From some cause, the expected attack was delayed several
hours. Meanwhile the enemy threw against our extreme right a
considerable force, which was met with energy, Henry's battalion
rendering, in its repulse, efficient service.

At length, about 1 p. m., on the concerted signal, our guns
in position, nearly one hundred and fifty, opened fire along the
entire line from right to left, salvos by battery being much practiced,
as directed, to secure greater deliberation and power. The enemy
replied with their full force. So mighty an artillery contest has
perhaps never been waged, estimating together the number and
character of guns and the duration of the conflict. The average
distance between contestants was about 1,400 yards, and the effect
was necessarily serious on both sides. With the enemy, there was
advantage of elevation and protection from earth works; but his fire
was unavoidably more or less divergent, while ours was convergent.
His troops were massed, ours diffused. We, therefore, suffered
apparently much less. Great commotion was produced in his ranks,
and his batteries were to such extent driven off or silenced as to have
insured his defeat but for the extraordinary strength of his position.

Proceeding again to the right, to see about the anticipated
advance of the artillery, delayed beyond expectation, I found, among
other difficulties, many batteries getting out of or low in ammunition, and the all-important question of supply received my earnest
attention. Frequent shell endangering the First Corps ordnance
train in the convenient locality I had assigned it, it had been removed
farther back. This necessitated longest time for refilling caissons.
What was worse, the train itself was very limited, so that its stock
was soon exhausted, rendering requisite demand upon the reserve
train, farther off. The whole amount was thus being rapidly
reduced. With our means to keep up supply at the rate required for
such a conflict proved practically impossible. There had to be,
therefore, some relaxation of the protracted fire, and some lack of
support for the deferred and attempted advance. But if this and
other causes prevented our sweeping the enemy from his position,
he was so crippled as to be incapable of any formidable movement.

Night closed upon our guns in their advanced position. And had our resources allowed ammunition for the artillery to play another day, the tremendous part it had performed on this his stronghold could scarcely have sufficed to save the enemy from rout and ruin.

10.   Although he was only a battalion commander in Longstreet's artillery reserve, Colonel Edward Porter Alexander commanded the artillery of Longstreet's Corps, and was put in charge of the artillery for the charge. In this paragraph from his essay on "The Great Charge and Artillery Fighting at Gettysburg," in *Battles and Leaders of the Civil War* Robert Underwood Johnson and Clarence Clough Buel, eds., (New York: The Century Magazine, 1888), Vol. III, 361, Alexander notes that he had received orders to place the First Corps' guns and was busy doing so at 3:00 a.m., and also describes the sleeping conditions that night.

There was a great deal to do meanwhile. Our sound horses were to be fed and watered, those killed and disabled were to be replaced from the wagon teams, ammunition must be replenished, and the ground examined and positions of batteries rectified. But a splendid moon made all comparatively easy, and greatly assisted, too, in the care of the wounded, many of whom, both our own and the enemy's, lay about among our batteries nearly all night. About 1 o'clock I made a little bed of fence-rails, as preferable to the trampled ground in the Peach Orchard, and got two hours' sleep. At 3 I began to put the batteries in position again and was joined by the Washington Artillery, which had been in reserve the day before. As daylight came I found I had placed about twenty guns so that the enemy's batteries on Cemetery Hill enfiladed the line, and I had a panic, almost, for fear the enemy could discover my blunder and open before I could rectify it. They would not, perhaps, see down into the valley as early as I could see them and all was right before they opened. They never could have resisted the temptation to such pot-shooting. Apparently to feel us, they fired a few shots, and hit one or two men and some horses; but we did not respond, wanting to save our ammunition for the real work, and we were grateful to them for their moderation, our ground being very unfavorable as regarded shelter.

11.   E. P. Alexander's *Military Memoirs of a Confederate* (New York: Scribner's, 1907) is one of the classics of Civil War

literature. It is perhaps the most serious, balanced, and sustained critique of the command of the Army of Northern Virginia by a participant. In this passage he gives his view of the charge. He states his belief that the Confederate artillery should have done a better job of enfilading the Federal infantry on Cemetery Ridge, and that the attack should have been centered on the Union right, not left. He also tells of Pendleton's offer of the howitzers to accompany Pickett's men, and then his withdrawal of them, and notes that there were 56 cannon idle during the bombardment(415-433).

In his official report Lee writes: — [Here he quotes Lee's official report included above, saying that "the general plan was unchanged."

This statement allows that the strongest features of the enemy's position were not yet apprehended. They were the ability of the enemy to concentrate their whole force upon any point attacked; and the impregnable character of the two Federal flanks. The two brigades sent from Rodes to reinforce Johnson were taken from the new position discovered by him early in the evening and already referred to, not only as the most favorable but as practically the only position from which the Federal line could have been attacked with any hope of success. The brigade sent from Early was sent from a force which could have effectively cooperated with an attack by Rodes. The effect of sending the three brigades was to emasculate the centre of our line and to concentrate several brigades where they were utterly useless.

. . . Lee's headquarters were beyond the Chambersburg pike, about four miles by road from the scene of battle on our right. During the night the Washington artillery was brought up and disposed with the rest of Longstreet's guns about the Peach Orchard, with the intention of resuming the battle in the morning. During the night Longstreet had sent scouts in search of a way by which he might turn the enemy's left and believed he had found one with some promise of success.

[Alexander next summarizes the views of Longstreet, Lee and Long already included]

. . . It seems remarkable that the assumption of Col. Long so easily passed unchallenged that Confederate guns in open and inferior positions could "suppress" Federal artillery fortified upon commanding ridges. Our artillery equipment was usually admitted to be inferior to the enemy's in numbers, calibres and quality of ammunition. Moreover, here, the point selected and the method of the attack would certainly have been chosen for us by the enemy had they had the choice. Comparatively the (Pender had been mortally wounded in the artillery duel of Ewell's corps during the afternoon of the 2d.) weakest portion of their line was Cemetery Hill, and the point of greatest interest in contention with this battle is the story of our entire failure to recognize this fact. The narrative may therefore pause while this neglected opportunity is pointed out.

There was one single advantage conferred by our exterior lines, and but one, in exchange for many disadvantages. They gave us the opportunity to select positions for our guns which could enfilade the opposing lines of the enemy. Enfilading fire is so effective that no troops can submit to it long. Illustrations of this fact were not wanting in the events of this day. What has been called the shank of the Federal fish-hook, extending south from the bend at cemetery Hill toward Little Round Top, was subject to enfilade fire from the town and its flanks and suburbs. That liability should have caused special examination by our staff and artillery officers, to discover other conditions which might favor an assault. There were and are others still easily recognizable on the ground. The salient angle is acute and weak, and within about 500 yards of its west face is the sheltered position occupied by Rodes the night of July 2d, which has already been mentioned.

From nowhere else was there so short and unobstructed an approach to the Federal line, and one so free from flank fire. On the northeast, at but little greater distance, was the position whence Early's two brigades the evening before had successfully carried the east face of the same salient. Within the edge of the town between the two positions was abundant opportunity to accumulate troops and to establish guns at close ranges.

As long as Gettysburg stands and the contour of its hills remains unchanged, students of the battle-field must decide that Lee's most promising attack from first to last was upon Cemetery Hill, by concentrated artillery fire from the north and assaults from the nearest sheltered ground between the west and northeast.

That this was not realized at the time is doubtless partly due to the scarcity of trained staff and reconnoitering officers, and partly to the fact that Ewell had discontinued and withdrawn the pursuit on the afternoon of the 1st, when it was about to undertake this position. Hence the enemy's pickets were not driven closely into their lines, and the vicinity was not carefully examined. Not a single gun was established within a thousand yards, nor was a position selected which enfiladed the lines in question.

Quite by accident, during the cannonade preceding Pickett's charge, Nelson's battalion of Ewell's corps fired a few rounds from a position which did enfilade with great effect part of the 11th Corps upon Cemetery Hill but the fire ceased on being sharply replied to. Briefly the one weak spot of the enemy's line and the one advantage possessed by ours were never apprehended.

In addition to the six brigades of Hill's Corps assigned to

Longstreet for his column of assault, one more, Wilcox of Anderson's division, was later added, making ten brigades in all, of which only three were Longstreet's and seven were Hill's. I was directed by Longstreet to post all of his artillery for a preliminary cannonade, and then to take a position where I could best observe the effect of our fire, and determine the proper moment to give the signal to Pickett to advance. The signal for the opening of the cannonade would be given by Longstreet himself after the infantry brigades were all in position.

A clump of trees in the enemy's line was pointed out to me as the proposed point of our attack, which I was incorrectly told was the cemetery of the town, and about 9 A.M. I began to revise our line and post it for the cannonade. The enemy very strangely interfered with only an occasional cannon-shot, to none of which did we now reply, for it was easily in their power to drive us to cover or to exhaust our ammunition before our infantry column could be formed. I can only account for their allowing our visible preparations to be completed by supposing that they appreciated in what a trap we would find ourselves. Of Longstreet's 83 guns, 8 were left on our extreme right to cover our flank, and the remaining 75 were posted in an irregular line about 1300 yards long, beginning in the Peach Orchard and ending near the northeast corner of the Spangler wood.

While so engaged, Gen. Pendleton offered me the use of nine 12-Pr. howitzers of Hill's Corps, saying that that corps could not use guns of such short range. I gladly accepted and went to receive the guns under command of Maj. Richardson. I placed them under cover close in rear of the forming column with orders to remain until sent for, intending to take them with the column when it advanced.

A few hundred yards to left and rear of my line began the artillery of the 3d corps under Col. Walker. It comprised 90 guns, extending on Seminary Ridge as far as the Hagerstown road, and two Whitworth rifles located nearly a mile farther north on the same ridge. In this interval were located 20 rifle guns of the 2d Corps under Col. Carter. Four more rifles of the same corps under Capt. Graham were located about one and a half miles northeast of Cemetery Hill they 24 guns of the 2d Corps were ordered to fire only solid shot as their fuses were unreliable.

There remained unemployed of the 2d Corps 25 rifles and 16 Napoleons, and of the 3d Corps, fifteen 12-Pr. howitzers. It is notable that of the 84 guns of the 2d and 3d Corps to be engaged, 80 were in the same line parallel to the position of the enemy and 56 guns stood idle. It was a phenomenal oversight not to place these guns, and many beside, in and near the town to enfilade the "shank of the fish-hook" and cross fire with the guns from the west.

The Federal guns in position on their lines at the commence-ment of the cannonade were 166, and during it 10 batteries were brought up from their reserves, raising the number engaged to 220 against 172 used upon our side during the same time.

The formation of our infantry lines consumed a long time, and the formation used was not one suited for such a heavy task. Six brigades, say 10,000 men, were in the first line. Three brigades only were in the second line — very much shorter on the left. It followed about 200 yards in rear of the first. The remaining brigade, Wilcox's, posted in rear of the right of the column, was not put in motion with the column, and being ordered forward 20 minutes or more later, was much too late to be of any assistance whatever. Both flanks of the assaulting column were in the air and the left without any support in the rear. It was sure to crumble away rapidly under fire. The arrangement may be represented thus:—

Brockenbrough, Davis, McGowan, Archer, Garnett, Kemper,
Lane, Scales, Armistead, Wilcox

No formation, however, could have been successful and the light one doubtless suffered fewer casualties than one more compact and deeper would have had.

A little before noon there sprung up upon our left a violent cannonade which was prolonged for fully a half-hour, and has often been supposed to be a part of that ordered to precede Pickett's charge. It began between skirmishers in front of Hill's Corps over the occupation of a house. Hill's artillery first took part in it, it was said, by his order. It was most unwise, as it consumed uselessly a large amount of his ammunition, the lack of which was much felt in the subsequent fighting. Not a single gun of our Corps fired a shot, nor did the enemy in our front.

When the firing died out, entire quiet settled upon the field, extending even to the skirmishers in front, and also to the enemy's rear; whence behind their lines opposing us we had heard all the morning the noise of Johnson's combats.

My 75 guns had all been carefully located and made ready for an hour, while the infantry brigades were still not set in their proper positions, and I was waiting for the signal to come from Longstreet, when it occurred to me to send for the nine howitzers under Richardson, that they might lead in the advance for a few hundred yards before coming into action. Only after the cannonade had opened did I learn that the guns had been removed and could not be found. It afterward appeared that Pendleton had withdrawn four of the guns, and that Richardson with the other five, finding himself in the line of the Federal fire during Hill's cannonade, had moved off to find cover. I made no complaint, believing that had the guns gone forward with the infantry they must have been left upon the field and perhaps have attracted a counter-stroke after the repulse of Pickett's charge. Meanwhile, some half-hour or more before the cannonade began, I was startled by the receipt of a note from Longstreet as follows:—

> Colonel: If the artillery fire does not have the effect to drive off the enemy or greatly demoralize him, so as to make our effort pretty certain, I would prefer that you should not advise Pickett to make the charge. I shall rely a great deal upon your judgment to determine the matter and shall expect you to let Gen. Pickett know when the moment offers.

Until that moment, though I fully recognized the strength of the enemy's position, I had not doubted that we would carry it, in my confidence that Lee was ordering it. But here was proposition that I should decide the question. Overwhelming reasons against the assault at once seemed to stare me in the face. Gen. Wright of Anderson's division was standing with me. I showed him the letter and expressed my views. He advised me to write them to Longstreet, which I did as follows —

> General: I will only be able to judge of the effect of our fire on the enemy by his return fire, as his infantry is little exposed to view and the smoke will obscure the field. If, as I infer from your note, there is any alternative to this attack, it should be carefully considered before opening our fire, for it will take all the artillery ammunition we have left to test this one, and if result is unfavorable we will have none left for another effort. And even if this is entirely successful, it can only be so at a very bloody cost.

To this note, Longstreet soon replied as follows:—

> Colonel: The intention is to advance the infantry if the artillery has the desired effect of driving the enemy's off, or having other effect such as to warrant us in making the attack. When that moment arrives advise Gen. Pickett and of course advance such artillery as you can use in aiding the attack.

Evidently the cannonade was to be allowed to begin. Then the responsibility would be upon me to decide whether or not Pickett should charge. If not, we must return to Va. to replenish ammunition, and the campaign would be a failure. I knew that our guns could not drive off the enemy, but I had a vague hope that with Ewell's and Hill's cooperation something might happen, though I knew little either of their positions, their opportunities, or their orders.

I asked Wright: " What do you think of it ? Is it as hard to get there as it looks?" He answered: "The trouble is not in going there. I went there with my brigade yesterday. There is a place where you can get a breath and re-form. The trouble is to stay there after you get there, for the whole Yankee army is there in a bunch."

I failed to fully appreciate all that this might mean. The question seemed merely one of support, which was peculiarly the province of Gen. Lee. I had seen several of Hill's brigades forming to support Pickett, and had heard a rumor that Lee had spoken of a united attack by the whole army. I determined to see Pickett and get an idea of his feelings. I did so, and finding Hill both cheerful and sanguine, I felt that if the artillery fire opened, Pickett must make the charge; but that Longstreet should know my views, so I wrote him as follows:—

"General: When our fire is at its best, I will advise Gen. Pickett to advance."

It must have been with bitter disappointment that Long-street saw the failure of his hope to avert a useless slaughter, for he was fully convinced of its hopelessness. Yet even he could have scarcely realized, until the event showed, how entirely unprepared were Hill and Ewell to render aid to his assault and to take prompt advantage of even temporary success. None of their guns had been posted with a view to cooperative fire, nor to follow the charge, and much of their ammunition had been prematurely wasted. And although Pickett's assault, when made, actually carried the enemy's guns, nowhere was there the slightest preparation to come to his assistance. The burden of the whole task fell upon the 10 brigades employed. The other 27 brigades and 56 fresh guns were but widely scattered spectators.

12. Lieutenant General A. P. Hill, commander of the Third Corps in the middle of the Confederate line, gives his version of his orders for the day. Hill had been one of the fiercest, most aggressive division commanders. It was said that when Lee rode with Longstreet, it was to speed him up, but that when he rode with Hill, it was to hold him back. Hill had initiated combat on July 1st, and had taken heavy losses. He was also suffering from a long-standing illness. His report echoes his sense of remoteness from the charge; he had no part to play, thus felt no responsibility, especially since two of his divisions were temporarily commanded

by Longstreet. Report of A. P. Hill, __, __, 1863. *OR*, 1, 27, 2, 608.

On the morning of the 3d, the divisions of my corps occupied the same position as on the 2d. The reserve batteries were all brought up, and put in position along the crest of the ridge facing the enemy's line. In addition, the battalion of Colonel Alexander, of Longstreet's Corps, was put in position in front of the right wing of Anderson's division, and on the ground won by Wilcox and Wright. I was directed to hold my line with Anderson's division and the half of Pender's (now commanded by General Lane), and to order Heth's division (commanded by Pettigrew), and Lane's and Scales' brigades, of Pender's division, to report to Lieutenant General Longstreet as a support to his corps in the assault on the enemy's lines. As the troops were filing off to their positions, Major General Trimble reported to me for the command of Pender's division, and took command of the two brigades destined to take part in the assault.

13.   **Lieutenant General Richard Ewell had taken over much of Jackson's Corps in the reorganization in May. On July 3rd he was in command of the left wing of the Army of Northern Virginia, and his men were engaged in action at Culp's Hill. In his official report written after the battle, Ewell reveals that he had orders to attack at dawn or thereabouts, and that he assumed Longstreet had similar orders. Report of Lieut. Gen. Richard S. Ewell, __, __, 1863, *OR*, 1, 27, 2, 447.**

. . . I was ordered to renew my attack at daylight Friday morning, and as Johnson's position was the only one affording hopes of doing this to advantage, he was re-enforced by Smith's brigade. . . Just before the time fixed for General Johnson to advance, the enemy attacked him, to regain the works capture by Steuart the evening before. They were repulsed with very heavy loss, and he attacked in turn, pushing the enemy almost to the top of the mountain. . . Half an hour after Johnson attacked, and when too late to recall him, I received notice that Longstreet would not attack until 10 o'clock, but, as it turned out, his attack was delayed till after 2 o'clock.

14. **Born in 1825, George E. Pickett was the scion of an old Virginia tidewater family who grew up to receive an appointment to West Point from an Illinois congressman, Abraham Lincoln. By**

1863 he had become a Major General and division commander in Longstreet's Corps. As the man in field command of the assault, his name is synonymous with the charge. Throughout the war he was in love with La Salle (Sallie) Corbell, and often wrote gushingly romantic letters. In them he asserted his undying love, and also described his military experiences and the emotions they engendered. After his death, Sallie Pickett published the letters, first in *McClure's* magazine and then in book form. Scholars have long debated their authenticity, but the most recent analysis, by Glenn Tucker, in *Lee and Longstreet at Gettysburg* (Dayton, Ohio: Morningside Bookshop, 1982), finds in their favor. In a letter written just before the charge, Pickett tells of his conversations with "Old Peter," as Longstreet was known, gives a slightly different account of the Lee-Longstreet meeting, and tells of his preparations for the charge. Arthur Crew Inman, ed., *Soldier of the South: General Pickett's War Letters To His Wife* (Freeport, N.Y.: Books for Libraries Press, 1971), 60-62.

. . . Well, Sallie mine, the long, wearying march from Chambersburg, through dust and heat beyond compare, brought us here yesterday (a few miles from Gettysburg). Though my poor men were almost exhausted by the march in the intense heat, I felt that the exigencies demanded my assuring Marse Robert that we had arrived and that, with a few hours' rest, my men would be equal to anything he might require of them. I sent Walter with my message and rode on myself to Little Round Top to see Old Peter, who, I tell you, was mighty glad to see me. And now, just think of it, though the old war-horse was watching A. P. Hill's attack upon the center and Hood and McLaws of his own corps, who had struck Sickles, he turned, and before referring to the fighting or asking about the march, inquired after you, my darling.

While we were watching the fight, Walter came back with Marse Robert's reply to my message, which was in part: "Tell Pickett I'm glad that he has come, that I can always depend upon him and his men, but that I shall not want him this evening."

We have been on the *qui vive*, my Sallie, since midnight; and as early as three o'clock were on the march. About half past three, Gary's pistol signaled the Yankees' attack upon Culp's Hill, and with its echo a wail of regret went up from my very soul that the other two brigades of my old division had been left behind. Oh, God! — if only I had them! — a surety for the honor of Virginia, for I can depend upon them, little one. They know your soldier and would follow him into the very jaws of death, and he will need them — right there, too, before he's through.

At early dawn, darkened by the threatening rain, Armistead, Garnett, Kemper and your soldier held a heart-to-heart powwow.

All three sent regards to you, and Old Lewis pulled a ring from his little finger and, making me take it, said, "Give this little token, George, please, to her of the sunset eyes, with my love, and tell her the old man says since he could not be the lucky dog he's mighty glad that you are."

Dear old Lewis — dear old "Lo," as Magruder always called him, being short for Lothario. Well, my Sallie, I'll keep the ring for you, and some day I'll take it to John Tyler and have it made into a breast-pin and set around with rubies and diamonds and emeralds. You will be the pearl, the other jewel. Dear old Lewis! Just as we three separated to go our different ways after silently clasping hands, our fears and prayers voiced in the "Good luck, old man," a summons came from Old Peter, and I immediately rode to the top of the ridge where he and Marse Robert were making a reconnaissance of Meade's position. "Great God!" said Old Peter as I came up. "Look, General Lee, at the insurmountable difficulties between our line and that of the Yankees — the steep hills — the tiers of artillery — the fences — the heavy skirmish line — And then we'll have to fight our infantry against their batteries. Look at the ground we'll have to charge over, nearly a mile of that open ground there under the rain of their canister and shrapnel."

"The enemy is there, General Longstreet, and I am going to strike him," said Marse Robert in his firm, quiet, determined voice.

About 8 o'clock I rode with them along our line of prostrate infantry. They had been told to lie down to prevent attracting attention, and though they had been forbidden to cheer they voluntarily arose and lifted in reverential adoration their caps to our beloved commander as we rode slowly along. Oh, the responsibility for the lives of such men as these! Well, my darling, their fate and that of our beloved Southland will be settled ere your glorious brown eyes rest on these scraps of penciled paper — your soldier's last letter, perhaps.

Our line of battle faces Cemetery Ridge. Our detachments have been thrown forward to support our artillery which stretches over a mile along the crests of Oak Ridge and Seminary Ridge. The men are lying in the rear, my darling, and the hot July sun pours its scorching rays almost vertically down upon them. The suffering and waiting are .all-lost unbearable.

. . . Well, my sweetheart, at one o'clock the awful silence was broken by a cannon-shot, and then another, and then more than a hundred guns shook the hills from crest to base, answered by more than another hundred — the whole world a blazing volcano — the whole of heaven a thunderbolt — then darkness and absolute silence — then the grim and gruesome, low spoken commands — then the forming of the attacking columns. My brave Virginians are to attack in front. Oh, God in mercy help me as He never helped before!

I have ridden up to report to Old Peter. I shall give him this letter to mail to you and a package to give you if — Oh, my darling, do you feel the love of my heart, the prayer, as I write that fatal word "if" ?

Old Peter laid his hand over mine and said: — "I know, George, I know — but I can't do it, boy. Alexander has my instructions. He will give you the order." There was silence, and his hand still rested on mine when a courier rode up and handed me a note from Alexander.

Now, I go; but remember always that I love you with all my heart and soul, with every fiber of my being; that now and forever I am yours — yours, my beloved. It is almost three o'clock. My soul reaches out to yours — my prayers. I'll keep up a brave heart for Virginia and for you, my darling.

Your Soldier
Gettysburg, July 3, 1863

15. In his official report, Major General J.E.B. Stuart, Lee's cavalry commander, describes his actions on July 3rd. While he does not specify that he was in the Union rear to coordinate with the charge, it is clear that that was the plan. Note that with the addition of the command of Brig. Gen. A. G. Jenkins, Stuart had with him virtually the entire cavalry of the Army, leaving behind only Brig. Gen. John Imboden's small reserve. He would be in place to cut off a main line of Federal retreat, or to advance and do significant damage in the rear as Pickett and his supporting troops broke through the center of the Federal lines. This was another crucial failure, and Stuart blames it on Jenkins. Unfortunately, Stuart would be killed 10 months later, and this is the only written evidence of his role in Pickett's Charge. Report of Major General J. E. B. Stuart, August 20, 1863, *OR*, 1, 27, 2, 697.

On the morning of July 3, pursuant to instructions from the commanding general (the ground along our line of battle being totally impracticable for cavalry operations), I moved forward to a position to the left of General Ewell's left, and in advance of it, where a commanding ridge completely controlled a wide plain of cultivated fields stretching toward Hanover, on the left, and reaching to the base of the mountain spurs, among which the enemy held position. My command was increased by the addition of Jenkins' brigade, who here in the presence of the enemy allowed themselves to be supplied with but 10 rounds of ammunition, although armed with the most approved Enfield musket. I moved this command and W. H. F. Lee's secretly through the woods to a position, and hoped to effect a surprise upon the enemy's rear, but Hampton's and Fitz. Lee's brigades, which had been ordered to follow me, unfortunately debouched into the open ground, disclosing the movement, and causing a corresponding movement of a large force of the enemy's cavalry.

16. **Born in Vermont in 1828 and educated at Dartmouth, Frank Aretas Haskell wrote *the* classic of all eyewitness accounts of Gettysburg, and one of the very best pieces of writing in American literary history. He had wandered west after college, joined a Wisconsin regiment, and became a staff officer under Major General John Gibbon, commander of the Second Division, Second Corps, Army of the Potomac. His work during the charge proved to be essential, and several officers, including Hancock, Gibbon and Harrow, wrote glowing accounts of his performance. He received a promotion to colonel of the 36th Wisconsin Infantry, and was killed at the battle of Cold Harbor in 1864. Shortly after Gettysburg he wrote a long essay on the battle to his brother, and it has been published in several editions. In this section he sketches the Federal generals and describes their planning on the evening of July 2nd. The manuscript is in the Pennsylvania Historical and Museum Commission in Harrisburg.**

After evening came on, and from reports received, all was known to be going satisfactorily upon the right, Gnl. Meade summoned his Corps Commanders to his Head Quarters for consultation. A consultation is held upon matters of vast moment to the country; and that poor little farm house is honored with more distinguished guests than it ever had before, or than it will ever have again, probably.

Do you expect to see a degree of ceremony, and severe military aspect characterize this meeting, in accordance with strict military rules, and commensurate with the moment of the matters of their deliberation? Name it: "Major General Meade, Commander of the Army of the Potomac, with his Corps Generals, holding a council of war, upon the field of Gettysburg," and it would sound pretty well, — and that was what it was; and you might make a picture of it and hang it up by the side of "Napoleon and his Marshals, and Washington and his Generals," may be, at some future time. But for the artist to draw his picture from, I will tell how this council appeared. Meade, Sedgwick, Slocum, Howard, Hancock Sykes, Newton, Pleasonton — commander of the Cavalry and Gibbon were the Generals present. — Hancock, now that Sickles is wounded has charge of the 3d Corps, and Gibbon again has the 2nd.

Meade is a tall, spare man, with full beard, which with his hair, originally brown, is quite thickly sprinkled with gray, — has a Romanish face, very large nose and a white large forehead, prominent and wide over the eyes which are full and large, and quick in their movements, and he wears spectacles. His fibres are all of the long and sinewy kind. His habitual personal appearance is quite careless and it would be rather difficult to make him look well dressed Sedgwick is quite a heavy man, — short, thick-set, and muscular, with florid complexion, dark, calm, straight looking eyes, with full, heavyish features, which with his eyes have plenty of animation when he is aroused, — he has a magnificent profile, — well cut, with the nose and forehead forming almost a straight line, curly short chestnut hair and full beard cut short, with a little gray in it. He dresses carelessly but can look magnificently when he is well dressed. Like Meade, he looks, and is, honest and modest. — You might see at once why his men, because they love him, call him "Uncle John," not to his face of course, but among themselves. Slocum is small, rather spare, with black straight hair, and beard, which latter is unshaven and thin, large full, quick black eyes, white skin, sharp nose, wide cheek bones, and hollow cheeks and small chin. His movements are quick and angular, — and he dresses with a sufficient degree of elegance. Howard is medium in size, has nothing marked about him, is the youngest of them all, I think, — has lost an arm in the war, — has straight brown hair and beard, — shaves his short upper lip, over which his nose slants down, dim blue eyes, and on the whole appears a very pleasant, affable, well dressed little gentleman. Hancock is the tallest, and most shapely, and in many respects is the best looking officer of them all. His hair is very light brown, straight and moist, and always looks, well, — his beard is of the same color, of which he wears the moustache and a tuft upon the chin; complexion ruddy, features neither large nor small, but well cut, with full jaw and chin, compressed mouth, straight nose, full deep blue eyes, and a very mobile, emotional countenance. He always dresses remarkably well, and his manner is dignified, gentlemanly and commanding. I think if he were in citizens clothes, and should give commands in the army to those who did not know him, he would be likely to be obeyed at once, and without any question as to his right to command. Sykes is a small, rather thin man, well dressed and gentlemanly, brown hair and beard which he wears full, with a red, pinched, rough looking skin, feeble blue eyes, large nose, with the general air of one who is weary, and a little ill natured. Newton is a well-sized, shapely, muscular, well dressed man, with brown hair, with a very ruddy, clean-shaved, a nice little dandy, with brown hair and beard,— a straw hat with a little jocky rim, which he cocks upon one side of his head, with an unsteady eye, that looks silly at you, and then dodges.

Gibbon, the youngest of them all save Howard, is about the same size as Slocum, Howard, Sykes and Pleasonton, and there are none of these who will weigh one hundred and fifty pounds. He is compactly made, neither spare nor corpulent, with ruddy complexion, chestnut brown hair, with a clean-shaved face, except his moustache, which is decidedly reddish in color, medium-sized, well-shaped head, sharp, moderately-jutting brows, deep-blue, calm eyes, sharp, slightly-aquiline nose, compressed mouth, full jaws and chin, with an air of calm firmness in his manner.

He always looks well dressed. I suppose Howard is about thirty-five, and Meade about forty-five, years of age; — the rest are between these ages, but not many are under forty. As they come to the council now there is the appearance of fatigue about them, which is not customary, but is only due to the hard labors of the past few days. They all wear clothes of dark blue, — some have top boots, and some not, and except the two-starred strap upon the shoulders of all save Gibbon, who has but one star, there was scarcely a piece of regulation uniform about them all. There were their swords, of various pattern, but no sashes — the Army hat, but with the crown pinched into all sorts of shapes, and the rim slouched down, and shorn of all its ornaments but the gilt band, — except Sykes who wore a blue cap, — and Pleasonton with his straw hat, with broad black band. Then the mean little room where they met, — its only furniture consisted of a large wide bed in one corner; a small pine table in the center, upon which was a wooden pail of water, with a tin cup for drinking, and a candle, stuck to the table by putting the end in tallow melted down from the wick; and five or six straight-backed rush-bottom chairs. The Generals came in, — some sat, some kept walking or standing, two lounged upon the bed, — some were constantly smoking cigars. And thus disposed, they deliberated, the army should fall back from its present position, to one in rear which it was said was stronger; — should attack the enemy on the morrow, wherever he could be found; — or should stand there upon the horse-shoe crest, still on the defensive, and await the further movements of the enemy.

The latter proposition was unanimously agreed to. Their heads were sound. The Army of the Potomac would just halt right there, and allow the Rebel to come up and smash his head against it, to any reasonable extent he desired, as he had to-day. After some two hours the council dissolved, and the officers went their several ways.

17. Perhaps the most effective and least heralded Union officer of the battle, Brigadier General Henry Hunt, was Chief of Artillery in the Army of the Potomac. His efficient management of his guns, including their positioning and the use of his reserves, stands in stark contrast to the disorganization and inefficiency of the Confederate artillery. Yet he received little recognition for his work, and was quickly forgotten after the war. In this essay he reviews Lee's strategy and conditions on the morning of the 3rd, and the positions of the Federal lines, then comments on the effort to interpret the meaning of the artillery bombardment. Hunt guides his gunners to fire slowly and accurately, and harbor their ammunition. Hancock wanted the artillery to fire continuously to keep up the morale of the infantry, but Hunt's orders would enhance their ability to virtually destroy Pickett's lines. His comments about Col. A. L. Long again points out the connections between the officers of both armies. His explanations for the lack of counter-attack make Meade's hesitancy understandable. Henry J. Hunt, "The Third Day At Gettysburg," *Battles and Leaders of the Civil War*, III, 369-376.

On the Federal side Hancock's Corps held Cemetery Ridge with Robinson's division, First Corps, on Hays's right in support, and Doubleday's at the angle between Gibbon and Caldwell. General Newton, having been assigned to the command of the First Corps, vice Reynolds, was now in charge on the ridge held by Caldwell. Compactly arranged on its crest was McGilvery's artillery, forty-one guns, consisting of his own batteries, reenforced by others from the artillery Reserve. Well to the right in front of Hays and Gibbon, was the artillery of the Second Corps under its Chief Captain Hazard. Woodruff's battery was in front of Ziegler's Grove; on his left, in succession, Arnold's Rhode Island, Cushing's United States, Brown's Rhode Island, and Rorty's New York. In the fight of the preceding, day the two last-named batteries had been to the front and suffered severely; Lieutenant T. Fred Brown was severely wounded, and his command devolved on Lieutenant Perrin. So great had been the loss in men and horses that they were now of four guns each, reducing the total number in the corps to twenty-six. Daniels's battery of horse artillery, four guns, was at the angle. Cowan's 1st New York battery, six rifles, was placed on the left of Rorty's soon after the cannonade commenced. In addition, some of the guns on Cemetery Hill, and Rittenhouse's on Little Round Top, could be brought to bear, but these were offset by batteries similarly placed on the flanks of the enemy, so that on the Second Corps line, within the space of a mile, were 77 guns to oppose nearly 150. They were on an open crest plainly visible from all parts of the opposite line. Between 10 and 11 a. m. everything looking favorable at Culp's

Hill, I crossed over to Cemetery Ridge, to see what might be going on at other points. Here a magnificent display greeted my eyes. Our whole front for two miles was covered by batteries already in line or going into position. They stretched — apparently in one unbroken mass — from opposite the town to the Peach Orchard, which bounded the view to the left, the ridges of which were planted thick with cannon. Never before had such a sight been witnessed on this continent, and rarely, if ever, abroad. What did it mean? It might possibly be to hold that line while its infantry was sent to aid Ewell, or to guard against a counter-stroke from his left. It most probably meant an assault on our center, to be preceded by a cannonade in order to crush our batteries and shake our infantry; at least to cause us to exhaust our ammunition in reply, so that the assaulting troops might pass in good condition over the half mile of open ground which was beyond our effective musketry fire. With such an object the cannonade would be long and followed immediately by the assault, their whole army being held in readiness to follow up a success. From the great extent of ground occupied by the enemy's batteries, it was evident that all the artillery on our west front, whether of the army corps or the reserve, must concur as a unit, under the chief of artillery, in the defense. This is provided for in an well-organized armies by special rules, which formerly were contained in our own army regulations, but they had been condensed in successive editions into a few short lines, so obscure as to be virtually worthless, because, like the rudimentary toe of the dog's paw, they had become, from lack of use, mere survivals — unintelligible except to the specialist. It was of the first importance to subject the enemy's infantry, from the first moment of their advance, to such a cross-fire of our artillery as would break their formation, check their impulse, and drive them back, or at least bring them to our lines in such condition as to make them all easy prey. There was neither time nor necessity for reporting this to General Meade, and beginning on the right, instructed the chiefs of artillery and battery commanders to withhold their fire for fifteen or twenty minutes after the cannonade commenced, then to concentrate their fire with all possible accuracy on those batteries which were most destructive to us — but slowly, so that when the enemy's ammunition was exhausted, we should have sufficient left to meet the assault. I had just given these orders to the last battery on Little Round Top, when the signal-gun was fired, and the enemy opened with all his guns. From that point the scene was indescribably grand. All their batteries were soon covered with smoke, through which the flashes were incessant, whilst the air seemed filled with shells, whose sharp explosions, with the hurtling of their fragments, formed a running accompaniment to the deep roar of the guns. Thence I rode to the Artillery Reserve to order fresh batteries and ammunition to be sent up to the ridge as soon as the cannonade ceased; but both the reserve and the train had gone to a safer place. Messengers, however, had been left to receive and convey orders, which I sent by them; then I returned to the ridge. Turning into the Taneytown pike, I saw evidence of the necessity under which the reserve had "decamped," in the remains of a dozen exploded caissons, which had been placed under cover of a hill, but which the shells had managed to search out. In fact, the fire was more dangerous behind the ridge than on its crest, which I soon reached at the position occupied by General Newton behind McGilvery's batteries, from which we had a fine view as all our own guns were now in action.

18.   John Gibbon had grown up in North Carolina and attended West Point. When the war came, three of his brothers sided with the South, while he stayed in the Union army. A 36-year-old Brigadier General at Gettysburg, he was known as one of the most effective combat officers, retaining his sense of self and a calm head no matter what the crisis. He gives us the best account of the strategic and tactical planning that occurred in Meade's headquarters on the evening of July 2nd.   John Gibbon, *Recollections of the War* (New York: G.P. Putnam, 1928), 140-145.

Soon after all firing had ceased, a staff officer from Army Headquarters met Gen. Hancock and myself and summoned us both to Gen. Meade's Headquarters where a council was being held. We at once proceeded there and soon after our arrival, all the corps commanders were assembled in the little front room of the Leister House; Newton, who had been assigned to the command of the 1st Corps over Doubleday, his senior, Hancock of the 2nd, Birney the 3rd, Sykes the 5th, Sedgwick who had arrived during the day with the 6th after a long march from Manchester, Howard, 11th; and Slocum, 12th, besides Gen. Meade, Gen. Butterfield, chief of staff, Warren, Chief of Engineers, A. S. Williams, 12th Corps, and myself, 2nd Corps. It will be seen that two corps were double represented, the 2nd Corps by Hancock and myself and the 12th by Slocum and Williams. These twelve were all assembled in a little room not more than 10 or 12 ft. square with a bed in one corner, a small table on one side and a chair or two. Of course all could not sit down. Some did, some lounged on the bed, some stood up whilst Warren, tired out and suffering from a wound in the neck, where a piece of shell had struck him, lay down in the corner of the room and went sound asleep and I don't think he heard any of the proceedings.

The discussion was at first very informal and in the shape of a conversation during which each one made comments on the fight and told what he knew of the condition of affairs. In the course of this discussion, Newton expressed the opinion that "this was no place to fight a battle in." Gen. Newton was an officer of Engineers (since Chief Engineer of the army) and was rated by me and, I suppose, by most of the others, very highly as a soldier. The assertion, therefore, coming from such a source, rather startled me and I eagerly asked what his objections to the position were. The objections he stated, as I recollect them, related to some minor details of the line, of which I knew nothing except so far as my own front was concerned and with those I was satisfied, but the prevailing impression seemed to be that the place for the battle had been in a measure, selected for us. "Here we are, now what is the best thing to do?" It soon became evident that everybody was in favor of remaining where we were and giving battle there. Gen. Meade himself, said very little except now and then to make some comment but I cannot recall that he expressed any decided opinion upon any point, preferring, apparently, to listen to the conversation. After the discussion had lasted for some time, Butterfield suggested that it would, perhaps, be well to formulate the questions to be asked and Gen. Meade assenting, he took a piece of paper on which he had been making some memoranda and wrote down a question. When he had done so he read it off and formally proposed it to the council.

I had never been a member of a council of war before (nor have I been since) and did not feel very confident that I was properly a member of this one, but I had engaged in the discussion and found myself, Warren being asleep, the junior member in it. By the custom of war the junior member votes first as on courts-martial, and when Butterfield read off his first question, the substance of which was should the army remain in its present position or take up some other, he addressed himself first to me for an answer. To say, "Stay and fight," was to ignore the objections made by Gen. Newton and I, therefore, answered somewhat in this way. "Remain here, and make such corrections in our position as may be deemed necessary but take no step which even looks like retreat." The question was put to each member and his answer taken down and when it came to Newton who was the fifth in rank, he voted pretty much in the same way as I had done and we had some playful sparring as to whether he agreed with me or I with him and all the rest voted to remain.

The next question written by Butterfield was, should the army attack or await the attack of the enemy? I voted not to attack and all the others voted substantially the same and on the third question — how long shall we wait?" I voted "until Lee moved." The answers to this last question showed the only material variation in the opinion of the members.

When the voting was over Gen. Meade said quietly, but decidedly "Such then, is the decision." And certainly he said nothing which produced, to my mind, a doubt as to his being perfectly in accord with the members of the council.

In 1881 (18 years after the battle) I was shown in Philadelphia by Gen. Meade's son a paper found among his effects after his death. It was folded and on the outside of one end was written in his well known handwriting, in ink, "- minutes of Council, July 2nd, '63." On opening it the following was found written in pencil in a handwriting unknown to me:

MINUTES OF COUNCIL, JULY 2d 1863
QUESTIONS ASKED
1. Under existing circumstances, is it advisable for this army to remain in its present position or to retire to another, nearer its base of supplies?
2. It being determined to remain in present position, shall the army attack or await the attack of the enemy?
3. If we await attack, how long?

REPLIES:

Gibbon: 1. Correct the position of army, but would not retreat.
2. In no condition to attack, in his opinion.
3. Until he moves.

Williams: 1. Stay.
2. Await attack.
3. One day.

Birney, same as Williams
Sykes, same as Williams.

Newton: 1. Correct position of army, but would not retreat.
2. By all means not to attack.
3. If we wait, it will give them a chance to cut our line. Remain.

Howard: 1. Remain.
2. Await attack until 4 p. m. tomorrow.
3. If they don't attack, them.

Hancock: 1. Rectify position without moving so as not to give up field.
2. Not attack unless our communications are cut.
3. Can't wait long, can't be idle.

Sedgwick: 1. Remain.

2. Await attack.
3. At least one day.

Slocum: Stay and fight.

Newton thinks it a bad position, Hancock puzzled about practicability of retiring, thinks by holding on (illegible) to mass forces and attack. Howard in favor of not retiring. Birney don't know. 3rd Corps used up and not in good condition to fight. Sedgwick (illegible). Effective strength about 9,000, 12,500, 9,000, 6,000, 8,500, 6,000, 7,000. total, 58,000.

D. B.

The memorandum at the bottom of the paper was doubtless made whilst the discussion was going on and the numbers at the foot refer probably to the effective strength of each corps.

Several times during the sitting of the council, reports were brought to Gen. Meade and now and then we could hear heavy firing going on over on the right of our line. It was nearly midnight before we separated and before we left the house I saw Gen. Meade in conversation with Gen. Birney and overhead the former say in rather a curt way, "Gen. Hancock is your superior and I claim the right to issue the order." From which I inferred that Birney had made some comments on the assignment of Hancock to command the 3rd Corps. I took occasion before leaving to say to Gen. Meade that his staff officer had regularly summoned me as a corps commander to the council, although I had some doubts about being present. He answered pleasantly, "That is all right, I wanted you here."

Gen. Meade was not himself the ranking officer in the army he commanded, both Reynolds and Sedgwick being his seniors, but Congress had by law, empowered the President to assign a junior to command. Meade told me that Secretary Stanton had telegraphed him that as Commander of the Army of the Potomac, he should be supported by the whole power of the War Department. It was upon this, I presume, that Gen. Meade took the responsibility of placing officers of his own choosing in places where he wanted them. Thus, on July 1st, he sent Hancock to command his senior (Howard), assigned me to command my senior in the 2nd Corps, Newton to command his in the 1st and in the midst of battle, sent Hancock to take command over Birney, the next in rank to Sickles in that Corps.

Before I left the house, Meade made a remark to me that surprised me a good deal, especially when I looked back upon the occurrence of the next day. By a reference to the votes in council it will be seen that the majority of members were in favor of acting on the defensive and awaiting the action of Lee. In referring to the matter, just as the council broke up, Meade said to me, "If Lee attacks tomorrow, it will be in your front." I asked him why he thought so and he replied "Because he has made attacks on both our flanks and failed and if he concludes to try it again, it will be on our centre." I expressed a hope that he would and told Gen. Meade with confidence that if he did, we would defeat him. Meade's reliance upon the doctrine of chances, that having tried each of our wings, Lee would, if he made a third trial, make it upon our centre, struck me as somewhat remarkable. But he was right.

As I have said it was near on to midnight when the council broke up and then Hancock, Newton and I repaired to a yard near the next house south of Meade's Headquarters (Brown's) and all three crawling into my headquarters ambulance, slept till waked up early the next morning by heavy picket firing on our left near Round Top. Everybody was soon astir, but the morning wore away and nothing very remarkable seemed to be taking place although every now and then the cannon on either side would open or a sudden spurt of picket firing take place, showing that both sides were alert and ready for slaughter — when the chiefs gave the word. I can hardly recall how the long hours of the morning wore away, or how we occupied our time, but recollect that the servants at my Division Headquarters went to work late in the morning to make us some coffee and prepare something to eat. One of them had "picked up" somewhere (no doubt without due process of law, for hungry men are not overscrupulous in regard to other men's rights or chickens) an old and tough rooster which was prepared for the pot and made into a stew and I recollect that I at once went to Meade's Headquarters and finding him looking worn and haggard, asked him if he had had any breakfast. He said no and I urged him to come to my Headquarters and share mine. He at first objected saying that he must remain at his Headquarters prepared to receive the reports which were constantly coming in and act on them. But I pointed out that we were close at hand in plain sight, that he would be absent but a few minutes, could leave word where he was and besides he must keep up his physical strength. He yielded to my solicitations and went with me sharing with us our coffee and stewed rooster, but almost immediately after returning to his Headquarters leaving our group of officers seated on the ground chatting over the battle and the probable events of the day. How long we sat there it is impossible to say but after a long silence along the line a single gun was heard off in my front and everyone's attention was attracted.

Section II

"They Would Have Made The Charge Without An Officer Of Any Description":

Preparing For The Charge

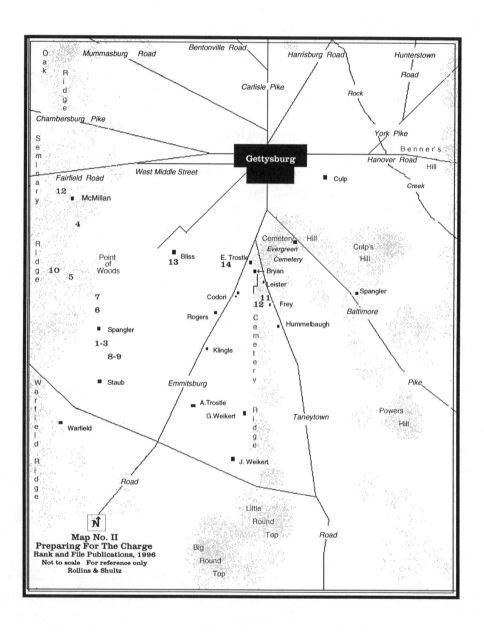

Mummasburg Road
Bentonville Road
Harrisburg Road
Hunterstown Road

Oak Ridge

Carlisle Pike

Rock

Chambersburg Pike

York Pike

Benner's

Seminary

Gettysburg

Hanover Road
Hill

Fairfield Road
West Middle Street
Culp

12 ■ McMillan
Creek

4

Ridge

Cemetery Hill
Culp's Hill

Evergreen
Cemetery

Point of Woods
13 ■ Bliss
E. Trostle
14

10 5
■ ← Bryan
Leister
Spangler

7
Codori
11
12 ■ Frey
Baltimore

6
Rogers
Hummelbaugh

■ Spangler
Cemetery

1-3
8-9
■ Klingle

■ Staub
Emmitsburg
Pike

Warfield Ridge
A.Trostle
G.Weikert
Taneytown
Powers Hill

■ Warfield
Ridge

■ J. Weikert

Seminary Ridge

Road

Little Round Top

N

Map No. II
Preparing For The Charge
Rank and File Publications, 1996
Not to scale   For reference only
Rollins & Shultz

Big Round Top
Road

1. Born in Virginia, Randolph Shotwell went north to study at Tuscarora Academy in Mifflin, Pennsylvania. When the war broke out he travelled to Virginia and joined the first regiment he found; it turned out to be Major Edmund Berkeley's 8th Virginia Infantry. He was 18 years old at Gettysburg, and won a promotion to Lieutenant for his bravery there. In this passage he gives us some insight into the life of a typical soldier. It is important to remember that even though Pickett's men had not fought on July 2nd, they had made a long, difficult march in the broiling sun and suffered much from heat and exhaustion. He hears some of the rumors that abounded in an army with no means of disseminating news, including the widespread one that a charge of the entire army would be made on the 3rd. He writes a poignant anecdote about receiving a letter from home while hearing the sounds of artillery in the distance. I have placed this out of its order by rank, at the beginning of this section because it sets the stage for the material that follows. The material excerpted here is from his autobiography, *Three Years in Battle and Three in Federal Prisons* in J. G. de Roulhal Hamilton, ed., *The Papers of Randolph Shotwell* (Raleigh: North Carolina Historical Commission, 1929-1931), 1-31.

— July 2d.—Four miles from the Battlefield of Gettysburg.

After a fatiguing march of 30 miles over a very rough turnpike, one has very little energy for note making, and tonight I confess to being as nearly worn out as a man can be without actually breaking down; yet I will devote the few remaining moments of twilight to recording another day's transactions as it may be the last that I shall have to note. I say it may be because at this moment as I write, the solemn forest is quivering under the deep reverberations of heavy cannonading, and the stream of gory looking soldiers coming back from the front, tell of the deadly conflict, which must be concluded tomorrow by the work of our own muskets and artillery.

We left camp south of Chambersburg at a very early hour this morning, and marching through town, filed off on the Baltimore turnpike. The townspeople no doubt felt a sensation of relief as our flags fluttered over the hills eastward; tho' any idea they may have had that we were retreating must have been dispelled by the enthusiastic cheers and gratified shouts that went up from the troops when they discovered the head of column tending eastward. "Here we go — right off for Baltimore!" — was the cry that ran along the lines and many companies sang the "Bonnie Blue Flag" or "Way Down South in Dixie."

Indeed, I rarely ever saw the troops more inspirited, which was much of a mystery to the phlegmatic, well-fed "Deutchers" as they could not imagine how any one so poorly fed, clothed, and paid — to say nothing of hardships, — could have any sort of liveliness of spirit.

As the day advanced, the sun took effect on the overladen men (carrying three days' rations, and extra ammunition), and quite a number were prostrated, while all of us suffered most severely. As we approached the Cashtown Gap about noon the vertical rays of the sun seemed like real Lances of steel tipped with fire! The broken rock of the McAdamized turnpike and the broad flat flagstones of mountain slate reflected the heat until a perfect steam arose in our faces as we trudged along and the choking dust gathered in throats and eyes causing infinite annoyance. At times the whole line or column seemed to stagger like "men overcome with new wine," as the Good Book mildly describes an attack of "Brandy on the Brain." In the middle of Cashtown Gap we halted for ten minutes' rest, and dinner. There was little shade and less breeze; and the sigh of exhaustion with which the men unshouldered their packs was only exceeded by the groan with which they were resumed, when the so called rest was over. It was now one o'clock P. M. and we had travelled 20 miles since dawn.

For my own part, having exceedingly sore feet, and not suspecting the proximity of a battle, I had resolved "not to be dragged to death" in this manner, but to take the first opportunity to leave ranks, retire to some shady spot, and "take mine ease" until after sunset; not doubting that the refreshment thus obtained would enable me to catch up with the command by nightfall, as it could hardly make many miles farther. However, before I could put my design into execution, I chanced to overhear General Garnett saying:— *"Pickett says we must go to Gettysburg tonight, at all risks; the battle is not decided, and if the enemy holds his ground; we must attack him tomorrow ourselves."* Here was news indeed! Of course I could not "fall out of ranks" at such a time, and with feelings akin to despair I strung up my energies to make the nine or ten miles yet before us. In all sincerity I can say that at that moment the thought of the afternoon's march was much more trying than the perils of tomorrow's battle.

To march 30 miles — some say 32 — under a broiling July sun — over rocky roads — up hill and down hill — without enough drinking water and loaded down with 120 pounds requires nerves and muscles of iron or gutta percha. Neither of which mine are!

We reached Cashtown at 4 P. M. It is a mere hamlet at the east face of the Gap. Here we found the reserve artillery and wagon trains in park. And here we first learned that there had been heavy fighting for the past two days resulting in a glorious victory for our arms; though the battle was not yet fully decided.

It seems that the Lincolnites have assembled the Pennsylvania Reserves, together with all the available troops from Washington, New York, Philadelphia, and Baltimore; all of whom have been hurried to reinforce Meade; so that he confronts us with a mighty army of more than 150,000 men.

Meade appears to have been marching to meet Lee when A. P. Hill jumped out from Cashtown Gap, and hit him in the face about a mile from where I write. Then Ewell came down from Carlisle and banged into his right flank, — forcing him to fall back to Gettysburg where he is now entrenched on a high ridge. This afternoon Longstreet attacked with two divisions, and held the ridge for a while but was overpowered. We however, have had the best of the fight so far; and have already captured between 4,000 and 5,000 prisoners, who are bivouacking under guard, about half a mile from us. The Federal General Reynolds has been killed. His fine black charger, with costly trappings and gold lace ornaments has just gone by, led by one of our men. He was much admired by those who noticed him.

Later: — Orders have been received to be ready to march at three o'clock tomorrow morning. This will give us but little rest; for we cannot get to sleep until the uproar of the wagons and artillery subsides, which will hardly be before ten o'clock.

A few minutes ago I was handed a letter from home. It had been nearly three weeks on the way. I wish I had not received it. How strange a contrast between the simple home affairs in the backwoods of North Carolina — of which the letter speaks — and the stirring, exciting situation in which it finds me. Here are thousands of weary soldiers lying on the grass, the light of countless camp fires illuminating the grove, the rumble of long trains upon the turn-pike, and the sullen "Boom!" "Boom!" "Boom!" "Boom!" of artillery in the distance. There the quiet parsonage is calmly bathed in twilight, with only the sound of tinkling cowbells, or the notes of music within hearing. Little did Father imagine the circumstances under which his letter would be read; though he bids me do my duty, and trust in Providence! The one I am doing, the other is rather more difficult. Little Jimmie Bose came to me a few minutes ago, and laid down on the edge of my blanket. Seeing him rather depressed, I asked him what troubled him. Said he: — "I wish you would take my money, and this little Journal and give it to mother if I get killed tomorrow." I tried to reason him out of his presentiment, but he seems almost certain of death. Says he was barefooted and could have stayed back in Loudon as his Mother wanted him to do, but he told her he wanted to come on with the Army and get himself a pair of new boots in Baltimore. She replied, "I fear you will never live to see Baltimore, Jimmie!" And said Jimmie: — "I expect she was right."

Nine o'clock P. M. — The noise of the battle has ceased, but the talking of the men who are cooking rations, prevents sleep. I am nearly dead for a drink of water, and it's fully half a mile to the spring! Alas! Alas!

As Ewell's weakened line was stubbornly resisting the successive waves of Blue coats hurled over the plateau upon them, many a mental question was asked: — "By all our hopes of victory, why don't Longstreet do something to call off these swarms of fresh troops that are overpowering us!"

The query has since become an historic one. According to General Lee's orders, Longstreet should have attacked on the right shortly after sunrise, coincident with Ewell's advance upon the left. But a second time that officer assumed the responsibility of disobeying orders, or of delaying action until the original programme of simultaneous assault, by both wings of the army had been practically nullified through the defeat of the corps which acted in accordance with Lee's directions.

The noble Lee, unwilling to censure his favorite lieutenant, finds a partial excuse for his dilatoriness as follows:

General Longstreet was delayed by a force occupying the high, rocky hill on the enemy's extreme left, from which his troops could be attacked from reverse as they advanced. His operations had been embarrassed the day previously from the same cause, and he now deemed it necessary to defend his flank and rear with the divisions of Hood and McLaws. He was therefore reinforced by Heth's division [under Pettigrew] and two brigades of Pender [Scales and Lane] to the command of which General Trimble was assigned. Gen. A. P. Hill was directed to hold his line with the rest of his command, to afford Longstreet farther assistance if required, and to avail himself of any success that might be gained.

It is asserted by excellent authority that Lee's orders provided for the participation of Longstreet's entire corps in this attack. Of this we shall speak hereafter.

General Pickett's division, of 5,500 Virginians, having bivouacked near the Stone Bridge, within four miles of the field, after a march of 30 miles from Chambersburg, was in motion before daybreak, and marching up a narrow valley west of Seminary Ridge, reached its appointed position on Seminary Ridge a little after sunrise, on the morning of the 3rd. Longstreet had ordered Pickett to form his line "under the best cover that he could get, from the enemy's batteries, and so that the center of the assaulting column should arrive at the salient of the enemy's position, General Pickett's line to be the guide, and General Pettigrew moving on the same line as Pickett, to assault the salient at the same time."

Pickett drew up his division in the hollow behind the line of batteries, which now crowned Seminary Ridge. The column of assault consisted of Garnett's brigade on the right, Kemper's on the left, and Armistead supporting both. Wilcox's brigade of Anderson's division, which was to accompany the attacking column as a cover to Pickett's flanks, was already in contact with the Federal skirmishers, having been sent to the front early in the morning to protect the batteries on the Ridge. It lay almost in front of Pickett's right brigade, ready to arise and go forward when the latter passed on its way to charge the Heights. Pettigrew, commanding Heth's division, formed his four brigades in single line, Archer's on the right, Pettigrew's under Marshall, next, Davis' next, and Brockenborough(sic) on the extreme left. This division had fought with unsurpassed gallantry on the 1st, and was now scarcely as strong as two good brigades; Archer's brigade especially, to use a common expression "being but a shadow of its former self." This fact should be borne in mind in connection with subsequent occurrences. The third division of the attacking column consisted simply of Scales and Lane's brigades (North Carolinians, both) of Pender's division under the command of General J. R. Trimble, who had arrived from the Valley of Virginia, just in time to be assigned to this honorable, but perilous command. His brigades were formed in rear of the right of Pettigrew's division; the intent being that he should reinforce the right or left wing of the assaulting column as occasion might require.

General Lee realized the weakness of the column for so hazardous an undertaking as is shown by his remark to Brigadier General Lane that he "needed more troops on the right very badly, but did not know where they were to come from."

From the foregoing, the reader will perceive that after the failure of Longstreet to co-operate with Ewell's assault upon the Federal right at Culp's Hill, a somewhat changed order of battle was adopted for the afternoon attack. Upon the presumption that Meade must have greatly weakened his center to reinforce the defeated troops on the extreme right and left — the weakest points of his position — General Lee decided upon a fourth and final attempt to dislodge him, on the following programme:

1st. — To arrange a column of 10,000 men, including Pickett's 5,000 fresh troops, behind the cover of Seminary Ridge, confronting the most advanced point, or salient of the enemy's works.

2d. — To assemble 100 or more pieces of artillery whose fire should be concentrated on the salient, and the adjacent lines to drive off the Federal batteries, and demoralize his infantry as far as possible.

3d. — When the artillery had done its best, to launch forth the assaulting column, followed and seconded by field batteries, to pierce the Federal lines and break his army into two parts; while at the first indication of commotion or disorder, among the enemy, all the other corps should spring forward, and convert the defeat into a rout.

It is easy to say *now* that this was an impracticable under-taking — that the Federal position and forces were too strong, and the attacking column altogether too weak for any such task. It is easy *now* to suggest a score of things that might have been done, or left undone. These *ex post facto* proofs of wisdom are the special province of a certain class of military and historical critics, who are "nothing if not critical."

Those who participated in the ill-fated charge, saw nothing of the "rashness," "blind folly," or "uselessness" of the attempt, but on the contrary were in splendid spirits and confident of sweeping everything before them. I refer, now, to the rank and file, of whom my recollection is that never was there anything like the same enthusiasm in entering battle.

Pickett's division had fewer "stragglers" than ever before, and while all the men realized that they were to have bloody work, none despaired of ultimate triumph. Reports of our successes on the first and second days were rife in the command, it was seen that we had driven the enemy for miles, and captured 5,000 prisoners, and all these things were an unquestioned guarantee of continued success. As the sun climbed towards the meridian, many of the men drew out their "corn dodgers" and bits of bacon, to make their frugal dinner, — to many the last meal on earth. Others spread their blankets on the gravelly hillside and stretched themselves for a nap. Everything looked quiet, dull and lazy, — as one sees the harvest-hands lolling under the trees at noontime. Up on the crest of the Ridge, 50 feet in advance of the infantry were the long lines of cannon and caissons, battery after battery as far as could be seen to right and left. Some of the gunners were examining their pieces: others sat idly about. A little in the rear of the caissons, the drivers were digging grave-like holes — six feet long, and one to two feet deep in which they purposed ensconcing themselves when the cannon-ade opened. Had we had the tools the infantry might also have thrown up a temporary protection for itself during the long hours of weary waiting for the order to "up and at 'em!"

2. In this passage from his memoirs, Adjutant James Crocker describes the feelings of a typical Confederate soldier on the morning of July 3rd. Knowing that more fighting would occur, they felt that perhaps the outcome of the entire war hung in the balance, and had considerable confidence that things would go their way. J. F. Crocker, *Gettysburg — Pickett's Charge and Other War Addresses* (Portsmouth, Va.: n.p., 1915), 37-44.

. . . From the teamsters to the general in chief it was known that the battle was yet undecided — that the fierce combat was to be renewed. All knew that victory won or defeat suffered, was to be at a fearful cost — that the best blood of the land was to flow copiously as a priceless oblation to the god of battle. The intelligent soldiers of the South knew and profoundly felt that the hours were potential — that on them possibly hung the success of their cause — the peace and independence of the Confederacy. They knew that victory meant so much more to them than to the enemy. It meant to us uninvaded and peaceful homes under our own rule and under our own nationality. With us it was only to be let alone. With this end in view, all felt that victory was to be won at any cost. All were willing to die, if only their country could thereby triumph. And fatal defeat meant much to the enemy. It meant divided empire — lost territory and severed population. Both sides felt that the hours were big with the fate of empire. The sense of the importance of the issue, and the responsibility of fully doing duty equal to the grand occasion, impressed on us all a deep solemnity and a seriousness of thought that left no play for gay moods or for sympathy with nature's smiling aspect, however gracious. Nor did we lightly consider the perils of our duty. From our position in line of battle, which we had taken early in the morning, we could see the frowning and cannon-crowned heights far off held by the enemy. In a group of officers, a number of whom did not survive that fatal day, I could not help expressing that it was to be another Malvern Hill, another costly day to Virginia and to Virginians. While all fully saw and appreciated the cost and the fearful magnitude of the assault, yet all were firmly resolved, if possible, to pluck victory from the very jaws or death itself. Never were men more conscious of the difficulty imposed on them by duty, or more determinedly resolve to perform it with alacrity and cheerfulness, even to annihilation, than were the men of Pickett's division on that day. With undisturbed fortitude and even with ardent impatience did they await the command for the assault. The quiet of the day had been unbroken save on our extreme left, where in the early morning there had been some severe fighting; but this was soon over, and now all on both sides were at rest, waiting in full expectancy of the great assault, which the enemy, as well as we, knew was to be delivered. The hours commenced to go wearily by. The tension on our troops had become great. The mid-day sun had reached the zenith, and poured its equal and impartial rays between the opposite ridges that bounded the intervening valley running North and South. Yet no sound or stir broke the ominous silence. Both armies were waiting spectators for the great event. Upwards of one hundred thousand unengaged soldiers were waiting as from a grand amphitheatre to witness the most magnificent heroic endeavor in arms that ever immortalized man. Still the hours lingered on. Why the delay? There is a serious difference of opinion between the general in chief and his most trusted lieutenant general as to the wisdom of making the assault.

3. Walter Harrison served as Pickett's Inspector General, and had some interesting comments on the mental state of the Southerners before the charge. Even the waiting for the charge was stressful, and little things, especially those that gave some relief from the tension and the heat, such as the quality of the water, became emblazoned on their memory. Walter Harrison, *Pickett's Men: A Fragment of War History* (New York: n.p., 1870, 91-107).

The strength of position of the enemy was frightful to look at. I had an opportunity of examining it carefully, before the attack was made, which few others had, and in this way. The left of Garnett's Brigade overlapped a little the right of Pettigrew's in the line of battle front, thus preventing Armistead's Brigade from coming up in the continuation of the first line. While forming this line, Gen. Armistead asked me to inquire of Gen. Pickett whether he wished him to push out, and form line in front of the right of Heth's Division, or to hold his position in rear for the present. Brave old Armistead was very tenacious of place to the front. Not seeing Gen. Pickett immediately, and anxious to satisfy Gen. Armistead, I rode up to Gen. Longstreet, whom I saw with Gen. Lee, on top of the ridge in front of us making a close reconnaissance of the enemy's position, and addressed Gen. Armistead's question to him. The great "war-horse" of the army, or as he was more familiarly called, "Old Peter," seemed to be in anything but a pleasant humor at the prospect "over the hill;" for he snorted out, rather sharply, I thought: "Gen. Pickett will attend to that, sir." Then, as I was going off — thinking perhaps, in his usual kind-heartedness, that he had unnecessarily snubbed a poor sub — he said: "Never mind, colonel, you can tell Gen. Armistead to remain where he is for the present and he can make up his distance when the advance is made." And this, as is well known, Armistead nobly did. My little trespass on military etiquette, if it brought with it a fair reproof, was the means of my obtaining a first and comprehensive view of the position of the enemy, and truly it was no cheering prospect.

His troops seemed to be heavily massed right on our only point of attack. Holding an advanced front, almost inaccessible in the natural difficulties of the ground, first by a line of skirmishers, almost as heavy as a single line of battle, in the lower ground; then the steep acclivity of the "Ridge" covered with two tiers of artillery, and two lines of infantry supports. These had to be passed over before reaching the crest of the heights where his heavy reserves of infantry were massed in double column.

A loose stone-fence or wall, common in the country, ran along the side of this ridge, offering cover and protection to his infantry, while a common rail-fence running through the bottom land, presented an obstacle to the advance of our men. From the crest of the hill, where our men first became exposed to the direct fire, down the descent, and up to the enemy's front must have been, I should think, half a mile, at least, of entirely open and exposed ground. Over this terrible space, within canister and shrapnel range, it would be necessary for our brave and devoted boys to go, before striking the foe at anything like close quarters. Ah! it looked — even in that morning's light, before a deadly shot had been fired, before a drop of blood had spotted that green meadow, which was so soon to be soaked with bloody carnage — like an open *guet apens* for slaughter, a passage to the valley of death; and the attacking force, like a truly "forlorn hope" on an extensive scale. But Gen. Lee's confidence in the men he had reserved for this desperate work, the well-proved metal of these veterans of many a hard-won field under his own eye, doubtless had satisfied him, even at that early day, that "Pickett's Men" could and would "carry anything they are put against."

The day was clear and bright. Nature, at least, was all smiling as she will smile, spite of the existing or portending woes of mortals; although her elements had already been well shaken by two days of desultory fighting, yet the serenity of this morn betokened little of the fierce conflict of passions, and deadly strife between men who should have been brethren in some common cause, as they were children of a common country. This inauspicious calm but preceded the most terrible storm of battle. After the formation of the lines of battle on the Confederate side, the whole forenoon was passed in comparative inactivity. The Federal line showed its teeth in grim silence, awaiting, like a tiger in his lair, the approach of his enemy, still strengthening and concentrating all of his forces for the death-grapple.

The Confederates were cheerful, but anxious at the delay. They were restless to be "up, and at 'em;" eager to have what they knew was inevitably before them commenced and ended. Both sides felt that this was to be a *combat acharne*; that the heavy skirmishing was over, and the moment of the grand action well-nigh arrived. The great question of that campaign, perhaps of the whole war, was hanging on the next few hours. Success or defeat to either side would be an almost final blow given and received. Not only the superior officers, but the subordinates and the men felt this; and the attacking party, at least, buoyant in their self-confidence, and appreciating the stern necessity of success, were impatient of restraint. It is said, that to the condemned, in going to execution, the moments fly. To the good soldier, to go into action, I am sure the moments linger. Let us not dare say, that with him, either individually or collectively, it is that mythical "love of fighting," poetical, but fabulous; but rather, that it is the nervous anxiety to solve the great issue as speedily as possible, without stopping to count the cost. The MacBeth principle — "Twere well it were done quickly," holds quite as good in heroic action as in crime.

Thus then the tried men selected for this desperate assault, waited in ardor-cooling inactivity, to rush boldly into victory or into death. Unhappily, none saw the first; but few escaped the last.

At one o'clock, P.M., a single gun from our side broke the stillness which had endured for hours: another gun! It was the preconcerted signal for more than a hundred pieces of artillery to belch forth their charges upon the lines of the enemy.

There is, or was, on the crest of the slope, and about two hundred yards in front of our line of battle, certain peach-orchard, which has been often mentioned in accounts of the battle of Gettysburg; and attached to that peach-orchard was a house, with a well of the coldest, hardest water that ever sprung out of limestone rock. I never shall forget that water. Whether it is the now celebrated "Gettysburg water," which is said to cure every ailment that human flesh and blood and bones and intestines cherish for the detriment of the poor sinners, I know not; but I *shall* know, if ever I taste the abominable bottled stuff. It was so cold, you could hardly drink it, by itself; and it would hardly amalgamate with Chambersburg whiskey. Perhaps if the whiskey had been of a *darker color*, we might have got up a miscegenation. I was sitting in this peach-orchard, with Gen. Garnett and Gen. Wilcox, first trying a piece of cold mutton which Gen. Wilcox had produced, then *trying* to drink the hard water; and then accomplishing without much difficulty a little pull at the Chambersburg whiskey, only to prevent the water from freezing my whole internal economy, and petrifying my heart of hearts, when this first signal-gun broke mysteriously upon the long tedium of the day. Having been previously informed of the signal, I told Gen. Garnett that we had better be getting back to our line, as the work was about to commence in earnest.

4. Birkett D. Fry, originally Colonel of the 13th Alabama, had assumed command of Brig. Gen. James J. Archer's brigade of Tennesseeans when Archer was captured on July 1st. In this passage he describes some of the preparations for the charge among the brigade and division officers, and indicates that his brigade was to be the center unit upon which all others would align themselves. Correct alignment would be crucial, since without it they would not be sure to attack the point of the Federal line that they assumed was the weakest, thus their chances of success would be diminished. Birkett D. Fry, "Pettigrew's Charge at Gettysburg," *SHSP,* VII(1879), 92-93.

During the forenoon of the 3d, while our division was resting in line behind the ridge and skirt of woods which masked us from the enemy, Generals Lee, Longstreet and A. P. Hill rode up, and dismounting, seated themselves on the trunk of a fallen tree some fifty or sixty paces from where I sat on my horse at the right of our division. After an apparently careful examination of a map, and a consultation of some length, they remounted and rode away. Staff officers and couriers began to move briskly about, and a few minutes after General Pettigrew rode up and informed me that after a heavy cannonade we would assault the position in our front, and added: "They will of course return the fire with all the guns they have; we must shelter the men as best we can, and make them lie down." At the same time he directed me to see General Pickett at once and have an understanding as to the *dress* in the advance. I rode to General Pickett, whose division was formed on the right of and in line with ours. He appeared to be in excellent spirits, and, after a cordial greeting and a pleasant reference to our having been together in work of that kind at Chapultipec, expressed great confidence in the ability of our troops to drive the enemy after they had been "demoralized by our artillery." General Garnett, who commanded his left brigade, having joined us, it was agreed that he would dress on my command. I immediately returned and informed General Pettigrew of this agreement. It was then understood that my command should be considered the centre, and that in the assault both divisions should align themselves by it. Soon after the two divisions moved forward about a hundred paces, and the men lay down behind our line of batteries.

5.   Lieutenant Colonel Rawley Martin, 53rd Virginia, Armistead's brigade, would undoubtedly have won a Confederate Medal of Honor if such a thing had existed. He begins his narrative of his experiences by emphasizing the enormous *esprit - de - corps* that was so evident and so important to the Confederates. While every individual saw and did different things, all seemed to share in the emotion of the moment, and Martin underscores the confidence of the Confederate troops, their serious frame of mind and their determination. They knew it would be bloody work, but they knew its importance. Rawley Martin, "Rawley Martin's Account," *SHSP*, XXXIX(1911), 184-194.

In the effort to comply with your request to describe Pickett's charge at Gettysburg, I may unavoidably repeat what has often been told before, as the position of troops, the cannonade, the advance, and the final disaster are familiar to all who have the interest or the curiosity to read. My story will be short, for I shall only attempt to describe what fell under my own observation. You ask for a description of the "feelings of the brave Virginians who passed through that hell of fire in their heroic charge on Cemetery Ridge." The *esprit de corps* could not have been better; the men were in good physical condition, self reliant and determined. They felt the gravity of the situation, for they knew well the metal of the foe in their front; they were serious and resolute, but not disheartened. None of the usual jokes, common on the eve of battle, were indulged in, for every man felt his individual responsibility, and realized that he had the most stupendous work of his life before him; officers and men knew at what cost and at what risk the advance was to be made, but they had deliberately made up their minds to attempt it. I believe the general sentiment of the division was that they would succeed in driving the Federal line from what was their objective point; they knew that many, very many, would go down under the storm of shot and shell which would greet them when their gray ranks were spread out to view, but it never occurred to them that disaster would come after they once placed their tattered banners upon the crest of Seminary Ridge.

I believe if those men had been told: "This day your lives will pay the penalty of your attack upon the Federal lines," they would have made the charge just as it was made. There was no straggling, no feigned sickness, no pretence of being overcome by the intense heat; every man felt that it was his duty to make that fight; that he was his own commander, and they would have made the charge without an officer of any description; they only needed to be told what they were expected to do. This is as near the feeling of the men of Pickett's Division on the morning of the battle as I can give, and with this feeling they went to their work. Many of them were veteran soldiers, who had followed the little cross of stars from Big Bethel to Gettysburg; they knew their own power, and they knew the temper of their adversary; they had often met before, and they knew the meeting before them would be desperate and deadly.

6. In a fascinating post-war letter to a former subordinate, Major Edmund Berkeley of the 8th Virginia, Garnett's brigade, gives us some insight into the personalities of Lee, Garnett, and Pickett. There are many stories of enlisted men throwing away their playing cards before battle to avoid having them found on them if they were wounded or killed, but this is one of the few by an officer. His description of the horses of the various officers reminds us of the importance of those animals to the Civil War armies, and especially the Southerners, who furnished their own mounts. Edmund Berkeley, "Rode With Pickett," *Confederate Veteran* (Nashville: Privately published, 1893-1932), XXIII(1915), 175. [hereafter cited as *CV*].

I received yours with much pleasure informing me that Lee Camp was going to secure a portrait of my dear old friend, the magnanimous Gen. Richard Garnett, the only general on either side who rests in an unidentified grave. My brothers and myself were perhaps on more perfect terms of intimacy with General Garnett than any other officers in the army, and my youngest brother served for a time on his staff. I buried on the Gettysburg battle field, before going into the charge, an old deck of cards that the General, Colonel Hunton, and my brothers and myself had played probably more than a hundred games with while we were near Fredericksburg. General Garnett's staff gave a supper to which none were invited except General Garnett, Colonel Hunton, my brothers and myself, and, believing General Lee had gone up town, we were very hilarious, and General Garnett being called on for a story and a song, gave a song called "The Fog and the Dew," and a story called "Mary Ann." I, being called on for a song, gave "Rum tum ta, touchie fol la." General Garnett seemed perfectly enthused and beat time to it with his knife on the table, and at its conclusion said to me: "Major, my dear fellow, don't you know, that's the first time I have heard that song since I left West Point." There were many other interesting occurrences in which we participated, and no more magnanimous man or one with a kinder heart fought in the war.

The morning after our supper at Fredericksburg, General Lee said to Peyton and Baldwin, "You had a very lively crowd in your tent last night," and when I heard of his hearing us, I was awfully afraid he might have heard some of the words of my song.

My brothers were near General Garnett when Pickett came up and spoke to him before we went into the charge. He said: "Dick, old fellow, I have orders to give you, but I advise you to get across those fields as quick as you can, for in my opinion you are going to catch hell." General Lee, knowing it would be almost certain death for an officer to go into the charge on horseback, advised all who could possibly walk to go on foot, and his advice was taken by all but five of his officers. Having been appointed one of a board by General Longstreet some time before leaving Virginia (the board consisting of Major Deering, Captain Fairfax, and myself) to appraise all the private horses in his corps, I knew all the five horses that were in the charge. General Garnett had been sick, and was strongly advised by the surgeons not to attempt to go in the charge, but, disregarding their protests, he put on a common old blue overcoat that completely concealed his uniform, and, mounting his magnificent thorough-bred gelding Red Eye (the second highest priced horse in the corp, $1,400), he went with us to near the Red House, where both he and his horse were killed, and appearing to be a common soldier, was covered up as one. Colonel Hunton, on his orderly's little dun gelding, was the first officer wounded, a Minie ball piercing his leg and going into the horses side, killing him, although he lived long enough to take the Colonel off the field. Capt. Simkins Jones, General Garnett's aide, had his bay mare killed under him, and was thereby enabled to help bear me from the field. General Kemper stopped his bay, or brown, horse by my side at the Red House, and was shot and the horse killed a few minutes afterwards. Lieutenant Colonel Williams, who, his men think, got farther than any mounted man, was killed, as was his little brown mare also, just beyond the Red House.

7. Lieutenant William Wood, 19th Virginia, describes the condition of the men while waiting in the hot sun for the charge to begin. The temperature was in the high 80s, with high humidity, and they were in wool uniforms. Note that at the end of the first paragraph he places his regiment at the foot of Cemetery Hill. Since that place was two miles away, he probably meant Seminary Ridge, since in fact that is where he was. This is not an infrequent mistake. William Nathaniel Wood, *Reminiscences of Big I* edited by Bell Irvin Wiley (Jackson, Tenn.: McCowat-Mercer Press, 1956), 43-48.

On the morning of July 2d our brigade hastened towards Gettysburg. The rank and file knew nothing of the fight then in progress, but from the activity of our movements a few guesses were made as to the near future. Arriving in the vicinity of Gettysburg on the evening of the same day, we gathered some information as to what had been going on. We bivouacked that night about three miles from the scene of action of the 1st and 2d without being disturbed by the nearness of the battlefield. Early in the morning of the 3d we prepared and ate our frugal meal. The usual jests and hilarity were indulged in, and soon after, when ordered into line, and we again took up the march, no gloomy forebodings hovered over our ranks. We marched possibly three miles and gradually approached the enemy. A shady, quiet march was this, protected from the enemy's view by woods and Cemetery Hill. We halted for a short time in the woods, but moved forward pretty soon into a field, near a branch. Here we filled our canteens and took things easy for twenty minutes, or possibly longer. Up to this time our march had been in column, but our next move was in line of battle to the front — halting immediately after crossing a road and getting over the fence on either side of the road. Remaining in this position but a few minutes, we moved forward again, and this time as we halted we dressed upon the colors, forming a line of battle. The other regiments of our brigade dressed upon us — ours being the centre regiment. We were ordered to lie down. Our position was, at this time, on the south side of Cemetery Hill and near its eastern end, and less than a hundred yards from the top in our front.

For how many hours we sweltered on the side of this hill that hot third day of July, 1863, I know not, but my own opinion is about five hours. The field-officers rode about us and held frequent short consultations. Leaving my command I walked up to the top of the hill and took a birds-eye view of the situation, just as Colonel Deering rode up to see about locating his artillery. I heard him say "that hill must fall" as he rode off to the right. I walked back to the regiment with "that hill must fall" ringing in my ears. Artillery came, it seemed to me, from every direction, and quickly prepared, on or near the hill top, for action. I never before saw such a display of artillery and felt, "that hill must fall." An hour or more passed in silence. The sun was making the hillside very uncomfortable.

8. Sergeant Major David Johnston, 7th Virginia, eloquently describes the spirits and concerns of many of the Confederates. Like James Crocker, he left two accounts of his experiences, and I have included excerpts from both. In the first, written in the 1880s, the sense of camaraderie that served to motivate them in the most trying of circumstances is central to his account of the men. They felt that this was perhaps the most important moment of the war; the outcome of the battle, the war, and of their hopes of

independence, seemed to hang in the balance. A measure of their esteem for Lee is Johnston's belief that the charge had to succeed because General Lee had ordered it, and therefore all would go well. David E. Johnston, *Four Years a Soldier* (Princeton, W. Va.: n.p., 1887), 249-272.

Happy, gentle, brave, jolly spirits; little do you anticipate the horrors of the next twenty-four hours! All was quiet during the night, and until reveille which was sounded before light the next morning; Friday, July 3rd, when we fell into ranks for roll call. Oh, how sad the last earthly roll call of so many of our brave, gallant men who on this eventful day were to pour out their life's blood for constitutional freedom and right, and to go to "that bourne from which no traveler ever returns." Many were to fall far from home and friends, in the land of strangers, and to be denied the privilege of even a decent burial. Sad were these thoughts to those who thought. With us on that morning were our good-hearted Captain Bane, happy, jolly Lieut. Walker, the brave, sturdy Sergt. Taylor; all ready to lead where duty required and dangers were to be met. With us also were our companions - in - arms, D. C. Akers, Daniel Bish, Jesse Barrett and John P. Sublet, with whom we had marched and fought for more than two years; and had stood side by side in the fury and midst of battle, had shared their common toils and dangers in a common cause in which we were all embarked. We were more than friends. We did not realize that bright July morning that the sun which had risen in all his glory and splendor upon these brave Virginia spirits would set upon their lifeless forms, and witness the saddest day the Confederacy had yet seen. As previously stated, the morning was bright and lovely, indeed, there was nothing to betoken fierce conflict and deadly strife. On our way to the battle field the men were cheerful and seemed to realize their weighty responsibilities and the importance — in fact, the imperative necessity of success, and that probably in their hands rested the destiny of the Republic. If the enemy could be beaten here in his own country, with the political and other troubles in the North growing out of the draft, etc., it seemed reasonable to suppose that subjugated, down-trodden Maryland would be free, and with her the Confederacy also. These matters were freely discussed by the men in the ranks who seemed fully aware of the gravity of the situation and the absolute impor- tance of victory, and perfect confidence was expressed in our ability to beat the enemy, if we could meet him on anything like fair and equal terms. Southern prowess, individuality and self-reliance had accomplished wonders in the past, and had become the admiration even of our enemies.

9. By 1914 Johnston's memoirs were long out of print, and with his comrades fast dying off and requests for his story continuing, he wrote another set. While they are similar, in the second he writes of the sense of suspense while they waited for the charge to occur, and again speaks of their overconfidence, their sense that they knew that this was an important moment, and that the outcome of the war seemed to hang in the balance. He also recalls Pickett's cry and its effect on the men. David Johnston, *The Story of a Confederate Boy in the Civil War* (Radford, Va.: David Johnston, 1914), 203-208.

. . . a soldier in the field rarely thought his time to die had exactly arrived — that is, it would be the other fellow's time and well it was so. Occasionally a man was met who had made up his mind that the next battle would be his last. Men have been known to have such presentiment and sure enough be killed in the next engagement. Such was true of our gallant Colonel Patton, who yielded up his promising young life in this battle.

The issue of the campaign and of the Civil War itself, as history shows, was now trembling in the balance. Victory or defeat to either side would be in effect a settlement of the issues involved; this the officers and men seemed clearly to realize. Under such conditions all were impatient of the restraint. To the brave soldier going into battle, knowing he must go, the moments seem to lengthen. This feeling is not born of his love for fighting, but it is rather the nervous anxiety to determine the momentous issue as quickly as possible, without stopping to count the cost, realizing if it must be done, "it were well it were done quickly." Over confidence pervaded the Confederate army, from the commanding general down to the shakiest private in the ranks. Too much over-confidence was the bane of our battle. For more than six long hours the men were waiting, listening for the sound of the signal guns. The stillness was at last broken: the shot was fired: down, according to program, went the men on their faces.

. . . Near 2:50 P.M., as the artillery fire had practically ceased, there came the order, "Fall in!" and brave General Pickett, coming close to where I lay wounded, called out: "Up, men, and to your posts! Don't forget today that you are from old Virginia!" The effect of this word upon the men was electrical. The regiments were quickly in line, closing to the left over the dead and wounded — the ranks now reduced by the losses occasioned by the shelling to about 4,400 men of the division, and I am satisfied that Kemper's brigade, the smallest of the division, did not then number over 1,250. The advance now began, the men calling out to the wounded and others: "Goodbye, boys! Goodbye!" Unable to move, I could not accompany this advance — did not see, hear, observe or know what thereafter happened only from the statement of others.

      10. An engineer in Early's division, W. H. Swallow recorded a conversation in which Isaac Trimble related Lee's determination and sense of the extreme importance of the charge. Also note here the fact that Swallow says the Pettigrew-Trimble lines made it from the woods on Seminary Ridge to the Emmitsburg Road in *eight* minutes. That means they were moving at Quickstep, 110 steps at 28" per step, according to the training manuals of the day. Thus, by Swallow's calculations they covered 85 yards per minute, or 680 yards in eight minutes. W. H. Swallow, "The Third Day At Gettysburg," *Southern Bivouac*, 4(February, 1886), 564-5.

      The distance from Seminary Ridge, where Heth's division crossed the plain, to the Federal works on Cemetery Hill, where a part of Archer's Tennessee brigade burst into them, is exactly one thousand two hundred and seventy- three yards. In the months of July and August, 1880, the writer measured the relative distances passed over by the column of attack a number of times with due regard to the speed of Heth's division, from which he reached the conclusion that the division must have passed from the top of Seminary Ridge to the Emmittsburg road in about eight minutes.

      Immediately after the column was formed Generals Lee, Longstreet, and Pickett rode along the lines several times, reviewing the troops and inspecting the different assignments. They then rode aside and had an earnest and animated conversation together. After which all three again rode along the column and retired together. Their whole conduct showed in a manner not to be mistaken, how extremely dangerous and full of doubt these officers regarded the proposed assault. General Trimble, who commanded Pender's division, and lost his leg in the assault, lay wounded with the writer at Gettysburg for several weeks after the battle, related the fact to the writer, that when General Lee was closing the inspection of the column in the front of Scales' brigade, which had been fearfully cut up in the first day's conflict, having lost very heavily, including all the regimental officers with its gallant commander, and noticing many of Scales' men with their heads bandaged, he said to General Trimble: "Many of these poor boys should go to the rear, they are not fit for duty." Passing his eyes searchingly along the weakened ranks of Scales' brigade, he turned to General Trimble and touchingly added "I miss in this brigade the faces of many dear friends."

      As he rode away he looked mournfully at the column and

muttered more to himself than to General Trimble, "the attack must succeed." During the time the column stood in line the suspense and anxiety of the troops was intensely great.

11. Across the valley in the Federal ranks, Lieutenant Frank Haskell spent the morning near the center of the Second Corps line. His description of the men as "an army of rag-gatherers" is striking, and his portrait of the Second Corps officers lunching on stewed chicken is one of the most quoted passages in his essay. He also describes the deployment of the Second Corps along the wall and at the angle, and a few incidents that occurred before the cannonade began. The last paragraph in this section is perhaps one of the most evocative written about the lull before the storm. Haskell, "Gettysburg."

I could not help wishing all the morning that this line of the two Divisions of the 2nd Corps were stronger,— it was, so far as numbers constitute strength, the weakest part of our whole line of battle. What if, I thought, the enemy should make an assault here to-day, with two or three heavy lines, — a great overwhelming mass, would he not sweep through that thin six thousand?

But I was not Gnl. Meade, who alone had power to send other troops there; and he was satisfied, with that part of the line as it was. He was early on horseback this morning, and rode along the whole line, looking to it himself, and with glass in hand sweeping the woods and fields in the direction of the enemy, to see if ought [?] of him could be discovered. His manner was ca[l]m and serious, but earnest. There was no arrogance of hope, or timidity of fear discernible in his face; but you would have supposed he would do his duty, conscientiously and well, and would be willing to abide the result. You would have seen this in his face. He was well pleased with the left of the line to-day, it was so strong, with good troops; — he had no apprehension for the right where the fight, now was going on, on account of the admirable position of our forces there; — he was not of the opinion that the enemy would attack the center, our artillery had such sweep there, and this was not the favorite point of attack with the Rebel; besides, should he attack the center, the General thought he could reinforce it in good season. I heard Gnl. Meade speak of these matters to Hancock and some others, at about nine o'clock in the morning, while they were up by the line, near the 2nd Corps.

No further changes of importance, except those mentioned, were made in the disposition of the troops this morning, except to replace some of the Batteries that were disabled yesterday, by others from the Artillery Reserve, and to brace up the lines well with guns wherever there were eligible places, from the same source. The line is all in good order again, and we are ready for general battle.

Save the operations upon the right, the enemy, so far as we could see, was very quiet all the morning. Occasionally the outposts would fire a little, and then cease as movements would be discovered which would indicate the attempt on the part of the enemy to post a Battery; — our Parrotts would send a few shells to the spot, then silence would follow.

At one of these times a painful accident happened to us, this morning; 1st Lieut. Henry Ropes, 20 Mass. in Gnl. Gibbon's Division, a most estimable gentleman, and officer, intelligent, educated, refined, one of the noble souls that came to the country's defense, while lying at his post with his regiment, in front of one of the Batteries, which fired over the infantry, was instantly killed by a badly made shell, which, or some portion of it, fell but a few yards in front of the muzzle of the gun. The same accident killed or wounded several others. The loss of Ropes would have pained us at any time, and in any manner; — in this manner his death was doubly painful.

Between ten and eleven o'clock over in a peach orchard in front of the position of Sickles yesterday, some little show of the enemy's infantry was discovered, — a few shells scattered the gray-backs, — they again appeared, and it becoming apparent that they were only posting a skirmish line, no further molestation was offered them. A little after this some of the enemy's flags could be discerned over near the same quarter, above the top, and behind a small crest of a ridge, — there seemed to be two or three of them, — possibly they were guidons, — and they moved too fast to be carried on foot. Possibly, we thought, the enemy is posting some Batteries there.— We knew in about two hours from this time better about the matter. Eleven o'clock came, — the noise of battle has ceased upon the right, — not a sound of a gun or musket can be heard on all the field, — the sky is bright with only the white fleecy clouds floating over from the West, — the July sun streams down its fire upon the bright iron of the muskets in stacks upon the crest, and the dazzling brass of the Napoleons — the army lolls, and longs for the shade, of which some get a hands breadth, from a shelter tent stuck upon a ramrod, — the silence and sultriness of a July noon are supreme. Now it so happened that just about this time of day a very original and interesting thought occurred to Gnl. Gibbon and several of his Staff that it would be a very good thing, and a very good time, to have something to eat. When I announce to you that I had not tasted a mouthful of food since yesterday noon, and that all I had had to drink since that time but the most miserable muddy warm water, was a little drink of whiskey that Major Biddle, Gnl. Meade's Aide-de-Camp, gave me last evening, and a cup of strong coffee that I gulped down as I was first mounting this morning; and further, that save the four or five hours in the night, there was scarcely a moment, since that time but what I was in the saddle, you may have some notion of the reason of my assent to this extraordinary proposition. Nor will I mention the doubts I had as to the feasibility of the execution of this very novel proposal, except to say that I knew this morning, that our larder was low; — not to put too fine a point upon it, that we had nothing but some potatoes and sugar, and coffee in the world. And I may as well say here, that of such, in scant proportions, would have been our repast, had it not been for the riding of miles by two persons, one an officer, to procure supplies, — and they only succeeded in getting some few chickens, some butter, and one huge loaf of bread, which last was bought of a soldier, because he had grown faint in carrying it, and was afterwards rescued with much difficulty, and after a long race from a four-footed hog, which had got hold of and had actually eaten a part of, it. "There is a divinity," &c.

Suffice it, this very ingenious and unheard of contemplated proceeding, first announced by the General, was accepted and at once undertaken by his Staff. Of the absolute quality of what we had to eat, I could not pretend to judge, — but I think an unprejudiced person would have said of the bread, that it was good, — so of the potatoes, before they were boiled; of the chickens, he would have questioned their age, but they were large and in good *running* orders, the toast was good, and the butter, — there were those who when coffee was given them, called for tea, and *vice versa,* and were so ungracious as to suggest that the water that was used in both, might have come from near a barn. Of course it did not. We all came down to the little peach orchard where we had stayed last night, and wonderful to see and tell, ever mindful of our needs, had it all ready, had our faithful John. There was an enormous pan of stewed chickens, and the potatoes, and toast, all hot, and the bread and the butter, and tea, and coffee.

There was satisfaction derived from just naming them all over. We called John an angel, and he snickered and said, he *"knowed"* we'd come. Gnl. Hancock is of course invited to partake, and without delay we commence operations. — Stools are not very numerous, — two in all — and these the two generals have by common consent. Our table was the top of a mess-chest, by this the Generals sat, the rest of us sat upon the ground, cross-legged like the picture of a smoking Turk, and held our plates upon our laps. How delicious was the stewed chicken. I had a cucumber pickle in my saddle bags, — the last of a lunch left there two or three days ago, — which George brought, and I had half of it. We were just well at it, when Genl. Meade rode down to us from the line, accompanied by one of his Staff, and by Gnl. Gibbons' invitation they dismounted and joined us. For the General commanding the Army of the Potomac, George, by an effort worthy of the person and the occasion, finds an empty cracker box for a seat. The Staff officer must sit upon the ground with the rest of us. Soon Generals Newton and Pleasonton, each with an Aide, arrive. By an almost super human effort a roll of blankets is found, which, upon a pirtch, is long enough to seat these Generals both, and room is made for them. — The Aides sit with us. And fortunate to relate, there was enough cooked for us all, and from Gnl. Meade to the youngest 2nd Lieutenant we all had a most hearty, and well relished dinner. Of the "past" we were "secure." The Generals ate, and after lighted cigars, and under the flickering shade of a very small tree, discoursed of the incidents of yesterday's battle, and of the probabilities of to-day. Gnl. Newton humorously spoke of Gnl. Gibbon as "this young North Carolinian," and how he was becoming arrogant and above his position because he commanded a Corps. Gnl. Gibbon retorted by saying that Gnl. Newton had not been long enough in such a command, only since yesterday, to enable him to judge of such things. Gnl. Meade still thought that the enemy would attack his left again to day, towards evening; but he was ready for them, — Gnl. Hancock, that the attack would be upon the position of the 2nd Corps. It was mentioned that Gnl. Hancock would again resume command of the 2nd Corps, from that time, so that Gnl. Gibbon would again return to the 2nd Division.

Gnl. Meade spoke of the Provost Guards, that they were good men, and that it would be better to-day to have them in the ranks, than to stop stragglers and skulkers, as these latter would be good for but little even in the ranks; and so he gave the order that all the Provost Guards should at once temporarily rejoin their Regiments. Then Gnl. Gibbon called up Capt. Farrel, 1st Minn. who commanded the Provost Guard of his division, and directed him, for that day, to join the regiment. "Very well, sir," said the captain, as he touched his hat, and turned away. He was a quiet excellent gentleman, and thorough soldier. I knew him well, and esteemed him. I never saw him again. He was killed in two or three hours from that time, and over half of his splendid company, were either killed or wounded.

And so the time passed on, each General now and then dispatching some order or message by an officer or orderly, until about half past twelve, when all the Generals, one by one, first Gnl. Meade, rode off their several ways. And Genl. Gibbon and his Staff, alone remained.

We dozed in the heat, and lolled upon the ground, with half open eyes. Our horses were hitched to the trees, munching some

oats. A great lull rests upon all the field. Time was heavy; ·
want of something better to do, I yawned and looked at m
— it was five minutes before one o'clock. I returned my wa
pocket, and thought possibly that I might go to sleep, and stretched
myself upon the ground accordingly. "Ex *uno d isce omnes.*'

12. A letter written by a sergeant in Harrow's brigade on the Federal left reveals that sleep and food often preoccupied the men while waiting for the fighting to begin. "John W. Plummer's Account," *Rebellion Record* **(New York: Putnam, 1862-1864), 179-181.**

We then lay down to get some sleep, with our equipment on and guns by our side; and I here say I never slept better and had more pleasant dreams in my life than I had on the battle-field of Gettysburg, with dead men and horses lying all around me; but the excitement and exhaustion had been so great that a man could sleep in any condition, and under any circumstances.

We got up about daylight, expected and awaited an attack from the enemy at any moment, but till afternoon all was quiet, except occasionally a shot from their or our batteries. Most of us got some during the forenoon, by going one or two at a time back to the rear, where they were allowed fires and cooking, which of course greatly refreshed us. A man's appetite generally, during a battle, is not very voracious. About half past twelve o'clock, as we had gathered around one of our Lieutenants to hear the yesterday's Baltimore *Clipper* read, bang! comes one of their shells over us, striking about twenty yards from us. That stopped the reading; each man took his place lay down, and for the next two hours hugged the ground just about as close as human beings are generally in the habit of doing.

13. The Bliss farm, located 600 yards west of the Federal lines and roughly half way between the lines, occupied the attention of both armies. The two sides struggled over it all morning, back and forth. Even in the larger battle of Gettysburg, this small fight, as described by Private Henry Stevens of the 14th Connecticut, illustrates the personal and often bizarre nature of combat. Henry Stevens, *Souvenir of the Excursions of the 14th Connecticut,* **(Washington, D.C.: Gibson Brothers, 1893), 15-24.**

The early morning firing of the third disturbed somewhat our slumbers on the ridge, but not enough to rouse us thoroughly, for the soldier learns to not trouble himself about what may happen while the picket line remains intact. Rest he needs, and he learns to secure it amid surroundings that might play havoc with a civilian's nerves. When the doughty Captain Arnold, commanding the battery the Fourteenth was supporting, had a brief tilt with a rebel battery, resulting in the blowing up of a caisson on each side and eliciting wild cheers along both lines, we were made thoroughly awake. Then Companies A and F were relieved from picket duty by Companies B and D. The work of these men on the picket line and the relief of the details was quite interesting and exciting to the observers in the rear and looked like a very pretty game — but to the participants it was not pretty. Our picket reserve station was in the Emmettsburg road in front of the regiment. The road was sunken there nearly two feet, affording some protection at the fence. The picket line was at a fence about two hundred yards in advance of the reserve, and the line of rebel pickets about the same distance further on, some of it by the trees at the Bliss orchard. Our men lay flat upon the ground by the fence, hidden and somewhat protected by the posts and lowest rails. Nothing was visible, usually, to fire at, yet when any movement was apparent a shot or two would follow from vigilant watchers; then the rising riflesmoke would attract retaliating shots. When the reliefs went to their places there was excitement. The relieving squad would leave the reserve rendezvous moving in any way possible to avoid the observation of the enemy, but when a place was reached where exposure was unavoidable each would take to running at highest speed, and upon reaching the fence would throw himself at once upon the ground. Then must the relieved ones get back to the reserve in a similar manner; and "relieving" seemed a misnomer.

The start of the pickets on either side, to or from their places, was a signal for a lively popping all along the line of their opponents as long as a man was in sight. Not many of the runners were struck, for to hit such a rapidly moving object is a difficult feat; but the pop! pop! crack! crack! would go on all the same; and the eagerness to hit would make some shooters careless, so furnishing themselves targets for some hidden watchers. Several men were wounded on the line, and Corporal Huxham of Company B was killed. When his squad was relieved he did not stir, and whenever Sergeants Stroud and Hirst went to him and touched him they found him dead, shot through the head. He was in position, his rifle resting on the fence, his finger on the trigger and his eye apparently glancing along the barrel in aiming. Shot at his post, his face toward the foe and his weapon directed against his enemy — the worthiest eulogy that can be expressed of the soldier.

In front of our skirmish line, a little to the right, eight hundred yards or more from our position at the wall, were two buildings, owned by William Bliss, a farmer. One was a large barn, almost a citadel in itself. It was an expensively and elaborately built structure, as barns go, seventy-five feet long and thirty-three feet wide, its lower story, or basement, ten feet high, constructed of stone, and its upper part, sixteen feet to the eaves, of bricks, the wall being carried to the gables. Within was an oak frame sufficiently heavy for a barn without walls. There was an overhang ten feet wide along the entire front for shelter of cattle, and the rear was banked to the first floor — whence the name "bank barn" — furnishing a drive-way for loads to that floor. There were five doors in the front wall of the basement and three windows in each end; several long, narrow, vertical slits in the upper story front and two rows of windows in each end. It was a paradise for sharp-shooters with long range rifles. Ninety paces north of it was the mansion, a frame building, two stories in height. As it had a front of three rooms width and two front doors, and there now remain two cellar excavations with a thick earth wall between, over which it stood, indicating a length of about fifty feet, we see the building must have been long and capacious. On the second of July, when our picket line was established between the Emmettsburg road and these buildings, the rebels settled a force of sharp-shooters in the latter, and the barn proved a veritable tower of strength to them but a terror to our batterymen on the ridge, as well as to our pickets on the line, for it allowed a drop-shot upon the latter. Captain Arnold complained that his men were suffering great annoyance and harm from the men in the barn and General Hays ordered its capture. Four companies of the 12th N. J. regiment were detailed for the duty. They charged in gallant style and captured it, with a good number of prisoners, losing several of their own men. With a strange kind of wisdom — from whom emanating we do not know — they soon retired, with their prisoners, to the main line, leaving the barn nicely inviting the Johnnies to come right in again; and soon they were sending their pretty leaden compliments as before. At 7.30 A. M. of the third five other companies of the 12th N. J. again captured the barn, taking two prisoners — and at once repeated the *retiring act*. This sagacious policy of seizing and at once abandoning had its effect, for the returning occupants soon sent the little stingers flying around as before. At last the thing became intolerable. Captain Arnold told the writer that it was such an injury to his men that he asked Colonel Smyth, the brigade commander, if that barn could not be burned. "The enemy would get behind the barn and do us more damage," was the reply. "The walls would be so hot men could not live in them," said the captain. "That is so," replied the colonel. Then an order was issued that the building be captured "to stay," and the Fourteenth [Connecticut], now reduced to about one hundred and twenty men exclusive of those on picket, was ordered to do it. Four companies of the left wing, to be commanded by Capt. S. A. Moore of Co. F, were first detailed for the purpose. Why a force only about one half as large as either of the parties previously sent for the same purpose was sent this time is one of the inscrutable things of the varying wisdom of war. Possibly it was thought that one Fourteenth man was equal to any other two. That it was a serious undertaking all could see, and no man coveted the job — but no choice is allowed the soldier. The detail was taken up towards the division headquarters and then down a lane one hundred and fifty yards to the Emmettsburg road, then across the road, and then into the field beyond, covered for about one hundred and fifty paces by a knoll. When the men came into view of the enemy, now well read in the business and prepared for them, there was a general firing at them from all along the skirmish line and from the host of sharp-shooters in the buildings. Then the desperate character of the sortie was fully revealed, but no man could recoil though death seemed inevitable. As to advance in any kind of formation would but furnish a better target to aim at, the order was to "go as you please," or scatter and run. Every man was put to his mettle and ran with all his might for the barn. Nearly six hundred yards were to be covered and it was soon accomplished at such speed, but several dropped on the way.

Such was the vim with which the rush was made that the rebs did not wait to greet their visitors, but "skeedaddled," as we used to say, out of the doors and other openings to take refuge in the orchard and house; the latter, which had not figured much in former attacks, now becoming quite formidable as a place of offense and defense. The little band, quite outnumbered, and beleaguered in the barn, could not leave the latter to attack the house because of the marksmen in the orchard and on the picket line, so the remaining four companies on the ridge were ordered to reinforce them and capture the house. Major Ellis commanded this detail, taking with him all except the color-guard. This detail was obliged to move more to the right after passing over the knoll and becoming exposed, and was subjected to a hot fire from the house and skirmish line, and for the last three hundred yards or more to a still hotter one on the right flank that the other had not encountered so fully. A lane, called "Long Lane," narrow and deep, runs out from Gettysburg about one mile to within about three hundred yards of the Bliss house and then turns at right angle up toward the position of the enemy. In this lane had been placed the brigades of Thomas and McGowan to support Rodes in an anticipated attack on Cemetery Hill on the evening of the second, and some say to support the left of Longstreet's assaulting column on the third. When Major Ellis' detail came within about three hundred and fifty yards of the house the whole right of Thomas' brigade began firing, and from them the detail received its worst cutting. Adjutant Doten once referred in a letter to the writer to his emotions in the "rush across that bullet swept plain," and when subsequently his correspondent took him to the Long Lane and pointed out the location of Thomas' brigade he said at once: "Now I know where that strong flank fire came from!" This flank fire could be termed volleys, and several were hit by it; but the majority, heated and panting, reached the goal, some entering the house and others continuing on to the barn. The men never could describe their feelings on those mad runs for life. We have never heard any really attempt it. The excitement, the frenzied effort, the terrible sense of imminent, savage danger could not be clearly called up nor could words express them — as Lieut. Fiske once wrote us: "When I try to write it I get stuck; in fact a battle is a plaguey poor thing to put on paper — some how it won't *fight*." There fell on the way Lieut. Seward of Co. I, shot through the body, and Lieut. Seymour, of the same company, shot through the leg. Both got off the field. Little Jeff Brainerd of Co. F while dashing along with break-neck speed fell with a mortal wound. He was the life of his company, full of rollicking fun, and when Capt. Broatch heared him "yell" and saw him leap into the air he thought it was "one of Jeff's antics." Poor, dear boy, when he touched the earth he rose no more unhelped. Sergt. Maj. Hincks as he rushed by heard his "shrill cry: My God! My God, I'm hit! — Oh, how it hurts me!" He was borne back and in a few minutes expired while saying to his chaplain, who was holding him and trying to soothe his agonies, "Tell my mother-tell-l-m-y." When the rebels were leaving the house as our men rushed up one of their latest shots gave to Sergt. Baldwin of Co. I a fatal wound, and another gave to John Fox of Co. A a serious wound in the thigh.

The house seemed a poor place for protection, bullets piercing the thin siding and windows, so some of the men left it, running to the barn or taking refuge at the wood-pile or elsewhere out of doors. But it was dangerous exposing head, hand or foot outside of either building, as the enemy had been so reinforced by constant additions from their main line that their guns were ready to cover every point, and the rear of the barn afforded but few openings to fire from. To make matters worse, a battery about five hundred yards in rear of the buildings began firing shells at them, and when their terrific crash was heard the men feared their own doom was sealed. Clements of Co. G was killed by one of these shells, and Lieut. Knowlton received from a scrap "a welt," as he described it, that nearly broke his back. T. W. Gardner of Co. H, while at one of the windows, was struck by a bullet that plowed a permanent furrow along the top of his head.

Though the men plied their rifles the best they could they seemed in a trap and doomed to stay until exterminated, for the order, as understood, was "to take and hold" the buildings. It was not known by them that any modifying order existed, though such had been given. As Col. Smyth was accompanying one detail over the Emmetsburg road Lieut. Seymour went to him and said: "If in event of our capturing the house and barn the rebs make it so hot we can't hold them shall we fire them?" "We don't know the word can't!" replied Col. S. Hardly had the lieutenant resumed his position at the head of his company when Col. Smyth rode up to him and said: "If they make it too hot for you, burn the buildings and return to the line." No other person than the lieutenant heard the instructions, and when he soon after fell helpless the line rushed on, giving him no chance to communicate the order to the commander — so our men, ignorant of its existence, held on in their beleaguered places.

At last those at headquarters seemed to become aware of the desperate straits of our men and Genl. Hays sent them instructions to burn the buildings and return to the main line. The order was borne by Capt. Postles of Col. Smyth's staff; a cavalier true, riding a large, powerful horse. He knew the undertaking was a daring one but he did not understand it fully until he reached a point where he took in at a glance the full line of fire he must run the gauntlet of. Then, as he once told the writer, he said to himself: "My God, there's no chance for me!" But, bold rider that he was, he struck spurs into his horse's flanks, those long, vicious looking rowels we always noticed jingling at his heels when he was on his tours of inspection. Knowing that his only chance lay in keeping his horse in swift motion, and dashed on with lightning speed, our men watching in breathless suspense and the rebels holding their guns at sight awaiting a moment's halting or change of direction of the rider to deliver their fire. When he reached the barn, knowing that still he must keep that "devil of a beast" in motion and give the Johnnies no opportunity to draw a bead on him, he made the spurs still do their wicked work, holding with tightest rein his furious charger until the frantic creature leaped wildly into the air, while he shouted his order into the ears of Major Ellis and received the salute of acknowledgment; then, saluting in return, he let out his hand and the horse shot out like a catapult charge and swept away with mighty bounds, the whole skirmish line of the enemy pouring quick volleys after him. His celerity saved him, as it is almost impossible to hit an object moving with such velocity — for when the bullet reaches the point aimed at the object aimed at is not there — and soon the gallant captain was safe within our lines unhurt, after one of the wildest and most danger-fraught runs ever chronicled. When he reached a point of safety he turned his panting steed facing the enemy and waved his hat to the disappointed "chivalry" — and they responded with a salvo of cheers.

The order received, preparations were instantly made for firing the buildings. Wisps of hay and straw were soon on fire and by numerous hands applied at different places in the barn, and in the house a straw bed was emptied upon the floor and the match applied. Then the men taking up tenderly their wounded and dead and gathering their arms, started on their perilous return, running nearly the same hazard as when advancing. When they reached the Emmettsburg road they turned and saw how well they had done their work of destruction, the flames then bursting fiercely out of house and barn. A little halting at the road by a small building in the shade to catch breath and to slake their terrific thirst at a well, and then the boys returned to the ridge to rest and reflect. There have been many strange claims made by men of other regiments to having burned the place after the battle most of the wall of the barn was standing, though "all the wood-work was burned out," and that the house was entirely destroyed.

. . . This affair of the Bliss buildings was one of the most thrilling and perilous of the experiences of the Fourteenth. We believe it to have been the most notable episode connected with the doings of any *individual regiment* occurring during the great battle of Gettysburg. It occurred in clear sight of both armies on the wide plain extending between them, eliciting their eager attention and inducing many interchanges of artillery sparring. Had the buildings been destroyed the first time captured by our troops many lives uselessly sacrificed would have been spared and much needless suffering avoided. It was one of the "fool things" of war. Yet it was a grand lesson to our boys, and it furnished one of the brightest points of their most glowing record. In that brilliant sortie some precious lives went out, some cripples were made, and every man that escaped hurt came back panting and wearied and reeling that "out of the jaws of death" had he come.

After the return to the ridge the men lay resting, or preparing their food, or penning notes for the anxious ones at home until the hour of sultriest noon was past. One bit of culinary enterprise, interesting victually if not vitally during this time to several men of one group, deserves chronicling as picturing a bit of soldier life and demonstrating the perfectness of military and moral discipline existing in the Fourteenth. That group gave undivided attention to an endeavor of fire and water to reduce the flesh of a veteran fowl in a pot to an impressionable condition. That fowl a little before was boldly bossing his little company in the barnyard of Mr. Bliss. Sergt. De Forest coveted it, his mouth moist in thought of the delicious fricassees it was evidently created for, but he was too conscientious and too soldierly to lay hands upon it until unquestioned authority was acquired. He approached adjutant Doten and gravely requested permission to take the fowl under his protection and introduce it (improved) to some of his comrades. The adjutant sympathized with man and bird and thought they should be friends, so he encouraged the alliance; and amid the crack of rifles and the banging of the artillery the sergeant pursued his game until victorious, and he bore it under his arm unharmed to the ridge. When the ball opened later that poultry was still in the pot "kicking" against reduction — and it is still a conundrum with us what became of Al De Forest's chicken.

. . . A hush seemed to have fallen on the whole field as the sun passed the meridian and men on either side were listlessly enduring the torrid heat on the unprotected ridges, when suddenly the ball opened and men instinctively knew a Titanic struggle had been initiated.

14. **Thomas Francis Galway, a 17 year-old private in the 8th Ohio Infantry, was stationed near the Emmitsburg Road, far in advance of the main Federal line. He jotted notes in his diary during the day and after the war published them in narrative form. The 11th Corps had been unfortunate enough to be surprised by Stonewall Jackson's flank march at Chancellorsville in May, and had been routed. They had been again routed on July 1st, and Galway's derisive view of the 11th Corps was common throughout the army. He also reminds us that Civil War soldiers often ate their rations as soon as they were issued, rather than holding on to them and eating them as intended, and thus were hungry later, as he was on July 3rd. Thomas Francis Galway, *The Valiant Hours* (Harrisburg, Pa.: Stackpole Books, 1961), 108-112.**

About a hundred and fifty yards to our left front was a large barn, such as are common throughout this rich part of Pennsylvania, where the barns are finer than the houses. Ever since daylight an incessant fire of sharpshooters had been kept up from its windows upon our artillery on the ridge behind us. This fire became at last so annoying that a battalion with its colors moved out from our left and with a good cheer charged the barn. For sometime before this charge, we ourselves had been so frequently the target for the shots from it that we had made many guesses amongst ourselves as to the number of men it sheltered. But we were not prepared for such a sight as we beheld when the New York regiment (I do not know its number) got to it. Certainly it was no exaggeration to say that two hundred Confederates issued from that barn and its surroundings, flying in confusion. The New Yorkers applied the torch and, as the flames burst through the thrifty farmer's barn-roof, we gave a cheer. Fired by the example of the men on our left, although as far as I know, without any orders, we charged straight ahead. We drove the enemy back down the other face of the low ridge on which he was posted, and up the slope to where we could plainly descry the masses of his line of battle, in all about two hundred yards. Here, however, we were met by successive discharges of canister from the batteries right ahead and by shells from their reserve artillery on Seminary Ridge beyond. This checked our advance and, while we were reforming, the rallied enemy skirmishers turned upon us again. We fell back slowly, firing, to our old position at the fence. All this happened between seven and eight in the morning.

The skirmish fire now became murderous. Having found that the enemy kept close to the ground so as to afford an uncertain target, owing to his dun clothes, we began, as the boys called it, to be scientific in our fire. In this way four or five neighbors in the line would load and, seeing a puff of smoke rise from some spot in front, would "watch for it." Being ready as soon as the smoke would rise, they would all aim at it and fire together. Generally, the poor "Johnny" was hit by this device. This was called "Turning a Jack," and continued amongst us.

The skirmishing was of that steady nature that comes from acquaintance with the ground and with the enemy's manner of fighting. The firing was rapid enough, and yet there was not much random work. It was almost as much as a man's life was worth to rise to his height from the ground. The advance of our line in the early morning had strewn the ground with our wounded, who, in our retreat to the fence, were necessarily left where they fell, now between the two fires. About thirty yards in front of my company stood a solitary tree which, I suppose, had been left as a shade for men in the harvest field. During the morning this tree became conspicuous on account of the well-aimed shots that came from it. We soon became aware that a couple of bold enemy sharpshooters had crawled up to it and were now practicing on any thoughtless man who offered himself as a mark. About the middle of the forenoon a cry of, "Don't fire, Yanks!" rang out, and we all got up to see what was coming. A man with his gun slung across his shoulder came out from the tree. Several of our fellows aimed at him but the others checked them, to see what would follow. The man had a canteen in his hand and, when he had come about half-way to us, we saw him (God bless him) kneel down and give a drink to one of our wounded who lay there beyond us. Of course we cheered the Reb, and someone shouted, "Bully for you! Johnny!" Whilst this was going on, we had all risen to our feet. The enemy too, having ceased to fire, were also standing. As soon as the sharpshooter had finished his generous work, he turned around and went back to the tree, and then at the top of his voice shouted, "Down Yanks, we're going to fire." And down we lay again.

About eleven, a couple of battalions of the Eleventh Corps, whose left had joined the right of our corps at the Baltimore pike right at the wall of the cemetery, advanced down the hill towards our right. The regiment that came closest to us was the 5th Ohio. The enemy treated them to a severe fire of shell and musketry as they approached the Emmitsburg pike where we lay. Seeing us lying in the ditch, where we were supporting our skirmishers out in front, they seemed to prefer the cool shade of the ditch to the right of us, to the heat of the air in front where they had been ordered to go. The officers seemed to be even less willing than the men to advance. Altogether they looked like children about to take a very bitter dose of medicine, who thought that by hesitating, some kind of accident would befall to save them from the disagreeable necessity. But we all rose and by taunts, sneers, and threats roused them to a sense of their manhood. A number of the braver among them, going ahead with bull-dog courage, the rest of them got up and went forward, keeping their heads down, though in the manner of new troops, as if walking against a driving rain. Of course they were walking against a rainstorm of lead, but by bending their heads they only managed to catch some of the terrible drops through the top of the cranium, in place of some other less vital part of the body. As they advanced towards the fence, several of their officers again lost courage and dropped to the ground, letting their men go ahead. But we soon drove them up with a shower of stones, and of oaths which perhaps were even more effective.

Towards noon the fighting raged all along the line. From the extreme right of the line of battle, at Culp's Hill, where was the 12th Corps, to the left at Round Top Hill, held by the 5th Corps and part of the 3d Corps, was about four miles. The sun shone down upon us from an unclouded July sky, and the heat, by the thirst that it caused, helped us forget our hunger. Before crossing the Potomac we had received six days rations, and again at Taneytown a small ration of hardtack was issued. But now it was all gone. I found myself scraping my fingers along the inside seam of my haversack, to find a few crumbs for my gnawing stomach.

Heavier and heavier grew the fire from infantry and artillery. Yet so exhausted had some of our men become that they slept through a good part of the forenoon. About noon all of the regiment except our company was withdrawn from the skirmish line, having been relieved by fresh troops. The ditch of the pike was now a familiar place to us. Here we sat, talked, and slept. Shells, solid shot, canister, and bullets were screaming and singing above us. Some of the more provident men had saved a little coffee and, having found water, started fires in our ditch. I was lucky enough to get from one of my men a cup of the reviving stuff.

Section III

"It Seemed That Death Was In Every Foot Of Space":

The Cannonade

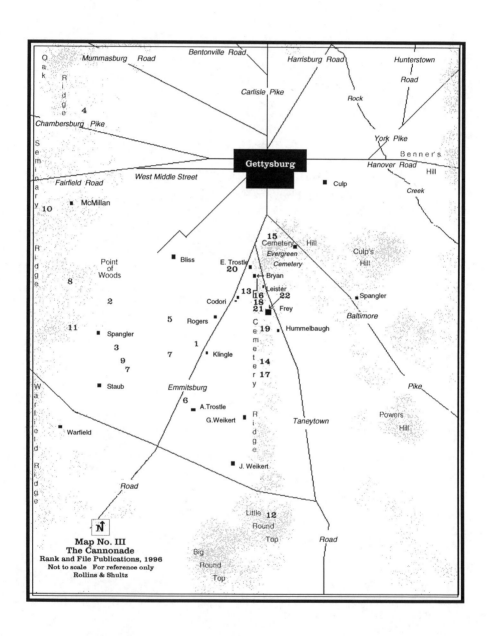

Gettysburg

Oak Ridge

Mummasburg Road

Bentonville Road

Harrisburg Road

Hunterstown Road

Carlisle Pike

Rock

Chambersburg Pike

4

York Pike

Benner's

Seminary Ridge

Fairfield Road

West Middle Street

Hanover Road

Hill

10

McMillan

Culp

Creek

15
Cemetery Hill

Culp's Hill

Bliss

E. Trostle
20

Evergreen
Cemetery

Point of Woods

8

2

Codori

Bryan

Leister

13

16 **22**

Spangler

18

5

Rogers

21

Frey

11

Spangler

3

1

Cemetery Ridge

19

Hummelbaugh

Baltimore

9

7

Klingle

14

7

17

Staub

Emmitsburg

Warfield Ridge

6

A.Trostle

G.Weikert

Taneytown

Pike

Powers Hill

Warfield

J. Weikert

Road

N

Little **12**
Round
Top

Road

Map No. III
The Cannonade
Rank and File Publications, 1996
Not to scale   For reference only
Rollins & Shultz

Big
Round
Top

1. Colonel Henry Coalter Cabell, commanding the artillery of McLaw's division of Longstreet's corps, was up most of the night placing his guns. They ended up on the high ground near Emmitsburg Road, and were there when Kemper's men passed through them on their way to Cemetery Ridge. Report of Col. H. C. Cabell, Commanding Artillery Battalion, August 1, 1863, *OR*, 1, 27, 2, 375-376.

The next day, finding that Captain Fraser's command was so much crippled by the loss of men, I placed two of his guns (3-inch rifles) in charge of Captain [B.C.] Manly. These two guns, under command of Lieutenant [J.H.] Payne, of Manly's battery, two 3-inch rifles of Captain [E.S.] McCarthy's battery, under command of Lieut. R. M. Anderson, and two Parrott guns of Captain Fraser's battery, under command of Lieutenant [W.J.] Furlong, were ordered to take position on the new and advanced line of battle.

These guns were placed several hundred yards in front of the infantry, near a small brick house, and fronted the road leading from Gettysburg to Emmitsburg. The line of artillery extended up the road for some distance. Captain [H.H.] Carlton's battery and a section of Captain McCarthy's battery (two Napoleons) were ordered to the left of the line, in front of Pickett's division, the guns being placed slightly *en echelon*, owing to the conformation of the line of battle. Their position was considerably to the left of the brick house, the interval being occupied by batteries of other battalions.

Captain McCarthy, who had, early in the morning, been placed 300 or 400 yards in advance, of the skirmishers, fired 20 rounds, and, with a section of another battery, succeeded in driving back an advancing line of the enemy.

The fire of the artillery was opened about 1 p. m. For over two hours the cannonading on both sides was almost continuous and incessant, far, very far, exceeding any cannonading I have ever before witnessed. The last-named batteries were opposite the cemetery position of the enemy. During this cannonading, Lieutenant [Henry] Jennings, a brave and gallant officer, fell, wounded, and, later in the day, Captain Carleton, who had in action so gallantly commanded his battery, fell, also wounded. The command of the battery fell upon, and was at once assumed by, First Lieut. C. W. Motes. The artillery ceased firing, and a part of Pickett's division passed over the ground occupied by these batteries in their celebrated charge. Captain Manly occupied, slightly shifting the position of his guns, the same position occupied the day before, and engaged the mountain batteries, particularly, with effect.

2. By rank, Colonel E. P. Alexander was a battalion commander in the artillery reserve of Longstreet's corps, under the command of Colonel J. B. Walton. Longstreet trusted Alexander, however, and thus he became, in effect, the primary artillery officer in the charge. Alexander's memoir is an important source for our knowledge of the communications between Alexander, Pickett, and Longstreet. His story is slightly different than Longstreet's. E. P. Alexander, *Military Memoirs*, 422-425.

It was just 1 P. M. by my watch when the signal guns were fired and the cannonade opened. The enemy replied rather slowly at first, though soon with increasing rapidity, having determined that Pickett should charge, I felt impatient to launch him as soon as I could see that our fire was accomplishing anything. I guessed that a half-hour would elapse between my sending him the order and his column reaching close quarters. I did not presume on using more ammunition than one hour's firing would consume, for we were far from supplies and had already fought for two days. So I determined to send Pickett the order at the very first favorable sign and not later than after 30 minutes' firing.

At the end of 20 minutes no favorable development had occurred. More guns had been added to the Federal line than at the beginning, and its whole length, about two miles, was blazing like a volcano. It seemed madness to order a column in the middle of a hot July day to undertake an advance of three fourths of a mile over open ground against the centre of that line.

But something had to be done. I wrote the following note and dispatched it to Pickett at 1.25: —

> General: If you are to advance at all, you must come at once or we will not be able to support you as we ought. But the enemy's fire has not slackened materially and there are still 18 guns firing from the cemetery.

I had hardly sent this note when there was a decided falling off in the enemy's fire, and as I watched I saw other guns limbered up and withdrawn. We frequently withdrew from fighting Federal guns in order to save our ammunition for their infantry. The enemy had never heretofore practiced such economy. After waiting a few minutes and seeing that no fresh guns replaced those withdrawn, I felt sure that the enemy was feeling the punishment, and at 1.40 I sent a note to Pickett as follows: —

> For God's sake come quick. The 18 guns have gone. Come quick or my ammunition will not let me

support you properly.

This was followed by two verbal messages to the same effect by an officer and sergeant from the nearest guns. The 18 guns had occupied the point at which our charge was to be directed I had been incorrectly told it was the cemetery. Soon only a few scattered Federal guns were in action, and still Pickett's line had not come forward, though scarcely 300 yards behind my guns.

I afterward learned what had followed the sending of my first note. It reached Pickett in Longstreet's presence. He read it and handed it to Longstreet. Longstreet read and stood silent. Pickett said, "General, shall I advance?" Longstreet knew that it must be done, but was unwilling to speak the words. He turned in his saddle and looked away. Pickett saluted and said, "I am going to move forward, sir," and galloped off.

Longstreet, leaving his staff, rode out alone and joined me on the left flank of the guns. It was doubtless 1.50 or later, but I did not look at my watch again. I had grown very impatient to see Pickett, fearing ammunition would run short, when Longstreet joined me. I explained the situation. He spoke sharply, — "Go and stop Pickett where he is and replenish your ammunition." I answered: " We can't do that, sir. The train has but little. It would take an hour to distribute it, and meanwhile the enemy would improve the time."

Longstreet seemed to stand irresolute (we were both dismounted) and then spoke slowly and with great emotion: "I do not want to make this charge. I do not see how it can succeed. I would not make it now but that Gen. Lee has ordered it and is expecting it."

I felt that he was inviting a word of acquiescence on my part and that if given he would again order, "Stop Pickett where he is." But I was too conscious of my own youth and inexperience to express any opinion not directly asked. So I remained silent while Longstreet fought his battle out alone and obeyed his orders. The suspense was brief and was ended by the emergence from the wood behind us of Garnett riding in front of his brigade. I had served on the Plains with him and Armistead in 1858, and I now met him for the first time since Longstreet's Suffolk campaign. He saluted and I mounted and rode with him while his brigade swept through our guns. Then I rode down the line of guns, asking what each gun had left. Many had canister only. These and all having but few shell were ordered to stand fast. Those with a moderate amount of suitable ammunition were ordered to limber up and advance.

During the cannonade the reserve ordnance train had been moved from the position first occupied, and caissons sent to it had not returned. Only about one gun in four could be ordered forward from the centre, but from the right Maj. Haskell took five from Garden's and Flanner's batteries, and Mjr. Eshleman, of the Washington artillery, sent four somewhat to Haskell's left.

3. Colonel Joseph Mayo commanded the 3rd Virginia Infantry in Kemper's brigade, and finished the charge in command of what was left of the brigade. The Colonel Patton referred to here was an ancestor of General George S. Patton of World War II fame. Joseph C. Mayo, "Pickett's Charge at Gettysburg," *SHSP*, XXXIV(1906), 328-335.

Before dawn the following morning, we moved to our place in the line, our march being carefully concealed from the enemy's view. Soon after we got into position, some two hundred yards in the rear of the batteries on Seminary Ridge, General Lee passed in front of us, coming from the right, and a little while afterwards every man in the ranks was made to know exactly what was the work which had been cut out for. I remember perfectly well General Kemper's earnest injunction to me to be sure that the Third Virginia was told that the commanding general had assigned our division the post of honor that day. He was a Virginian; so were they. Then the arms were stacked and the men allowed to rest at will; but one thing was especially noticeable; from being unusually merry and hilarious they on a sudden had become as still and thoughtful as Quakers at a love feast. Walking up the line to where Colonel Patton was standing in front of the Seventh, I said to him, "This news has brought about an awful seriousness with our fellows, Taz." "Yes," he replied, "and well they may be serious if they really know what is in store for them. I have been up yonder where Dearing is, and looked across at the Yankees."

Then he told me a good joke he had on our dashing and debonair chief of artillery. He had ridden out on the skirmish line to get a closer observation of the enemy's position, when a courier galloped up with a message from General Lee. Naturally he supposed Mars Robert wished to ask him what he had seen of those people that was worth reporting; but he was woefully mistaken. This was all the General had to say: "Major Dearing, I do not approve of young officers needlessly exposing themselves; your place is with your batteries." While we were talking an order came to move up nearer the artillery. This was done, and the final preparations made for the advance. Here let me say that General Kemper's memory was at fault when he said in his letter to Judge David E. Johnston, dated

February 4, 1886, that he and General Garnett were the only officers of Pickett's Division who went into that battle mounted. He himself gave Col. Lewis B. Williams, of the First, permission to keep his horse, as he was too unwell to walk, and after the General was shot down I saw two of his staff, Captain William O. Fry and Orderly Walker, still on horseback.

    . . . The first shot or two flew harmlessly over our heads; but soon they began to get the range and then came — well, what General Gibbon, on the other side, called "pandemonium." First there was an explosion in the top of our friendly tree, sending a shower of limbs upon us. In a second there was another, followed by a piercing shriek, which caused Patton to spring up and run to see what was the matter. Two killed outright and three frightfully wounded, he said on his return. Immediately after a like cry came from another apple tree close by in the midst of the Third. Company F had suffered terribly; First Lieutenant A. P. Gomer, legs shattered below the knee; of the Arthur brothers, second and third lieutenants, one killed and the other badly hit; Orderly Sergeant Murray mortally wounded, and of the privates, one killed and three wounded. Then, for more than an hour it went on. Nearly every minute the cry of mortal agony was heard above the roar and rumble of the guns. . . . Doubtless there would have been some consolation to know, as we afterwards learned, that our blue-coated friends over the way were in the same, if not in a worse predicament. General Gibbon, who with Hancock's Corps held the position we were about to storm says of the execution done by our batteries that it exceeded anything he had dreamed of in artillery warfare; and I believe it is now an admitted historical fact that from the time that the "nimble gunner with limstock the devilish cannon touched," that awful din at Gettysburg was the most fearful sound that ever pealed from the "red throat of roaring war." Colonel Patton called my attention to the gallant bearing of Major Dearing, as he galloped, flag in hand, from gun to gun of his battalion and suggested that it would be safer for us to close up on the artillery, but I told him he must not think of moving without orders and, besides, it was evident that the enemy's fire was rapidly abating, and that the storm would soon be over. The words were barely spoken before it came again; our turn now. I thought at first that it was my adjutant, John Stewart, as a handful of earth mixed with blood and brains struck my shoulder; but they were two poor fellows belonging to Company D (one of them, I remember, had a flaming red head), and another, as we believed, mortally hurt, Sergeant-Major Davy Johnston, of the Seventh. Strange to say, he was at the time lying between Colonel Patton, and myself.

    That was among the last shots fired, and as the terrific duel was drawing to a close, General Pickett came riding briskly down the rear of the line, calling to the men to get up and prepare to advance, and "Remember Old Virginia." Our dear old Third, it was a heart-rending sight which greeted me as I moved along your decimated ranks! — while quickly, and without a word of command, the men fell into their places; especially to see our color-bearer, Murden, as fine a type of true soldiership as ever stepped beneath the folds of the spotless stars and bars, now lying there stark and stiff, a hideous hole sheer through his stalwart body, and his right hand closed in a death grip around the staff of that beautiful new flag which to-day for the first and last time had braved the battle and the breeze.

4. Lieutenant Colonel Thomas H. Carter, commander of artillery in Rodes' division, Ewell's Corps, describes firing on the Federal lines on Cemetery Ridge from an area some two and a half miles north, near the Rail Road Cut. This is the type of highly destructive and demoralizing enfilade fire that Alexander would later comment that could have been even more effective if the Confederate artillery had been better positioned, and the reserve guns better utilized. Report of Lieut. Col. Thomas H. Carter, Commanding Artillery Battalion, August 5, 1863, *OR*, 1, 27, 2, 603.

On Friday, July 3, ten guns were posted on the right and left of the railroad cut, and their fires directed on the batteries planted on the Cemetery Hill. This was done to divert the fire of the enemy's guns from Hill and Pickett's troops in their charge across the valley, and also to divert their fire from three batteries of the First Virginia Artillery, under Captain Dance, and temporarily in my command. These three batteries had been ordered to fire, in conjunction with a large number of guns on their right, on a salient part of the enemy's line prior to the charge of infantry. The effect of this concentrated fire on that part of the line was obvious to all. Their fire slackened, and finally ceased. It was feebly resumed from a few guns when Pickett's and Hill's troops advanced, but the most destructive fire sustained by these troops came from the right and left of this salient. The smooth-bore guns of my battalion were held in readiness to move in rear of Gettysburg College, but were not needed.

5. Major James Dearing, commander of artillery in Pickett's division, whose bravery is recorded in several other accounts included in this anthology, describes firing his ammunition until

it was exhausted. Note that he had his guns fire slowly, by battery, to insure accuracy and effectiveness against specific targets. Report of Maj. James Dearing, Commanding Artillery Battalion, August 16, 1863, *OR*, 1, 27, 2, 388-389.

About daybreak the next morning (the morning of July 3), it marched to the field of battle, and was, later in the morning, put in position on the crest of the hill immediately in front of the enemy's position, which was assailed by General Pickett's division. On my left and rear was Colonel Cabell's Artillery Battalion, and on my right and rear was the Washington Artillery Battalion. Early that morning, the enemy threw forward a strong line of skirmishers in front of my position, and, having no infantry to drive them away, Captain [R. M.] Stribling's battery was ordered to drive them in, which was done by firing about a dozen rounds. Several of my men and horses were wounded by these sharpshooters. There was no more firing from my battalion until the signal guns for the commencement of the general attack were fired. Maj. J. P. W. Read, who was superintending the firing of Captain Stribling's battery in the morning, was wounded in the head by a fragment of shell. Though not dangerous, the wound was painful. Major Read did not leave the army on account of this wound, but has been with it all of the time. When the signal guns were fired, I at once brought my battalion in battery to the front, and commenced firing slowly and deliberately. To insure more accuracy and to guard against the waste of ammunition, I fired by battery. The firing on the part of my battalion was very good, and most of the shell and shrapnel burst well. My fire was directed at the batteries immediately in my front, and which occupied the heights charged by Pickett's division. Three caissons were seen by myself to blow up, and I saw several batteries of the enemy leave the field. At one time, just before General Pickett's division advanced, the batteries of the enemy in our front had nearly all ceased firing; only a few scattering batteries here and there could be seen to fire. About this time my ammunition became completely exhausted, excepting a few rounds in my rifled guns, which were used upon a column of infantry which advanced on General Pickett's right flank. I had sent back my caissons an hour and a half before for a fresh supply, but they could not get it. Two of my batteries and a part of Captain [G. V.] Moody's battery, of Colonel Alexander's battalion, under command of Captain Moody, remained under a very heavy fire for upward of an hour without being able to fire a single shot. My own batteries remained on the field after every round of ammunition was exhausted and until I could receive some fresh batteries which Colonel Alexander sent to me. Captain Moody's four 24-pounder howitzers, two of Captain [Joe] Norcom's guns, and one of Captain [M. B.] Miller's, and Captain [O. B.] Taylor's battery were sent to me. I put them in position, and succeeded in driving back the column of infantry which was at that time advancing. This was near 6 o'clock, as nearly as I can recollect. After the enemy was driven back at this point, nothing but desultory picket firing could be heard on that part of the line for the rest of the day. In this engagement, Captain Stribling's battery had 3 men wounded and 10 horses killed and left on the field. Captain [M. C.] Macon had 3 men killed, 3 wounded, and 8 horses killed and left on the field; Captain [W. H.] Caskie, 3 men wounded and 7 horses killed and left on the field; Captain [J. G.] Blount had 5 men killed and wounded, and 12 horses killed. There were others so slightly wounded as not to unfit them for duty, and, consequently, not reported. Captain Moody and the others who served under my orders that day will, of course, hand in their reports to their respective battalion commanders. The behavior of officers and men was all that could be desired by any commander. They were all cool, collected, and in earnest, and perfectly indifferent to danger. In the field and staff, Major Read was wounded, as above mentioned, early in the morning. The horse of my color-bearer and courier was shot under him while bearing the flag along the line. There were no other casualties.

6. **Major Benjamin Eshleman, commanding the famed Washington Artillery of New Orleans in Alexander's battalion, describes the positioning of artillery during the charge. His guns, like other Confederate artillery, ran out of ammunition. The story of William Forrest, a teamster in the Army, gives us insight into the level of commitment of the entire army on July 3rd. Report of Maj. B. F. Eshleman, Washington (Louisiana) Arty., August 11, 1863, OR, 1, 27, 2, 433-436.**

About midnight, I received orders from Colonel Alexander, commanding reserve artillery, to take position on the field before daylight, and with his assistance I placed my battalion, consisting of eight Napoleon guns and two 10 pounder howitzers, as follows, viz: Three Napoleons (Third Company), Lieutenants Andrew Hero, jr., and [Frank] McElroy, and one Napoleon (First Company, Lieutenant H. C.] Brown, all under command of Captain [M . B.] Miller, about 100 yards to the left of the peach orchard, and on the immediate left of Captain [0. B.] Taylor's battery, of Alexander's battalion; two Napoleons (Fourth Company), Captain Norcom and Lieutenant Battles, on Captain Miller's left, and two Napoleons (Second Company), Captain [J. B.] Richardson and Lieutenant [Samuel] Hawes, on the left of Captain Norcom. The two howitzers—one of the Second and one of the Fourth Company—were held in reserve, under command of Lieutenant [George E.] Apps, Fourth Company.

As soon as day broke and the enemy's lines became visible, it was apparent that to provide against an enfilade fire, the left of my line had better be thrown a little to the rear. Colonel Alexander, having approved the proposed change, Captain Norcom's battery was retired about 30 yards, and Captain Richardson's moved about 200 yards to the left and to the rear of Norcom, forming en echelon by batteries. Major Dearing afterward took position with his battalion on my left, and five guns of Colonel Cabell's battalion were placed in position between Captains Norcom and Richardson.

During the morning, the enemy threw forward heavy lines of skirmishers, endeavoring to gain the ravine and cover of the woods in my front. My guns, with those of Captain Taylor, opened upon them moderately with evident effect. The enemy's batteries replied, but I paid little attention to them, seldom answering their fire at their batteries, in order to save my ammunition for the grand attack.

Early in the day my attention was called by Captain Richardson to a 3-inch rifled gun (that had been abandoned by the enemy the previous day) standing between the lines, about 300 yards in advance of our line of skirmishers. The horses had all been killed and lay firmly harnessed to the piece. William Forrest and Jim Brown (drivers), of Captain Richardson's company, immediately volunteered and earnestly requested permission to bring it off. Having given them directions how to proceed, I allowed them to do so, and the piece was drawn off under a heavy fire from the enemy's sharpshooters. Several shots struck the carriages, but the men and horses were unharmed. The limber contained about 60 rounds of ammunition, and the gun was immediately placed in position by Captain Richardson.

I was deprived of the services of Capt. Joe Norcom early in the day, who, being struck by a piece of shell, had to retire from the field after turning over the command to Lieut. H. A. Battles.

Between 1 and 2 p. m. you ordered me to give the signal for opening along the entire line. Two guns in quick succession were fired from Captain Miller's battery, and were immediately followed by all the battalions along the line opening simultaneously upon the enemy behind his works. The enemy answered vigorously, and a most terrific artillery duel ensued. Notwithstanding a most galling fire from the enemy's artillery from behind his works, and an enfilading fire from the mountain on my right, my men stood bravely to their work, and by their steady and judicious firing caused immense slaughter to the enemy. About thirty minutes after the signal guns had been fired, our infantry moved forward over plateau in our front. It having been understood by a previous arrangement that the artillery should advance with the infantry, I immediately directed Captain Miller to advance his and Lieutenant Battles' batteries. Captain Miller having suffered severely from the loss of men and horses, could move forward only three pieces of his own battery and one of Lieutenant Battles' section. Then, with one piece of Major Henry's battalion under the direction of Major [J, C.] Haskell, he took position 400 or 500 yards to the front, and opened with deadly effect upon the enemy. With the exception of those five guns, no others advanced. Captain Taylor, on my right; and Major Dearing, on my left, at this juncture ran out of ammunition and withdrew, leaving my battalion alone to bear the brunt of this portion of the field. The battery of Colonel Cabell's command, on Captain Richardson's right, had also ceased firing.

. . . Too much cannot be said in praise of William Forrest (driver) of Captain Richardson's company, for the gallant manner in which he acted in getting off the Yankee gun. Having secured the gun, and finding ammunition, it was necessary, in order to put it to immediate use, to have horses and harness. Forrest was indefatigable in his exertions till he had captured from between the lines horses and harness sufficient to haul the gun, having several times approached within near range of the enemy's sharpshooters. He was afterward wounded by a Minie ball in the arm at the battle of Williamsport, Md. My casualties were: Wounded, 3 officers. Killed, 3; wounded, 23, and missing, 16, non-commissioned officers and privates; 37 horses killed and disabled; 3 guns disabled; 1 limber blown up. I omitted to state in the proper place that Lieutenant Apps, shortly after putting his howitzers in position, was struck by a piece of shell, and his horse killed under him. He was obliged to leave the field.

7. Adjutant James Crocker recalls that the largest number of cannon ever arrayed on the North American continent--well over 200--emitted clouds of smoke so thick that they obscured the July sun. J.F. Crocker, *Gettysburg*, 37-44.

At last, in our immediate front, at 1 P. M., there suddenly leaped from one of our cannons a single sharp, far-reaching sound, breaking the long-continued silence and echoing along the extended lines of battle and far beyond the far-off heights. All were now at a strained attention. Then quickly followed another gun. Friend and foe at once recognized that these were signal guns. Then hundreds of cannon opened upon each other from the confronting heights. What a roar — how incessant! The earth trembled under the mighty resound of cannon. The air is darkened with sulphurous clouds. The whole valley is enveloped. The sun, lately so glaring, is itself obscured. Nothing can be seen but the flashing light leaping from the cannon's mouth amidst the surrounding smoke. The air which was so silent and serene is now full of exploding and screaming shells and shot, as if the earth had opened and let out the very furies of Avernus. The hurtling and death-dealing missiles are plowing amidst batteries, artillery and lines of infantry, crushing, mangling and killing until the groans of the men mingle with the tempest's sound. The storm of battle rages. It is appalling, terrific, yet grandly exciting.

8. Lieutenant John Lewis, 9th Virginia, describes the emotions he felt during the cannonade, and Armistead's morale-building presence. John H. Lewis, *Recollections from 1860 to 1865* (Portsmouth, Va.: Privately Printed, 1893), 84-85.

Up to this time, near 1 o'clock, all had been quiet; artillery had been moving into line and taking position; but there was not even an occasional shot to disturb the quiet. About 1 o'clock the sound of two Whitworth guns broke the stillness, and immediately 125 guns, all along the line, joined in. In a few moments the Federals opened with about 80 guns and Joined in the infernal din that fairly shook the mountains. The smoke soon darkened the Run, and the scene produced was similar to a gigantic thunder-storm, the screeching of shot and shell producing the sound of the whistling blast of winds. Man seldom ever sees or hears the like of this but once in a lifetime; and those that saw and heard this infernal crash and witnessed the havoc made by the shrieking, howling missiles of death as they plowed the earth and tore the trees will never forget it. It seemed that death was in every foot of space, and safety was only in flight; but none of the men did that. To know the tension of mind under a fire like that, it must be experienced; it can not be told in words. There is nothing to which I could compare it so as it would be made plain to one who had never been there. For two long hours this pandemonium was kept up, and then, as suddenly as it commenced, it ceased. For a few moments all was quiet again. Then was to come the work of death. (I was a member of Armistead's brigade.) The command "attention" was heard, and the men rose from the ground, where they had been lying during the fire of artillery.

If I should live for a hundred years I shall never forget that moment or the command as given by General Louis (Lewis) A. Armistead on that day. He was an old army officer, and was possessed of a very loud voice, which could be heard by the whole brigade, being near my regiment. He gave the command, in words, as follows— "Attention, second battalion! battalion of direction forward; guides center; march!" I never see at any time a battalion of soldiers but what it recalls those words. He turned; placed himself about twenty paces in front of his brigade, and took the lead. His place was in the rear, properly. After moving he placed his hat on the point of his sword, and held it above his head, in front of him.

9. The number of men killed or wounded during the cannonade is unknown, but Sergeant David Johnston of the 7th Virginia in Kemper's brigade graphically describes the chaos, terror, and suffocating heat and noise of the cannonade. It led strong men to prayer, and ended for him with a serious injury. This is the same David Johnston to whom Mayo had referred in the previous document. David E. Johnston, *Four Years a Soldier*, 249-272.

. . . down upon our faces we lay; and immediately belched forth the roar of more than an hundred guns from the Confederate batteries, immediately in our front, to which the enemy, with a greater number, promptly replied, with telling effect upon our lines, the exact position of which they seemed to have ascertained, -- if in no other way, by means of their signals on Round Top. The very atmosphere seemed broken by the rush and crash of projectiles, solid shot, shrieking, bursting shells. The sun, but a moment before so brilliant, was now almost darkened by smoke and mist enveloping and shadowing the earth, and through which came hissing and shrieking, fiery fuses and messengers of death, sweeping, plunging, cutting, ploughing through our ranks, carrying mutilation, destruction, pain, suffering and death in every direction . Turn your eyes whithersoever you would, and there was to be seen at almost every moment of time, guns, swords, haversacks, human flesh and bone, flying and dangling in the air, or bouncing above the earth, which now trembled beneath us as if shaken by an earthquake. Some of our men with the teams two or three miles away, declared that the window sash in the windows shook and chattered as if shaken by a violent wind. Over us, in front of us, behind us, and in our midst, and through our ranks, poured shot, shell and the fragments thereof, dealing out death on every hand; yet the men stood bravely to their posts -- that is, those that had not been knocked out of place by shot -- and all this in an open field, beneath the burning rays of a July sun. The reader must not suppose that no one was alarmed or felt squeamish, for doubtless, man a poor fellow thought time had about come -- and pray? yes; great big, bearded men prayed loud too, and they were in earnest -- it was really a praying time, for if men ever needed the care and protection of a merciful, loving, Heavenly

Father, it was now. Men prayed on that field that never prayed before. This fearful artillery duel continued for about one hour and fifty-five minutes without ceasing, though it almost seemed an age. So rapid was the firing and so great the number of guns engaged, that the fire from one could not be distinguished from another; in fact, there was one continuous roar, and it really seemed that between the fires a bird could scarcely have flown without being struck, yet the gallant Maj. (afterwards Gen.) Dearing, commandant of the battalion of artillery in our front, with flag in hand, rode to and fro among his guns, encouraging his men. Our position was a trying one; much more so than if we had been engaged in a close combat with the enemy, and almost as perilous; for certainly we should not have felt the terrible strain so much could we have given back the blows with our own strong arms.

About a quarter to 3 o'clock, the fire from the batteries of the enemy began to slacken, and our own, out of ammunition, began to withdraw, but the enemy had a battery to our left from which we received an enfilading fire, which was quite accurate, having almost the exact range, which was, perhaps, guided by the signal corps on Round Top, from which our position was evidently plainly visible.

. . . Referring to the wounding of myself and others as the artillery duel was closing, I will state the surroundings, etc. As Sergeant-Major my position was on the left of the regiment, which threw me in the shade of an apple tree which stood in the field on the left of our regiment and on the right of the 3rd regiment. When the signal guns were fired Col. Patton of our regiment and Col. Jo. Mayo of the 3rd regiment lay down under the apple tree and I lay down rather between two soldiers of the 3rd regiment and Lieutenant James Brown of our regiment, with my head a little higher or further up the hill than the two soldiers referred to, and about on a parallel with Lieut. Brown's. As the batteries began to withdraw and the enemy's fire slackened, we found that one of these batteries formed to our left was the one that had been doing us considerable damage -- in fact, almost enfilading our line. I began to breathe a little more freely and raised my head off the ground and looked around, whereupon Lieut. Brown said to me, "you had better put your head down or you may get it knocked off." I replied, "well, Lieut., a man had as about as well die that way as to suffocate for want of air." I had barely spoken these words when a terrific explosion occurred, which for a moment deprived me of my breath and of sensibility, but it was momentary, for in a moment or so I found myself lying off from my former position and grasping for breath. Around me were brains, blood and skull bones; my first thought was that my Colonel's head had been blown off, but this was dispelled the next moment by his asking me if I was badly hurt, to which I replied I thought I was and called for that which a wounded which I replied I thought I was and called for that which a wounded soldier always first wants, a drink of water. The Col. sprang up and called to some one to bring water. By this time I had turned about and discovered that the heads of the two men who lay on my left side had been blown off just over the ears, and that the shell had exploded almost directly over me, a little below my left shoulder blade, breaking sever[al] of my ribs loose from my backbone, bruising severely my left lung and cutting my grey jacket almost into shreds and filling it with grains of powder. Lieut. Brown was severely wounded by the same shot -- making two killed and two wounded. In a few moments two of my old company -- Harry Snidow, the other not recollected -- came to me, raised me up, gave me water, put a blanket on the ground near the tree and placed me on it in a kind of sitting position; just then came Gen. Pickett and the order to advance, as previously stated. In less than ten minutes the wounded men came pouring back over the hill, among them a Lieut. of the brigade whose face was familiar, but his name I could not call; he picked up a limb which had been cut from the tree under which I lay and threw it over the headless bodies of the two men at my feet, doubtless, thinking that such a sight to a wounded man would have a tendency to make him sick. I said to him "Lieut., never mind that, but have me carried off," which he promised to do, and in a short time the corps of litter bearers bore me back some two hundred yards where I found Drs. Oliver and Worthington, our regimental surgeon and assistant. My wound was examined and the Doctors gave me a quantity of morphine. About dark I was placed in an ambulance and carried some few miles from the battle field to the field hospital, whither Gen. Kemper was also removed and placed in a farm house while the rest of us were placed in an old barn with some of the men detailed as nurses to take care of us. We got no attention of any moment that night. It was thought Gen. Kemper would not live during the night his sufferings were so great -- almost beyond endurance.

10. **The Confederates suffered significant casualties during the cannonade. Dr. John Holt, a physician from Mississippi, relates the story of the death of Private Jeremiah Gage of the "University Greys," Company A of the 11th Mississippi. Quoted in Maud Morrow Brown,** *The University Greys: Company A, Eleventh Mississippi Regiment, Army of Northern Virginia, 1861-1865* **(Richmond: Garrett and Massie, 1940), 37-40.**

Early on the morning of July 3d, I selected the nearest possible cover for wounded behind a raised roadway about two and one half feet high, constructed to allow wagons to be driven in upon the lower floor of a barn and unloaded. Fortunately it ran parallel with the Federal Batteries opposite, and the crest of the ridge for about thirty yards.

About 1 o'clock in the day I was with my regiment down the slope in front of our line of artillery, when a sergeant major of a nearby battery came along and asked if any one had a watch on time. I told him I believed my watch was on time but why did he want to know. He replied that the Captain of his battery sent him, "because at half-past one o'clock a signal gun on our extreme right will let loose all this artillery and that over yonder." As the minute hand touched half-past, I ran up toward the battery yelling: "Half-past! Time is up!" About two minutes later a solemn boom rolled from the far right. Instantly the whole crest of Seminary Ridge, Round Top, Little Round Top and Culp's Hill burst into simultaneous explosion: tongues of fire leaping from their sides, with the crash of Krakatoa and Pele in violent eruption blazing at once. The atmosphere suddenly became a screaming, shrieking, bellowing pandemonium of shells and flying fragments.

I went up to my little first-aid hospital behind the barn road embankment, and under its cover, seated myself for business. . . .

Presently the wounded began to come in crouchingly; for many were killed and wounded before the charge began. The first to arrive, born on a litter, was a princely fellow and favored son of the Eleventh Mississippi. I saw in an instant a condition of terrible shock. Keeping everybody close to the ground, I turned to him and he pointed to his left arm. I quickly exposed it and found that a cannon ball had nearly torn it away between the elbow and the shoulder. I made some encouraging remark when he smiled and said: "Why, Doctor, that is nothing; here is where I am really hurt," and he laid back the blanket and exposed the lower abdomen torn from left to right by a cannon shot, largely carrying away the bladder, much intestine, and a third of the right half of the pelvis; but in both wounds so grinding and twisting the tissues that there was no hemorrhage. I then surveyed his personality, observing the tender devotion on the part of his litter bearers, and I saw a singularly attractive creature. Through his deathly pallor I could detect a sunburned blond, who in health would show a strong and ruddy countenance; a large head with a tousled shock of reddish golden locks like a mane, with the musculature and form of an athlete. Deferentially polite, there was something singularly self-confident and manly about him, answering distinctly the descriptive marks of that Shepherd, the younger son of Jesse about the time he chose five smooth stones out of the brook. "For he was ruddy and withal of a beautiful countenance, and goodly to look to."

Without the slightest change of voice, he asked: "Doctor,

how long have I to live?" "A very few hours," I replied. "Doctor, I am in great agony; let me die easy, dear Doctor; I would do the same for you." His soul peered from the depths of his blue eyes in an appeal of anguish that cut me to the heart, and I replied, "You dear, noble fellow, I will see to it that you shall die easy."

No word or detail of this scene has faded from my memory. There was no thought of the dramatic; it was dreadfully genuine and naturally spontaneous, in the unconscious creating and acting of a grander tragedy than we might ever hope to play. For my own feelings and as physician I can make no disclosure of his name and tell this reminiscence.

I called for, and my hospital knapsack bearer, Jim Rowell, quickly handed me a two ounce bottle of black drop — a concentrated solution of opium, much stronger than ladanum.

I poured a tablespoonful of it into a tin cup, with a little water, and offered it; but before his hand could reach it, a thought flashed into my mind, and withdrawing the cup, I asked, "Have you no message to leave?"

It startled him, and in a low moaning wail, he cried: "My mother, O, my darling mother, how could I have forgotten you? Quick! I want to write."

By that time, all who were crouching under the low shelter, were crowded around, oblivious of their own injuries and weeping silently.

I took my seat on the ground close beside him and lifted him over, reclining on my chest, his face close to mine to steady his head, his right elbow in the hollow of my right hand to support and steady his arm, and a pencil slipped into his hand; Jim Rowell had provided the sheet of paper, held on the smooth lid of the hospital knapsack improvised as a desk. He wrote rapidly — all of this transpired in haste — murmuring to himself the words, audible to me for I looked another way.

He began with place and date "On the battlefield, July 3rd, 1863." He wrote little more than half a page into which he poured with vehemence his whole soul of tenderest love never faltering for a word; and a message toward the last, with a name that he wrote silently, conscious of the presence of strangers; but the message was too personal and sacred to him for me to trespass. For it was holy ground.

The last line he softly repeated aloud: "I dip this letter in my dying blood." With that he turned down the blanket and seizing the letter pressed the back of it upon his oozing, bloody wound, and handed it to me; giving his mother's address and begging to be sure she got that letter.

. . . . I arose from the ground and had him supported, when he turned to me with a reminder of my promise and of his hopeless pain. I handed him the cup and he feebly waved it saying: "Lc around, boys, and let us have a toast. I do not invite you to drink with me, but I drink the toast to you, and to the Southern Confederacy, and to victory!" And he grabbed it to the last drop, returning the cup, saying, "I thank you."

We laid him back on some improvised soft head - rest, and I rushed off to work among the wounded.

In about an hour, passing hastily, I lifted the cover from his face, to find him sleeping painlessly.

Three hours later, as the tide of battle turned and the Southern Confederacy had touched its highest watermark and ebb - tide began, I passed again and laid aside the cover from his face, to find that the spirit of our reincarnated Sir Galahad had taken its flight in triumphal ascension to Him who instituted and consecrated the Holy Grail. Oh, the excruciating pathos and very agony of the glory!

His death surpassed in tenderness of love, in philosophical resignation, in courage and willing sacrifice of self, if it were possible, even that of Socrates, as revealed to us in the Phaedo.

Upon the receding wave of the great charge, came a heavy drift of shattered humanity.

(After Doctor Holt had received Mrs. Armistead's letter of inquiry, *The Times - Democrat* sent Flo Field to interview her. On Sunday, June 29th, 1937, the interview, from which the following extract and the letter are taken, was published.)

The sisters would be reluctant to give the contents of this dying message to the public were it not an intimate historic note which shows the sort of hero heart that beat in young Southern manhood. When one reads this letter one must remember this: that it was written amid the roar and horror of battle: written by a youth who knew he had only a few hours to live: written as he was supported in the doctor's arms, with a knapsack as desk: written in mortal agony.

Gettysburg Penn.
July 3rd.
My dear Mother

This is the last you may ever hear from me. I have time to tell you that I died like a man. Bear my loss best you can. Remember that I am true to my country and my greatest regret at dying is that she is not free and that you and my sisters are robbed of my worth whatever that may be. I hope this will reach you and you must not regret that my body can not be obtained. It is a mere matter of form anyhow. This is for my sisters too as I can not write more.

Send my dying release to Miss Mary . . . you know
who.

　　　　　J S. GAGE

Mrs. P. W. Gage　　　　　Co. A, 11th Miss.
Richland,
Holmes County,
Miss.
This letter is stained with my blood.

**11. Private Erasmus Williams of the 14th Virginia prepared to
defend himself during the cannonade, but an officer in his company didn't, and paid for it. Erasmus Williams to John Daniels,
n.d., John Daniels Papers, University of Virginia.**

　　. . . Early on the morning of the 3rd, we advanced marching
by column and then formed line of battle in rear of the Confederate
artillery and infantry. After my part of the brigade was posted in the
open, I soon got out a case knife which I carried, and with my
bayonet began digging a hole and throwing the dirt in front of me.
One of the Lieutenants of the 14th was standing up in rear with his
back against a sapling. He laughed at me for digging a hole, and said
good naturedly "why Williams, you are a coward." "you can call me
what you please," said I, "but when the time comes I will show up
all right, and when the artillery begins the hole I am digging will be
a good place for me to be in." So I kept on until I had a good little
fort for the accommodation of one.
　　Not long after this I heard Col. Hodges, of my regiment, say
to Capt. Logan of my company, "cannonade is going to commence
presently and a signal gun will begin it." A little later the colonel fell
upon the field and was "dead upon the field of honor."
　　I had been campaigning a little on my own account, and
passing a house went in. I found two or three Confederates there,
but all the people gone; so I helped myself to a jowl of meat and a half
gallon of salt, which were very acceptable as reinforcements to my
rations, not only to me but to my company for the rations were scant.
　　So I settled myself in my little fortification and awaited
events. The Lieutenant behind me kept guying my and said "I am
going to stand right up here and witness the whole proceeding."
Smiling and chatting, he took things as easy and less cautiously
than I did. In a little while the signal fired, and there came a terrific
blast all along the lines from the enemy's guns in reply. In a few
minutes I was covered with dirt from the shot and shell striking near
me. Presently, indeed almost instantly, the defiant Lieutenant was

swept away by a shot or shell, and his blood sprinkled all over me. A shell stuck in the ground right by me with the fuse still burning. I had just time to stretch my hand and pull out the fuse, else both I and others might have been killed by its explosion. A little later and after we were moving to the charge, a shell from the enemy's batteries to our right struck our line, killed Capt. Logan and nine in our company.

12. One of the most important differences between the armies during most of the war, and certainly at Gettysburg, was their use of artillery. A private in the 107th New York observed that the essential difference between the two was that "there is one thing that our government does that suits me to a dot. That is, we fight mostly with artillery. The rebels fight mostly with infantry." Much of the truth of that statement is due to the work of Brigadier General Henry J. Hunt, one of the few men of rank on either side who seemed to fully understand, and have the ability to implement, the full capabilities of the artillery. He concentrated several batteries together on key features of the terrain to maximize their firepower against attack at any point. Hunt formed his guns into two lines of 40-50 guns each, one south of the copse of trees, one on Cemetery Hill, with a commanding view of the entire field. He saw to it that ammunition and the guns in the Artillery Reserve were well placed and quickly available. As commander of the Federal artillery at Gettysburg, he is perhaps one of the great unsung heroes of the battle on the Union side. His efficient and effective work stands in stark contrast to "Parson" Pendleton's bumbling ineptitude. In this essay, Hunt tells the story of the preparations for the Charge and its repulse. Henry J. Hunt, "The Third Day At Gettysburg," *Battles and Leaders of the Civil War*, V. III, 369-376.

I had just given these orders to the last battery on Little Round Top, when the signal-gun was fired, and the enemy opened with all his guns. From that point the scene was indescribably grand. All their batteries were soon covered with smoke, through which the flashes were incessant, whilst the air seemed filled with shells, whose sharp explosions, with the hurtling of their fragments, formed a running accompaniment to the deep roar of the guns. Thence I rode to the Artillery Reserve to order fresh batteries and ammunition to be sent up to the ridge as soon as the cannonade ceased; but both the reserve and the train had gone to a safer place. Messengers, however, had been left to receive and convey orders, which I sent by them; then I returned to the ridge. Turning into the

Taneytown pike, I saw evidence of the necessity under which the reserve had "decamped," in the remains of a dozen exploded caissons, which had been placed under cover of a hill, but which the shells had managed to search out.   In fact, the fire was more dangerous behind the ridge than on its crest, which I soon reached at the position occupied by General Newton behind McGilvery's batteries, from which we had a fine view as all our own guns were now in action.

Most of the enemy's projectiles passed overhead, the effect being to sweep all the open ground in our rear, which was of little benefit to the confederates — a mere waste of ammunition, for everything here could seek shelter.   And just here an incident already published may be repeated, as it illustrates a peculiar feature of civil war.   Colonel Long, who was at the time on General Lee's staff, had a few years before served in my mounted battery expressly to receive a course of instruction in the use of field-artillery.   At Appomattox we spent several hours together, and in the course of conversation I told him I was not satisfied with the conduct of this cannonade which I had heard was under his direction, inasmuch as he had not done justice to his instruction; that his fire, instead of being concentrated on the point of attack, as it ought to have been and as I expected it would be, was scattered over the whole field.   He was amused at the criticism and said: "I remembered my lessons at the time, and when the fire became so scattered, wondered what you would think about it!"

I now rode along the ridge to inspect the batteries.   The infantry were lying down on its reverse slope, near the crest, in open ranks, waiting events.   As I passed along, a bolt from a rifle-gun struck the ground just in front of a man of the front rank, penetrated the surface and passed under him, throwing him "over and over." He fell behind the rear rank, apparently dead, and a ridge of earth where he had been lying reminded me of the backwoods practice of "barking" squirrels.   Our fire was deliberate, but on inspecting the chests I found that the ammunition was running low, and hastened to General Meade to advise its immediate cessation and preparation for the assault which would certainly follow.   The headquarters building, immediately behind the ridge, had been abandoned, and many of the horses of the staff lay dead.   Being told that the general had gone to the cemetery, I proceeded thither.   He was not there, and on telling General Howard my object, he concurred in its propriety, and I rode back along the ridge, ordering the fire to cease.   This was followed by a cessation of that of the enemy, under the mistaken impression that he had silenced our guns and almost immediately his infantry came out of the woods and formed for the assault.   On my way to the Taneytown road to meet the fresh batteries which I had ordered up, I met Major Bingham, of Hancock's staff, who informed me that General Meade's aides were seeing me with orders to "cease firing" so I had only anticipated his wishes. The batteries were brought up, and Fitzhugh's, Weir's, Wheeler's, and Parsons's were put in near the clump of trees. Brown's and Arnold's batteries had been so crippled that they were now withdrawn, and Brown's was replaced by Cowan's.

13. Brigadier General John Gibbon's classic description of the cannonade from the center of Cemetery Ridge includes a sense of the noise of the guns and shells, and an interesting vignette of his conversations with soldiers. He also reveals the confusion caused by the event and his attempt to comprehend its meaning. His walk down in front of the ridge underscores the high fire of the Confederate artillery. Gibbon, *Recollections*, 146-153.

Almost instantly afterwards the whole air above and around us was filled with bursting and screaming projectiles, and the continuous thunder of the guns, telling us that something serious was at hand. All jumped to their feet and loud calls were made for horses, which orderlies hurried forward with, already saddled and waiting. Mine did not come at once and anxious to get upon my line, I started on a run, up a little swale leading directly up to the center of it. Some features of that hurried trip are indelibly impressed upon my memory. The thunder of the gun was incessant, for all of ours had now opened fire and the whole air seemed filled with rushing, screaming and bursting shells. The larger round shells could be seen plainly as in their nearly completed course they curved in their fall towards the Taneytown road, but the long rifled shells came with a rush and a scream and could only be seen in their rapid flight when they "upset" and went tumbling through the air, creating the uncomfortable impression that, no matter whether you were in front of the gun from which they came or not, you were liable to be hit. Every moment or so one would burst, throwing its fragments about in a most disagreeably promiscuous manner, or, first striking the ground, plough a great furrow in the earth and rocks, throwing these last about in a way quite as dangerous as the pieces of the exploding shell. At last I reached the brow of the hill to find myself in the most infernal pandemonium it has ever been my fortune to look upon. Very few troops were in sight and those that were, were hugging the ground closely, some behind the stone wall, some not, but the artillerymen were all busily at work at their guns, thundering out defiance to the enemy whose shells were bursting in and around them at a fearful rate, striking now a horse, now a limber box and now a man. Over all hung a heavy pall of smoke underneath which could be seen the rapidly moving legs of the men as they rushed (the reason, as I afterwards learned, was that a shell struck my faithful orderly, Sheldan of Battery B, killing him instantly). To and fro between the pieces and a the line of limbers, carrying forward the ammunition. One thing which forcibly occurred to me was the perfect quiet with which the horses stood in their places. Even when a shell, striking in the midst of a team, would knock over one or two of them or hurl one struggling in his death agonies to the ground, the rest would make no effort to struggle or escape but would stand stoicly by as if saying to themselves, "*It is fate,* it is useless to try to avoid it." Looking thus at Cushing's Battery my eyes happened to rest upon one of the gunners standing in rear of the nearest limber, the lid open showing the charges. Suddenly, with a shriek, came a shell right under the limber box, and the poor gunner went hopping to the rear on one leg, the shreds of the other dangling about as he went.

As I reached the line just to the left of Cushing's Battery, I found Gen. Webb seated on the ground as coolly as though he had no interest in the scene and somehow it seemed to me that in such a place men appear to take things a good deal as I had remarked the horses took them. Of course, it would be absurd to say we were not scared. How is it possible for a sentient being to be in such a place and not experience a sense of alarm? None but fools, I think, can deny that they are afraid in battle.

"What does this mean?" I asked Webb shook his head. In fact it was a question about which we all felt anxious, but no one could answer it yet. It might mean preparation for retreat; it might signify the prelude to an assault.

How long did this pandemonium last? Measured by our feelings it might have been an age. In point of fact it may have been an hour or three or five. The measurement of time under such circumstances regular as it is by the watch, is exceedingly uncertain by the watchers. Getting tired of seeing men and horses torn to pieces and observing that although some of the shells struck and burst among us, most of them went high and burst behind us, the idea occurred to me that a position farther to the front would be safer and rising to my feet, I walked forward accompanied by my aide (Lt. Haskell). I had made by a few shells when three of Cushing's limber boxes blew up at once, sending the contents in a vast column of dense smoke high in the air, and above the din could be heard the triumphant yells of the enemy as he recognized this result of his fire. Passing the clump of trees referred to as marking this point of our line, we walked forward to the fence, where the men were lying close behind it and motioning them to make room for me, I stepped over the wall, went to a little clump of bushes standing just in front of the line and looked out there to see if I could detect any movement going on in that direction. Nothing could be seen but the smoke constantly issuing from the long line of batteries and nothing heard but the continuous roar of hundreds of guns, the screaming of countless projectiles, as they rushed through the air in all directions and the bursting of shells. These all went over our heads and generally burst behind us. Whilst standing here and wondering how all this din would terminate, Mitchell, an aide of Gen. Hancock, joined me with a message from Hancock to know what thought the meaning of this terrific fire. I replied I thought it was the prelude either to a retreat or an assault. After standing here for some time and finding the enemy did not lessen the elevation of his pieces we walked down to the left still outside of the line of battle, the men peering at us curiously from behind the stone wall as we passed along. As we approached the left of my division the line made a slight inclination to the front, beyond which was the spring alluded to in the description of the ground. As we neared the piece of marshy ground below it I called Lt. Haskell's attention to a man who had evidently left his regiment in front to get some water. Around his neck were hung several canteens and he was crawling back through the wet ground, keeping as close to the earth as possible, evidently fearful of the shot and shell soaring over his head. As we came nearer I called out to him. "Look out, my man, you might get hit!" At the sound of my voice, he turned his head, still keeping it as close to the ground as possible, to look at me and then, as if inspired by a new idea, rose to his feet and walked deliberately back to his regiment; no doubt arguing with himself that if two could walk erect there was little danger to a third. Passing round the left of my line, I was proceeding behind it up towards the right, when I noticed a man coming across the field carrying another, evidently wounded, on his back. Just as they came opposite to us, they encountered a low stone wall over which the one was trying to climb with the other still on his back. I stopped and told Haskell to assist them and we then continued on our way.

14. **Lieutenant Colonel Freeman McGilvery played an important and largely unheralded role in the repulse of the charge. His work with the 39 (or more) guns south of the copse of trees concentrated an enormous fire on the undefended men of Kemper, who passed within easy range in front of them. He also describes his slow, well-aimed counter-battery fire and its effects. His estimate of 35,000 Confederates is way off. Report of Lieut. Col. Freeman McGilvery, 1st Maine Light Artillery, Cmdg. First Volunteer Brigade, —, —, 1863, *OR*, 1, 27, 1, 883-884.**

During the night I ascertained the whereabouts of all my batteries, and early on the morning of July 3 brought them into line on the low ground on our left center, fronting the woods and elevated position occupied by the enemy along the Gettysburg and Emmitsburg road a point at which it was plain to be seen they were massing artillery in great force.

The line of batteries under my command, commencing on the left, which rested on an oak wood, occupied by our infantry, were, in numbers and kind of guns, as follows: Ames' battery, six light 12 pounders; Dow's Sixth Maine Battery, four light 12-pounders; a New Jersey battery, six 3-inch guns, one section New York [Pennsylvania] Artillery, Lieutenant Rock [Captain Rank], two 3-inch guns; First [Second] Connecticut, four James rifled and two howitzers; Hart's Fifteenth New York Independent Battery, four light 12-pounders; Phillips' Fifth Massachusetts, six 3-inch rifled guns; Thompson's battery, F and C, consolidated Pennsylvania Artillery, five 3-inch rifled guns; total, thirty-nine guns. In front of these guns I had a slight earthwork thrown up, which proved sufficient to resist all the projectiles which struck it, and the commanders of batteries were repeatedly ordered that, in the event of the enemy opening a cannonading upon our lines to cover their men as much as possible, and not return the fire until ordered.

At about 12.30 o'clock the enemy opened a terrific fire upon our lines with at least one hundred and forty guns. This fire was very rapid and inaccurate, most of the projectiles passing from 20 to 100 feet over our lines. About one-half hour after the commencement some general commanding the infantry line ordered three of the batteries to return the fire. After the discharge of a few rounds, I ordered the fire to cease and the men to be covered. After the enemy had fired about one hour and a half, and expended at least 10,000 rounds of ammunition, with but comparatively little damage to our immediate line, a slow, well-directed fire from all the guns under my command was concentrated upon single batteries of the enemy of those best in view, and several badly broken up and successively driven from their position to the rear.

15. Major Thomas Osborn commanded the nearly 50 guns of the 11th Corps artillery on Cemetery Hill. He had a spectacular view of the charge, and left a particularly vivid account of the action in his area. From his viewpoint, Cemetery Hill seemed to be the center of the storm of lead, surrounded by Confederate artillery. He gives a superb account of the effect of the Confederates' enfilade fire, and his effective return-fire. Osborn underscores the enormous self-control it took for officers to command themselves and their men amidst the intensity of the moment, to stifle "every impulse of nature." He also discloses that the men in at least one

battery failed to control their fear and dumped their ammunition and retreated to the "safety" of the Reserve area. There is much here that doesn't appear in other memoirs, including the account of Meade amidst the roar, and his suggestion to Hunt to stop firing and lure the Confederates into charging. His estimation of the effectiveness of his guns is also noteworthy. The regulations required that cannon be placed 14 feet apart in line of fire, so his statement that they were half that, or 7 feet, should leave the reader with the picture of guns nearly hub-to-hub on Cemetery Hill. Thomas Osborn, "Experiences at the Battle of Gettysburg," Colgate University Archives. Published in Herbert Crumb, Ed., *The Papers of Thomas Osborn: The Eleventh Corps Artillery at Gettysburg* (Hamilton, N.Y.: Edmonston Publishers, 1992). Published with Permission.

During all the forenoon there was an ominous silence on the part of the enemy. It was reported to us from the Headquarters of the Army that the enemy could be seen moving along Seminary Ridge to a point opposite the left wing of the army. Batteries were being put into position all along Seminary Ridge to bear upon that wing of our army and commanding our entire front. The report was correct. Before the afternoon battle opened, with our glasses we could see Lee's batteries in position on Seminary Ridge, standing at regulation intervals covering a line of two miles. It was the longest and finest line of light batteries ever planted on a battlefield. We were fully aware that this line of batteries meant mischief to us and that immediately behind it was a corresponding body of infantry.

At precisely one o'clock in the afternoon we saw a puff of smoke from a gun fired from the hills upon our front and right, and about two and a half miles from us. Soon after, in less than a minute, the sharp whistle of a Whitworth bolt or shot, aimed at the crest of Cemetery Hill, passed a few feet over our heads. The report from a Whitworth gun and the sound of the long steel bolt used for a solid shot, as it passes through the air, is readily recognized and distinguished from the reports of all other guns. By the time this Whitworth shot had passed us and gone to the rear of the army without doing harm, more than two hundred and fifty guns from Lee's line opened upon Meade's army.

More than half of these were turned upon the small space of Cemetery Hill which I occupied with five batteries. They were turned upon the guns of my command. The crest of the hill was so limited that even the guns I had were placed at half regulation distance. I at once appreciated that the admirable position taken by Howard and especially the hill upon which he had placed his own command was fully recognized by the enemy as the point of greatest strength in the line. It was plain that Lee's primary object was to drive the artillery from that hill. He put his guns into position in the form of a crescent in such a manner that nearly all of them could bear upon Cemetery Hill. A little later, perhaps twenty minutes or a half hour, 36 guns were in position on our right so as to bring them directly on the flank of my line. They commanded my guns to absolute perfection.

With the opening of these last guns, the enemy's line of artillery was practically in a semi-circle around us. My batteries on the hill were then raked from every side, except the rear and the direct left. In addition to the military necessity of driving my guns from Cemetery Hill, we were upon the crest of an elevation and in plain view from every part of the enemy's line. We were an especially tempting object for every gun the enemy had, and more than half of them were devoted exclusively to us.

Instantly upon the enemy's guns opening fire, all the guns on Meade's front opened. Meade had as many guns in line as did Lee. The firing on both sides was exceedingly rapid, going up from two to four shots a minute from each gun on both sides.

That is about as rapidly as the chief of the gun could take good aim.

Allowing that three shots a minute were fired by each gun, which was for a considerable time below the average, there were 1,500 shots a minute passing between the armies. If it should be thought that I overstate the number of shots which can be fired in a minute from a single muzzle loading gun, I will say that Battery D under pressure at the Battle of Chancellorsville fired nine shots a minute from every gun, or 54 shots a minute from six guns, and every one with good aim.

It does not take longer for a well-drilled battery to load and fire a cannon than for a sportsman to load and fire a fowling piece. The gun, under pressure, can be loaded and fired as fast as one man can bring ammunition from the ammunition chest which is generally about ten steps in rear of the gun.

At the moment the artillery fire opened, I had only the five batteries on the hill or guns, but I acted upon General Hunt's instructions and called on the Artillery Reserve for about as many more, making all told on Cemetery Hill a little short of 50 guns. The space occupied was so small that the guns were placed at half distance and the batteries close together. I was determined to hold the hill no matter how severe the fire might be.

It is now conceded that never in any battle in the world was the fire of light artillery so heavy as that at Gettysburg. Every gun on the line in both armies was doing its best. The fire of both armies was excellent. Looking down our own line or along the enemy's line, there was not a half minute that one could not see the smoke from an exploded ammunition chest. A shell or solid shot striking a chest exploded it, and the white smoke from the powder shot up in a solid cloud which could be seen from every part of the army. These explosions were an indication of the accuracy of the fire and the damage being done by the fire of the opposing armies. More shot and shell killed men and horses than hit the small ammunition chests.

The sound was, of course, deafening, though little attention was paid to it. I am under the impression that the infantry paid far more attention to the sound of the guns than the artillery men did. I have often heard infantry officers speak of it, though I have but a faint recollection of it myself.

While the firing was at its height in our front and along the main line to our right, bringing a fire upon our line from a considerable angle, a group of guns (after the battle I learned to have been 36) opened square upon our right flank so as to rake my line its entire length. From the first shot they had our range and elevation exactly, and the havoc among my guns, men, horses and ammunition chests was fearful. Guns were hit and knocked off their carriages, ammunition chests were blown up and horses were going down by the half dozen. To meet this fire, I drew out from the line three batteries and swung them half around to face this new fire. The hill was so narrow that the guns were put as close together as they could be worked. These three batteries, in turn, got the range and elevation of the enemy's guns at the first fire, upon which the enemy lost our elevation at once and did very little more damage. After our guns began to play upon them, they fired very wildly. After the battle we visited the ground those batteries occupied and found they had been literally destroyed. Men, horses and the debris of the batteries showed that all those batteries were ruined. I had only 14 guns to their 36. However, my command suffered a good deal from their fire but was not moved by it.

Our fire to the front and on the flank rapidly used up the ammunition, and I ordered the ammunition chests refilled from the army ordnance train while the fighting was in full progress. This was done by sending one, two or more caissons at a time to the train to have the chests filled.

As a rule, the fire of the enemy on all our front against Cemetery Hill was a little high. Their range or direction was perfect, but the elevation carried a very large proportion of their shells about twenty feet above our heads. The air just above us was full of shells and the fragments of shells. Indeed, if the enemy had been as successful in securing our elevation as they did the range there would not have been a live thing on the hill fifteen minutes after they opened fire. The batteries on our right flank did secure both range and elevation perfectly, but in a few minutes we so demoralized them that they lost the elevation but not the direction, and they too fired high. As it was, we suffered severely.

Under all human conditions where the surroundings are exceptionally pressing or serious, more or less ludicrous incidents will occur. This terrific artillery battle, which all knew was the immediate forerunner of victory or defeat, was no exception to that rule. I will mention a couple of them now and then go on with the narrative of the battle. During such time, the force of will which an officer must bring to bear upon himself in order not only to control his men but also to govern himself, is wonderful. He must by sheer force of will shut up every impulse of his nature, except that of controlling the officers and men subject to his command. He must discard all care of his personal safety and even his own life. The most difficult person to control is always himself.

. . . While this fire on Cemetery Hill was at its very height General Meade rode into the batteries at great speed followed by two or three staff officers. As he came within hearing he shouted, "Where is Major Osborn?! Where is Major Osborn?!" As he came near me, I answered him. He then shouted, apparently greatly excited, "What are you drawing ammunition from the train for?" I said that some of the ammunition chests were giving out. He then said, "Don't you know that it is in violation of general orders and the army regulations to use up all your ammunition in a battle?" I replied that I had given that no thought and that General Hunt had directed me to draw what I might require from the ordnance train. He then said, "What do you expect to do here?" I replied that I was expected to hold the hill, and that I expected to do so, if the infantry would stand by me. To this he retorted, "You cannot hold your men here." I replied, "I will stay here, General, and so will my men."

He then rode off with as great a speed as he had come. He gave me no orders. Apparently he was greatly excited, but his command in the battle, from beginning to end, showed that his judgment was good and not influenced by his excitable nature. I have no doubt that Meade was as brave personally as any of the officers mentioned, but he was a passionate man and excitable, and in officer-like bearing upon a battlefield he bore no comparison to the others. This scene was far more ludicrous than serious. His reference to the army regulations and general orders under these circumstances was, to say the least, a little peculiar. Yet he gave me no orders, nor objected to my getting all the ammunition I might deem necessary. At the time and after, I was under the impression that no one except those I mentioned were near, but years after, General Howard told me that he was standing near and heard all that passed between General Meade and myself.

Another incident occurs to me which at the time roused my temper considerably. In reply to my requisition from the Reserve Artillery for more batteries, an Ohio battery was sent to me, which

I placed at the extreme left on my line and near a clump of forest trees, a little natural grove into which Cemetery Hill broke off abruptly. The battery had been under fire but a few minutes when information was brought to me that the men were throwing ammunition out of the chests into that bunch of timber. This was in order to get clear of it and then represent that it was expended and so retire from the field. I went to the battery, gave the captain some orders in emphatic English and then left him. A few minutes later several of the men called out, "Look, Major, see the cowards." I did look and saw that Ohio battery with all the men mounted on the ammunition chests going at full speed, the horses running down the Baltimore Pike, the drivers whipping their horses at every jump. I never saw that battery again, and as it did not belong to my command, I did not report it to its proper superiors. Doubtless, the captain reported to the commander of the Reserve Artillery that he was in the hottest of the fight and that he and all his men were heroes. At all events, the giant monument on Cemetery Hill stands today to the credit of that battery.

Still another personal incident comes to me which impressed itself upon my mind because my personal vanity was a little set back. Captain Wadsworth, a son of General Wadsworth, was an aide on the staff of General Meade. . . . While the artillery fire was still at its highest, he came to me with some directions and to make some inquiries for headquarters. I was at the moment on a nice horse thoroughly accustomed to me. His horse was the same. We halted close together in the midst of the batteries, the horses headed in opposite directions and our faces near together. Neither horse flinched. The forelegs of each horse were in line with the hind legs of the other, and we stood broadside to the enemy's fire. While we were talking, a percussion shell struck the ground directly under the horses and exploded. The momentum of the shell carried the fragments along so that neither horse was struck nor did either horse move. When the shell exploded, I was in complete control of my nerves and did not move a muscle of my body or my face. Neither did Wadsworth, but I dropped my eyes to the ground where the shell exploded, and Wadsworth did not. I never quite forgave myself for looking down to the ground when that shell exploded under us. I do not believe that there was a man in the entire army, save Captain Wadsworth, who could have a ten pound shell explode under him without looking where it struck.

There were many other incidents of that afternoon which were photographed on my memory, but most of them were of a sad nature and involved suffering at an hour when no heartbeat of sympathy could be expressed. One in illustration of this order will be enough. One regular soldier who had served with me as an orderly for a considerable time was struck with a shell just as I arrived at his battery. His entire shoulder was torn out. He saw me as he fell, and with a word of affection and farewell, bled to death in a minute or two. This is sufficient of the many incidents of suffering which were every minute before our eyes on Cemetery Hill that afternoon.

General Hunt, Chief of Artillery of the Army, came upon the hill almost immediately after General Meade of whom I have spoken, but he dismounted to canvass the desperate state of affairs as the entire artillery of both armies was working up to its capacity, and there was no variation in the fire upon Cemetery Hill. As I was in charge of the artillery, Hunt was talking to me when Generals Howard and Schurz joined us. We were talking over the course of this fearful artillery duel and what might be Lee's plans, as the artillery fire was evidently intended to precede some more desperate movement of the infantry. It was conceded by all that the mass of Lee's army was concentrated behind Seminary Ridge and in front of Meade's left wing, between three-fourths of a mile and a mile from it. In our conversation we assumed these facts which afterward proved to be correct. We also believed that Lee's primary object was to drive the guns off of Cemetery Hill. This, Lee's Chief of Artillery has since written to me was a fact, as those guns more than any others in our army commanded the open plain over which his great charge was to be made.

I said to these officers that I believed that if we should stop firing along our entire line suddenly and as though the artillery on Cemetery Hill was driven off the field, Lee would at once develop his plans—that if the General would give me permission, I would stop my batteries at once. Hunt said that he thought I was correct, and if Howard agreed to it, he would give the order. Howard thought the suggestion a good one and said that he would like to see the experiment tried. Hunt asked me if I could keep my men on the hill if I stopped their work, and expressed the belief that I could not hold them. I told him that I could do so and to give himself no uneasiness on that score. He then gave the order to stop firing and said that he would ride down the line and stop all the batteries.

Then he left the hill, riding at great speed. All of this took but a few minutes; meanwhile there was no cessation of fire from any part of the field in either line, and shells were reaching the hill from 800 to 1,000 a minute. A few feet above our heads the air was nearly as full of shells and fragments of shells as it is of flakes in a snowstorm, and every second or two a shell struck among the batteries and men on the hill.

I went to my battery on the right, Wiedrich's, ordered him to cease firing and for every officer and man to lie flat upon the ground covering themselves as best they could by the unevenness of the ground, and to remain there until further orders. From Wiedrich's battery I walked along the line and gave the same order to each battery, whether they belonged to my own command or were borrowed from the Artillery Reserve. This required but a very few minutes and every gun on the hill was silent, and the enemy's officers with their glasses could see none of our men on the hill. Hunt rode very rapidly along the line, and the batteries stopped one after another in quick succession. Meanwhile, the enemy's shells came in nearly as rapidly as before. In the same magazine article of which I have spoken, General Hunt claims to have originated the idea of stopping the fire of the artillery to tempt Lee to develop his plans. This moment was in fact the turning point in the battle in our favor, and Hunt made the most of it for himself. Fortunately, both Howard and Schurz were present at the time, and both have since publicly stated the facts to be as I have given them and would confirm them upon inquiry.

We had but a few minutes to wait after the artillery ceased firing for developments. I think it was not more than ten minutes before the enemy's line of battle showed itself coming over Seminary Ridge at the point where we supposed Lee's troops were massed. As the line of battle came into view, it appeared to be about three-fourths of a mile in length and was moving in perfect line. The moment that line appeared coming down the slope of Seminary Ridge, every battery on Meade's line opened on it. Lee believed that he had silenced all our batteries while, with the exception of one or two a couple of hundred yards beyond my left, none had been so seriously injured that they were not able to continue their fire. The enemy's artillery kept up their fire on our line, but none of our batteries paid any further attention to it. They devoted their attention exclusively to the advancing line of battle.

16. There was nothing for Federal infantry to do but wait and hope, as Lt. Frank Haskell of Gibbons' staff explains, and he describes their attitudes in a memorable passage. His description of the quiet in front of the lines underscores the inaccuracy of the Confederate artillery. Haskell, "Gettysburg."

What sound was that? — There was no mistaking it! — The distinct sharp sound of one of the enemy's guns, square over to the front, caused us to open our eyes and turn them in that direction, when we saw directly above the crest the smoke of the bursting shell, and heard its noise. In an instant, before a word was spoken, as if that was the signal gun for general work, loud, startling, booming, the report of gun after gun, in rapid succession, smote our ears, and their shells plunged down and exploded all around us. We sprang to our feet. — In briefest time the whole Rebel line to the West, was pouring out its thunder and its iron upon our devoted crest. The wildest confusion for a few moments obtained among us. The shells came bursting all about. —The servants ran terror-stricken for dear life and disappeared. The horses, hitched to the trees or held by the slack hands of orderlies, neighed out in fright, and broke away and plunged riderless through the fields. The General at the first, had snatched his sword, and started on foot for the front. I called for my horse; no body responded. I found him tied to a tree near by, eating oats, with an air of the greatest composure, which under the circumstances, even then struck me as exceedingly ridiculous. He alone of all beasts or men near, was cool. I am not sure but that I learned a lesson then from a horse. Anxious alone for his oats, while I put on the bridle and adjusted the halter, he delayed me by keeping his head down; so I had time to see one of the horses of our mess-wagon struck and torn by a shell; — the pair plunge, — the driver has lost the rein, — horses, driver, and wagon go into a heap by a tree. — Two mules close at hand, packed with boxes of ammunition, are knocked all to pieces by a shell. Gnl. Gibbon's groom has just mounted his horse, and is starting to take the General's to him, when the flying iron meets him and tears open his breast, — he drops dead, and the horses gallop away. No more than a minute since the first shot was fired, and I am mounted and riding after the General. The mighty din that now rises to heaven and shakes the earth, is not all of it the voice of the rebellion; for our guns, the guardian lions of the crest, quick to awake when danger comes, have opened their fiery jaws, and begun to roar, — the great hoarse roar of battle. I overtake the General half way up to the line, — before we reach the crest his horse is brought by an orderly, leaving our horses just behind a sharp declivity of the ridge, on foot we go up among the Batteries. How the long streams of fire spout from the guns, — how the rifled shells hiss, how the smoke deepens and rolls. But where is the Infantry? Has it vanished in smoke? Is this a nightmare, or a juggler's devilish trick? All too real. The men of the Infantry have seized their arms, and behind their works, behind every rock, in every ditch, wherever there is any shelter, they hug the ground, silent, quiet, unterrified, little harmed. The enemy's guns now in action, are in position at their front of the woods along the second ridge, that I have before mentioned, and towards their right, behind a small crest in the open field, where we saw the flags this morning. Their line is some two miles long, concave on the side towards us, and their range is from one thousand to eighteen hundred yards. A hundred and twenty-five Rebel guns, we estimate, are now active, firing twenty-four pound, twenty, twelve and ten pound projectiles, solid shot and shells, spherical, conical, spiral. The enemy's fire is chiefly concentrated upon the position of the 2nd Corps. From the

Cemetery to Round Top, with over a hundred guns, and to all parts of the enemy's line, our Batteries reply, of twenty and ten pound Parrotts, ten pound rifled Ordnances and twelve pound Napoleons, using projectiles as various in shape and name as those of the enemy. Capt. Hazard, commanding the Artillery Brigade of the 2nd Corps, was vigilant among the Batteries of his command, and they were all doing well.

All was going on satisfactorily. We had nothing to do, therefore, but to be observers of the grand spectacle of battle. Capt. Wessels, Judge Advocate of the Division, now joined us, and we sat down just behind the crest, close to the left of Cushing's Battery, to bide our time, to see, to be ready to act, when the time should come, which might be at any moment. Who can describe such a conflict as is raging around us! To say that it was like a summer storm, with the crash of thunder, the glare of lightning, the shrieking of the wind, and the clatter of hail-stones, would be weak. The thunder and lightning of these two hundred and fifty guns, and their shells, whose smoke darkens the sky, are incessant, all pervading, in the air above our heads, on the ground at our feet, remote, near, deafening, ear-piercing, astounding; and these hail-stones, are massive iron charged with exploding fire. And there is little of human interest in a storm; — it is an absorbing element of this. You may see flame and smoke, and hurrying men, and human passion, at a great conflagration; but they are all earthly, and nothing more. These guns are great infuriate demons, not of the earth, whose mouths blaze with smoky tongues of living fire, and whose murky breath, sulphur laden, rolls around them and along the ground, the smoke of Hades. These grimy men, rushing, shouting, their souls in phrenzy, plying the dusky globes, and the igniting spark, are in their league, and but their willing ministers. We thought, that at the second Bull Run, at the Antietam, and at Fredericksburg on the 11th of December, we had heard heavy cannonading; — they were but holy day salutes compared with this. Besides the great ceaseless roar of the guns, which was but the background of the others, a million various minor sounds engaged the ear. The projectiles shriek long and sharp, — they hiss, — they scream, — they growl, — they sputter, — all sounds of life and rage; and each has its different note, and all are discordant. Was ever such a chaos of sound before.

We note the effect of the enemy's fire among the Batteries, and along the crest. We see the solid shot strike axle, or pole, or wheel, and the tough iron and heart of oak snap and fly like straws. The great oaks there by Woodruff's guns heave down their massive branches with a crash, as if the lightning had smote them. The shells swoop down among the Battery horses, standing there apart, — a half a dozen horses start, — they tumble, — their legs stiffen,

— their vitals and blood smear the ground. And these shot and shells have no respect for men either. We see the poor fellows hobbling back from the crest, or unable to do so, pale and weak lying on the ground, with the mangled stump of an arm or leg, dripping their life blood away, or with a cheek torn open, or a shoulder smashed. And many, alas! hear not the roar as they stretch upon the ground, with upturned faces, and open eyes, though a shell should burst at their very ears. Their ears, and their bodies this instant are only mud. We saw them but a moment since there among the flame, with brawny arms and muscles of iron, wielding the rammer and pushing home the cannon's plethoric load.

Strange freaks these round shot play! — We saw a man coming up from the rear with his full knapsack on, and some canteens of water held by the straps, in his hands. He was walking slowly and with apparent unconcern, though the iron hailed around him. A shot struck the knapsack, and it and its contents flew thirty yards in every direction, — the knapsack disappeared like an egg, thrown spitefully against a rock. The soldier stopped, and turned about in puzzled surprise, — put up one hand to his back to assure himself that the knapsack was not there, and then walked slowly on again unharmed, with not even his coat torn. — Near us was a man crouching behind a small disintegrated stone, which was about the size of a common water-bucket. He was bent up, with his face to the ground, in the attitude of a pagan worshiper, before his idol. It looked so absurd to see him thus, that I went and said to him: "Do not lie there like a toad — Why not go to your regiment and be a man?" He turned up his face with a stupid, terrified look upon me, and then without a word turned his nose again to the ground. An orderly that was with me at the time, told me a few moments later, that a shot struck the stone, smashing it in a thousand fragments, but did not touch the man, though his head was not six inches from the stone.

All the projectiles that came near us were not so harmless. Not ten yards away from us, a shell burst among some small bushes, where sat three or four orderlies holding horses; — two of the men and one horse were killed. Only a few yards off a shell exploded over an open limber box in Cushing's Battery; and almost at the same instant, another shell, over a neighboring box. In both the boxes the ammunition blew up with an explosion that shook the ground, throwing fire, and splinters, and shells far into the air and all around, and destroying several men. We watched the shells bursting in the air, as they came hissing in all directions. Their flash was a bright gleam of lightning radiating from a point, giving place in the thousandth part of a second, to a small, white, puffy cloud, like a fleece of the lightest, whitest wool. These clouds were very numerous. We could not often see the shell before it burst; but some times, as we faced towards the enemy, and looked above our heads, the approach would be heralded by a prolonged hiss, which always seemed to me to be a line of something tangible, terminating in a black globe, distinct to the eye, as the sound had been to the ear. The shell would seem to stop; and hang suspended in the air an instant, and then vanish in fire and smoke and noise. We saw the missiles tear and plow the ground. All in rear of the crest for a thousand yards, as well as among the Batteries, was the field of their blind fury. Ambulances, passing down the Taneytown Road, with wounded men, were struck. — The Hospitals near this road were riddled. — The house which was Gnl. Meade's Head Quarters was shot through several times; and a great many horses of officers and orderlies were lying dead around it.

Riderless horses, galloping madly through the fields, were brought up, or down, rather, by these invisible horse-tamers, and they would not run any more. Mules with ammunition, pigs wallowing about, cows in the pastures, whatever was animate or inanimate, in all this broad range, were no exception to their blind havoc. The percussion shells would strike, and thunder, and scatter the earth and their whistling fragments; the Whitworth bolts would pound, and ricochet, and how far away sputtering, with the sound of a mass of hot iron plunged in water; and the great solid shot would smite the unresisting ground with a sounding "thud," as the strong boxer crashes his iron fist into the jaws of his unguarded adversary. Such were some of the sights and sounds of this great iron battle of missiles. Our Artillery men upon the crest, budged not an inch, nor intermitted, but, though caisson and limber were smashed, and guns dismantled, and men and horses, killed, there amidst smoke and sweat, they gave back without grudge or loss of time in the sending, in kind whatever the enemy sent, globe, and cone, and bolt, hollow or solid, — an iron greeting to the rebellion, — the compliments of the wrathful Republic. An hour has droned its flight, since first the war began, — there is no sign of weariness or abatement on either side. So long it seemed, that the din and crashing around began to appear the normal condition of nature there, and fighting, man's element. The General proposed to go among the men, and over to the front of the Batteries, so at about two o'clock he and I started. We went along the lines of the infantry, as they lay there flat upon the earth, a little to the front of the Batteries. — They were suffering little, and were quiet, and cool. How glad we were that the enemy were no better gunners, and that they cut the shell fuses too long. To the question asked the men: "What do you think of this?" — the replies would be: "O, this is bully," — "We are getting to like it," — "O, we don't mind this." And so they lay under the heaviest cannonade that ever shook the continent, and among them a thousand times more jokes, than heads, were cracked.

We went down in front of the line some two hundred yards, and as the smoke had a tendency to settle upon a higher plain than where we were, we could see near the ground distinctly all over the field, as well back to the crest where were our own guns, as to the opposite ridge where were those of the enemy. No Infantry was in sight save the skirmishers, and they stood silent, and motionless, — a row of gray posts through the field on one side, confronted by another of blue. Under the grateful shade of some elm trees, where we could see much of the field, we made seats of the ground, and sat down. Here all the more repulsive features of the fight were unseen by reason of the smoke. Man had arranged the scenes, and for a time had taken part in the great drama; but at last as the plot thickened, conscious of his littleness, and inadequacy to the mighty part, he had stepped aside and given place to more powerful actors. So it seemed; for we could see no men about the Batteries. On either crest we could see the great flaky streams of fire, and they seemed numberless, of the opposing guns, and their white banks of swift convolving smoke; but the sound of the discharges was drowned in the universal ocean of sound. Over all the valley, the smoke, a sulphury arch, stretched its lurid span; and through it always, shrieking on their unseen courses, thickly flew a myriad iron deaths.

With our grim horizon on all sides round toothed thick with Battery flame, under that dissonant canopy of warring shells, we sat, and saw, and heard in silence. What other expression had we that was not mean, for such an awful universe of battle.

A shell struck our breast work of rails up in sight of us, and a moment afterwards we saw the men bearing some of their wounded companions away from the same spot; and directly two men from there came down toward where we were, and sought to get shelter in an excavation near by where many dead horses, killed in yesterday's fight, had been thrown. General Gibbon said to these men, more in a tone of kindly expostulation, than of command: "My men, do not leave your ranks to try to get shelter here. All these matters are in the hands of God, and nothing that you can do will make you safer in one place than in another." — The men went quietly back, to the line, at once. The General then said to me "I am not a member of any church, but I have always had a strong religious feeling; and so in all these battles I have always believed that I was in the hands of God; and that I should be unharmed or not, according to his will. For this reason, I think it is, I am always ready to go where duty calls, no matter how great the danger." Half past two o'clock, an hour and a half since the commencement, and still the cannonade did not in the least abate; but soon thereafter some signs of weariness, and a little slackening of fire began to be apparent upon both sides. First we saw Brown's Battery retire from the line, too feeble for further battle. Its position was a little to the front of the line. Its commander was wounded, and many of its men were so, or worse, — some of its guns had been disabled, — many of its horses killed — its ammunition was nearly expended. Other Batteries in similar cases, had been withdrawn before, to be replaced by fresh ones, and some were withdrawn afterwards. Soon after the Battery named had gone, the General and I started to return, passing towards the left of the Division, and crossing the ground where the guns had stood. The stricken horses were numerous, and the dead and wounded men lay about, and as we passed these latter, their low piteous call for water would invariably come to us, if they had yet any voice left. I found canteens of water near, — no difficult matter where a battle has been — and held them to livid lips, and even in the faintness of death, the eagerness to drink told of their terrible torture of thirst. But we must pass on. Our Infantry was still unshaken, and in all the cannonade suffered very little — The Batteries had been handled much more severely. I am unable to give any figures. A great number of horses had been killed, — in some Batteries more than half of all. Guns had been dismounted, — a great many caissons, limbers, and carriages had been destroyed, — and usually from ten to twenty-five men to each Battery had been struck, at least along our part of the crest. All together the fire of the enemy had injured us much, both in the modes that I have stated, and also by exhausting our ammunition, and fouling our guns, so as to render our Batteries unfit for further immediate use. The scenes that met our eyes on all hands among the Batteries were fearful. All things must end, and the great cannonade was no exception to the general law of earth. In the number of guns active at one time, and in the duration and rapidity of their fire, this Artillery engagement, up to this time must stand alone and pre-eminent in this war. It has not been often, or many times, surpassed, in the battles of the world. Two hundred and fifty guns, at least, rapidly fired, for two mortal hours! Cypher out the number of tons of gunpowder and iron that made those two hours hideous!

Of the injury of our fire upon the enemy, except the facts that ours was the superior position, if not better served and constructed Artillery, and that the enemy's Artillery, hereafter during the battle, was almost silent, we know little. Of course during the fight we often saw the enemy's caissons explode, and the trees sent, by our shot, crashing about his ears, but we can from these alone infer but little of general results. At three o'clock almost precisely the last shot hummed, and bounded, and fell, and the cannonade was over. The purpose of General Lee in all this fire of his guns, — we know it now, we did not at the time, so well — was to disable our Artillery and break up our Infantry, upon the position of the 2nd Corps, so as to render them less an impediment to the sweep of his own Brigades and Divisions over our crest, and through our lines. He probably supposed our Infantry was massed behind the crest, and the Batteries; and hence his fire was so high, and his fuses to the shells were cut so long, too long. The Rebel General failed in some of his plans in this behalf, as many Generals have failed before, and will again.

17. The 5th Massachusetts Battery, commanded by Captain Charles Phillips, was part of McGilvery's line of guns placed just south of the copse of trees and near where the present Pennsylvania monument now stands. They were apparently unnoticed by the Confederates during the cannonade, and received little fire from their guns. *History of the Fifth Massachusetts Battery* **(Boston: Luther E. Cowles, Publisher, 1902), 652-661.**

Captain Phillips in his letter written at Littlestown, Penn., July 6, 1863, in relation to the fight of July 3d proceeds as follows:

The next morning I went into position at daylight, and everything remained quiet till one o'clock. Finding that the rebels were massing artillery in our front, the Major ordered us to throw up a parapet, which we afterwards found conduced very much to our comfort. About one they commenced the most tremendous cannonading I ever heard. They must have had 80 or so guns in position. As artillery ammunition was rather short, we had been ordered not to reply to their batteries, and so we could lie still and enjoy it. My men were entirely sheltered by our parapet, and about the only damage done was to kill 8 or 10 horses.

Viewed as a display of fireworks, the rebel practice was entirely successful, but as a military demonstration it was the biggest humbug of the season.

About half past one General Hancock ordered us to reply, thereby showing how little an infantry officer knows about artillery. The rebels were not doing us any harm, and if they wanted to throw away their ammunition I do not see why we should prevent them. However, we obeyed orders. Fortunately, Major McGilvery came up and stopped us before we had fired a great while.

From the letter of Captain Phillips sent with the plans from the camp near Kelly's Ford Nov. 21, 1863:—

The rebel batteries were arranged along the crest in our front, the peach orchard being full of them. From the woods on our left to the right of our Brigade we threw up a little breastwork of rails and dirt, about two feet high, very useful and convenient. A Division of infantry were placed on this line between our guns, and only one man in the whole Division was hurt by the rebel artillery fire, and he was foolishly lying about 10 feet behind the breastwork. About noon the rebels opened a grand cannonade from their whole line, and for an hour and a half we had a grand Fourth of July performance.

18. Sergeant John Plummer, of the 1st Minnesota, describes the cannonade from the perspective of an infantryman on the Federal left, south of the copse of trees. He reminds us that the men in Pickett's Charge were normal human beings, and that the routine parts of life did not disappear in battle. "John W. Plummer's Account." *Rebellion Record*, 1862-1864, 179-181.

We then lay down to get some sleep, with our equipment on and guns by our side; and I here say I never slept better and had more pleasant dreams in my life than I had on the battle-field of Gettysburg, with dead men and horses lying all around me; but the excitement and exhaustion had been so great that a man could sleep in any condition, and under any circumstances. We got up about daylight, expected and awaited an attack from the enemy at any moment, but till afternoon all was quite, except occasionally a shot from their or our batteries. Most of us got some food during the forenoon, by going one or two at a time back to the rear, where they were allowed fires and cooking, which of course greatly refreshed us. A man's appetite generally, during a battle, is not very voracious. About half past twelve o'clock, as we had gathered around one of our Lieutenants to hear the yesterday's Baltimore *Clipper* read, bang! comes one of their shells over us, striking about twenty yards from us. That stopped the reading; each man took his place lay down, and for the next two hours hugged the ground just about as close as human beings are generally in the habit of doing. The first gun was the signal for a hundred more to open, at less than half a mile distance, while till then their existence was perfectly unknown to us. Such an artillery fire has never been witnessed in this war. The air seemed to be filled with the hissing, screaming, bursting missiles, and all of them really seemed to be directed at us. They knew our exact position, for before we lay down they could with the naked eye plainly see us, and where our lines were, and tried to explode their shells directly over us; but fortunately most of them just went far enough to clear us, while many struck in front of us and bounded over us. We lay behind a slight rise of ground, just enough, by lying close, to hide us from the view of the rebels. A good many shell and pieces struck mighty close to us, and among us, but strange to say, none of us were injured, while the troops that lay behind us had many killed and wounded. Our batteries replied, but for the first time in our experience, they were powerless to silence the rebels, and in fact, many of our guns were silenced. So many of their horses and men were killed that they could not work their guns, and drew them off the field. Caisson after caisson blew up, and still the rebels' fire was fierce and rapid as ever. I kept thinking, surely they cannot fire much longer; their guns will get so hot they will have to stop, and they cannot afford, so far from their base, to waste so much ammunition. It was awful hot where we lay, with the sun shining down on us, and we so close to the ground that not a breath of air could reach us. We kept wishing and hoping they would dry up, as much to get out of the heat as the danger, for the latter we thought little of, after they had fired a while; but Lee had an object to attain by throwing away so much ammunition. He calculated by concentrating his fire on our centre that he could use up our batteries, drive away and demoralize our infantry lines, for owing to the shape of our lines, a shell coming from the rebels, if it failed to do any damage to the front lines, could scarcely fail to go into the reserves that lay back of us; and in fact many more were killed in the rear than in the front, though their fire was directed at the front line and batteries nearly altogether. Had he succeeded in doing what he expected, and got the position we occupied, we were defeated, and so badly that I much doubt our ability to stop their progress towards Baltimore, or anywhere they chose to go. But Mr. Lee got fooled for once, and threw away a mighty sight of good ammunition, and derived little benefit from it.

19. In a rambling and disjointed essay, Private Ralph Sturtevant of the 13th Vermont recalls the intensity of the cannonade causing men to go to extraordinary lengths to avoid the shells, often unsuccessfully. Friends were hit, and men gritted their teeth and crawled out of the way of the shells. Yet some still had the courage to get up and man the artillery's guns. R. O. Sturtevant, *Pictorial History of the 13th Vermont* (Burlington: The Self-Appointed Committee of Three, 1913), 259-264.

. . . The cracking of carbines on the advancing picket line, the buzz and hissing noise of the sharpshooters' bullets and the ricochet of cannon balls bounding along all about us, and the bursting shrapnel overhead quite fully absorbed our attention. We only noted the passing occurrences in our immediate locality watching the aides and orderlies on their foaming steeds galloping over the field bent on reaching some given point, paying no attention to shot or shell that filled the air. It must have been near two o'clock in the afternoon when we realized unusual activity along Seminary Ridge and Emmitsburg Road then occupied by General Longstreet's and Hill's corps.

About this hour, while our brigade was still in rear of Cemetery Hill in support, one of the many shells that passed over the hill on its errand of death and dismay burst in the ranks of the 13th regiment mortally wounding Captain Merritt B. Williams, of Company G; others also were injured but not as seriously. The author of these pages calls to mind the vivid scenes of this occasion still fresh in memory. Captain Williams was a schoolmate at Bakersfield Academy in 1860, '61, and '62, and was an intimate and abiding friend, and I hastened on observing some commotion in the rank of Company G nearby to ascertain the cause and found Captain Williams lying on the ground in mortal pain apparently struggling in the throes of death surrounded by his comrades tenderly and anxiously rendering every possible attention to revive the fainting hero. Lieutenant Albert Clark of his company gave him brandy and he opened his eyes and feebly said, "I am shot and feel as if my last hour had come." This was indeed sad, but such scenes were common sights before the battle was over. Captain Williams was placed on a stretcher and carried to a nearby field hospital for surgical attention. I never expected to see him alive again, but he lived to return to his native state, town and home where he was affectionately nursed, and cared for by loving wife and doting mother and sister during long weeks of pain and suffering until death the 27th day of Sept., 1863. . . . While Captain Williams was being carried from that part of the field where he fell, a whole regiment (what was left of it) came running down from the top of Cemetery Hill to escape the deadly shower of shot and shell that hailed down among them. They were simply frightened and were seeking cover against danger, regardless of duty. Our brigade, just previous to this unusual occurrence in front of us, had been advanced nearer to the base of Cemetery Hill to avoid the numerous exploding shells that came over the hill and scattered their deadly missiles among us. Colonel Randall placed himself in front of these boys seeking shelter behind the Hill and checked their stampede and tried to shame them and restore confidence by referring to his boys of the 13th, saying to them loud enough so all not too far away could hear, pointing to his regiment, "See these boys, they don't run and they were never in a battle; you ought to be ashamed to run because a few shells are being fired over this way, better hasten back to your position on Cemetery Hill." The officers of that regiment, with Colonel Randall's assistance, induced them to return to their position and back they went up the hill in good order no doubt feeling ashamed for their momentary undue weakness and folly. While this episode was pending, orders came from General Stannard, who was then in charge of infantry supports of the troops on the left brow of Cemetery Hill, to Colonel Randall to detach five companies of his regiment and hasten them under command of Lieutenant Colonel Munson to him on Cemetery Hill. The left wing was thereupon made up of Companies D, F, H, I and K, and the same were expeditiously detached and hastily sent to General Stannard, and by his direction placed in support of a battery on the west front of Cemetery Hill leaving the other five companies of the regiment, together with the 14th and 16th regiments, behind the hill where they remained until late in the afternoon. . . . The five companies detached moved directly up the south slope of Cemetery Hill into the Taneytown Road, marched up the road towards Gettysburg village a short distance and filed to the right over a tumbled down stone wall and took position, at first, in rear of a battery on the very crest of Cemetery Hill where we were much exposed to enfilading cannonading of the Confederate batteries west, north and east.

The batteries west and front of our then position occupying a commanding situation on the east slope of Seminary Ridge distant perhaps one-half mile and in good range, were evidently handling their guns with great skill, judging from the accurate and rapid landing of shot and shell about us. Although during the forenoon while in the rear of Cemetery Hill we had heard and seen plenty of shell as they whizzed and passed overhead, some exploding near the ground, but here in our new position there was nothing to protect us save the stone wall nearby. We of the left wing were on the very top of the hill where we could see and be seen. It seemed as if we were, when approaching to position, marching into the very jaws of death. We were glad when the order was given to lie down in line of two ranks and there remain without firing until ordered. This order was obeyed to the letter and no one hesitated. We soon discovered why there had been a break and scamper down the hill just before we started for this position. Those boys who came running down the hill, before we started up, were likely veterans and knew when to run for cover to escape being shot, without waiting for orders.

It was really a hot place; every shell evidently exploded where the gunners in charge of the battery calculated. They were good marksmen, horses were hit and taken to the rear disabled. The ground plowed up in furrows, the grave stones nearby tumbled and shattered to the ground, cannoneers killed or wounded in quick succession, the pieces of shell fell thick and fast among us, and so frequently and numerous that some were quite apprehensive of being killed and prudently hugged the ground and raised neither hand nor foot to unnecessary exposure. There must have been a large number of cannon concentrating their fire against the west slope and crest of Cemetery Hill. We of the Second battalion had not been long here before we observed Generals Doubleday and Stannard hastily approach and examine the surroundings, evidently expecting, because of the severity and persistent shelling against Cemetery Hill, that preparations were being made for a charge at that point. The nearby batteries just across the valley and directly in our front said in the language of a battlefield, "We will disable those batteries on Cemetery Hill, scatter and frighten the raw recruits supporting, and then charge and take the hill." And because of these indications Generals Doubleday and Stannard were on the alert. They did not seem to pay any attention to the bursting shells or bullets that whizzed about them, they sought the most elevated position, climbed up and stood on top of the wall with their field glasses, eagerly surveyed the field from right to left (the battle lines of both armies were in plain sight from this position) to discover if any advance of the enemy toward the position in their charge · (Cemetery Hill) was in progress. We watched them closely and noticed that they held their field glasses in one direction for some moments as if some movement of the enemy particularly attracted their attention. They dropped their glasses and pointed across the field and held what appeared to be a hasty conversation, and then came directly past where we lay in position stopping a movement to converse with Lieutenant Colonel Munson and then passed down towards General Stannard's headquarters. This was late in the afternoon and still the cannons on both sides were as spirited and determined as at first. . . . We expected every moment to hear the Rebel yell and see the lines of gray coming up the hill, and we calculated just how and where we would stand to use bayonets if any should attempt to scale the wall; our bayonets had been fixed to guns before we took position. We had been thoroughly instructed in bayonet drill during the winter and spring and were ready to take a hand at making or parrying thrust if occasion required it. Our position here was of the best to see the maneuvering of the troops and the fighting ranks for miles along the battle lines and on the field of both armies, especially to our left, west of Little Round Top. The fighting in that locality had been incessant and desperate for hours. It was in plain view and not over three-fourths of a mile away. We could distinctly see, (except when too much smoke) as well as hear the continuous roar of cannon, the rattle of musketry and the yell and cheer as the lines swayed to and fro, as one side charged and then the other. While intensely watching the fighting in this direction, endeavoring to ascertain whether we were being driven back, our attention was cane to the fact that a nearby battery had for some reason suspended firing; only two or three gunners stood beside their guns steadily gazing across the valley, apparently as fixed in position as the cannon beside them.

Lieutenant Stephen Brown of Company K saw the forlorn situation and hastened to them to ascertain the trouble, (only a few yards away), and after a brief interview, which we of Company K watched with interest, came running back and reported to Captain Blake and suggested assistance and asked permission to take some of the boys and go up and help them fire the guns of that battery. Henry Meigs, Smith Decker, Daniel Manahan, James Hagan and probably others of Company K promptly volunteered, and led by Lieutenant Brown ran to their assistance. Some carried shells from the Caisson situated just down the hill, part way up, and the others to the gunners and assisted them in firing their guns until the chest of that Caisson was empty. Our battalion heartily cheered as our boys actively supported that battery, and enabled it to send its compliments to the cannoneers across the valley that had slain their comrades, and for a time silenced the guns of the battery in their charge. Lieutenant Brown and his boys returned to our position safe and sound with powdersmoked hands and faces. Some had holes and rents in the clothing they wore. They had a thrilling experience, and which with great animation and pride each enthusiastically related to his immediate comrades on their return. The author, as an eye witness to this incident, recalls it as one of the most daring, unusual and valiant incidents that he witnessed during the battle. I have many times wondered what these statue-like gunners thought when they first saw Lieutenant Brown approaching them uniformed as an infantry officer with a common camp hatchet in his right hand swinging it in the air as he leaped, Indian like, to their side. They must have thought him crazy, or that he belonged to a regiment of wild Indians from the plains west of the Mississippi.

Lieutenant Brown, as before referred to, carried a hatchet because he had no sword at the time. He had been for a trivial reason placed under arrest and deprived of his sword, and therefore was now armed with his comrade's camp hatchet as a necessity . . .

We of the front battle lines lay flat on the ground between the long lines of cannon on the right, in front and rear, and were intensely interested not only in the artillery combat but in the prospect of the coming hand to hand struggle that we knew would surely follow. The blowing up of Caissons first on one side and then on the other were frequent and greeted with cheers from the side that caused them. The missiles of hurtling shell struck thick and fast among our prostrate ranks with deadly effort and the dead and wounded remained on the field until the battle was over. . . .

It is said that this artillery duel continued for two hours without any signs of weakness or yielding. While the cannon roared and the bursting shell filled the air, the boys of the 13th crawled carefully along the ground to the rail fence westward that was built in the forenoon, in order to change our front battle line that had evidently been located by the cannoneers and to be ready when the cannonading ceased. This forward movement of the 13th regiment was not according to strict military rule, but a helter skelter zig zag crouching, crawl and run each taking his own way to reach the rail breastwork as best he could and as quick as possible and take position in companies on reaching there. The stone and bushes and rails and smoke on the way obscured our move and no one was killed in making this change. This new position was important. We were further down the slope and in less danger from the enemy's shell, and there was a clear open field in front right and left, and an admirable chance to fire on approaching columns. Some of the boys were a little frightened and others slightly wounded in this advance and all as soon as they reached the rail breastworks flattened out behind them to await the end of the artillery battle.

20. Private Galway of the 8th Ohio, down near the Emmitsburg Road, had an unusual perspective on the cannonade and charge. Thomas Frances Galway, *The Valiant Hours,* **112-114.**

At ten minutes to one precisely, by my watch, after a lull in the cannonade, a heavy gun was heard from the enemy's line. Instinct told us at once that that gun had fired a signal. Yesterday afternoon a desperate fight had been waged on our left, which resulted in nothing except carnage. Last night Ewell, with Jackson's old corps, had assaulted our right, with like result. We all felt that *now* they would make a last effort against us, who were at the center. So when the heavy gun had boomed its signal the enemy's line, a general bucking up could be seen along ours. We had just received fresh ammunition, and our men at once began to arrange their cartridges and caps for the coming "trouble." A pause of a few seconds followed the firing of the signal gun, when there broke out on the still air so terrific a cannonade as I had not heard since the morning when our guns bombarded Fredericksburg. From ten minutes to one until half-past two this cannonade made those Pennsylvania hills vibrate again with its awful sound. We lay on our backs in the ditch, our heads to the enemy. We could see our artillerymen with their jackets off and their sleeves rolled up, at work at their guns. And an inspiring sight it was. The enemy's artillery fire soon became destructive enough. Now and again a shell would strike one of our battery ammunition chests, blowing it up with a tremendous detonation. Still our artillery kept at their work, giving out Indian yells whenever they saw that their shots had taken good effect. We were between the fires, but beneath the paths of the shells. The infantry on both sides seemed to be letting artillery do the work, knowing that their own more desperate efforts would soon be called for. After a while so monotonous became the roar of the artillery that it produced drowsiness amongst us, and I went to sleep, as I was told later. Most of my regiment did as I did. Several of our men were hit in the meantime, amongst them Charley Gallagher, who had crossed the road and laid down in the shade of a tree. He was severely wounded while fast asleep. I slept for about ten minutes, then awoke. Shortly afterwards I was struck in the foot by a spent shell fragment. After recovering from the pain of the impact, and whilst laughing at the matter, I was slapped in the thigh by a fragment of an enemy shell. This knocked me over, but I picked myself up, to hear the same melancholy man whom I had helped off at Antietam, tell me that the next hit would, he feared, be a fatal one. Prophets of evil are always.

This terrible cannonade had now lasted about forty minutes, when a sharp musketry fire started, beginning on our skirmish line in front. We sprang to our feet. Just to our left, on the south side of the road, was a poor little farm house. We saw the sharpshooters who had been there all the morning aiming off towards our left front. A staff captain rode down to our regiment with orders to advance.

21. Private Daniel Bond of the 1st Minnesota, Harrow's brigade, lay on the ground in line south of the copse of trees. He describes the cannonade from that location. Daniel Bond, "Bond Recollection," undated manuscript, Minnesota Historical Society.

. . . The silence seemed to grow more and more intense. *Bang! Bang!* two signal guns sent shot into our lines. How can mortal men write or mortal tongue tell or mortal mind conceive what followed! Along our whole front especially in front of our corps on the left centre where a hundred and forty five War Dogs opened their brazen throats and fired in volley not as artillery but as the continual rattle of musketry, with all the weight of sound and metal from a ten pound parrot to a 32 pound Howitzer. Had all the demons of the infernal regions been let loose they could scarcely have excelled what their intelligent pupil man had here produced for peopling those lower regions with souls unfitted to enter the gates of happiness. The hot shot hissing and crossing each other in their prey course over our heads. As a good simile of it was given by another I will quote his words as more appropriate than any I can say myself. "It seemed that all the devils in hell were let loose and were holding high carnival over us." As we lay flat on our faces they would strike the ground in front of us and bounding over[.] The force with which a shell strikes the ground cannot be appreciated by any one who has not seen and heard. But stretch your imagination to its utmost limit and then multiply it indefinitely and you will fall short of the truth. I have nothing to liken it to and consequently must leave it totally to your imagination. I can only say that all such descriptions as "ploughing up the ground" are so very weak at to be foolish. If you have ever seen a tree struck by lightening you can form some idea but there is nothing else which citizens ever see that will do for a simile. Our heads will go on their way growling in anger too terrible for description. Again they would explode in our front and the ugly missiles could come down with a sound unpleasant to the ears and fall with a propensity that in hours of less excitement would cause the hearer to think of the uncertainty of human life. Again they would sing in with so very close that one would momentarily cling more closely to mother earth. Here they would strike in a caisson. And high in air would go a cloud of smoke and wait for the scattered fragments of shells and timbers would fly the air would give so that it would seem that we were raised from the ground. Our batteries were not idle but rapidly and accurately did they respond and repeatedly did we see the clouds of smoke rise from the rebel lines showing that their limbers and caissons were not more safe than ours though they were using nearly two guns to our one but our artillery always was better than that of the rebels. We were laying between the two fires and firing over our heads we seemed to be in the only safe place on that field for horses and men fell every where else but right where our regt lay. Had we lay at two or three rods behind where we did we must have lost nearly half our men in that artillery fire and a like result would have followed had we been two rods in advance. The reason of this is there was a slight elevation of ground just in front of us and as it was, not more than 800 yards to the rebel guns the shell were passing on nearly a level and would strike the hill or pass over. And so it happened that they did not get to exploding at the right point and I believe that not a one in our regt. was hurt by that fierce cannonade from which we were now after two hours and a half to be relieved. They are coming!! Oh! what a joyful sound! You may think strange that I say so but was the greatest relief that I had ever then experienced, and in fact I never was so relieved but once since and that will be seen in the course of my journal.

22. **Stationed at a hospital behind the Federal lines, Assistant Surgeon Francis Moses Wafer of the 108th New York had an unusual perspective on the cannonade and the charge. His diary is in fragments, and difficult to read in spots. Diary of Francis Moses Wafer, Queen's University Library, Kingston, Ontario, Canada.**

After a short time of most oppressive and ominous stillness some trees in the edge of the woods that covered the rebel position were suddenly cut down when numerous batteries which they had concealed opened at once upon our centre. It has been estimated that upwards of [?] guns opened at this moment, all concentrated upon the position which was chiefly held by the 2nd Corps. When this cannonade commenced and for the remainder of the day I was at a small stone farm house on the Taneytown road — about half a mile in rear of the regiment and near the centre or focus of the curve which our line formed at this point. The concentrated [fire?] of the enemys guns naturally converged to this [place?] giving me ample opportunity to judge of its effects. Our artillerymen sprang to their posts at once and replied with more than their usual pluck and spirit but it soon became evident that they were being rapidly overpowered, worsted and fairly battered out of sight. I could plainly see their caissons being frequently blown up, although the explosions of these could not be heard in the general crash yet the sudden bursting up of fleecy cloud of smoke invariably told the story. The horses rolled in heaps everywhere tangled in their harness with their dying struggles _ — wheels knocked off, guns capsized and artillerists going to the rear or lying on the ground bleeding in every direction. The few large oaks that hung over Woodruff['s] battery were torn in splinters, their limbs dropping in some cases on men of the 108th N. Y. Several batteries had concentrated their fire on this battery in order to silence it, but although nearly all the horses were destroyed and one gun of the six dismounted, yet the gallant commander fought them until he had not a round of ammunition left except a few rounds of canister shot only available at short range, for which it was reserved.

With every gun in our line that could be brought to bear on the rebel batteries replied at once — yet the enemy persevered in directing their fire against the centre — consequently its whole weight came crushing on the 2nd corps and all other troops that were hurried up to reenforced this part of the line. It has been estimated that more than 200 guns were now i action on both sides. The sights and sounds now became awfully & indescribably grand. No intermission between the exploding was very long [?] appreciable & sometimes whole volleys of cannon were quite distinct. About this time as Genl. Hancock was actively engaged preparing his line for the impending attack a shell tearing through a board fence close to the General — drove a splinter [from the] fence into his thigh, the splinter containing a rusty nail which lodged in the wound, the wound being of such a painful character that he had to leave the field. Genl. Gibbon succeeded him but he also was wounded & thrown out of the fight before the battle ended. This terrible cannonade lasted more than one hour and a half and to one who was under it — it seemed miraculous that life could exist within its range and so the enemy thought evidently by their subsequent behavior & indeed seemed disposed to [?] their sagacity on this occasion no more than others. They saw our guns as plainly becoming feebler either through being overpowered or else their ammunition was blown up & expended & many empty caissons — when sufficiently [?] found alive [they] were sent to the rear to obtain ammunition from the train. In moving to the rear somewhat rapidly through the heavy fire looked like a flight & discouraged many who did not then know the cause. But a sight better suited to assure us now met our eyes. A portion of the troops of the 6th corps that had gone in to the assistance of Genl. Slocum in the morning was moved with their guns to the left centre. It was truly a sublime sight to look [?] as they moved to the front at the double quick step reeking with perspiration [?] to one of the most scathing fires that ever martial men endured for at this point [?] shriek of shells through the air — their dull beating sound as they [?] from the earth — which their blows made tremble perceptibly. . . .

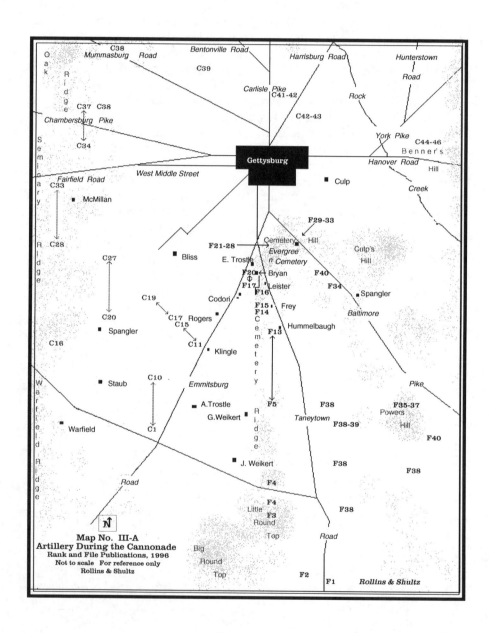

Oak
Ridge

C38
Mummasburg   Road
C39

Bentonville   Road

Harrisburg   Road

Hunterstown

Road

Carlisle   Pike
C41-42

Rock

C42-43

C37   C38

Chambersburg   Pike

C34

Seminary   Ridge

York   Pike
C44-46

Benner's

Gettysburg

Hanover   Road

Hill

West   Middle   Street

Culp

Creek

Fairfield   Road
C33

McMillan

C28

F29-33

C27

Bliss

Cemetery   Hill

F21-28

Evergreen   Cemetery

E. Trostle

Culp's
Hill

F20

Bryan

F40

C19

Codori

F17   Leister

F34

Spangler

C17   Rogers

C15

F16

Spangler

F15   Frey

F14

Baltimore

C20

C16

C11

Klingle

Cemetery   Ridge

F13   Hummelbaugh

C10

Staub

Emmitsburg

Warfield   Ridge

C1

A. Trostle

G. Weikert

Warfield

Road

F5

Pike

F38

F35-37

Powers

Taneytown

F38-39

Hill

F40

J. Weikert

F38

F38

F4

F4

Little

F3

F38

Round

Top

Road

N

Map No. III-A
Artillery During the Cannonade
Rank and File Publications, 1996
Not to scale   For reference only
Rollins & Shultz

Big

Round

Top

F2

F1

Rollins & Shultz

Section IV

"Everything Was A Wild Kaleidoscopic Whirl":

The Charge of Pickett's Division

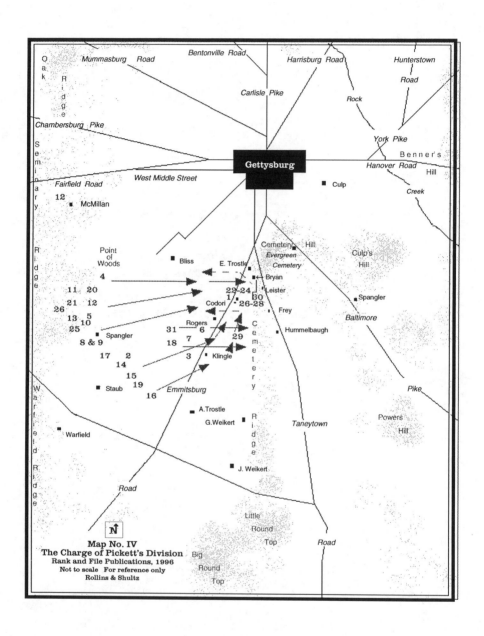

Oak Ridge

Mummasburg Road
Bentonville Road
Harrisburg Road
Hunterstown
Road

Carlisle Pike

Rock

Chambersburg Pike

Seminary

York Pike
Benner's

Gettysburg

Hanover Road
Hill

Fairfield Road
West Middle Street

Culp

Creek

12
McMillan

Ridge

Point
of
Woods

Cemetery Hill

Evergreen
Cemetery

Culp's
Hill

Bliss
E. Trostle

4

Bryan

11 20
22-24
30
Leister

21 12
1
Codori
26-28

Spangler

26
13 5
10
Frey

Baltimore

25
Cemetery

Rogers

Spangler
31   6

Hummelbaugh

8 & 9
18   7
29

17   2
3
Klingle

14

15

19
Staub
Emmitsburg

16

A.Trostle

G.Weikert
Ridge

Warfield
Taneytown

Powers
Hill

J. Weikert

Road

Pike

Little
Round
Top
Road

N

Map No. IV
The Charge of Pickett's Division
Rank and File Publications, 1996
Not to scale   For reference only
Rollins & Shultz

Big
Round
Top

1. Major General George Pickett commanded the right wing of the assault. Distraught over the failure of the charge and blaming it on a lack of proper support, his post-battle report was evidently harshly critical of someone, for Lee asked him to tear it up and write another. One of Pickett's staff, Captain Robert Bright, kept close to his commander during the day, and lived to tell some good stories. His account of Pickett's conversation with a Colonel Gordon foreshadows the early retreat of some of the men, and reminds us that even some of the bravest did not make it to the wall. Bright notes the number of mounted men in the charge, despite Lee's orders, and his account of Longstreet telling Bright that he should go to Pickett and tell him to order Wilcox forward is another example of Longstreet's ineffectiveness on this day. Bright's description of Pickett's position during the charge is important to those who want to know where the field commander spent his time and how close he got to the ridge. Finally, he records Lee's conversations with Pickett and Kemper after the charge. Captain Robert A. Bright, "Pickett's Charge at Gettysburg," *CV*, XXXVIII(1930), 263-266.

Early in the morning (July 3) Pickett's Virginians, forty-seven hundred muskets, with officers added, five thousand strong, moved from the camping ground of the second day, two miles in rear, to the battle field, and took position behind the hill from which we charged later in the day. Then came the order from headquarters: "Col. E. P. Alexander will command the entire artillery in action to-day, and Brigadier General Pendleton will have charge of the reserve artillery ammunition of the army." Later, General Pickett was informed from General Longstreet's headquarters that Colonel Alexander would give the order when the charge should begin. Several hours later the batteries on both sides opened. Had this occurred at night, it would have delighted the eye more than any fireworks ever.

Shortly before the artillery duel commenced, I returned from looking over the ground in our front, and found General Pickett talking to a strange officer, to whom he introduced me, saying: "This is Colonel Gordon, once opposed to me in the San Juan affair, but now on our side." In explanation of this I will state here that the San Juan affair occurred on the Pacific Coast when General Pickett was captain in the United States Army, and when he held the island against three English ships of war and 1,000 English regulars, he having one company of United States infantry and part of another company. General Winfield Scott was sent out by this government to settle the trouble. After the introduction, Colonel Gordon, who was an Englishman, continued speaking to General Pickett, and said: "Pickett, my men are not going up to-day." The General said:

"But, Gordon, they must go up; you must make them go up."
Colonel Gordon answered: "You know, Pickett, I will go as far with
you as any other man, if only for old acquaintance sake, but my men
have until lately been down at the seashore, only under the fire of
heavy guns from ships, but for the last day or two they have lost
heavily under infantry fire and are very sore, and they will not go up
to-day." This officer was on foot, there was no horse in sight, and
he must have come from Pettigrew's Brigade on our left, only some
two hundred yards distant. I have written and asked about the
commanded which this officer belonged, but have met with no
success. Three times General Pickett sent to Colonel Alexander,
asking: "Is it time to charge?" The last messenger brought back this
answer: "Tell General Pickett I think we have silenced eight of the
enemy's guns, and now is the time to charge." (Some Federal officers
after the war informed me that they had only run these guns back
to cool.) General Pickett ordered his staff officers, four in number
(Maj. Charles Pickett, Captain Baird, Captain Symington, and
myself), to Generals Armistead, Garnett, and Kemper, and to
Dearing's Artillery Battalion, which earlier in the day had been
ordered to follow up the charge and keep its caissons full. Orders
to the other staff officers I did not hear. But I was sent to General
Kemper with this order: "You and your staff and field officers to go
in dismounted; dress on Garnett and take the red barn for your
objective point." During the charge I found Kemper and Garnett,
apparently, drifting too much to the left, and I believe it was because
the red barn was too much to Kemper's left. General Pickett would
have altered the direction, but, our left being exposed by the retreat
of Pettigrew's command, our men and ten thousand more were
needed to the left. When I reached General Kemper, he stood up,
removing a handkerchief from under his hat, with which he had
covered his face to keep the gravel knocked up by the fierce artillery
fire from his eyes. As I gave the order, Robert McCandish Jones, a
friend and schoolmate of mine, called out: "Bob, turn us loose, and
we will take them." Then Col. Louis Williams, of the 1st Virginia
Regiment, came to me and said, "Captain Bright, I wish to ride my
mare up," and I answered: "Colonel Williams, you cannot do it. Have
you not just heard me give the order to your general to go up on foot?"
He said: "But you will let me ride. I am sick to-day, and, besides
that, remember Williamsburg." Now, Williamsburg was my home,
and I remembered that Colonel Williams had been shot through the
shoulder in that battle and left at Mrs. Judge Tucker's house on the
courthouse green. This I had heard, for I missed that fight; so I
answered: "Mount your mare, and I will make an excuse for you."
General Garnett, who had been injured by a kick while passing
through the wagon train at night, had been allowed to ride; Colonel
Hunton, of the same brigade, also rode, being unable to walk. He

fell on one side of the red barn and General Kemper on the other side. So there were eight mounted officers, counting General Pickett and the staff, mounted in the charge. Colonel Williams fell earlier in the fight. His mare went riderless almost to the stone wall and was caught when walking back by Capt. William C. Marshall, of Dearing's Battalion. His own horse, Lee, having been killed, he rode Colonel Williams' mare away after the fight. When I returned to General Pickett from giving the order to General Kemper, Symington, Baird, and Charles Pickett were with the General, they having less distance to carry their orders than I, as Kemper was on our right, and Armistead not in first line, but in echelon. The command had moved about fifty yards in the charge, and General Pickett and staff were about twenty yards in rear of the column. When we had gone about four hundred yards, the General said to me: "Captain, you have lost your spurs to-day instead of gaining them." Riding on his right side, I looked at once at my left boot, and saw that the shank of my spur had been mashed around, and the rowel was looking toward the front, the work of a piece of shell, I suppose, but that was the first I knew of it. Then I remembered the irishman's remark, that one spur was enough, because if one side of your horse went, the other would be sure to go. When we had charged about 750 yards, having about 500 more to get over before reaching the stone wall, Pettigrew's Brigade broke all to pieces and left the field in great order. At this time we were mostly under a fierce artillery fire; the heaviest musketry fire came farther on. General Pettigrew was in command that day of a division, and his brigade was led by Colonel Marshall, who was knocked from his horse by a piece of shell as his men broke, but he had himself lifted on his horse, and when his men refused to follow him up, he asked that his horse be turned to the front. Then he rode up until he was killed. If all the men on Pickett's left had gone on like Marshall, history would have been written another way. General Pickett sent Captain Symington and Captain Baird to rally these men.

They did all that brave officers could do, but could not stop the stampede. General Pickett directed me to ride to General Longstreet and say that the position against which he had been sent would be taken, but he could not hold it unless reinforcements were sent to him. As I rode back to General Longstreet, I passed small parties of Pettigrew's command going to the rear; presently I came to quite a large squad, and, very foolishly, for I was burning precious time, I halted them, and asked if they would not go up and help those gallant men now charging behind us. Then I added, "What are you running for?" and one of them, looking up at me with much surprise depicted on his face, said: "Why, good gracious, Captain, ain't you running yourself?" Up to the present time I have not answered that question, but will now say, appearances were against me.

I found General Longstreet sitting on a fence alone; the fence ran in the direction we were charging. Pickett's column had passed over the hill on our side of the Emmettsburg Road, and could not then be seen. I delivered the message as sent by General Pickett. General Longstreet said, "Where are the troops that were placed on your flank?" and I answered: "Look over your shoulder and you will see them." He looked and saw the broken fragments. Just then an officer rode at half speed, drawing up his horse in front of the general, and saying: "General Longstreet, General Lee sent me here, and said you would place me in a position to see this magnificent charge. I would not have missed it for the world." General Longstreet answered: "I would, Colonel Freemantle; the charge is over. Captain Bright, ride to General Pickett and tell him what you have heard me say to Colonel Freemantle." At this moment our men were near to but had not crossed the Emmettsburg Road. I started, and when my horse had made two leaps, General Longstreet called: "Captain Bright!" I checked my horse, and turned half around in my saddle to hear, and this was what he said: "Tell General Pickett that Wilcox's Brigade is in that peach orchard [pointing], and he can order him to his assistance." Some have claimed that Wilcox was put in the charge at its commencement — General Gordon says this; but this is a mistake. When I reached General Pickett, he was at least one hundred yards behind the division, having been detained in a position from which he could watch and care for his left flank. He at once sent Captain Baird to General Wilcox with the order for him to come in; then he sent Captain Symington with the same order, in a very few moments, and last he said, "Captain Bright, you go," and I was about the same distance behind Symington that he was behind Baird. The fire was so dreadful at this time that I believe that General Pickett thought not more than one out of the three sent would reach General Wilcox. When I rode up to Wilcox he was standing with both hands raised waving and saying to me: "I know; I know." I said: "But, General, I must deliver my message." After doing this, I rode out of the peach orchard, going forward where General Pickett was watching his left. Looking that way myself, I saw moving out of the enemy's line of battle, in head of column, a large force; having nothing in their front, they came around our flank as described above. Had our left not deserted us, these men would have hesitated to move in head of column, confronted by a line of battle. When I reached General Pickett, I found him too far down toward the Emmettsburg Road to see these flanking troops, and he asked of me the number. I remember answering 7,000 but this proved an overestimate. Some of our men had been faced to meet this new danger, and so doing somewhat broke the force of our charge on the left. Probably men of the 1st Virginia will remember this. I advised the general to withdraw his command before these troops got down far enough to left face, come into line of battle, sweep around our flank, and shut us up. He said: "I have been watching my left all the time, expecting this, but it is provided for. Ride to Dearing's Battalion; they have orders to follow up the charge and keep their caissons filled; order them to open with every gun and break that column and keep it broken." The first officer I saw on reaching the battalion was Capt. William C. Marshall. I gave him the order with the direction to pass it down at once to the three other batteries. Marshall said: "The battalion has no ammunition. I have only three solid shot." I then asked why orders to keep caissons filled had not been obeyed, and he answered: "The caissons had been away nearly three quarters of an hour, and there was a rumor that General Pendleton had sent the reserve artillery ammunition more than a mile in rear of the field." I directed him to open with his solid shot; but I knew all hope of halting the column was over, because solid shot do not halt columns. The second shot struck the head of column, the other two missed, and the guns were silent. I found General Pickett in front about three hundred yards ahead of the artillery position, and to the left of it, and some two hundred yards behind the command, which was then at the stone wall over which some of our men were going — that is, the 53rd Regiment, part of Armistead's Brigade, led by Col. Rawley Martin, who fell next to the gallant General Armistead — had reached the enemy's guns and captured them. All along the stone wall, as far as they extended, Kemper and Garnett's men were fighting with but few officers left. I informed the general that no help was to be expected from the artillery, but the enemy were closing around us, and nothing could now save his command. He had remained behind to watch and protect that left, to put in first help expected from infantry supports, then to break the troops which came around his flank with the artillery; all had failed. At this moment our left (Pickett's Division) began to crumble, and soon all that was left came slowly back — 5,000 in the morning; 1,600 were put in camp that night; 3,400 killed, wounded, and missing. We moved back, and when General Pickett and I were about three hundred yards from the position from which the charge had started, Gen. Robert E. Lee, the peerless, alone, on Traveller, rode up and said: "General Pickett, place your division in rear of this hill and be ready to repel the advance of the enemy should they follow up their advantage." (I never heard General Lee call them the enemy before; it was always those or these people.) General Pickett, with his head on his breast, said: "General Lee, I have no division now. Armistead is down, Garnett is down, and Kemper is mortally wounded." Then General Lee said: "Come, General Pickett, this has been my fight, and upon my shoulders rests the blame. The men and officers of your command have written the name of Virginia as high to-day as it has ever been written before." (Now, talk about "Glory enough for one day"; why, this was glory enough for one hundred years.) Then turning to me, General Lee said: "Captain, what officer is that they are bearing off?" I answered, "General Kemper"; and General Lee said, "I must speak to him," and he moved Traveller toward the litter. I moved my horse along with his, but General Pickett did not go with us. The four bearers, seeing it was General Lee, halted, and General Kemper, feeling the halt, opened his eyes. General Lee said: "General Kemper, I hope you are not very seriously wounded." General Kemper answered, "I am struck in the groin, and the ball has ranged upward; they tell me it is mortal;" and General Lee said: "I hope it will not prove so bad as that. Is there anything I can do for you, General Kemper?" The answer came, after General Kemper had seemingly with much pain raised himself on one elbow: "Yes, General Lee; do full justice to this division for its work to-day." General Lee bowed his head and said: "I will." I wish to mention here that Capt. William I. Clopton, now judge, of Manchester, told me after the war that while General Pickett was trying to guard his left, he saw twenty-seven battle flags, each with the usual complement of men, move out on our right flank, but we did not see this, as all our thoughts were fixed on our left flank. Captain Symington and Captain Baird could each give many interesting incidents if they could be induced to write for publication. My article of the 20th of December, 1903, in the *Times-Dispatch* should be read before this account to show how and when General Pickett's command reached Gettysburg. Should I write again, it will be about the 4,000 prisoners we guarded back to Virginia, Kemper's supposed death bed, and General Lee's note to General Pickett, a few days after Gettysburg. To those seeking the truth about this great battle, I will say, the very great losses in other commands occurred on the first and second day. The third day, at this exhibition, was most decidedly Virginia day, and a future Virginia Governor, Kemper by name, was present. I wish here to state that some of the men of Garnett's Brigade told me they saw up at the stone wall, fighting with them, some men and officers, mostly the latter, of two other States, and in answer to my questions as to numbers and organization, answered, numbering in all, less than sixty, and without formation of any military kind, Alabamians and North Carolinians.

2. **The only brigade commander in Pickett's division to survive the charge, Brigadier General James Kemper went on to become Governor of Virginia after the war. In this letter to a former comrade he describes his ordeal and how, though wounded, he made it back to Seminary Ridge. J. L. Kemper to W. H. Swallow,**

February 4, 1886, Gettysburg National Military Park.

. . . On the morning of the 3d of July, Pickett's division of three brigades marched, from its bivouac of the night before, right in front, Kemper's being the leading brigade. Reaching the ridge on which our artillery was posted and being posted, we were directed to choose positions behind the ridge, and near its crest, and to cause the men to lie down as a precaution against the enemy's artillery. Garnett and Armistead, chose positions some little distance apart and nearer the crest of the ridge, than the position I selected. Very soon after the fire of the artillery ceased, a young officer of Pickett's staff galloped to my position and said "Gen. Pickett orders you to advance your brigade immediately."

That was the only order I received during the battle, and on receiving it I looked up and saw that Garnett and Armistead were already in line and apparently ready to advance, and it was evident they had received the order to advance before it was communicated to me. Quickly forming my brigade and moving it to the front; I observed there was a considerable interval that was apparently increasing as it seemed to me those two brigades were advancing in somewhat divergent lines.

At once I moved my brigade into the interval and thus made the line of battle of the division a connected and continuous line and at once I communicated with both Garnett and Armistead who, seeing what I had done and promptly cooperating with me, rectified their alignment by mine, and all during the subsequent advance right and left brigades dressed on the centre brigade. . . . From first to last I saw nothing of Archer, or of Pettigrew, or of Davis, or of Heth's division, or of Pender's (commanded that day, as I think, by Trimble) or of any confederate commands, excepting only those three brigades of Pickett's division. I do not mean to say or to intimate that those commands failed in efficient support of Pickett's division, or failed in any particular, of duty or gallantry. You doubtless realize how an officer in battle is absorbed in his own separate duties and how oblivious he is of the separate operations of other commands. I only mean to say that from the beginning to the end of that charge, up to the time when Pickett's division found itself in the cul-de-sac of death unto which it had been hurled, where it met an overpowering fire in front, and raking fires both from the right and the left, I never saw any command or any troupe on the confederate side except the three brigades of Pickett's division.

In response to your inquiries, I have to say that, according to my knowledge, information and belief, it would not be fair to say any part of Pickett's division was first to file[?] back or to be broken or to retreat. A great proportion of the division being slaughtered; its strength being broken and destroyed, the survivors of the three brigades gave back simultaneously. I think I was shot from my horse about the instant at which the general rout began. I know that I was then near enough to the enemy's line to observe the features and expressions of the faces of the men in front of me, and I thought I observed and could identify the soldier who shot me. Quickly after I fell, a federal officer with several men took possession of me, placed me on a blanket, and started to take me (as the officer said) to a federal surgeon, when some of my men came up and firing across my body, recaptured me and carried me in the same blanket to our own rear. I beg you to notify me if I have failed to answer any of your enquiries intelligibily and explicitly enough, and I beg you will not construe any word of this letter to the prejudice of any of our confederate comrades.

3. **Brigadier General Cadmus Wilcox reports the failure of his attempt to support Pickett, and notes the lack of effective artillery fire. Report of Brig. Gen. Cadmus M. Wilcox, Cmdg. Brigade, July 17, 1863,** *OR,* **1, 27, 2, 619-620.**

With reference to the action of the 3d instant, I beg to report that, early in the morning, before sunrise, the brigade was ordered out to support artillery under the command of Colonel Alexander, this artillery being placed along the Emmitsburg turnpike, and on ground won from the enemy the day before. My men had had nothing to eat since the morning of the 2d, and had confronted and endured the dangers and fatigues of that day. They nevertheless moved to the front to the support of the artillery, as ordered. The brigade was formed in line parallel to the Emmitsburg turnpike and about 200 yards from it; artillery being in front, much of it on the road, and extending far beyond either flank of the brigade. My men occupied this position till about 3.20 p. m. Our artillery opened fire upon the enemy's artillery, and upon ground supposed to be occupied by his infantry. This fire was responded to promptly by the enemy's artillery, and continued with the greatest ferocity on either side for about one hour. In no previous battle of the war had we so much artillery engaged, and the enemy seemed not to be inferior in quantity.

During all this fire, my men were exposed to the solid shot and shell of the enemy but suffered comparatively little, probably less than a dozen men killed and wounded. The brigade lying on my right (Kemper's) suffered severely. Our artillery ceased to fire after about one hour. The enemy continued to fire for awhile after ours had ceased. I do not believe a single battery of the enemy had been disabled so as to stop its fire.

Pickett's division now advanced, and other brigades on his

left. As soon as these troops rose to advance, the hostile artillery opened upon them. These brave men (Pickett's) nevertheless moved on, and, as far as I saw, without wavering. The enemy's artillery opposed them on both flanks and directly in front. Every variety of artillery missiles was thrown into their ranks.

The advance had not been made more than twenty or thirty minutes, before three staff officers in quick succession (one from the major-general commanding division) gave me orders to advance to the support of Pickett's division. My brigade, about 1,200 in number, then moved forward in the following order from right to left: Ninth, Tenth, Eleventh, Eighth, and Fourteenth Alabama Regiments. As they advanced, they changed direction slightly to the left, so as to cover in part the ground over which Pickett's division had moved. As they came in view on the turnpike, all of the enemy's terrible artillery that could bear on them was concentrated upon them from both flanks and directly in front, and more than on the evening previous. Not a man of the division that I was ordered to support could I see; but as my orders were to go to their support, on my men went down the slope until they came near the hill upon which were the enemy's batteries and entrenchments.

Here they were exposed to a close and terrible fire of artillery. Two lines of the enemy's infantry were seen moving by the flank towards the rear of my left. I ordered my men to hold their ground until I could get artillery to fire upon them. I then rode back rapidly to our artillery but could find none near that had ammunition. After some little delay, not getting any artillery to fire upon the enemy's infantry that were on my left flank, and seeing none of the troops that I was ordered to support, and knowing that my small force could do nothing save to make a useless sacrifice of themselves, I ordered them back. The enemy did not pursue. My men, as on the day before, had to retire under a heavy artillery fire. My line was reformed on the ground it occupied before it advanced.

4. **Brigadier General Ambrose Wright had a unique perspective on Pickett's Charge. His brigade had charged up the same slopes on the previous day, had gained a foothold, but been unable to stay there. On the morning of the 3rd, he told his wife in a letter of July 7th, later published in his hometown newspaper, he had heard the rumor "that a general attack was to be made along our whole line, first making feints upon the enemy's extreme right and left, and then concentrating the fire of the 120 guns which I have just spoke of upon their centre, to make a vigorous assault with a heavy fire upon that portion of their line, (the centre) which we had carried the day before." He then watched the charge from Semi-**

nary Ridge and was astonished at the artillery's lack of ammunition and the lack of infantry support. [Ambrose Wright], "From Wright's Brigade," *Augusta Daily Constitutionalist*, July 23, 1863.

. . . Now the infantry is brought up for the assault, Pickett's Division in advance, then Heth's, (now commanded by Gen. Pettigrew, senior Brigadier) in echelon on the left. On the men swept. Our Brigade being held in reserve, enabled us to take a position where we had a fair view of the whole field, and I am sure that I have never seen troops start better than this storming party did. Pickett pushed firmly and steadily forward, going over the identical ground our Brigade had passed the day before. Pettigrew followed in fine order. Our artillery now ceased firing, and upon inquiry, I learned they had exhausted their ammunition! And at such a time! There is Pickett and Pettigrew half across the valley; the enemy have run up new guns and are pouring deadly fire into their ranks.—The enemy's infantry have opened upon them—they fall on every side— Generals, Colonels, Captains, Lieutenants, privates, as thick as autumn leaves they strew the plain. And our guns, will they not they[sic] re-open? Is there no succor for those brave spirits who are so nobly and steadily bearing their country's flag in that terrible fight? Surely our artillery will help them now - this is the crisis! My God! all is as silent as death along our whole line of artillery; one hundred twenty pieces of cannon standing mute and dumb while the very flower of the Confederate army is grappling on unequal terms in a struggle of life and death with an enemy strongly posted on a mountain fastness, and admirably protected by well served artillery. I ask myself, "can they stand this fire much longer?" and I see Pickett still vigorously pushing on dealing a deadly fire at every step. The enemy fell back from his front—they take shelter behind the stone wall—still Pickett advances. On the left Pettigrew's line wavers—it pauses—all is lost—it falls back—it runs. Some of the officers attempt to rally their men, but a great many are scampering away in front of their men; helter skelter, pellmell, here they come. But one thought seems to activate them all, and that is to gain a safe place in the rear. Pickett left alone, still rushes forward upon the enemy—he has gained the stone wall—has gone over it—is in the enemy's works—has silenced their guns. I can see with my glass our battle flag waving in the enemy's batteries, where but a moment since the Yankee colors floated in the breeze. Take care, brave Virginian, you are in a trap; the support on your right and left has fallen back. Our Brigade was caught there yesterday, and there upon their right a heavy column of Yankee infantry is deploying around a point of woods to gain their rear—it is done—they are surrounded. They now attempt to cut their way out, but many are killed and wounded, and many more are taken prisoners. I learn that a stand of colors fell into the enemy's hands, and the grater[sic] part of the regiments. And thus again after whipping the enemy, after driving him from and capturing his guns, our gallant men are driven back because they were not properly supported. Seeing Pickett falling back with the enemy pursuing, without orders, Wright's Brigade went to his support, and protected his retreat. In this movement we lost several men, including Lieut. Rice of Capt. Sneed's company, who lost a leg, and Lieut. Bell, of Capt. Corker's company, who also lost a leg by a Yankee shell.

While this attack was being made on the enemy's centre, Hood's and McLaw's Divisions were thundering away on his right, inflicting heavy loss upon the enemy. I cannot understand why Ewell's corps and all of A. P. Hill's were not engaged in this day's fighting. I am satisfied that if they had been, our victory would have been complete. As it was, while we inflicted terrible loss upon the enemy—greatly larger than our won[sic]—we failed to carry his position.

5. Private James Clay, 18th Virginia in Garnett's brigade, describes the death of Brig. Gen. Richard Garnett, in front of the wall. His body was never recovered. "About the Death of General Garnett," *CV*, XXXIII(1905), 81.

Gen. Garnett was killed while leading his brigade in Pickett's charge across the field and up the slope between the two contending battle lines. Immediately after the great artillery duel, during which many of the enemy guns were silenced, orders came for the general advance of Pickett's Division, but it was not until we had covered nearly the entire distance between the two lines that Gen. Garnett received his death wound.

I was struck down by a fragment of shell about one hundred yards from the clump of trees near the farthest point reached by our brigade — now indicated by a bronze tablet. Semiconscious, my blood almost blinding me, I stumbled and fell among some rocks, severely injuring my knee. The last I saw of Gen. Garnett he was astride his large black horse in the forefront of the charge and near the stone wall, just beyond which is marked the farthest point reached by the Southern troops. The few that were left of our brigade advanced to this point.

Gen. Garnett was waving his hat and cheering the men on to renewed efforts against the enemy. He wore a black felt hat with a silver cord. His sword hung at his side. Capt. Campbell, retiring from the front with a broken arm, came to me. During the next fifteen minutes the contending forces were engaged in a life-and-death struggle, our men desperately using the butts of their rifles. At this time a number of the Federals threw down their arms and started across the field to our rear. Two of them came to the clump of rocks where Capt. Campbell and I were and asked to be allowed to assist us to our rear, obviously for mutual safety, and the kind offer was accepted. These men told us that our brigade general had been killed, having been shot through the body at the waist by a grapeshot. Just before these men reached us Gen. Garnett's horse came galloping toward us with a huge gash in his right shoulder, evidently struck by a piece of shell. The horse in its mad flight jumped over Capt. Campbell and me.

Gen. Garnett wore a uniform coat, almost new, with a general's stars and wreath on the collar, and top boots, with trousers inside, and spurs. It is therefore inexplicable that his remains were not identified.

6. Colonel E. P. Alexander moved some of his guns to the top of a rise on and west of Emmitsburg Road. He had an excellent view of the entire charge on the right flank, and wrote about it in detail. Alexander, *Military Memoirs*, 425-432.

Returning to the centre I joined the few guns advancing from the batteries there, and moved forward to a swell of ground just west of the Emmitsburg road, whence we opened upon troops advancing to attack the right flank of Pickett's division. Eshleman and Haskell to the left front of the Peach Orchard soon also opened fire. The charging brigades were now close in front of the Federal lines and the musketry was heavy. As we watched, we saw them close in upon the enemy in smoke and dust, and we ceased firing and waited the result. It was soon manifest in a gradual diminution of the fire and in a stream of fugitives coming to the rear pursued by some fire but not as much, it seemed to me, as might have been expected. After perhaps 20 minutes, during which the firing had about ceased, to my surprise there came forward from the rear Wilcox's fine Ala. brigade, which had been with us at Chancellorsville, and, just 60 days before, had won the affair at Salem Church. It had been sent to reinforce Pickett, but was not *in the column*. Now, when all was over, the single brigade was moving forward alone, and there was no one there with authority to halt it. They were about 1200 strong and on their left were about 250, the remnant of Perry's Fla. brigade. It was at once both absurd and tragic. They advanced several hundred yards beyond our guns, under a sharp fire. Then they halted and opened fire from some undergrowth and brushwood along a small ravine. Federal infantry soon moved out to attack their left, when Perry fell back past our guns; Wilcox moved by his right flank and making a circuit regained our lines at the Peach Orchard. His loss in this charge was 204 killed and wounded. Perry's loss was about proportional, with some prisoners in addition. While Wilcox's brigade was making its charge, Gen. Lee rode up and joined me. He was entirely alone, which could scarcely have happened except by design on his part. We were not firing, but holding position to prevent pursuit by the enemy. I have no doubt that Lee was apprehensive of this, and had come to the front to help rally the fugitives if that happened. He remained with us perhaps an hour and spoke to nearly every man who passed, using expressions such as: "Don't be discouraged." "It was my fault this time." "Form your ranks again when you get under cover." "All good men must hold together now." I had with me as an aide, Lt. Colston, ordnance officer of my battalion. At one time loud cheering was heard in the Federal lines and Lee asked Colston to ride to the front and find out the cause. Colston's horse was unused to the spur and, balking, Colston had a stick handed him and used it. Lee said: " Oh, don't do that. I once had a foolish horse and I found gentle measures so much the best." Colston presently reported that the Federals were cheering an officer riding along their line. Lee remarked that he had thought it possible that Johnson's division in the Federal rear might have gained some success. Evidently he was not yet informed that Johnson, about noon, had withdrawn to a defensive position. Kemper was brought by on a litter. Lee rode up and said, "General, I hope you are not badly hurt." Kemper replied, "See, General, I'm afraid they have got me this time." Lee pressed his hand, saying: "I trust not! I trust not." Col. Fremantle, of her majesty's Coldstream Guard's, had also joined the parts. We sat on horseback on the slope below the guns where we could see over the crest, but the group of horses was not visible to the enemy.

When all the fugitives had passed and there was still no sign of counter-stroke, Lee rode off. I continued to hold my line of guns with few damages until after dark. There were some advances by Federal skirmish lines, which we kept in check with our guns, sometimes having to use cannister sharply. But the Federal guns did not interfere, for which we were duly grateful.

During the afternoon I quietly withdrew guns, one at a time, sending them to be refitted, and by 10 o'clock our whole line had been retired about to the position from which the attack began on the 2d.

Now that we have reached the turning-point of our campaign, we may revert to some incidents of note in the progress of the battle.

. . . Gen. Howard in the *Atlantic Monthly, July* 1876, writing of this occasion, says, "One regiment of Steinwehr's was fearfully cut to pieces with a shell." It doubtless received an enfilading shot from the firing here described. The official reports enable us to identify this firing as done at a range of 2500 yards by three rifled guns of Milledge's battery of Milledge's battalion of Ewell's reserve artillery. Nelson had three batteries carrying 13 guns, and the 48 rounds fired by Milledge were the only shots fired by the battalion during the campaign. It was not, however, Nelson's fault, but his superior's. His report says: —

> About 12 M. I was ordered to draw the attention of the enemy's batteries from our infantry, in connection with Capt. Graham, commanding Rockbridge artillery, and fired about 20 or 25 rounds from a point to the left and somewhat in advance of Capt. Graham's position. On Friday night I encamped about one-half mile in rear of my position on that Day.

The Ordnance report of the 2d corps identifies the guns and gives the rounds fired as 48.

Mention has been made of the five guns advanced by Maj. Haskell from the Peach Orchard, and the four from the Washington artillery a little to their left. Their guns moved so far outside of Pickett's charge that they were able to fire obliquely upon the Federals opposing it. Haskell on the extreme right was even able to enfilade portions of the Federal reenforcements. . . .

The enfilading shots described by Col. Rice doubtless came from the batteries under command of Maj. Haskell. No official report was made, but I quote from a personal letter of Maj. Haskell some years later:

> Just before Pickett's division charged, you rode up and after inquiring what ammunition I had, you ordered me to move forward with five guns, part of which were then from each battery. We advanced about 300 to 500 yards when I saw a large mass of infantry to our left front beginning to deploy, apparently to strike the right flank of Pickett's division. I at once opened fire on this infantry, which almost immediately scattered or withdrew, unmasking a large number of guns. Gen. Hunt told me after the war there were over 20. In a very few minutes these guns had disabled several of mine, killing and wound-

ing quite a number of men and horses. Our ammunition being exhausted, I ordered such guns as could
be moved to withdraw, ordering Garden and Flanner
to return as quickly as possible with litters for the
wounded, and teams and limbers for the disabled
guns. This they did, getting everything out.

The four guns under Capt. Miller and Lt. Battle fared nearly
as badly. Maj. Eshleman, seeing that they were being rapidly cut up,
withdrew them; but two of the guns, three of the teams, a Lt., and
several men were put *hors de combat* in the movement. But one
official report from Pickett's division has been published, that of
Garnett's brigade, by Maj. C. S. Peyton, 19th Va., who was the only
field officer of the division not killed or wounded. Pickett wrote a
report which reflected unjustly upon the brigades of Hill's corps,
among which the break first occurred. Lee returned the report,
asking Pickett to modify it, which Pickett delayed and finally
neglected to do. I quote from Peyton's report, dated July 9, as
follows:— [Peyton's report is included below].

. . . All accounts of the charge agree that its failure began
when the advance had covered about half the distance to the Federal
line. At that point the left flank of Pettigrew began to crumble away
and the crumpling extended along the line to the right as they
continued to advance until two-thirds of the line was gone, before
the remainder, beginning at Fry's brigade, was finally absorbed in
the collision with the enemy. That result was inevitable. Under the
conditions it should have been foreseen. The Federal line on our left
overlapped our line by nearly a half-mile. It was crowded with guns,
and their oblique fire upon the unsupported left could be endured
but for a short period, particularly, as several fences crossed their
line of advance, causing constant disturbance of their ranks. The
artillery of the 3d corps, firing from Seminary Ridge, which had been
vainly expected to silence this portion of the enemy's line, was now
itself practically silent, on account of its imprudent expenditure in
the duel about 11 A.M. Lee's report says:—

> Our artillery, having nearly exhausted their ammu-
> nition in the protracted cannonade that preceded
> the advance of the infantry, were unable to reply or
> render the necessary support to the attacking party.
> Owing to this fact, which was unknown to me when
> the assault took place, the enemy was enabled to
> throw a strong force of infantry against our left,
> already wavering under a concentrated fire of artil-
> lery from the ridge in front and from Cemetery Hill on
> the left. It finally gave way, and the right, after

penetrating the enemy's lines, entering his advanced works and capturing some of his artillery, was attacked simultaneously in front and on both flanks, and driven back with heavy loss.

Evidently the reliance for the support of our left flank had been the fire of the 82 guns from Seminary Ridge. It was as oversanguine as that expressed by Col. Long in the morning conference on the right, and it failed to note that the enemy might hold guns in reserve. This was done on the present occasion. Hunt, the Federal chief of artillery, had withdrawn many guns to await the charge which he knew was coming. The crumbling away of Pettigrew's left precipitated the advance of Wilcox. Pickett, who was riding with his staff in rear of his division, saw that the brigades on the left were breaking and sent two aides to endeavor to rally them, which they were unable to do. A third was sent at the same moment to Longstreet to say that the position in front would be taken, but that reenforcements would be required to hold it. Longstreet, in reply, directed Pickett to order up Wilcox, and Pickett sent three messengers in succession to be sure that the order was promptly acted upon. As the fugitives from Pettigrew's` division came back, Wright's brigade of Anderson's division was moved forward a few hundred yards to cover their retreat. Later, after Wilcox had fallen back, by Lee's order, Wright was moved across to the rear in support of Wilcox, in case the enemy should make an advance, which at times seemed probable during the entire afternoon. It must be ever held a colossal mistake that Meade did not organize a counter-stroke as soon as he discovered that the Confederate attack had been repulsed. He lost here an opportunity as great as McClellan lost at Sharpsburg. Our ammunition was so low, and our diminished forces were, at the moment, so widely dispersed along our unwisely extended line, that an advance by a single fresh corps, the 6th, for instance, could have cut us in two. Meade might at least have felt that he had nothing to lose and everything to gain by making the effort.

7. Colonel David Lang, in command of Perry's brigade after Perry had been wounded, was under the command of Wilcox on this day. Report of Col. David Lang, Commanding Brigade, July 29, 1863, *OR*, 1, 27, 2, 632-633.

Throwing forward pickets, the brigade remained quietly in this position until daylight of the 3d, when I received orders from General Anderson to connect my right with General Wilcox's left, and conform my movements during the day to those of his brigade. I was at the same time notified that I would receive no further orders.

About 7 a. m. General Wilcox moved forward to the support of a portion of General Longstreet's artillery, then being placed in position; and, in accordance with orders, I moved up with his left, and put my command in front and at the foot of the hill upon which the batteries were in position, at the same time advancing my skirmishers to the crest of the next hill. Here we remained quietly until nearly 2 p. m., when the batteries opened a furious bombardment upon the enemy's stronghold, which lasted till nearly 4 p. m., when Pickett's division, of Longstreet's corps, charged the enemy's position, but were soon after driven back in confusion.

Soon after General Pickett's troops retired behind our position, General Wilcox began to advance, and, in accordance with previous orders to conform to his movements, I moved forward also, under a heavy fire from artillery, but without encountering any infantry until coming to the skirt of woods at the foot of the heights. Just before entering the woods, a heavy body of infantry advanced upon my left flank.

The noise of artillery and small-arms was so deafening that it was impossible to make the voice heard above the din, and the men were by this time so badly scattered in the bushes and among the rocks that it was impossible to make any movement to meet or check the enemy's advance. To remain in this position, unsupported by either infantry or artillery, with infantry on both flanks and in front and artillery playing upon us with grape and canister, was certain annihilation. To advance was only to hasten that result, and, therefore, I ordered a retreat, which, however, was not in time to save a large number of the Second Florida Infantry, together with their colors, from being cut off and captured by the flanking force on the left. Owing to the noise and scattered condition of the men, it was impossible to have the order to retreat properly extended and I am afraid that many men, while firing from behind rocks and trees, did not hear the order, and remained there until captured.

Falling back to our artillery, we reformed in our old line, and remained here quietly until night, when I received orders from Major-General Anderson to fall back to the original line of battle in the woods. Here we remained, without any other interruption than a little picket fighting on the 4th, until the night of the 4th, when at dark, in accordance with orders from General Anderson, I withdrew my command and joined the army, then marching on the road to Fairfield.

8. With Kemper severely wounded, Colonel Joseph Mayo filed the official report for the brigade. It is not included in the *OR*. Report of Col. Joseph Mayo, July 25, 1863, George Edward Pickett Papers, William R. Perkins Library, Duke University.

> Head Qrs, Kemper's Brigade
> 25 July 1863
> Major C. Pickett a. a. g.
> Major:

I have the honor to submit the following report of the part borne by this command in the battle of the 3rd Inst. near Gettysburg Pa. Arrived at the scene of operations about 11 O'clock in the morning, this Brigade was formed in line of battle in a field in rear of the position occupied by the Artillery Battalions of Eschelman, the left connecting with Garnett's Brigade. The 24th Va. Regt (Col. Wm R. Terry Comdg) occupied the right of the line; the 3rd Va. (Col. Jos Mayo jr Cmdg) the left; the centre was occupied by the 1st Va (Col. Lewis B. Williams jr Comdg) the right centre by the 11th Va (Major Kirkwood Otey Comdg) and the left centre by the 7th Va (Col. W. T. Patton Comdg)[.] Skirmishers were then thrown out about 50 paces in front. These dispositions made, the troops were ordered to lie down & await the preparations for the advance. Preliminary to this our batteries opened a terrific fire upon the enemy's works, which was replied to with vigor. During the cannonade, which lasted nearly two hours, fearful havoc was made in our lines, the 3d and 7th Regts suffering with particular severity. Many too were completely prostrated[?] by exposure to the blazing sun in the open field. At 3 O'clock the firing ceased and the advance was ordered.

Slowly, steadily and in perfect order, over the hill and across the plain which separated us from the enemy which was swept by the terrible fire of his numerous batteries, the Brigade moved forward to storm the heights beyond. Receiving their fire until they had approached within a hundred yards of his works, our men poured into the enemy one well-directed volley and then at the command of Gen. Kemper rushed with a cheer upon the works, closely followed by the noble brigades of Garnett and Armistead. The entrenchments were carried, the enemy was driven from his guns; but one shattered look[?], showed at what fearful sacrifice the work was done. We had scarcely a line of skirmishers now to oppose the enemy's reinforcements, which were pouring down from the right and left on this devoted band. Our right flank was entirely exposed & but for the promptness with which a small portion of the 11th and 24th Regts were thrown back at right angles to our line, under the direction of Col. Terry and Capt. Fry the enemy would have [reached?] our rear. At this critical juncture when seconds seemed more precious than hours of any former time, many an anxious eye was cast back to the hill from which we came in the hope of seeing supports near at hand and more than once I heard the [desperate?] exclamation, "why don't they come!" But no help came, and with a loss of two thirds of the men and more than 75 per cent of the officers, our Division was compelled to relinquish the position it had so nobly won and face back to the rear of our batteries. It is not necessary for me to say anything of the behaviour of the troops, as they fought under the eye and in the immediate presence of the Maj. Genl. Comdg. and he knows how they performed the task assigned to them.

Accompanying this report is a list of the casualties of the Brigade.

I am Major
Very Respectfully
Jo. Mayo Jr
Col. Comdg.

9. Mayo began the charge in command of the 3rd Virginia, and ended it in command of Kemper's brigade. He notes the gap between Kemper and Garnett and the rolling hills of the landscape which prevented men from seeing the entire line. Note that his regiment, on the left of Kemper's brigade, passed the Codori farm on the west side, and that the right of the line passed it on the east, already on the Federal side of the Emmitsburg Road. Joseph C. Mayo, "Pickett's Charge at Gettysburg," *SHSP,* XXXIV(1906), 328-335.

. . . as the terrific duel was drawing to a close, General Pickett came riding briskly down the rear of the line, calling to the men to get up and prepare to advance, and "Remember Old Virginia." Our dear old Third, it was a heart-rending sight which greeted me as I moved along your decimated ranks! — while quickly, and without a word of command, the men fell into their places; especially to see our color-bearer, Murden, as fine a type of true soldiership as ever stepped beneath the folds of the spotless stars and bars, now lying there stark and stiff, a hideous hole sheer through his stalwart body, and his right hand closed in a death grip around the staff of that beautiful new flag which to-day for the first and last time had braved the battle and the breeze. The devoted little column moved to the assault, with Garnett, and Kemper in front, and Armistead behind in close supporting distance. Soon after clearing our batteries it was found necessary to change direction to the left. While conducting the movement, which was made in perfect order under a galling flank fire from the Round Top, General Pickett, for the second time, cautioned me to be sure and keep the proper interval with General Garnett; Armistead was expected to catch up and extend the line on the left. Then we swept onward again straight for the Golgotha of Seminary Ridge, half a mile distant, across the open plain. As we neared the Emmettsburg road, along which, behind piles of rails, the enemy's strong line of skirmishers was posted, General Kemper called to me to give attention to matters on the left, while he went to see what troops those were coming up behind us. Glancing after him, I caught a glimpse of a small body of men, compact and solid as a wedge, moving swiftly to the left oblique, as if aiming to uncover Garnett's Brigade. They were Armistead's people, and as Kemper cantered down their front on his mettlesome sorrel they greeted him with a rousing cheer, which I know made his gallant heart leap for joy. At the same moment I saw a disorderly crowd of men breaking for the rear, and Pickett, with Stuart Symington, Ned Baird and others, vainly trying to stop the rout. And now the guns of Cushing and Abbott double-stocked by General Gibbon's express order, reinforced the terrific fire of the infantry behind the stone fence, literally riddling the orchard on the left of the now famous Cordori house, through which my regiment and some of the others passed.

"Don't crowd, boys," -- "Pretty hot" -- "Perfectly Ridicklous"

    While clearing this obstruction, and as we were getting into shape again, several things were impressed on my memory. First, the amusement it seemed to afford Orderly Waddy Forward, who might, if he pleased, have stayed behind with the horses, to see me duck my head as a ball whizzed in an ace of my nose; next, to see Captain Lewis, of Company C, looking as lazy and lackadaisical, and, if possible, more tired and bored than usual, carrying his sword point foremost over his shoulder, and addressing his company in that invariable plaintive tone, half command, half entreaty, "Don't crowd, boys; don't crowd." "Pretty hot, Captain," I said in passing. "It's redicklous, Colonel; perfectly redicklous"—which, in his vocabulary, meant as bad as bad could be; then Captain Tom Hodges directing my attention to a splendid looking Federal officer, magnificently mounted, straining his horse at full speed along the crest of a hill a hundred yards in our front, and both of us calling to the skirmishers, "Don't shoot him! don't shoot him!" and, lastly, the impetuous Kemper, as rising in his stirrups and pointing to the left with his sword, he shouted, "There are the guns, boys, go for them." It was an injudicious order; but they obeyed with a will, and mingled with Garnett's people pushed rapidly up the heights.
    Within a few steps of the stone fence, while in the act of shaking hands with General Garnett and congratulating him on

being able to be with his men (he had been seriously ill a few days before), I heard some one calling to me, and turning my head, saw that it was Captain Fry. He was mounted, and blood was streaming from his horse's neck. Colonel Terry had sent him to stop the rush to left. The enemy in force (Standard's Vermonters) had penetrated to our rear. He told me that Kemper had been struck down, it was feared mortally. With the help of Colonel Carrington, of the Eighteenth, and Major Bentley, of the Twenty-fourth, I hastily gathered a small band together and faced them to meet the new danger. After that everything was a wild kaleidoscopic whirl. A man near me seemed to be keeping tally of the dead for my especial benefit. First it was Patton, then Collcote, then Phillips, and I know not how many more. Colonel Williams was knocked out the saddle by a ball in the shoulder near the brick-house, and in falling was killed by his sword. His little bay mare kept on with the men in the charge. I can see her now as she came limping and sadly crippled down the bill. I saw her again at Williamsport in care of his faithful man Harry, who asked me what I thought old master would say when she was all belonging to Mars Lewis he had to take home. Seeing the men as they fired, throw down their guns and pick up others from the ground, I followed suit, shooting into a flock of blue coats that were pouring down from the right, I noticed how close their flags were together. Probably they were the same people whom Hood and McLaws had handled so roughly the day before. "Used up," as General Meade said of them. Suddenly there was a hissing sound, like the hooded cobra's whisper of death, a deafening explosion, a sharp pang of pain somewhere, a momentary blank, and when I got on my feet again there were splinters of bone and lumps of flesh sticking to my clothes. Then I remembered seeing lank Tell Taliaferro, adjutant of the Twenty-fourth, jumping like a kangaroo and rubbing his crazy bone and blessing the Yankees in a way that did credit to old Jube Early's one-time law partner, and handsome Ocey White, the boy lieutenant of Company A, taking off his hat to show me where a ball had raised a whelk on his scalp and carried away one of his pretty flaxen curls, and lastly, "Old Buck" Terry, with a peculiarly sad smile on his face, standing with poor George and Val Harris and others, near where now is the pretty monument of Colonel Ward, of Massachusetts. I could not hear what he said, but he was pointing rearward with his sword, and I knew what that meant.

As I gave one hurried glance over the field we had traversed, the thought in my mind was repeated at my side, "Oh! Colonel, why don't they support us?" It was Walker, General Kemper's orderly, unhorsed, but still unscathed and undaunted, awkward, ungainly, hard-featured, good-natured, simple-minded, stouthearted-Walker, one of the Eleventh boys, I believe; only a private doing his duty with might and main and recking no more of glory than the ox that has won the prize at a cattle, show. At the storming of the Redan when Wyndam's forlorn hope tumble into the ditch and couldn't get out, owing to the scarcity of ladders, and the few they had were too short, the men huddled together dazed and bewildered, and were mowed down like dumb beasts by the Muscovite rifles, because there were no officers left to lead them. There was a notable exception, an Irishman, scrambling up the scarp, he shouted, "Come up, boys follow the captain." The captain fell, but Pat went on to immortality. It was not so that day at Gettysburg.

Unknown Private Who Fell Beyond

Twenty paces beyond the spot which is marked to tell where stout old Armistead fell, the foremost hero of them all, a humble private, without a name, bit the dust. The man in blue who told the story had a seam in his cheek. "I tried to save him, but he would not give up, so I had to kill him to save my own life." . . . Calling to the group around me to spread themselves, I led the way back to the woods in rear of our guns on Seminary Ridge. Realizing painfully our own sad plight, we were, of course, anxiously concerned for the rest of our people. But soon Mars Robert came along, followed by his faithful aides, the two Charleses — Venable and Marshall. How ineffably grand he appeared — a very anointed king of command, posing for the chisel of a Phidias, and looking on him we knew that the army was safe.

10. English observer Colonel Arthur Fremantle saw Long-street at the end of Pickett's Charge and records his reaction. Arthur Fremantle, *Three Months In The Southern States*, 264-267.

Soon after passing through the toll-gate at the entrance of Gettysburg, we found that we had got into a heavy cross-fire; shells both Federal and Confederate passing over our heads with great frequency. At length two shrapnel shells burst quite close to us, and a ball from one of them hit the officer who was conducting us. We then turned round and changed our views with regard to the cupola — the fire of one side being bad enough, but preferable to that of both sides. A small boy of twelve years was riding with us at the time: this urchin took a diabolical interest in the bursting of the shells, and screamed with delight when he saw them take effect. I never saw this boy again, or found out who he was.

The road at Gettysburg was lined with Yankee dead, and as

they had been killed on the 1st, the poor fellows had already begun to be very offensive. We then returned to the hill I was on yesterday. But finding that, to see the actual fighting, it was absolutely necessary to go into the thick of the thing, I determined to make my way to General Longstreet. It was then about 2.30. After passing General Lee and his Staff, I rode on through the woods in the direction in which I had left Longstreet. We soon began to meet many wounded men returning from the front; many of them asked in piteous tones the way to a doctor or an ambulance. The further I got, the greater became the number of the wounded. At last I came to a perfect stream of them flocking through the woods in numbers as great as the crowd in Oxford-street in the middle of the day. Some were walking alone on crutches composed of two rifles, others were supported by men less badly wounded than themselves, and others were carried on stretchers by the ambulance corps; but in no case did I see a sound man helping the wounded to the rear, unless he carried the red badge of the ambulance corp. They were still under a heavy fire; the shells were continually bringing down great limbs of trees, and carrying further destruction amongst this melancholy procession. I saw all this in much less time than it takes to write it, and although astonished to meet such vast numbers of wounded, I had not seen enough to give me any idea of the real extent of the mischief. When I got close up to General Longstreet, I saw one of his regiments advancing through the woods in good order; so, thinking I was just in time to see the attack, I remarked to the General that "I wouldn't have missed this for any thing." Longstreet was seated at the top of a snake fence at the edge of the wood, and looking perfectly calm and imperturbed. He replied, laughing, "the devil you wouldn't! I would like to have missed it very much!; we've attacked, and been repulsed: look there !" For the first time I then had a view of the open space between the two positions, and saw it covered with Confederates slowly and sulkily returning towards us in small broken parties, under a heavy fire of artillery. But the fire where we were was not so bad as further to the rear; for although the air seemed alive with shell, yet the greater number burst behind us. The General told me that Pickett's division had succeeded in carrying the enemy's position and capturing his guns, but after remaining there twenty minutes, it had been forced to retire, on the retreat of Heth and Pettigrew on its left. No person could have been more calm or self-possessed than General Longstreet under these trying circumstances, aggravated as they now were by the movements of the enemy, who began to show a strong disposition to advance. I could now thoroughly appreciate the term bulldog, which I had heard applied to him by the soldiers. Difficulties seem to make no other impression upon him than to make him a little more savage. Major Walton was the only officer with him when I came up — all the rest had been put into the charge. In a few minutes Major Latrobe arrived on foot, carrying his saddle, having just had his horse killed. Colonel Sorrell was also in the same predicament, and Captain Gorce's horse was wounded in the mouth.

11. Lieutenant Colonel Rawley Martin of the 53rd Virginia crossed the wall with Armistead and, though severely wounded, lived to tell what happened. Rawley Martin, "Rawley Martin's Account," *SHSP,* **XXXIX(1911), 184-194.**

From this point, I shall confine my description to events connected with Armistead's brigade, with which I served. Soon after the cannonade ceased, a courier dashed up to General Armistead, who was pacing up and down in front of the 53d Virginia Regiment, his battalion of direction (which I commanded in the charge and at the head of which Armistead marched), and gave him the order from General Pickett to prepare for the advance. At once the command "Attention, battalion!" rang out clear and distinct. Instantly every man was on his feet and in his place; the alignment was made with as much coolness and precision as if preparing for dress parade. Then Armistead went up to the color sergeant of the 53d Virginia Regiment and said "Sergeant, are you going to put those colors on the enemy's works to-day?" the gallant fellow replied: "I will try, sir, and if mortal man can do it, it shall be done." It was done, but not until this brave man, and many others like him, had fallen with their faces to the foe; but never once did that banner trail in the dust, for some brave fellow invariably caught it as it was going down, and again holding it aloft, until Armistead saw its tattered folds unfurled on the very crest of Seminary Ridge.

The Advance

After this exchange of confidence between the general and the color-bearer, Armistead commanded: "Right shoulder, shift arms. Forward, march." They stepped out at quick time, in perfect order and alignment—tramp, tramp, up to the Emmittsburg road; then the advancing Confederates saw the long line of blue, nearly a mile distant, ready and awaiting their coming. The scene was grand and terrible, and well calculated to demoralize the stoutest heart, but not a step faltered, not an elbow lost the touch of its neighbor, not a face blanched, for these men had determined to do their whole duty, and reckoned not the cost. On they go; at about 1,100 yards the Federal batteries opened fire; the advancing Confederates encounter and sweep before them the Federal skirmish line. Still forward they go; hissing, screaming shells break in their front, rear, on their flanks, all about them, but the devoted band, with the blue line in their front as their objective point, press forward, keeping step to the music of the battle. The distance between the opposing forces grows less and less, until suddenly the infantry behind the rock fence poured volley after volley into the advancing ranks. The men fell like stalks of grain before the reaper but still they closed the gaps and pressed forward through that pitiless storm. The two advance brigades have thus far done the fighting. Armistead has endured the terrible ordeal without firing a gun; his brave followers have not changed their guns from the right shoulder. Great gaps have been torn in their ranks; their field and company officers have fallen; colorbearer after colorbearer has been shot down but still they never faltered.

The Critical Moment

At the critical moment in response to a request from Kemper, Armistead, bracing himself to the desperate blow, rushed forward to Kemper's and Garnett's line delivered his fire and with one supreme effort planted his colors on the famous rock fence. Armistead himself with his hat on the point of his sword that his men might see it through the smoke of battle rushed forward scaled the wall and cried "Boys give them the cold steel!" By this time the Federal host lapped around both flanks and made a counter advance in their front and the remnant of those three little brigades melted away. Armistead himself had fallen, mortally wounded, under the guns he had captured, while the few who followed him over the fence were either dead or wounded. The charge was over, the sacrifice had been made, but, in the words of a Federal officer: "Banks of heroes they were; they fled not, but amidst that still continuous and terrible fire they slowly, sullenly recrossed the plain — all that was left of them — but few of the five thousand."

Where Was Pickett

When the advance commenced General Pickett rode up and down in rear of Kemper and Garnett, and in this position he continued as long as there was opportunity of observing him. When the assault became so fierce that they had to superintend the whole line, I am sure he was in his proper place. A few years ago Pickett's staff held a meeting in the city of Richmond, Va., and after comparing recollections they published a statement to the effect that he was with the division throughout the charge; that he made an effort to secure reinforcements when he saw his flanks were being turned, and one of General Garnett's couriers testified that he carried orders from him almost to the rock fence. From my knowledge of General Pickett I am sure he was where his duty called him throughout the engagement. He was too fine a soldier, and had fought too many battles not to be where he was most needed on that supreme occasion of his military life.

The ground over which the charge was made was an open terrain, with slight depressions and elevations, but insufficient to be serviceable to the advancing column. At the Emmettsburg road, where the parallel fences impeded the onward march, large numbers were shot down on account of the crowding at the openings where the fences had been thrown down, and on account of the halt in order to climb the fences. After passing these obstacles, the advancing column deliberately rearranged its lines and moved forward. Great gaps were made in their ranks as they moved on but they were closed up as deliberately and promptly as if on the parade ground; the touch of elbows was always to the centre, the men keeping constantly in view the little emblem which was their beacon light to guide them to glory and to death.

Instances Of Courage

I will mention a few instances of individual coolness and bravery exhibited in the charge. In the 53d Virginia Regiment, I saw every man of Company F (Captain Henry Edmunds, now a distinguished member of the Virginia bar) thrown flat to the earth by the explosion of a shell from Round Top, but every man who was not killed or desperately wounded sprang to his feet, collected himself and moved forward to close the gap made in the regimental front. A soldier from the same regiment was shot on the shin; he stopped in the midst of that terrific fire, rolled up his trousers leg, examined his wound, and went forward even to the rock fence. He escaped further injury, and was one of the few who returned to his friends, but so bad was his wound that it was nearly a year before he was fit for duty. When Kemper was riding off, after asking Armistead to move up to his support, Armistead called him, and, pointing to his brigade, said: "Did you ever see a more perfect line than that on dress parade?" It was, indeed, a lance head of steel, whose metal had been tempered in the furnace of conflict. As they were about to enter upon their work, Armistead, as was invariably his custom on going into battle, said "Men, remember your wives, your mothers, your sisters and you sweethearts." Such an appeal would have made those men assault the ramparts of the infernal regions.

After The Charge

You asked me to tell how the field looked after the charge, and how the men went back. This I am unable to do; as I was disabled at Armistead's side a moment after he had fallen, and left on the Federal side of the stone fence. I was picked up by the Union forces after their lines were reformed, and I take this occasion to express my grateful recollection of the attention I received on the field, particularly from Colonel Hess, of the 72d Pennsylvania (I think). If he still lives, I hope yet to have the pleasure of grasping his hand and expressing to him my gratitude for his kindness to me. Only the brave know how to treat a fallen foe.

I cannot close this letter without reference to the Confederate Chief, General R. E. Lee. Somebody blundered at Gettysburg but not Lee. He was too great a master of the art of war to have hurled a handful of men against an army. It has been abundantly shown that the fault lay not with him, but with others, who failed to execute his orders.

12. Major Charles Peyton, commanding the 19th Virginia, was the only regimental commander in Pickett's division not killed or wounded during the charge, and the only one whose report is in the _OR_. He describes his experience, honors Garnett, and describes the valor of Captain Michael Spessard. Report of Maj. Charles S. Peyton, Nineteenth Virginia Infantry, commanding Garnett's brigade, Pickett's division, _OR_, 1, 27, 2, 385-387.

MAJOR: In compliance with instructions from division headquarters, I have the honor to report the part taken by this brigade in the late battle near Gettysburg, Pa., July 3.

Notwithstanding the long and severe marches made by the troops of this brigade, they reached the field about 9 a. m., in high spirits and in good condition. At about 12 m. we were ordered to take position behind the crest of the hill on which the artillery, under Colonel [E. Porter] Alexander, was planted, where we lay during a most terrific cannonading, which opened at 1.30 p. m., and was kept up without intermission for one hour.

During the shelling, we lost about 20 killed and wounded. Among the killed was Lieutenant-Colonel [John T.] Ellis, of the Nineteenth Virginia, whose bravery as a soldier, and has innocence, purity, and integrity as a Christian, have not only elicited the admiration of his own command, but endeared him to all who knew him.

At 2.30 p. m., the artillery fire having to some extent abated, the order to advance was given, first by Major-General Pickett in person, and repeated by General Garnett with promptness, apparent cheerfulness, and alacrity. The brigade moved forward at quick time. The ground was open, but little broken, and from 800 to 1,000 yards from the crest whence we started to the enemy's line. The brigade moved in good order, keeping up its line almost perfectly, notwithstanding it had to climb three high post and rail fences, behind the last of which the enemy's skirmishers were first met and immediately driven in. Moving on, we soon met the advance line of the enemy, lying concealed in the grass on the slope, about 100 yards in front of his second line, which consisted of a stone wall about breast high, running nearly parallel to and about 30 paces from the crest of the hill, which was lined with their artillery.

The first line referred to above, after offering some resistance, was completely routed, and driven in confusion back to the stone wall. Here we captured some prisoners, which were ordered to the rear without a guard. Having routed the enemy here, General Garnett ordered the brigade forward, which it promptly obeyed, loading and firing as it advanced.

Up to this time we had suffered but little from the enemy's batteries, which apparently had been much crippled previous to our advance, with the exception of one posted on the mountain, about 1 mile to our right, which enfiladed nearly our entire line with fearful effect, sometimes as many as 10 men being killed and wounded by the bursting of a single shell. From the point it had first routed the enemy, the brigade moved rapidly forward toward the stone wall, under a galling fire both from artillery and infantry, the artillery using grape and canister. We were now within about 75 paces of the wall, unsupported on the right and left, General Kemper being some 50 or 60 yards behind and to the right, and General Armistead coming up in our rear.

General Kemper's line was discovered to be lapping on ours, when, deeming it advisable to have the line extended on the right to prevent becoming flanked, a staff officer rode back to the general to request him to incline to the right. General Kemper not being present (perhaps wounded at the time), Captain [W.] Fry, of has staff, immediately began his exertions to carry out the request, but, in consequence of the eagerness of the men in pressing forward, it was impossible to have the order carried out. Our line, much shattered, still kept up the advance until within about 20 paces of the wall, when, for a moment, it recoiled under the terrific fire that poured into our ranks both from their batteries and from their sheltered infantry. At this moment, General Kemper came up on the right and General Armistead in rear, when the three lines, joining in concert, rushed forward with unyielding determination and an apparent spirit of laudable rivalry to plant the Southern banner on the walls of the enemy. His strongest and last line was instantly gained; the Confederate battle-flag waved over his defenses, and the fighting over the wall became hand to hand, and of the most desperate character; but more than half having already fallen, our line was found too weak to rout the enemy. We hoped for a support on the left (which had started simultaneously with ourselves), but hoped in vain. Yet a small remnant remained in desperate struggle, receiving a fire in front, on the right, and on the left, many even climbing over the wall, and fighting the enemy in his own trenches until entirely surrounded; and those who were not killed or wounded were captured, with the exception of about 300 who came off slowly but greatly scattered, the identity of every regiment being entire lost, and every regimental commander killed or wounded.

The brigade went into action with 1,287 men and about 140 officers as shown by the report of the previous evening, and sustained a loss as the list of casualties will show, of 941 killed, wounded, and missing, and it is feared, from all the information received, that the majority (those reported missing) are either killed or wounded

It is needless, perhaps, to speak of conspicuous gallantry where all behaved so well. Each and every regimental commander displayed a cool bravery and daring that not only encouraged their own commands, but won the highest admiration from all those who saw them. They led their regiments in the fight, and showed, by their conduct that they only desired their men to follow where they were willing to lead. But of our cool, gallant, noble brigade commander it may not be out of place to speak. Never had the brigade been better handled, and never has it done better service in the field of battle. There was scarcely an officer or man in the command whose attention was not attracted by the cool and handsome bearing of General Garnett, who, totally devoid of excitement or rashness, rode immediately in rear of his advancing line, endeavoring by his personal efforts, and by the aid of his staff, to keep his line well closed and dressed. He was shot from his horse while near the center of the brigade, within about 25 paces of the stone wall. This gallant officer was too well known to need further mention.

Captain [C. F.] Linthicum, assistant adjutant-general, Lieutenant [John S.] Jones, aide-de-camp, and Lieutenant Harrison, acting aide-de-camp, did their whole duty, and won the admiration of the entire command their gallant bearing on the field while carrying orders from one portion of the line to the other, where it seemed almost impossible for any one to escape.

The conduct of Captain [Michael P.] Spessard, of the Twenty-eighth Virginia, was particularly conspicuous. His son fell, mortally wounded, at his side; he stopped but for a moment to look on his dying son, gave him his canteen of water, and pressed on, with his company, to the wall, which he climbed, and fought the enemy with his sword in their own trenches until his sword was wrested from his hands by two Yankees; he finally made his escape in safety.

In making the above report, I have endeavored to be as accurate as possible, but have had to rely mainly for information on others whose position gave them better opportunity for witnessing the conduct of the entire brigade than I could have, being with, and paying my attention to, my own regiment.

13. Adjutant James Crocker describes what it was like to march across the valley, and the impact of the death of Armistead on the men who surrounded him. J.F. Crocker, *Gettysburg*, 37-44.

After two hours of incessant firing the storm at last subsides. It has been a grand and fit prelude to what is now to follow. All is again silent. Well knowing what is shortly to follow, all watch in strained expectancy. The waiting is short. . . . The order ran down through the brigade, regimental and company officers to the men. The men with alacrity and cheerfulness fell into line. Kemper's brigade on the right, Garnett's on his left, with Heth's division on the left of Garnett, formed the first line. Armistead's brigade moved in rear of Garnett's, and Lane's and Scale's brigades of Pender's division moved in the rear of Heth, but not in touch nor in line with Armistead. As the lines cleared the woods that skirted the brow of the ridge and passed through our batteries, with their flags proudly held aloft, waving in the air, with polished muskets and swords gleaming and flashing in the sunlight, they presented an inexpressibly grand and inspiring sight. It is said that when our troops were first seen there ran along the line of the Federals, as from men who had waited long in expectancy, the cry: There they come! The first impression made by the magnificent array of our lines as they moved forward, was to inspire the involuntary admiration of the enemy. Then they realized that they came, terrible as an army with banners. Our men moved with quick step as calmly and orderly as if they were on parade. No sooner than our lines came in full view, the enemy's batteries in front, on the right and on the left, from Cemetery Hill to Round Top, opened on them with a concentrated, accurate and fearful fire of shell and solid shot. These plowed through or exploded in our ranks, making great havoc. Yet they made no disturbance. As to the orderly conduct and steady march of our men, they were as if they had not been. As the killed and wounded dropped out, our lines closed and dressed up, as if nothing had happened, and went on with steady march. I remember I saw a shell explode amidst the ranks of the left company of the regiment on our right. Men fell like ten-pins in a ten-strike. Without a pause and without losing step, the survivors dressed themselves to their line and our regiment to the diminished regiment, and all went on as serenely and as unfalteringly as before. God! it was magnificent — this march of our men. What was the inspiration that gave them this courage — this gallant bearing — this fearlessness — this steadiness — this collective and individual heroism? It was home and country. It was fervor of patriotism — the high sense of individual duty. It was blood and pride of state — the inherited quality of a brave and honorable ancestors.

On they go — down the sloping sides of the ridge — across the valley — over the double fences — up the slope that rises to the heights crooked with stone walls and entrenchments, studded with batteries, and defended by multiple lines of protected infantry. The skirmish line is driven. And now there bursts upon our ranks in front and on flank, like sheeted hail, a new storm of missiles — canister, shrapnel and rifle shot. Still the column advances steadily and onward, without pause or confusion. Well might Count de Paris describe it as an irresistible machine moving forward which nothing could stop. The dead and wounded officers and men — mark each step of advance. Yet under the pitiless rain of missiles the brave men move on, and then with a rush and cheering yell they reach the stone wall. Our flag is planted on the defenses. Victory seems within grasp, but more is to be done. Brave Armistead, coming up, overleaps the wall and calls on all to follow. Brave men follow his lead. Armistead is now among the abandoned cannon, making ready to turn them against their former friends. Our men are widening the breach of the penetrated and broken lines of the Federals. But, now the enemy has made a stand, and are rallying. It is a critical moment. That side must win which can command instant reinforcements. They come not to Armistead, but they come to Webb, and they come to him from every side in overwhelming numbers in our front and with enclosing lines on either flank. They are pushed forward. Armistead is shot down with mortal wounds and heavy slaughter is made of those around him. The final moment has come when there must be instant flight, instant surrender, or instant death. Each alternative is shared. Less than 1,000 escape of all that noble division which in the morning numbered 4,700; all the rest either killed, wounded or captured. All is over. As far as possible for mortals they approached the accomplishment of the impossible. Their great feat of arms has closed. The charge of Pickett's division has been proudly, gallantly and right royally delivered.

14.   Captain John Holmes Smith began the charge in command of a company and ended it in command of the 11th Virginia. His regiment formed the right flank of Kemper's brigade. His account underscores the rolling nature of the landscape, and the effectiveness of the Federal skirmishers. The "hasty trench" he refers to puts his location just south of the copse of trees, where the stone wall disappeared for a time. Smith also emphasizes the fact that they all believed that reinforcements would come to help establish the breakthrough at the wall. "John Holmes Smith's Account," *SHSP*, XXXII(1904), 190-194.

Signal Guns

About 1 o'clock there was the fire of signal guns, and there were outbursts of artillery on both sides.   Our artillery on the immediate front of the regiment was on the crest of the ridge, and our infantry line was from one to 250 yards in rear of it. We suffered considerable loss before we moved. I had twenty nine men in my company for duty that morning.   Edward Valentine and two Jennings brothers (William Jennings) of my company were killed; De Witt Guy, sergeant, was wounded, and some of the men — a man now and a man then — were also struck and sent to the rear before we moved forward — I think about ten killed and wounded in that position.   Company E, on my right, lost more seriously than Company G, and was larger in number.

Longstreet's Presence

Just before the artillery fire ceased General Longstreet rode in a walk between the artillery and the infantry, in front of the regiment toward the left and disappeared down the line. He was as quiet as an old farmer riding over his plantation on a Sunday morning, and looked neither to the right or left. It had been known for hours that we were to assail the enemy's lines in front. We fully expected to take them. Presently the artillery ceased firing. Attention! was the command. Our skirmishers were thrown to the front, and "forward, quick time, march," was the word given. We were ordered not to fire until so commanded. Lieutenant-Colonel Kirkwood Otey was thus in command of the regiment when we passed over the crest of the ridge, through our guns there planted, and had advanced some distance down the slope in our front.   I was surprised before that our skirmishers had been brought to a stand by those of the enemy; and the latter only gave ground when our line of battle had closed up well inside of a hundred yards of our own skirmishers. The enemy's skirmishers then retreated in perfect order, firing as they fell back. ·

The enemy's artillery, front and flank, fired upon us, and many of the regiment were struck.

Up The Hill

Having descended the slope and commenced to ascend the opposite slope that rises toward the enemy's works, the Federal skirmishers kept up their fire until we were some four hundred yards from the works. They thus being between two fires — for infantry fire broke out from the works — threw down their arms, rushed into our lines, and then sought refuge in the depression, waterway or gully between the slopes.

There was no distinct change of front; but "close and dress to the left" was the command, and this gave us an oblique movement to the left as we pressed ranks in that direction.

Our colors were knocked down several times as we descended the slope on our side. Twice I saw the color-bearer stagger and the next man seize the staff and go ahead; the third time the colors struck the ground as we were still on the down slope. The artillery had opened upon us with canister. H. V. Harris, adjutant of the regiment, rushed to them and seized them, and, I think, carried them to the enemy's works.

At The Works

When the enemy's infantry opened fire on us — and we were several hundred yards distant from them as yet — we rushed towards the works, running, I may say, almost at top speed, and as we neared the works I could see a good line of battle, thick and substantial, firing upon us. When inside of a hundred yards of them I could see, first, a few, and then more and more, and presently, to my surprise and disgust, the whole line break away in flight. When we got to the works, which were a hasty trench and embankment, and not a stone wall at the point we struck, our regiment was a mass or ball, all mixed together, without company organization. Some of the 24th and 3d seemed to be coming with us, and it may be others. Not a man could I see in the enemy's works, but on account of the small timber and the lay of the ground, I could not see very far along the line, either right or left, of the position we occupied. There were, as I thought at the time I viewed the situation, about three hundred men in the party with me, or maybe less. Adjutant H. V. Harris, of the regimental staff, was there dismounted. Captain Fry, Assistant Adjutant-General of General Kemper, was also there on foot, with a courier, who was a long-legged, big-footed fellow, whom we called "Big Foot Walker," also afoot. Captain R. W. Douthat, of Company

F, I also noticed, and there were some other regimental officers whom I cannot now recall.

Big Foot Walker

We thought our work was done, and that the day was over, for the last enemy in sight we had seen disappear over the hill in front; and I expected to see General Lee's army marching up to take possession of the field. As I looked over the work of our advance with this expectation, I could see nothing but dead and wounded men and horses in the field beyond us, and my heart never in my life sank as it did then. It was a grievous disappointment. Instantly men turned to each other with anxious inquiries what to do, and a number of officers grouped together in consultation, Captain Fry, Captain Douthat, Adjutant Harris, and myself, who are above noted, amongst them. No field officer appeared at this point that I could discover. We promptly decided to send a courier for reinforcements. No mounted man was there. "Big Foot Walker" was dispatched on that errand. Fearing some mishap to him, for shots from the artillery on our right, from the enemy's left, were still sweeping the field, we in a few moments sent another courier for reinforcements.

We were so anxious to maintain the position we had gained, that we watched the two men we had sent to our rear across the field, and saw them both, the one after the other, disappear over the ridge from which we had marched forward.

Wait For Twenty Minutes

Unmolested from the front or on either side, and with nothing to indicate that we would be assailed, we thus remained for fully twenty minutes after Walker had been sent for reinforcements — waited long after he had disappeared on his mission over the ridge in our rear. Seeing no sign of coming help, anticipating that we would soon be attacked, and being in no condition of numbers or power to resist any serious assault, we soon concluded — that is, the officers above referred to — to send the men back to our lines, and we so ordered. Lest they might attract the fire of the guns that still kept up a cannonade from the enemy's left, we told the men to scatter as they retired, and they did fall back singly and in small groups, the officers before named retiring also. Only Captain Ro. W. Douthat and myself remained at the works, while the rest of the party we were with, retired. I remained to dress a wound on my right leg, which was bleeding freely, and Douthat, I suppose, just to be with me. I dropped to the ground under the shade of the timber after the men left, pulled out a towel from my haversack, cut it into strips, and bandaged my thigh, through which a bullet had passed. This wound had been received as we approached the enemy's skirmishers on the descending slope, one of them having shot me. I thought at the time I was knocked out, but did not fall, and I said to James R. Kent, sergeant: "Take charge of the company, I am shot." But soon finding I could move my leg and that I could go on, no bones being broken, I went to the end of the charge.

Getting Away

While I was still bandaging my leg at the works, my companion, Captain Robert W. Douthat, who had picked up a musket, commenced firing and fired several shots. Thinking he had spied an enemy in the distance, I continued bandaging my leg, and completed the operation.

When raising myself on my elbow I saw the head of a column of Federal troops about seventy-five yards toward our right front, advancing obliquely toward us. I was horrified, jumped up and exclaimed to Douthat: "What are you doing?" as he faced in their direction. He dropped his gun and answered: "It's time to get away from here," and I started on the run behind him, as we both rapidly retired from the advancing foes. We made good time getting away, and got some distance before they opened fire on us — perhaps 100 or 150 yards. We ran out of range, shot after shot falling around us, until we got over the Emmettsburg road toward our lines. After we had got over the fences along the road the fire didn't disturb us. No organized body of troops did I meet in going back. I wondered how few I saw in this retreat from the hill top. I reached ere long the tent of a friend, Captain Charles M. Blackford, judge advocate of our Second Corps, at Longstreet's headquarters, and this was the last of the battle of Gettysburg time. I didn't hear of Lieutenant-Colonel Otey being wounded until after the battle was over, though I have since understood it was shortly after the advance commenced. I, the Captain of Company G, was the only commissioned officer with the company that day. I may properly mention an incident or two.

Wounded

Now the battery of the descending slope was advanced. Sergeant James R. Kent, of my company, suddenly plunged forward in a ditch, and I asked of him: "How are you hurt, Kent?" for I knew he was hit. He answered: "Shot through the leg." About the time we sent "Big Foot Walker" back for reinforcements, "Blackeyed Williams," as we called him, a private of my company, cried to me: "Look here, Captain," at the same time pulling up his shirt at the back and showing a cut where a bullet had a full mark about its depth in the flesh. Quite a number of the men on the hill top had been struck one way or another, and there were many nursing and tying up their wounds. Kent's leg had been fractured — the small bone — and he was captured. Before an advance I went several times to the crest where our artillery was planted, and could see the enemy in our front throwing up dirt on the line which we afterwards took. Just before the cannonade commenced Major James Downing rode along the line of guns in our immediate front, carrying a flag.

15.   Captain Henry Owen, 18th Virginia, describes the counterattack by Stannard's brigade from the perspective of a Confederate in Garnett's brigade. Henry T. Owen to Col. H. A. Carrington, 27 January 1878, Frank Yates Collection.

. . . Again you say we were driven out of the enemy's intrenchment by a body of the enemy. I suppose not more than a brigade, *which struck us on the right flank after we reached the wall &c.*

Now in regard to this flanking party I think I am well posted and you will understand me to have the highest respect for every officer's report, especially as we all know that no two men ever could see all the incidents of a battle alike.

When we came into line upon the crest of Cemetery Ridge where the assaulting columns were forced there were troops upon the right & upon the left of our Division. Longstreet does not mention this but Major Daniel in his address before the survivors of the A.N.Va. states that "Wilcox was upon our right and Heath or a part of his command upon or left." The distance from crest to crest of the two heights is said to be 2000 yards. When half way down the slope we were ordered to "oblique" to the left which threw us more to the center of the field. While marching obliquely I looked to the left and saw the troops sent as our support falling back in great disorder. When we again "fronted" and assumed the direct front march I looked to the right and saw only the 8th Va. Regt. and the support had completely vanished. I then knew as well as I do now that Pickett's Div. was alone. Now about that flanking party. When we were about six hundred yards from the stone wall a Sergt. Dalton of my Co. asked me "what troops are those on our right, are they our men or yankees?" I looked and made him no answer for a few minutes and then said just loud enough for him to hear me (he is still living) "Yankees March straight ahead and say nothing." I measured the distance with my eye as accurately as the best surveyors compass and chain ever constructed could do.

There off on our right was the grandest sight I have ever seen — A body of yankees 800 or 1000 yards away coming at a double quick "right shoulder shift." Uniforms looking black in the distance muskets glittering in the sunlight and battle flags fluttering in the breeze created by their quickened motion. I saw at once they were the men let loose by the withdrawal of our support on the right. Their line was perpendicular to our own and they were hastening to strike us before we reached the stone wall. I saw it was to be a race and as Genl. Garnet came along saying several times "faster, faster men." I put my men to the doublequick and each time was ordered on guide time. I have always thought that Garnet perhaps saw this flanking party but there is no way now of ever deciding that point. Your position being more to the centre of the line you did not feel the shock of this attack on our right, which struck us at least 100 yards from the stone wall and I saw their men up in 60 or 70 yards of the right flank of the 8th Va. and deliberately fire into our whole line. In a few minutes all was confusion and companies belonging in the 8th Va. were in a few minutes fighting on my left while I found myself with a part of my company upon the left of Capt. Cocke and a part of his Co. E. and we on the right advanced upon the stone wall 15 or 20 deep. I saw men turn deliberately and coolly commence upon this new enemy while others shot to the front. At one time I saw two men cross their muskets one fired to our right the other to our left. There was a part of the 8th Va. & part of A.B.C. & E. that fought this body upon the right and never reached the stone wall. I think the nearest I got to the wall was about 50 yards. I had 5 or 6 only of my company, the other going to the right & front. Capt. Cocke probably as many and with other companies. I suppose 100 or perhaps 150 were all we had these were scattered and fought without any order or command. This body did not advance for twenty minutes I suppose and when we fell back we had to run down the face of their line I thought for a quarter of a mile. I knew from the first that not one soldier in a hundred would see this flanking party while advancing upon an enemy in full view in their front. I tried to estimate their numbers by their flags which seemed to be fifteen or twenty and they were six or eight lines deep. I have always estimated their numbers at 10,000 (double our force). They certainly came from the extreme left of the enemy's line. Major Daniel says in speaking of the charge "that when half way down the slope the line was halted and reformed." Now I do not remember any halt and think he is mistaken perhaps our oblique movement to the left to get nearer the centre of the field has mislead him or his informant. If you can recollect that we did halt and reorganize the lines please say so and I shall be satisfied of the fact.

16. In a previously unpublished post-battle report, Captain W. W. Bentley of the 24th Virginia recalls the torrent of iron and lead that raked his lines while they marched several hundred yards across the fields west of the Emmitsburg Road. W. W. Bentley to Capt. W. Fry, July 9, 1863, George Edward Pickett Papers, Perkins Library, Duke University.

Hd. Qtrs. 24th Va. Regt. July 9, 1863.
Captain
In the absence of Col. Terry & Maj. Hambrick it is made my duty to report that on the morning of the 3rd inst. this regiment occupying the right of Kemper's brigade moved to the front & was drawn up on line of battle just in rear of a line of artillery confronting the enemy strongly intrenched on an eminence near Gettysburg, Pennsylvania.

About noon our batteries opened upon the enemy & then commenced a terrific cannonade which lasted near two hours. The men & officers who were lying upon the ground in an open field enduring the heat of a broiling sun suffered considerably from the iron hail of the enemy's batteries. When our artillery ceased firing Col. Terry gave the order to prepare to advance which was promptly obeyed. The first movement was by the left flank to the depth of a regt. & then by the front. The regt. advanced deliberately in good order at common time receiving as we cleared the top of the hill upon which our artillery was posted the musketry fire of the enemy which was not returned by the men until we had gotten nearer. We moved alternately by the front & by the left flank under a most deadly fire of infantry & artillery. With the three or four company officers & a few men the regt. stemmed the torrent of iron & leaden hail with great gallantry & returned the fire with some effect. When we had gotten some four or five hundred yards to the left we reached a point a few paces from the enemy's works which afforded some cover and protection & there Col. Terry with a few men and officers endeavored to rally the regt. A few minutes later the forces on our left gave way & the enemy were closing in upon our left & right when Col. Terry gave the order to retreat. . . .

17. In this previously unpublished post-battle report, Captain A. N. Jones of the 7th Virginia describes planting a Confederate battle flag on the stone wall and staying there for 15 minutes. Report of Capt. A. N. Jones, 7th Va. Infantry, July 5, 1863, George Edward Pickett Papers, Perkins Library, Duke University.

Sir

I have the honor to report that this regiment (7th) took position in company with the other regiments of the brigade in rear of the artillery at about 1 o'clock PM, the 1st Regt. (Colo. Williams) being on the right, 3rd Regt (Colo Mayo) being on its left. At 3 o'clock PM the artillery opened upon the enemy and was warmly replied to by his shells inflicting a severe loss upon the regiment. I suppose it was about 4 PM when the order to charge the enemy was given. This regiment moved forward steadily and earnestly and stood the shock of battle with fortitude. Its ranks were thinned at every step, and its officers were being rapidly cut down, but this did not check their steady advance which was pressed forward till our flag was planted upon the breastworks of the enemy. At this critical hour of the conflict, heavy reinforcements were moved upon us by the enemy, and the sanguinary conflict was renewed with redoubled violence; and after fifteen minutes we were driven from the enemy's works; with heavy loss in men and gallant officers. The colors of this regiment were gallantly borne and were only relinquished when death took the power from its bearer to protect them longer. I enclose herewith a list of casualties of this command an by leave to call your [remainder missing]

18. Captain James Johnson, 5th Florida in Lang's brigade, saw the limit of human endurance in Pickett's Charge. James Johnson to ?, n.d., William Walker Collection.

During the morning we were ordered to the front to support our artillery, which was being massed for an attack upon Cemetery Ridge, with the hope of silencing their guns and preparing the way for that famous charge of Pickett's division. Cemetery Ridge had been heavily fortified during the night of the 2nd by the enemy. When our position was taken we dug a shallow trench with our swords and bayonets for protection. Around us were one hundred and fifty cannon, and we estimated the enemy's at one hundred. At about one o'clock the artillery duel, which is said to have been the heaviest in the annals of the war, began. The roar of our cannon and the bursting shells from the enemy's was something indescribable and terrific. I would look at the cannon around us, some of which were not over twenty feet away; could see the smoke and flame belch from their mouths, but could not distinguish a particular sound, it was one continuous and awful roar. The ground seemed to rock. It lasted for about one and a half hours, then slackened. Looking back to the rear, I see two long lines of men advancing; it is Pickett's division in that memorable charge. On they came; they passed over us; they start in a run; the rebel yell is raised; then the rattle of musketry takes the place of the roar of the cannon. They are enveloped in a dense smoke; and the terrible roar of artillery tells us that the enemy are pouring grape and shrapnel into those brave lines.

There is a point beyond which human endurance and courage can not go. The sound grows nearer; Pickett is falling back; his shattered line passed over us again; not one half are there; that wonderful charge has failed. The smoke lifts revealing the long lines of blue coats advancing. The order comes to us, "Attention." We spring to our feet, forward, and we are marching to meet the enemy. They halt, about face, and return to their fortifications, as much as to say, "if you are ready for us, we have had enough for one day." And we go back to our position. The artillery are moving off and some of the brigades supporting us are ordered to other points. Col. Lang said to me, "if the enemy should attack us, we could not hold this position. There are some officers on horseback over to our right; see if you can't explain to them the situation and get us some support." I started on a run. Upon getting nearer I saw it was Gen. Lee and his staff, Lee with his field glasses scanning the enemy's lines. Just as I got to them, Gen. Willcox galloped up and with tears streaming down his face, he said "General Lee, I came into Pennsylvania with one of the finest brigades in the army of Northern Virginia and now my people are all gone. They have all been killed." Lee turned to him a sad face, and said, "It is all my fault, General." I then told him of our condition pointing to it, and asked for support. His manner and expression changed, and turning to one of his staff officers, said, "go to those woods and order support to them." I turned and went back as fast as I could go, but no support came and no advance of the enemy. This ended the fighting of the 3rd, and virtually the battle of Gettysburg, for there was no fighting on the 4th.

I witnessed two incidents in Pickett's charge worthy of mention. As the lines passed over us going to the front, a man dropped on me in the little trench we were in. I thought he was killed or wounded. He said, "No sir, but I can't go forward. I know I am disgracing my family, but I can't go." I gave him a slight punch with my sword and told him to roll off and go to the rear. I pointed him the way, and he unbuckled his cartridge belt; leaving that and his musket, he started. And I thought it would take a pretty swift bullet to overtake him.

When the lines had passed over us and gone a considerable distance, I saw coming toward me a lieutenant; the dense smoke concealed him until he was near; his left arm had been shattered at the elbow, the bone protruding, and the blood spurting from the arteries. I knew he would soon bleed to death unless something was done for him. I took a handkerchief; tied it loosely around the arm then took a bayonet and putting it between the arm and handerchief(sic) twisted it until the blood stopped. He seemed so much absorbed in listening to the charge in front, that he paid no attention to the arm. I asked him how the battle was going when he left, and he said, "the front line is fighting as bravely as men ever fought, but the second, damn them, are not; and I belong to the second line."

19. Lieutenant John Lewis, 9th Virginia, came up on the far right of Kemper's line, crossed the wall with Armistead, and lived to tell about it. John H. Lewis, *Recollections*, 78-85.

The division moved forward at command, in common time, and as it cleared the woods its work was seen before it. Long lines of bristling bayonets and the blackened mouth of numerous artillery, which at the time were quietly awaiting to deal death and destruction to us. But the men in that line, by their steady step and well-dressed lines, seemed to be determined to do or die.

(The writer of this was a second lieutenant and file-closer at that time; that is, in rear of his company, and could see all that was in front.)

All was quiet; we had cleared the woods, and advanced about 200 yards. (We had about one mile to go before reaching the Federal lines.) Suddenly about fifty pieces of artillery opened on our lines. The crash of shell and solid shot, as they came howling and whistling through the lines, seemed to make no impression on the men. There was not a waver; but all was as steady as if on parade. "Forward" was the command, and "steady, boys" came from the officers, as we advanced. Crash after crash came the shot and shell. Great gaps were being made in the lines only to be closed up; and the same steady, move forward; the division was being decimated. Its line was shortening, but as steady as ever, the gallant Armistead still in the lead, his hat working down to the hilt of his sword, the point having gone through it. He seemed to be as cool as if on drill, with not a sound of cannon near. We were nearing the Emmittsburg road. There were two fences at that road, but they were no impediment. The men go over them, and reform and forward again. At this point the crash of musketry was added to the roar of artillery. Men were falling in heaps. Up to this time no shot had been fired by this division.

Within 800 yards of the Federal works Garnett's brigade gave their usual yell and strike the double--quick. At 100 yards they deliver their fire and dash at the works with the bayonet.

Kemper's brigade takes up the yell, fire, and dashes at them with the bayonet. Armistead, who is a little to the left and rear catches the enthusiasm, joins the yell, and, on the run, Armistead fell back to the rear to give his brigade a chance to fire. They fire and rush at the works and to the assistance of Garnett and Kemper. There are shouts, fire, smoke, clashing of arms. Death is holding high carnival. Pickett has carried the line. Garnett and Kemper are both down. Armistead dashes through the line, and, mounting the wall of stone, commanding "follow me," advances fifty paces within the Federal lines, and is shot down. The few that followed him and had not been killed fall back over the wall, and the fight goes on. Death lurks in every foot of space. Men fall in heaps, still fighting, bleeding, dying. The remnant of the division, with scarce any officers, look back over the field for the assistance that should have been there; but there are no troops in sight; they had vanished from the field, and Pickett's division, or what is left of it, is fighting the whole Federal center alone.

We see ourselves being surrounded. The fire is already from both flanks and front but yet they fight on and die. This can not last. The end must come; and soon there is no help at hand. All the officers are down, with few exceptions, either killed or wounded. Soon a few of the remnant of the division started to the rear, followed by shot, shell, and musket-balls.

Out of 4,800 men in line that morning there was not more than 600 left to tell the tale of our annihilation. Fully sixty per cent were dead or wounded and the balance in the hands of the enemy. This ended the battle of Gettysburg.

I had passed over that field of fire and death. I had followed Armistead until I saw him fall. I had walked back over the wall, and being the only officer at that point I assumed command. The men fought with desperation, cool and courageous, until surrounded on all sides. I finally gave order to all to look out for themselves, and my duties ceased as an officer from that time. Believing it my duty to at that wall as long as there was any hope, I remained until the question was whether I would die or be captured. I chose the latter, and found myself a prisoner of war.

20. Lieutenant William Wood, 19th Virginia, Garnett's brigade, describes the sensation of being wounded in the charge. William Nathaniel Wood, *Reminiscences of Big I*, 43-48.

How long this terrific cannonading lasted I know not, but it did cease. "Attention!" was heard along the infantry line, and every man sprang to his feet, and then was observed a singular excitement. All along the line men were falling from seeming sunstroke with dreadful contortions of the body, foaming at the mouth, and almost lifeless. Some were possibly shamming but much, real, downright suffering from the sun's hot rays was experienced. But why this effect just as they rose and felt the breeze? They were taken to the shade and order restored in the ranks. "Forward, guide centre, march!" and we moved forward to the top of the hill — just in front of our artillery, and halted. Here we formed a beautiful line of battle and were in full view of the enemy. Glancing my eyes over the field I felt, "That hill must fall" still applied to the future. Forward again! and, look yonder! Kemper's brigade in splendid array, moving steadily forward. To the left and rear is Armistead's brigade seemingly more hurried as they come into line. What a line of battle! How they keep together! "That hill must fall." Onward we move in common marching time. No excitement. No loud commands. "Steady, boys," "Don't fire," "Close up," "Never mind the skirmish line," as that of the enemy hastened to shelter. Over the plain we marched. Surely the hill has fallen. No, look! They are bringing fresh artillery to bear upon us. Again the shrieking shot and bursting shell, and now the blazing musketry.

Forward, still forward. How thin the ranks are getting. Down the gradual descent we hurry. Over the fence we scramble. We bound diagonally across the Emmetsburg Pike and feel that the hill has fallen.

Just beyond the Emmetsburg pike was the bottom, the greatest depression between the two armies. The bottom was speedily reached and up Cemetery Hill we start. Grape and canister scour the ground. Down! down! go the boys. The remainder press forward. The enemy's line — a stone and dirt wall — is just in front. Suddenly the firing in our front ceases and the brave boys renew their efforts to reach the goal. Just then, when within twenty yards of the rock fence, I received a blow on the right leg. Am I wounded? Leaning against a rock, I ascertain it to be only a bruise, and again went forward with the small remnant. Stopping at the fence, I looked to the right and left and felt we were disgraced. Where were those who started in the charge? With one single exception I witnessed no cowardice, and yet we had not a skirmish line. Less than two hundred yards to my right the enemy was forming a line of battle on our side of the fence. Their right was at the fence, their left was being rapidly extended into the field to our rear. I watched them as they began to move in our direction. To remain was life in prison. To retreat was probable death in crossing the field, but possible safety within our lines, and without a moment's hesitation I turned my back to the fence and started across that nearly three quarters of a mile over which we had so recently come. Warm, tired and thirsty I limped down the hill, and felt like taking shelter behind a pile of rails that lay invitingly in my way just as the enemy opened upon us again. Resisting the temptation, I was walking rapidly when a twinge in the side and a ball of wadding from my coat and vest caused me to think a ball had gone through me. I slackened my speed and expected every second to feel the blood trickling down. At last I reached our line and hastened to the shade. The first voice I heard was that of Lucien Jones, asking if I thought my wound serious. My reply was, "I think I am shot through," and asked his condition. He replied, "I am mortally wounded, but fell in the discharge of duty and near the cannon's mouth." He died the next day. I immediately entered upon an investigation of my injuries. Removing my coat I observed it was much torn by the ball. My vest was also torn in front. With intense anxiety and bated breath I removed my shirt and found there the same evidences of a musket ball's reckless speed. I also observed blood stains as I dropped it on the ground. Further investigation revealed a scratch only. In returning across the field between the lines, I saw enough to account readily for the thin line that reached the much-talked of stone fence, and when General Pickett silently extended his hand, and as he turned aside almost sobbed out the words, "My brave men! My brave men!" I felt that after all we were not disgraced. The men were easily rallied, and a line of battle formed for any emergency. We had, for the first time, failed to do what we attempted, but the earnestness of the effort was attested by the great loss sustained. Our brigade commander, General R. B. Garnett, was killed near the enemy's line. He went into action on horseback, not being able to walk. He was a noble specimen of manhood and was greatly admired by those who knew him. His memory is perpetuated in my household by my youngest child bearing his name. Our regimental losses were as follows: Henry Gantt, colonel, wounded early in action, escaped and recovered; John T. Ellis, lieutenant colonel, killed as mentioned. Our major, Charles Peyton, went to the rock fence and returned without injury. Acting Adjutant James D. McIntire was badly wounded but escaped capture. The officers of Company A were three in number and fared as follows: Captain John C. Culin, as usual, was wounded, but escaped capture; Lieutenant Wood, slightly wounded; Lieutenant John Hill, captured and died in prison. Sergeant James R. Buck and Corporal George Thomas Johnson were captured, but not wounded. Privates John D. Durrett badly wounded and William M. Dudley and James H. Dudley captured; John A. Bowen killed; John W. Houchens wounded and captured; Polk Points wounded but escaped. Two or three more whose names are not mentioned were missing. The company was small, indeed, the next morning as an effort was made to get the men together. Major Peyton was senior officer of the regiment — fit for duty — if not of the brigade.

21. Lieutenant Wyatt Whitman of the 53rd Virginia marched with Armistead's brigade across the valley. Quoted in Maud Carter Clement, *The History of Pittsylvania County Virginia* (Baltimore: Regional/Genealogical Publishing Company, 1987), 248-250.

The Brigade moved promptly forward and arrived at the top of the hill which until now had protected us. As we advanced toward the valley the enemy's artillery re-opened fire upon us and it seemed to me the whole of Cemetery Ridge was a blaze of fire and the blaze continued until the Confederate forces had marched through this valley, which was four or five hundred yards wide, and gotten within charging distance of the stone wall.

General Kemper's Brigade was in front and when we were about half through this valley Kemper rode up to Armistead who was in front and said to him, 'Armistead, I am going to charge those heights and carry them and I want you to support me.' Armistead replied, "I'll do it! Look at my line. It never looked better on dress parade."

This took place under the heaviest artillery fire that in my opinion the world ever saw, and still under this fire Armistead's Brigade was marching at quick step, as if on parade. Just at this point Armistead took off his hat, put it on the point of his sword, and kept it there through the entire charge. He kept fifteen or twenty steps in front of his brigade all the way, was cheering all the time and calling his men to follow. After getting within 40 yards of the stone fence (not a gun had been fired by the Confederates up to this time) there came an order all along the line to charge, and we did charge, and just behind the stone wall rose up the Yankee infantry and poured into our ranks such a murderous fire as no human tongue can describe. Kemper's and Garnett's Brigades had almost entirely disappeared now, for forming the front line of attack they had received the brunt of the enemy's merciless fire and were Lying wounded and dead upon the valley across which we had come. After a desperate fight the Yankee's gave way and as they fell back from the stone wall our men began to climb over.

When the brigade reached the stone wall there were very few men left, and General Armistead turning to Lieutenant Colonel Rawley W. Martin said: "Colonel, we can't stay here."

To which Colonel Martin replied: "Then we'll go forward."

And over the wall the remaining few went, but there were only seven or eight men left now, General Armistead, Col. Martin, Lieutenant H. L. Carter, Thomas Tredway, James C. Coleman, and a few others. Lieutenant Carter grasped the regimental colors from the hands of Robert Tyler Jones, the wounded bearer, and ran forward among the enemy's artillery which had been abandoned. But reinforcements coming up, the enemy returned, retook the guns, there being no one to hold them, and opened fire again on our line. General Armistead was fatally wounded while trying to turn one of the enemy's guns; Col. Martin was severely wounded; his friend Thomas Tredway, who ran to his assistance was shot and fell across his body. The others fell also and Lieutenant Carter finding himself alone in the enemy's lines, surrendered himself and the flag of the 53rd, which had been carried to the farthest point in the enemy's lines that day

22. Sergeant James H. Walker's essay is perhaps more general than we would like, but still contains some interesting information. Especially important is his recollection of a band stepping off with Kemper's brigade. James H. Walker, "The Charge of Pickett's Division by a Participant," n.d., Virginia State Library.

. . . The men knew the thing was most desperate, for they had been told that two attempts had been made, one by McLaw's division and the other by Hood's, and both had been repulsed with heavy loss, although the men knew this, apparently there was no dread upon the face of any man.

They seemed determined to win for Virginia and the Confederates States, a name which would be handed down to posterity in honor and which would be spoken of with pride by not only Virginia but by all America.

And they succeeded, for not only have their foes accorded them the crown of laurel, but England herself spoke words of praise, then and now, whose anglo saxon blood nerved them to such a brave deed.

But to return to the scene of action. The artillery after throwing round shot and shell into each other for an hour, suddenly ceased on the part of the confederates. The enemy also discontinued firing, and the stillness of death succeeded a noise and tumult, which must have been equal to that with which the Gods assailed the titans.

The Virginians were soon made aware that the artillery had not succeeded in driving the enemy from his strong and seemingly impregnable position for the word came down the line from the right, where Genl. Pickett was, that they were to charge. All were on their feet in a moment, and ready, not a sound was heard. Not a shot was fired from any part of the field.

The command "Forward" was given, and in two minutes they had left the woods which had concealed them during the artillery fight. As we emerged from cover, and passed through and artillery which was immediately on the verge of the woods, the latter raised their hats and cheered us on our way. As soon as the artillery on the hill discovered the line advancing, they opened fire. They were when first seen about a mile immediately in front, with nothing between us but two fences.

The division advanced steadily in quick time. A band on the extreme right playing in the same manner that it would, had the division been passing in review. They continued to march forward and the band continued to play.

The shells flew far over us at first, but this lasted but a moment. They soon obtained the range, and then death commenced his work of destruction. All of the division had been quite near him before, but on this occasion he seemed to be pressing on them so steadily and closely, it was enough to make the bravest quail under his ghastly appearance. But they went on without flinching. Now they have passed half the distance up the hill, and the enemy pours grape and canister into the ranks, causing such wide gaps, the division has to be better dressed to the right, obliquing and filling up their gaps they continue to push forward. The infantry now pour their fire into them from behind a stone wall, and their ranks begin to melt away, men are falling in every direction but still they press on with the wild yell peculiar to confederate soldiers. They do not hear the band now, it is drowned in the fearful uproar. Round shot, shell, canister, and rifle balls are poured into them at close range from the front, and a battery on Round Top raked the line from the right. General Armistead is in front of his brigade, with his hat on his sword and holding it up as a guide. As they were within two hundred yards of the batteries a yell was given and a dash made for them. The artillery left their pieces, and the whole line of thirty-two guns was carried at the point of the bayonet, General Armistead falling dead, shot, with his hand on one of the guns. Cemetery Hill was won, and all honor is due to ~~Pickett's Virginians. They did all that was expected, and this charge will be remembered by future Americans, as the English remember that of the "Light Brigade" and the French that of the "Old Guard."~~

23. Sergeant Randolph Shotwell of the 8th Virginia, Garnett's brigade, became part of the skirmish line moving across the valley ahead of the main column, then took part in the charge. Randolph Shotwell, "Virginia and North Carolina in the Battle of Gettysburg," *Our Living and Our Dead,* **IV(1876), 90-95. Shotwell makes several errors: there were about 6,000 Federals on Cemetery Ridge, not 20,000; Pickett was not wounded; Armistead did not die in front of the wall, but crossed it, as others attest.**

It is about 1 P. M. All over the South the farmers are coming in from the harvest fields in obedience to the long-drawn tooting of "old Aunt Dinah's" dinner-horn, and mothers as they place the "vacant chairs" around the well-worn table are wondering how long 'will be 'ere "the boys" come back from that far away trip to the northward. How strange the contrast from these quiet Southern home-scenes to that, now enacting in this Pennsylvania valley, and wherein "the boys" are about to participate! The cannonading has ceased. "Let us stop to see what the Rebels are up to" — says the Federal chief of artillery. "We have silenced the enemy — his is perfectly demoralized" — says our own chief. The duello has lasted nearly two hours, and our gunners have not a shot to divert the attention of Meade's batteries while we are advancing — a sad mishap!

Riding coolly down the lines, now, comes Gen. Pickett, well mounted, rather *dandyish* in his ruffles and curls, but ready to ride to the death if need be. He pauses at the head of our brigade. "Have you any further instruction?" asks Garnett puffing at his cigar with splendid unconcern. "No, Dick, I don't recollect anything else" — says Pickett — "*unless it be to advise you to make the best kind of time in crossing the valley; its a h—l of an ugly place over yonder.*" As they converse, Col. Hunton orders my company to deploy as skirmishers — advance and drive in the enemy's sharpshooters — pull down a couple of cross-fences that would obstruct the charge of the division — and await further instructions. So we are to have the honor of piloting the corps into that "h—l of an ugly place" — I reflect, as we move forward over the brow of the hill, and I am not sure the glory repays the risk; though it is better to be in motion, even under fire, then lying in suspense. Passing between the smoking cannon, that should now, of all times, be bellowing fiercely, we are cheered by the powder-grimed cannoniers(sic), who have mounted their pieces to witness the fight.

Measuring by the eye, from the crest of the ridge to the Federal works on the opposite slope, one would estimate at a little over a mile, descending swiftly over the Emmettsburg road near the eastern side of the valley; then ascending somewhat steeply towards the summit of Cemetery Ridge with its crown of earth-works, surmounted by scores of flags, telling of the masses gathered under them. Just beyond the sunken road is an unfinished brick house, with one or two outhouses, which are the only obstructions of the view or the *range* between the lines. I have but a moment to glance at the scene ere we are hotly engaged with the Federal sharpshooters; firing on Paddy's rule in a "skirmage" — "Whinever ye see a head, hit for it." Soon we reach the last fence, and pull it down, throwing the rails in piles, and lying in the tall grass behind them to await the advance of the main column. More than one of us has already been 'phlebotomized' by the Federal bullets.

Pickett's Advance

Presently behind the hill a stentorian voice is heard giving the command — "Forward! — Guide -on-the-Right — MARCH!" Gen. Pickett appears on the crest among the artillery and sends his brother, Charlie, to bid us keep about 120 yards in advance of the division. Now we hear the murmur and jingle of a large corps in motion. Colonels on horseback ride slowly over the brow of the ridge; followed by a glittering forest of bright bayonets. The whole column is now within sight, coming down the slope with steady step and superb alignment. The rustle of thousands of feet amid the stubble stirs a cloud of dust, like the dash of spray at the prow of a vessel. The flags flutter and snap — the sunlight flashes from the officer's swords — low words of command are heard — and thus in perfect order, this gallant array of gallant men marches straight down into the valley of Death! Two armies, for a moment, look on, apparently spellbound; then the spell is broken by the crash of one hundred guns trained upon the advancing troops. Shot, shell, spherical case, shrapnel and cannister — thousands of deadly missiles racing through the air to thin our ranks! A bomb explodes in front of a regiment — three men fall lifeless, — five men limp, moaning, to the rear — "Close up men!" — the gap disappears and there is no falter in the line. Two or three men drop out of different companies — "killed by sharpshooters" — "Close up men!" An officer's head is blown off by a round shot — the men step over his body — "Close up!" — "Not too fast on the left" — "Major take command, Colonel is down" — on moves the devoted column into the jaws of Destruction! Lee, standing with Longstreet, and a group of staff officers, on Seminary Ridge, watching this last attempt to break the enemy's lines, must have felt a throb of the heart at each peal of the ravaging artillery.

Pettigrew and Pender

As has been stated the divisions of Pickett, Pettigrew and Pender were to move successively, *en echelon*, not *following* each other as has been generally understood. When I first noticed Pettigrew's column, it was emerging from the skirt of timber on the brow of the ridge about 800 yards to our left and rear. So great an interval was due, I suppose to the fact that Gen. Pettigrew, and most of his brigadiers were *new* in their positions, having been called to the command by casualties of the previous days; hence did not get in motion so promptly as usual. In advancing these troops encountered the same storm of mangling missiles, including a rapid enfilading fire from the apex of Cemetery Hill, that fairly melted away the two left brigades of the division before it reached the sunken road. Pettigrew's old brigade, under the noble Marshall, and the remnants of Archer's, however, came on with springing steps, not far behind the left of Pickett's line.

Here it may be mentioned that a conflict of orders occasioned considerable interval between the divisions. In the morning orders were given to "dress to the left" — the meaning of which will be understood by all old soldiers. Afterwards Pickett's men were instructed to "dress to the right," and as the others went to the left the interval grew larger as the columns advanced. This change of direction, probably, gave rise to the common statement that Heth failed to "follow and support" Pickett.

The Simoon of Death

When half the valley had been traversed by the leading column, there came such a storm of grape and canister as seemed to take away the breath, causing whole regiments to stoop like men running in a violent sleet. Shower upon shower of the fatal shot rattle through the ranks, or scream through the air overhead till one wonders that a single human being can escape. But there is no pause, scarcely a waver; on, on, on! Within six hundred yards of the Yankee breastworks! The "grid-lock" flag waves every fifty paces, but no a blue coat is seen, save the gunners plying their pieces. Five hundred yards of the works! Four hundred! No sign of the foe. Three hundred! Can he have fled? Two hundred! — (passing the sunken road) and, with a shout we start to run up the slope. Lo! from behind the breastworks on the crest arises a dense rank of blue coats, whose polished musket barrels are seen to glitter for an instant. then bursts forth a puff, a blinding, withering, wasting blaze, a long sheet of lightening, as if from the summit of the hill had suddenly sprung a vomiting volcano of deadly gases! Think of more than twenty thousand muskets hurling their fatal contents in a single volley! Think of the havoc such a volley must make in the compact columns swarming up the ascent! At 40 paces it was almost impossible for the poorest of the Yankee marksmen to avoid hitting some one of the advancing throng. It were strange indeed that any of the latter escaped unscathed. All around me were men weltering in their life-blood, some on their faces, some on their backs, some writhing and moaning, others still forever! Half the flags of the division fell with the first fire, but quickly they were raised by the survivors and borne forward. At twenty paces from the works, those who had not fired their muskets in the confusion of the first volley, poured a fusillade upon the Yankees with so much effect that I thought the day was ours, as whole companies ran back towards the upper line. At this juncture Gen. Garnett was riddled with bullets; Kemper carried off with a shattered leg; Pickett wounded; all the field and staff officers killed or disabled; and more than two-thirds of the men *hors du combat.* I felt stunned, dazed, bewildered, but picked up a musket and fired repeatedly. All the foregoing had occupied less than five minutes. Armistead's brigade now swept up to the works, and the General, at their head, waving his hat, attempting to jump upon the works, but fell dead in the ditch. His men with some of my regiment, clambered atop the breastworks, and seemed to have possession of them. At this a long line of bayonets rushed down from the rear of the artillery and everything went to pieces. *Suave qui pent!* — and be quick about it!

To retreat was nearly as dangerous as to advance, and scores of men threw themselves behind some piles of stone in front of the works, and held up their hands in token of surrender. Liberty looked too sweet to lose without an effort; and I started back but halted in the road to see the result of Pettigrew's assault upon the left.

A portion of the division, as has been stated, did not go farther than the road, being terribly cut up and scattered by a severe flanking fire. Judging by a momentary glance, about one thousand or twelve hundred North Carolinians and Tennesseans swept over the road, and up to the enemy's works. At their head was the noble Marshall, acting Brigadier of Pettigrew's brigade, who fell within a few feet of the Yankee bayonets, and was buried by them. His horse was ridden off by a Tennessean showing how the two States were mixed in the fray. Thinking the North Carolinians had secured a lodgement on the crest, I picked up a musket and started to move towards the left. But on firing the gun (which probably had three charges rammed down one upon the other, as was common in the excitement of battle) it kicked so violently as to nearly cause me to turn a somersault. When I recovered myself the enemy was pouring a terrible volley into the retreating Confederates, and all was over. Farther to the left Lane's and Scale's brigades of North Carolinians were struggling for the heights, but their movements were not discernible from the point I occupied.

Wilcox's brigade, I neglected to state, was to follow Pickett on his right to prevent a flank attack, and it now came to the road a little to my right, exchanging several volleys with the enemy. This demonstration was mainly useful in allowing time for the fragments of the two attacking divisions, with many of their slightly wounded to get out of range of the Federal sharpshooters. With the same object in view, a number of us, officers and men together, paused in a gulley on the north of the road, and peppered every Yankee who dared show his head over the works. During this time I saw a man, lying behind a pile of stone within fifteen feet of the works, tear a flag from its pole and conceal it in his breast. The enemy, imagining there were a good many of us in the ditch, threw out a regiment to take us in flank. At this I started for our lines, amid a shower. Of those who started with me none escaped, though one or two threw themselves in the grass, I think, to avoid the severe fire.

24. Sergeant Dennis Easley of the 14th Virginia saw Armistead go down, and recalls that not all the Confederates in the attack were able to brave the storm of lead that greeted them on their way across the valley. D. B. Easley, "With Armistead When He Was Killed," *CV*, XX(1912), 379.

I was sergeant in Company H, 14th Virginia Infantry, and before starting in the charge our captain specified three or four men who were habitual "play-outs" and instructed the file closers to "take them into that fight or kill them," he didn't care which, and if we killed them he would be responsible. I selected an old schoolmate as he had done more talking and less fighting than any one in the company. We did not go far before he claimed to be wounded; but when I insisted on seeing the wound, he got up and ran. Finally he dived through the space between the 14th and 57th Virginia and ran down the front of the 57th. I saw Sergeant Garner cock his gun and run down the rear of the 57th Regiment.

Ours was the left company of the 14th Regiment. The order was, "Guide center!" and just before I caught up they crowded too much to the center, and the right company of the 57th lapped behind our company and cut me off. I saw a gap in our line to the right and hurried through it and unexpectedly I ran into a whole line of Yankees. I brought down my bayonet, but soon saw that every man had his arms above his head; so I crowded through them with no other idea than to locate my company. By the time I was through them I struck the stone fence in a battery of brass pieces. I mounted the fence and got one glance up and down the line, while General Armistead mounted it just to my left, with only a brass cannon between us.

I forgot my company and stepped off the fence with him. We went up to the second line of artillery, and just before reaching those guns a squad of from twenty-five to fifty Yankees around a stand of colors to our left fired a volley back at Armistead and he fell forward, his sword and hat almost striking a gun. I dropped behind the gun and commenced firing back at them till they located me and poured another volley. They shot my ramrod off where it entered the stock.

I then ran back to the stone fence to get another gun. General Armistead did not move, groan, or speak while I fired several shots practically over his body; so I thought he had been killed instantly and did not speak to him. I have since learned that he lived till next day.

I am not claiming any credit for being there, and acknowledge that I was out of my place, for General Armistead was killed on the left of the 14th in a space between it and the 57th.

25. Easley recalls more of the events that occurred inside the Angle. D. B. Easley to Howard Townsend, July 24, 1913, D. B. Easley Papers, U. S. Military History Institute, Carlisle Barracks.

Scottsburg, Va. July 24th 1913
Mr. Howard Townsend,
                              Cedar St. N.Y.
Dear Sir,
. . . I have a more definite recollection of what happened after crossing the Emmitsburg Road than any other part of the charge, for I was looking after the welfare of an old school-mate about to that point where he took off down the front rank of the 57th and got away from me. I there got a good look at the Federal line to my right which seemed to be solid and in good order, and right here is something which I do not understand myself. There was nothing in our line to the right of our regiment: the 14th Va. Inft. Armistead's right regiment, but the tablets place Kemper's Brigade to the right of Armistead's, and I saw the colors of the 13th Va. Garnett's regiment within ten feet of the 14th at the stone wall. [Ed.: the 13th was not in Pickett's Charge.]

I have never heard that Kemper's Brigade failed us and I do not believe they did, but I cannot imagine where they were. I know that Armistead's tablet is farther to the left than his line extended. But to resume my story my company was on the left of the 14th next to the 57th Va. The order was "Guide Center," and just as I was catching up the 57th Va. gave way to the right, and closed up the little space between the regiments; first pressed against my company and then lapped behind it cutting me off. I then dived through a little gap in the company to our right, and ran to the front looking back, but my company seemed to have disappeared, I do not know how far I ran but not far till I ran into the squad of Yankees. I did not do anything brave or desperate, my only idea was to locate my company and get with them, and I do not recollect hearing a ball whistle from the time I ran forward till the volley was fired which killed Armistead. I ran squarely into the Yankees before seeing them and brought down my bayonet before seeing they had up "The sign of distress." There was nothing for me to do but crowd through them, and then I struck the stone wall. I glanced to the right and left but the wall was vacant with the exception of the two squads, and my recollection is they huddled around the colors, and they seemed to have given us a little more breathing room to our right. I could not locate our left. I struck the wall with two brass guns to my right, and two to my left pointing over the wall.

There were others to my right and left. I took in all this at a glance and then saw Armistead. We went up to the second line of guns almost as close together as if we had been marching in ranks. He fell to our left of the gun and I stepped in to the right. I might say here that our line was crossing the wall when I looked back; possibly half of them over. They went back to a man. The squad that killed Armistead was just about where the monument of the 71st Penn. is located, . . . I dropped in behind the gun and commenced firing back at the squad that killed him using the gun as a rest. I fired several shots and then they paid their respects to me pouring back a volley similar to the one that killed Armistead. I was behind the gun between it and the wheels but something seemed to strike me all over. They must have fired too low and knocked gravels against me. I felt of myself and when I found I was not hurt I grabbed for my ramrod to return their compliment and found it was shot off just where it enters the stock. I did not see that I could do much without a ramrod and so bore to the left in order to avoid them and sent back to the stone wall, looking for a gun. One of our men gave me his gun saying "He was wounded." I rammed a ball about half way down when it hung, and I began driving the rammer against the stone fence when he turned over and said "don't load it; it's loaded" I went off the handle and said "Where are you wounded anyhow; I don't see anything the matter with you." He turned over and groaned and made no answer. I clubbed the musket and started to burst his head with it, but happened to think and raising it as high as I could dropped it on the back of his head. From the way he growned[sic] he though[t] a shell struck him. I grabbed another gun with the bayonet twisted like a cork screw, and blew through it. I expected if I had fired it the bullet would have hit the bayonet, but just as I got it I loaded three bayonets came against me and they hauled me in. I have bored you enough but I forgot to say that Armistead did not groan or move while I fired several shots near him, and I thought him dead, but he was an old man 63 and was probably exhausted, and that I only got the skin broken in two places, though I could hardly walk with my knee next day but I do not recollect anything hitting it.

26. Corporal James Carter of the 53rd Virginia reports his view of Armistead and the flag of the 53rd. James T. Carter, "Flag of the Fifty-Third Va. Regiment," *CV,* **X(1902), 263.**

. . . When the cannonading ceased, the brigade advanced to the top of the hill, where a halt was made for a short time; at that time Gen. Armistead came up to color-sergeant Blackwell, of the Fifty-Third Virginia Regiment, which was the batalion[sic] of direction of Armistead's Brigade, and pointing to the enemy's breastworks, said: "Sergeant, I want you and your men to plant your colors on those works. Do you think you can do it?" The sergeant replied, "Yes, sir, if God is willing." Then the General, taking out a small flask, told him to take some, which he did. My position that day was on Blackwell's left, with Gen. Armistead and Col. Martin in front of me.

Then we continued to advance, moving forward in two lines, Kemper and Garnett forming the first line, with Armistead for support. We advanced under a heavy fire of both artillery and small arms, and when about seventy-five yards from the stone wall, Gen. Kemper, on a handsome bay horse, rode up to Gen. Armistead (who was not over five feet from me) and said to him: "General, I am going to storm those works, and I want you to support me." Armistead said that he would, and calling Gen. Kemper's attention to the perfection of his line, said: "Did you every see anything better on parade?" Kemper saluted, and replied, "I never did." Then Armistead placed his hat on the point of his sword, and waving it around gave the command: "Forward, double quick!" The saber soon cut through his hat, which slipped down to the hilt, but he continued to wave it, and urged his men forward.

Color-Sergeant Blackwell was now shot down, I seized the colors, but another of the guard, Scott, snatched them out of my hand, and ran about fifteen feet out in front of the brigade and waved them — all this while that terrible storm of bullets was pouring in — he was instantly shot, and Robert Tyler Jones ran forward and picked them up. I was wounded here and fell. Up to this time our Brigade had not fired a gun. When Jones took the colors he was shot in the arm, but continued to advance until he reached the stone wall, where he leaped on top and waved the flag triumphantly. But the was again shot, and fell forward severely wounded.

When the brigade reached the wall there were very few men left, and Armistead, turning to Lieut. Col. R. W. Martin, said: "Colonel, we can't stay here." Col. Martin replied, "Then we'll go forward!" and over the wall the remaining few went, but there were only seven or eight left — Gen. Armistead, Col. Martin, Lieut. H. L. Carter, Lieut. J. W. Whitehead, Thomas Treadway, James A.

Coleman, and some others.

When Jones fell forward, Lieut. H. L. Carter seized the colors and ran forward among the enemies artillery, which they had abandoned, retook the guns, there being no one to hold them, and opened fire again on our line. Gen. Armistead was killed while trying to turn one of the guns on the enemy. Col. Martin was wounded, his left leg being shattered by a ball; his friend, Thomas Treadway, who ran to his assistance, was shot and fell across his body. The others fell also, and Lieut. Carter finding himself alone in the enemy's lines, surrendered, and was sent a prisoner to the rear, leaving the flag among the guns, with seventeen bullet holes in his clothes, and yet without a scratch.

27.   Private J. R. McPherson, 28th Virginia, Garnett's brigade, was wounded before reaching the stone wall. While the beginning and conclusion is probably an eyewitness account of his experiences, the information about Spessard and the others who made it to the wall is probably what he heard after the battle from those who survived.   J.R. McPherson, "A Private's Account of Gettysburg," *CV*, VI(1898), 148-149.

In making the charge Gen. Pickett rode in front of his men and gave the command: "Forward!" Every man responded. When we reached the little hill where our batteries were we could see what we had to encounter, but on we went, until within about three hundred yards of the Federal line. Then a galling fire of musketry was poured into our ranks, but we gave them as good as they sent.

Near this point I received a severe wound in my right arm. On the boys went and into the enemy's works , from which they had fled. My captain, M. P. Spessard, encountered three Yankees at the works, who had hid there. One of them wrung the sword from Spessard's hand and ordered him to surrender, but, instead, he ran the Yankees from the works with stones, and then made good his escape, leaving his only son mortally wounded. Capt. Spessard was promoted for his gallantry. The Federals had limbered up their artillery, and were retreating from the field; but when they found that we had no reenforcement they rallied, and, with the aid of a fresh corps, captured a number of Pickett's men in the works, while the remainder suffered great loss in retreating, the Federals using grape and canister on us. When I returned to the edge of the woods, in rear of our cannon, there I saw a line of infantry in commotion. The officers were trying to advance them. We had no support on that part of the line.

Our loss was heavy. My company went into the charge with

about forty men, and next morning only five answered roll-call.

28. Colorbearers played a key role in all Civil War combat. By 1863, the flag, always an emotional symbol, had become the very embodiment of the regiment it represented. Men went to great lengths to display courage in keeping it at the forefront of the unit. The conspicuousness of their actions also made them memorable, as Private Charles T. Loehr of the 1st Virginia recalled long after the battle. Charles T. Loehr, "The 'Old First' Virginia at Gettysburg," *SHSP*, XXXII(1904), 33-40.

Much has been written about this historic event and chiefly by those who are writers, but get their information from all kinds of publications, while those who were actors in the bloody drama have had but little to say, and they are fast passing on to answer the roll call of their comrades gone before.

The story of Pickett's charge will ever be remembered and generations yet to come will point to it as one of the grandest acts of heroism in American history.

The Old First Virginia formed part of Kemper's brigade. It held the center position in the brigade line. The 3d of July, 1863, was extremely hot and the brigade had to endure the sweltering sun, lying in rear of Seminary Ridge in open field, while to its left were the brigades of Garnett and Armistead in the woods.

The distance from the position of Kemper's brigade to the angle of the stone wall, the point of attack, was just one mile across an open hilly plain crossed by the Emmetsburg road, thus the enemy from their position on Roundtop Hill could see and count every man we had when we advanced to the charge. Moreover, on these hills the enemy placed their batteries, which fired with fatal effect on our men as they charged.

Just before our artillery opened, there was a detail of fifteen men from each regiment made to act as skirmishers. These moved at once forward in rear of the batteries near which Wilson's brigade was in position. At 1 o'clock our artillery opened the battle and a few minutes afterward the Federal guns joined in and the very ground shook. It was simply awful the bursting of the shells, the smoke, and the heat combined made things almost unendurable for our men lying in long rows in rear of the ridge.

Many of our men were wounded by the shelling and it was a relief when finally the artillery ceased its terrible work and orders came for Pickett's men to charge. The skirmish line (to which the writer was attached) moved forward towards the enemy's skirmish line. Some two hundred yards in the rear came the line of battle, Richard B. Garnett's brigade on the left and Kemper's brigade on the right while Armistead's came close in the rear.

It was a splendid exhibition. The alignment was nearly perfect. After advancing some three hundred yards the enemy's artillery opened on the columns and shells came screaming through the ranks of Pickett's men. As the men fell the ranks closed and forward went the line leaving the dead and wounded in its track.

Seminary Ridge

The move was made in a left oblique direction to reach the point of attack which was the angle of a stone wall or fence on the ridge of Seminary Hill. When the line reached this point it became irregular. Many of the officers fell before this point was gained. Colonel Joseph of the Third ordered the brigade to face to the right just as the wall was reached.

There were heavy columns of the enemy coming from that direction while Garnett's men came in contact with the enemy behind the wall; then Armistead's men rushed across the wall and pursued the enemy who abandoned the battery some 300 feet in rear of the wall. Then came short lull in the battle but firing was kept up and men fell to rise no more.

About 150 Federals were captured at the angle and taken off the field. It was at this time that General Lewis A. Armistead was killed having his left hand on one of the guns of Cushing's battery and in his right hand he held his sword on which he had placed his hat. Thus a hero meets a hero's death.

The line around the angle was being fast thinned out and now was the time for reinforcements to push on the victory within our grasp, but none were there to aid Pickett's men in their struggle to hold the position for which they had fought so hard.

The supporting line on Pickett's left struck the enemy's line further to our left, reaching there long before Pickett, their line being nearly one-half shorter, and as Pickett's men advanced the line our left was seen to be in full retreat, having suffered heavily. The men of Pickett's division — that is, about one-tenth of what was left — retraced their steps, falling back in small groups, firing as they retreated.

General Pickett was seen in the midst of his survivors when the battle was over, but at the close Wilcox's brigade came rushing down. It came about half way when it met the concentrated fire of the enemy and fell back faster than it came; adding only to the losses and accomplishing naught.

Sergeant Major J. R. Polak states that he was ordered by Colonel Williams to bring up the ambulance corps, as men were falling right and left needed attention. He went off on "Nelly" (Colonel Williams's horse) to execute the orders given him, and on his return the regiment, with the rest of the division, were all charging, and all he could do was to return Colonel Williams's horse and take his place in the ranks. Colonel Williams at once mounted and wheeled in front of the regiment and was almost immediately struck down. Then Major Langley took command; he was soon disabled. Then Captain took command with the same result. Then Captain Davis jumped in front of the line and was bowled over almost immediately. Then I remember we pushed to the wall, and could almost see the Yankee gunners leaving their pieces and running in our lines for safety. Whilst we were waiting with our line for reinforcements, I had a short talk with Lieutenant Cabell about the massing of the Yankees in our front, and the next thing I saw was Colonel Patton of the Seventh Virginia, struck, and when I asked him if he was hurt he tried to answer, but the blood gushed out of his mouth, and made it impossible.

The next thing that I remember was that no reinforcements came and that the Yankees came over the works and we "got," at least I did. I was slightly wounded in the face and in the arm, and found it somewhat difficult to jump what looked to me a ten rail fence, but I managed this all the same. When I got my breath about a quarter of a mile from the field, I saw General Lee riding unattended, and after a few minutes of observation he rode back and returned with General Longstreet, and then established a point for the returning men to fall back on

The Color Guard

The account given of Lieutenant William Lawson, who was the color bearer of the regiment is as follows: When the order was given to fire and the color bearer and guard consisting of Color Bearer William M. Lawson, Sergeants Pat Woods, Theodore R. Martin, Corporal John Q. Figg, and Private Willie Mitchell moved four paces to the front of the line and kept in their position until one after the other was shot down. About half way Willie Mitchell was wounded, but he declined to go back and kept on. About one hundred yards further he was killed. Pat Woods, Theodore R. Martin and John Q. Figg were shot down and the line came close to the stone fence. The color bearer had his right arm shattered by a bullet, and the colors fell from his hand among the dead and dying. J. R. Polak attempted to raise and secure the colors, but was also wounded. Those that were able now fell back and the colors remained where they fell near the angle of the stone wall.

Willie Mitchell was only about sixteen years of age. He was a member of Company D., having joined that company in December,

1862, at the battle of Fredericksburg. He was the son of John Mitchell, the "Irish Patriot," and had just finished his course at the University of Paris. William M. Lawson, the color bearer, lost his arm near the shoulder, leaving only a stump, which was hardly healed when he reported for duty to his regiment. After being released from prison he was promoted to lieutenant for gallant conduct.

Sergeant Pat Woods was shot through the body and remained in prison for some time. He was a most reckless, daring Irishman. There were no better men than Sergeant Theodore R. Martin and John Q. Figg. both of these were severely wounded. Sergeant John Q. Figg was afterwards promoted to color bearer and made a splendid record for himself in the battles that followed in 1864 and 1865 until the close of the war.

29. Writing long after the war, Private George Clark, a Judge in Texas, recalls the confusion surrounding the movements of Wilcox's brigade, his wounding during the charge, and reveals a bitter resentment against the breakdown in the plans that led to Wilcox and Perry starting late and veering off course. George Clark, "Wilcox's Alabama Brigade at Gettysburg," *CV*, XVII(1909), 230-231.

At an early hour on the morning of July 3 the brigade was formed and moved up somewhat in the rear of Seminary Ridge. The artillery was beginning to form on our front along the Emmetsburg Pike, and the brigade was halted in the rear of the artillery then beginning to form and told that this would be its position during the bombardment which was to take place during the day. The men began to make themselves as comfortable as practicable, when the brigade commander, unaccompanied by his staff, went forward on foot to the crest of the ridge and was seen to be surveying the enemy's position opposite on Cemetery Ridge through his field glass. After a short while he returned; and forming the brigade in line, he moved it forward until it reached a space of about forty yards behind the artillery which was being planted near the crest. When this was done, there were ominous shakes of the head among the boys as to the wisdom of such a move, and expressions were heard to the effect that "Old Billy Fixin" (the brigadier's nickname) was not satisfied with having lost one-half his brigade the day before, but was determined to sacrifice "the whole caboodle" to-day. The wisdom of the change was demonstrated by the bombardment.

Immediately upon our advance Pickett's division came up

and occupied our original position with his left brigade, the other two brigades of his division extending farther to the right.

After hours of waiting, the bombardment opened with a fury beyond description. The earth seemed to rise up under the concussion, the air was filled with missiles, and the noise and din were so furious and overwhelming as well as continuous that one had to scream to his neighbor lying beside him to be heard at all. The constant roar of nearly four hundred cannon on both sides, with the explosion of the shells and frequently the bursting of a caisson wagon, was terrific beyond description. Men could be seen, especially among the artillery, bleeding at both ears from concussion, and the wreck of matter and the crush of worlds seemed to be upon us.

After an hour or so, or perhaps longer, Pickett's men were ordered up and began their forward movement to storm the enemy's position on Cemetery Ridge. His division had suffered considerably during the bombardment, especially the brigade which occupied the old position of Wilcox in our rear; but the men moved forward in fine order and, passing to the right of our brigade, mounted the crest of the ridge and started down the gradual incline toward the enemy's lines of intrenchments with quick pace and steady step. Just as they passed our right flank orders were given to our brigade to rise and move rapidly by the right flank, which was promptly done, and then the brigade faced and moved forward rapidly to the right of Pickett. Just previous to our reaching Pickett's right his division seemed to take somewhat of a left oblique and soon disappeared from my view, and I only have its brave deeds from history.

The Alabama brigade proceeded to charge Meade's army alone. What such an absurd movement meant was never known to the officers then, nor has it ever been satisfactorily explained since. It was rumored afterwards that orders had been issued to stop our movement, but were never delivered; but the whole affair is involved in mystery even to this day. Be that as it may, the brigade moved forward rapidly; but one could hear frequent expressions from the men to the effect: "What in the devil does this mean?" For a few moments practically no loss occurred in our forward movement; but the Federal artillery soon got their range, and a storm of shot and shell was poured upon us. Shrapnel shot would burst in front of us and great gaps be made in our ranks, but the ranks would close and the line move forward. . . .

At last we came within the range of grape and canister, and a hurricane of such missiles seemed to burst from a hundred cannon on our little line of about eight hundred, rank and file, and plow their deadly path through our ranks. We finally reached a scrubby timbered drain just under the enemy's position, and were passing through it as rapidly as possible when further participation, in so far as I was concerned, altogether ceased. A grape shot struck me down, and the struggle ended in so far as I was concerned. The retreat was ordered, and I was left alone to contemplate the horrors of war and the reckless and criminal folly of a military order which was subsequently repudiated by every officer from third lieutenant to the commanding general.

What happened to myself subsequently can be of little interest to any living man. Suffice it to say that I escaped capture and imprisonment by the gallant conduct of four of my good comrades, who, when the brigade was re-formed, ascertained my absence and its cause and gallantly came back and picked me up on a litter and carried me off the field. These four men are all dead now; but the memory of this good deed will abide with me so long as I am capable of tender and grateful recollection.

On a mound on Cemetery Heights there has been erected a monument marked "The High-Water Mark of the Confederacy." It was designed to mark the farthest point reached by the Confederates, and glancing at the inscription one can read thereon: "Wilcox's Alabama Brigade — Esto Perpetua."

30. Private Erasmus Williams of the 14th Virginia crossed the wall with Armistead, helped turn around a Federal gun, and then made it back alive. Erasmus Williams to John Daniels, n.d., John Daniels Papers, University of Virginia.

While we were advancing on the heights, we could see at times only smoke and flame. When we got near a stonewall, our lines rushed forward, and Gen. Armistead jumping over it cried out "turn the guns!"

I caught hold of one of the enemy's cannon under this order and my left forefinger was caught and torn, and the wound looks as if a knife had cut it well nigh in two. We got the gun turned towards the enemy, and I was in a few feet of Gen. Armistead at the time. Col. R. W. Martin, of the 53rd of our brigade, was also within a few feet of Armistead. He was a brave young fellow and among the foremost. As we looked over the field we could see now the enemy advancing in front and on our left and right at the same time, and when we looked back we could see that no reinforcements were coming. If either Wilcox's brigade or any other body of good troops could have arrived at this time, I think we could have held our ground, for we were there at the wall and over it for something like fifteen or twenty minutes, though of course with so many things going on with rapid succession it is hard to measure time. In a few minutes I said to Major Martin "Look Major, the yankees are flanking us, we must get out from here." "No," he said, "hold on men, rally, rally, right here." Presently Gen. Armistead fell to the ground, and by the side of the gun which we had turned about by his order, and as the yankees were pressing forward and on our flanks the men commenced to quit. As the yankees came nearer and nearer, I commenced to recede, still keeping my face towards them and cried out again to Major Martin, "We must get away from here, Major." Major Martin was about to get up on the stonewall toward the Confederate side, when he fell but a few yards from where Armistead had fallen before him. There was nothing to do but get away as best we could, so I struck across a field to our rear, and had gotten scarce twenty-five or thirty yards when I was shot through my left wrist. The balls were falling all around us, and it was "save himself who can." I kept on going, and in a little while got back to the hole I had dug on the line. I picked up my case knife and knapsack which I had left there, and went on still farther towards the rear. Presently I saw an ambulance coming along down the hill from the battle field, and it proceeded on a road on the Confederate side of the line. Cannon shot were falling about, and one took off the top of it and smashed it up. The body that was in it rolled out on the ground, but the driver was unhurt, and he jumped up and called to me "come here and help me to carry off this man." "I am shot myself" I said, "and unable to help anybody." The driver insisted, "You must help me " he said, "take hold and let's carry this wounded man along the road beyond." I could see the road was right in the line of the enemy's cannonade which was still progressing. I said "no, but if you take him around this hill I will try to help him with my right hand." So together we picked up as best we could the wounded soldier. I looked at the wounded man and said "I believe he is already dead, it is not worth while carrying him anywhere." "No you must help me," again he exclaimed, and catching hold of the blanket with him we went around the hill and laid him down at the hospital. I asked the driver before I left "who is this?" He said "it is Gen. Kemper." I got my arm tied up, and as no bones were broken, I got along about as well as any of the wounded, and finally tramping along I got to Virginia and back to my home.

31. Some of the men scheduled to make the charge could not, and Private John Dooley discussed the emotions of one who did control his fear. In one of the best descriptions of the march of the men in the ranks, he gives a sense of the things that were on their minds during the charge, as well as the sounds. Joseph T. Durkin, ed., *John Dooley, Confederate Soldier: His War Journal* (Georgetown: Georgetown University Press, 1945), 101-107.

Get Ready, Pickett!

Our artillery has now ceased to roar and the enemy have checked their fury, too. The time appointed for our charge is come.

I tell you, there is no romance in making one of these charges. You might think so from reading "Charlie O'Malley," that prodigy of valour, or in reading of any other gallant knight who would as little think of riding over *gunners sich like* as they would of eating a dozen oysters. But, when you rise to your feet as we did today, I tell you the enthusiasm of ardent breasts in many cases *ain't there*, and instead of burning to avenge the insults of our country, families and altars and firesides, the thought is most frequently, *Oh, if I could just come out of this charge safely how thankful would I be!*

We rise to our feet, but not all. There is a line of men still on the ground with their faces turned, men affected in 4 different ways. There are the gallant dead who will never charge again; the helpless wounded, many of whom desire to share the fortunes of this charge; the men who have charged on many a battlefield but who are now helpless from the heat of the sun; and the men in whom there is not sufficient courage to enable them to rise, — but of these last there are but few.

Up, brave men! Some are actually fainting from the heat and dread. They have fallen to the ground overpowered by the suffocating heat and the terrors of that hour. Onward — steady — dress to the right give way to the left — steady, not too fast — don't press upon the center — how gentle the slope! steady — keep well in line — there is the line of guns we must take — right in front — but how far they appear! Nearly one third of a mile, off on Cemetery Ridge, and the line stretches round in almost a semicircle. Upon the center of this we must march. Behind the guns are strong lines of infantry. You may see them plainly and now they see us perhaps more plainly.

To the right of us and above the guns we are to capture, black heavy monsters from their lofty mountain sites belch forth their flame and smoke and storms of shot and shell upon our advancing line; while directly in front, breathing flame in our very faces, the long range of guns which must be taken thunder on our quivering melting ranks. Now truly does the work of death begin. The line becomes unsteady because at every step a gap must be closed and thus from left to right much ground is often lost.

The Turning Point At Gettysburg

Close up! Close up the ranks when a friend falls, while his life blood bespatters your cheek or throws a film over your eyes!

Dress to left or right, while the bravest of the brave are sinki
no more! Still onward! Capt. Hallinan has fallen and I take
So many men have fallen now that I find myself within a few ᵣᵤ
my old Captain (Norton). His men are pressing mine out of place.
I ask him to give way a little to the left, and scarcely has he done so
than he leaps into the air, falling prostrate. Still we press on — oh,
how long it seems before we reach those blazing guns. Our men are
falling faster now, for the deadly musket is at work. Volley after
volley of crashing musket balls sweeps through the line and mow us
down like wheat before the scythe.

On! men, on! Thirty more yards and the guns are ours; but
who can stand such a storm of hissing lead and iron? What a relief
if earth, which almost seems to hurl these implements of death in
our faces, would open now and afford a secure retreat from
threatening death. Every officer is in front, Pickett with his long
curls streaming in the fiery breath from the cannons' mouth.
Garnett on the right, Kemper in the center and Armistead on the left;
Cols., Lieut. Cols., Majors, Captains, all press on and cheer the
shattered lines.

Just here — from right to left the remnants of our braves
pour in their long reserved fire; until now no shot had been fired, no
shout of triumph had been raised; but as the cloud of smoke rises
over the heads of the advancing divisions the well known southern
battle cry which marks the victory gained or nearly gained bursts
wildly over the blood stained field and *all that line of guns is ours.*

John Dooley Is Struck Down

Shot through both thighs, I fall about 30 yards from the
guns. By my side lies Lt. Kehoe, shot through the knee. Here we lie,
he in excessive pain, I fearing to bleed to death, the dead and dying
all around, while the division sweeps over the Yankee guns. Oh, how
I long to know the result, the end of this fearful charge! We seem to
have victory in our hands; but what can our poor remnant of a
shattered division do if they meet beyond the guns an obstinate
resistance?

Defeat

There listen — we hear a new shout, and cheer after cheer
rends the air. Are those fresh troops advancing to our support? No!
no! That huzza never broke from southern lips. Oh God! Virginia's
bravest, noblest sons have perished here today and perished all in
vain!

Oh, if there is anything capable of crushing and wringing the
soldier's heart it was this day's tragic act and all in vain! But a little

well timed support and Gettysburg was ours. The Yankee army had been routed and Pickett's division earned a name and fame not inferior to that of the Old Guard of Bonaparte. I will not attempt to describe.

Section V

"Great Praise Is Due The Enlisted Men":

The Federal Left

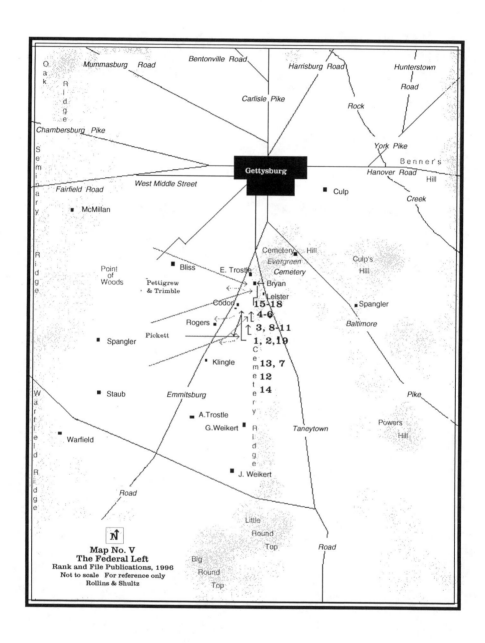

Map No. V
The Federal Left
Rank and File Publications, 1996
Not to scale For reference only
Rollins & Shultz

1. Kemper's brigade stepped off south of the Spangler farm, crossed the Emmitsburg Road as their right flank brushed the Klingle farm, left obliqued near Plum Run and then marched up the Emmitsburg Road. Their right flank passed some 300 yards in front of the Federal artillery commanded by Lieutenant Colonel Freeman McGilvery, and the brigades of Colonel Norman Hall and Colonel William Harrow. They made a nearly unmissable target and took a murderous fire all the way from the Plum Run area to the Angle. Once past the Codori farm, they were hit by a counter-charge in their flank and rear. Brigadier General George Stannard commanded the brigade of Vermont troops on the left of the Federal line. These men executed the most difficult and dangerous maneuver of the entire charge. After making a right wheel to hit Kemper, they turned 360 degrees and pitched into the left flank of the two brigades led by Brigadier General Cadmus Wilcox, who were attempting to support Kemper. Report of Brig. Gen. George J. Stannard, *OR*, 1, 27, 1, 349-50.

At about 2 p. m. the enemy again commenced a vigorous attack upon my position. After subjecting us for one and one-half hours to the severest cannonade of the whole battle, from one hundred guns or more, the enemy charged with a heavy column of infantry, at least one division, in close column by regiments. The charge was aimed directly upon my command, but owing apparently to the firm front shown them, the enemy diverged midway, and came upon the line on my right. But they did not thus escape the warm reception prepared for them by the Vermonters. During this charge the enemy suffered from the fire of the Thirteenth and Fourteenth, the range being short. At the commencement of the attack, I called the Sixteenth from the skirmish line, and placed them in close column by division in my immediate rear. As soon as the change of the point of attack became evident, I ordered a flank attack upon the enemy's column. Forming in the open meadow in front of our lines, the Thirteenth changed front forward on first company; the Sixteenth, after deploying, performed the same, and formed on the left of the Thirteenth, at right angles to the main line of our army, bringing them in line of battle upon the flank of the charging division of the enemy, and opened a destructive fire at short range, which the enemy sustained but a very few moments before the larger portion of them surrendered and marched in--not as conquerors, but as captives. I then ordered the two regiments into their former position. The order was not filled when I saw another rebel column charging immediately upon our left. Colonel Veazey, of the Sixteenth, was at once ordered to attack it in its turn upon the flank. This was done as successfully as before. The rebel forces, already decimated by the fire of the Fourteenth Regiment,

Colonel Nichols, were scooped almost *en masse* into our lines. The Sixteenth took in this charge the regimental colors of the Second Florida and Eighth Virginia Regiments, and the battle-flag of another regiment.

2. Colonel Wheelock Veazey commanded the 16th Vermont in Stannard's brigade on the left of the Federal line. He describes his unit's actions, including the manning of artillery guns and the maneuvers that led to the repulse of Wilcox. Wheelock Veazey to G. G. Benedict July 11, 1864, Vermont Historical Society.

The enemy also opened with a large amount of artillery said to be 140 pieces. My men were lying flat down, and most of the fire with that of our own artillery which was on the crest in our rear passed over us. I lost several men, however, by it. This continued about 2 hours. The effect of this cannonading on my men was the most remarkable ever witnessed in any battle, many of them, I think, the majority fell asleep. It was with the greatest effort only that I could keep awake myself, not withstanding the cries of my wounded men & my anxiety for the more fearful scene which I knew must speedily follow. About 4 p. m. the enemy, Pickett's Division advanced. My pickets held the enemy's skirmish line until their main line of battle came upon us when we gradually drew in on the reserve, and at the same time, the 14th was moved forward to the right of my reserve and opened by a volley on their own lines. The 13th soon came down to the right of the 14th & by this time I had got my regiment together & we delivered but few volleys before the enemy moved by the flank to their left and forward towards the lines on our right, which were considerably to our rear, and soon began to uncover our front when I received an order to move by flank to the right and forward towards the right and left of the 13th. I united with the 13th by moving to their left, exposed their right flank, & my regiment in moving upon their line, gradually changed or made an oblique change of front forward on the first company, and we charged forward on the enemy and completely destroyed their lines. Very many of the enemy were killed, but more were captured and probably still more ran away, except on their right which was particularly exposed as the left of my regiment extended across their line after our change of front & forward movement. I think we moved from where my reserve rested about fifty rods. That was my estimate at the time & I have been over the ground since. As soon as we had destroyed their first line or lines, another brigade, Wilcox's, appeared on the charge at double quick their left being just in front of the position where my reserve had rested, therefore obliquely to my rear as we were then situated. I immediately faced my regiment to the rear & began to move back when I met a staff officer.   I think yourself or Mr. Hooker, with an order to move to my original position and open fire on this new line. I marched in the direction ordered about 35 rods, and then by the left flank & changed direction obliquely to the left, which produced a change of front as you will notice, a novel way indeed but adopted in order to gain upon the enemy in the movement & to avoid the confusion that might arise under such terrible artillery fire & began nearly a third of my men had already fallen, by adopting any movement laid down in the tactics to effect a change of front. This movement brought my front facing obliquely on the enemy's left flank, from 30 to 40 rods distant. Here I met Genl. Stannard and obtained permission of him, after repeated requests (for he at first thought it would be rash to send one).

       ... At a quarter before four A M of the 3d day, the enemy sent a line of skirmishers against my picket line, and the skirmishing continued more or less nearly all the forenoon.   My line was reinforced by a dozen sharpshooters. At about the same hour a battery in our front opened upon one in our rear which was being supported by the 14th Vt. and blew up one of the caissons. The enemy in our front were so watchful and active and kept up such a constant fire on the pickets when any movement in our line was attempted, that it was deemed impracticable and too dangerous to try to relieve the line by a fresh detail, and the result was that the men had to remain on the line throughout the day and endure great suffering from hunger and thirst and exhaustion.   During the forenoon the great battle on the right was fought, which created a good deal of alarm as it seemed to be directly in our rear, by reason of the curve in our line of battle to the right. At length the firing in that direction subsided, and the stillness every where through the middle of the day was almost painful. This continued until about two o'clock in the afternoon when the enemy opened along our front and far to the right and left with one hundred and fifty pieces of artillery. Our artillery which was on the elevated ground in our rear, soon replied, and then for two hours there took place that great artillery duel, pronounced by military historians the greatest that ever occurred between field artillery. As the picket line was in the depression between the two crests where the artillery of the two armies was posted, the missiles mostly passed over us, yet a few of the men were hit. The effect of this cannonading on them was the most remarkable I ever witnessed in any battle. A large number of the reserves fell asleep. It was only with the greatest effort that I could keep awake, notwithstanding the peril, the groans of the wounded and my anxiety on account of the awful collision of the infantry lines which I knew would speedily take place. About four o clock the artillery fire subsided and the rebel infantry columns soon emerged from the smoke and advanced steadily but rapidly down the slopes and with a skirmish line in advance quickly struck our own picket and skirmish line. The men held their position against the enemy's skirmishers and until their main line came upon them and then gradually fell back and gathered on the reserves which were on the crest with our artillery. The enemy seemed to be aiming directly upon the position of our picket reserves, until they had nearly reached it, when they changed their course sufficiently to pass by our right. About this time we saw the 14th Vermont had been pushed forward to our right and a little to our rear, and were firing into the flank of the enemy. By the divergence of the enemy to their left (our right) they exposed their right flank to a flank attack by our brigade. The 16th was still in the same position which the reserves of the skirmish line occupied. The skirmishers had all come in and joined the reserves and that regiment had begun to fire obliquely to the right into the flank of the rebels when an order was received from Gen. Stannard to move to the right of the 14th by passing behind them and unite on the left of the 13th and charge the flank of the enemy. This was quickly accomplished. I found the 13th to the right and little to the rear of the line of the 14th and engaged in making an oblique change of front forward In order to unite on the left. I made a corresponding movement, and the two regiments were thus brought into line facing obliquely to the right and facing the flank of the enemy. The charge was made at about the time the enemy struck, and at one point, broke the front line of battle to our right As we advanced in that charge the enemy were in great masses, without much order, and were rushing rapidly upon the lines to our right, and regardless of the exposure of their right flank. Our regiments fired a few volleys as they moved forward under the combined movement on the enemy's front and flank those great masses of men seemed to disappear in a moment. As we moved down upon them the left of my regiment extended well around their flank, and we took large numbers of prisoners. The ground over which we passed after striking their flank was literally covered with dead and wounded men. While thus engaged in this flank movement to the right I observed another force of the enemy charging down at double quick away to the left and rear of our then position and apparently aiming towards the position we held before making this flank attack to the right. The direction of this new line, afterwards found to consist of Perry and Wilcox's brigades, would take them by my left and rear as we were then situated. I immediately conceived that I should change front obliquely to the left and charge the left flank of the new line when it came within striking distance, just as we had charged the right of Pickett's division. I heretofore immediately called to the men to fall in, as they were then broken into squads gathering up prisoners, and we had started on the new movement when I received an order from Gen. Stannard to double quick back to our original position and get in front of this new line. This order would take me in the same direction for some rods that I contemplated going, and we kept on in that direction but in moving I had changed the front of my regiment to the left and so as to face obliquely towards the left flank of this new line; and just then came upon Gen. Stannard and explained my plan of a charge. He at first opposed it on the ground that it would be rash and too much to ask of men to go alone so far to the front against so large a force; but he soon yielded and said, "go ahead." At that moment the enemy had reached the bottom of the ravine, their left flank being not more than thirty to forty rods distant, and they were crouching behind the low bushes and rocks which afforded some shelter from our artillery and infantry fire in front. The ground from our position towards the enemy was fairly smooth and a little descending and upon the order the men cheered and ran forward at a run without firing a shot and quickly struck the rebel flank and followed it until the whole line had disappeared. The movement was so sudden and rapid that the enemy could not change front to oppose us. A great many prisoners were taken but I cannot tell the number as they were sent to the rear without a guard as I had no men to spare for that purpose, and none were needed as the prisoners were quite willing to get within the shelter of our lines and away from the exposure to which they were then subjected as well as we from the rebel artillery which followed us with merciless vigor. As fast as they were captured they were told where to go and then went, and without standing on the order of their going. We also took two stands of regimental colors. This was the last effort of the infantry of the enemy. After following down his line as stated until it had substantially disappeared I moved the regiment to the left through and behind the shelter of the bushes and trees to get out of range of the rebel artillery which had gained a destructive range upon us. We had been then but a few moments when I was ordered to move a few rods to the right and in this movement we were again exposed to the artillery severely and lost several men. I consequently moved again farther to the right and got a little out of range, and soon after this, the firing subsided, and there was no more fighting except a little skirmishing far to our left. Our forty rounds of ammunition were mostly used up but this was mainly done before our first flank movement to the right and while making it. In the second flank charge to the left but few shots were fired and those were after we struck the enemy before they became fully aware we were on their flank. I could see their line break ahead of us and the men rush to the rear, and thereby they escaped being captured. The fire of the 14th was very destructive on Pickett's division to the right, but Col. Nichols informed me that Perry and

Wilcox came down so rapidly and so quickly got under cover of bushes that he produced but little effect upon them, and our charge being across his front prevent him from firing after that. Four companies of his regiment were sent down on my left after we passed under shelter of the bushes as above stated. You have our losses in the reports. That they were not larger I attribute to the fact that we were almost constantly moving and that our work consisted mainly of flank charges, which if rapid and successful, are usually without great loss. If not successful they are likely to be very disastrous. We were also very much enveloped in the smoke of the battle and were thus obscured from view. I failed to see a single man falter in the least throughout the battles but every one seemed a host as the orders to charge were given. They made the changes of front first to the right and then to the left with almost the precision of a parade, and as though the fire upon them was from blank cartridges in a sham fight. At the close of the battle, they were farther to the front than when the battle opened, except when they were upon the skirmish line, and farther than any other regiment on that part of the field within our sight.

3. Colonel Theodore Gates commanded the 80th New York, also known as the 20th New York State Militia. These were 1st Corps troops, stationed just left of Harrow's brigade, south of the copse of trees. Gates describes the superb field of fire they had on Kemper. As the Confederates moved north along Emmitsburg Road, Gates pulled his men out of line and moved them to the right to the copse of trees area to continue the fight. This "following the parade" movement rippled all along the line south of the copse of trees. Report of Col. Theodore B. Gates, commdg. 20th New York State Militia, *OR*, 1, 27, 1, 321-323.

About 5 a. m. on the 3d, the enemy opened with artillery, and for some time kept up a brisk fire upon our position. This finally ceased, and until about 1 p. m. no further firing took place on this part of the line.

During the interval, the Vermont troops threw up a breastwork to my left and about 100 feet in advance of my line, masked by the small grove before mentioned. The regiment of that brigade on my right took position in rear of this new work, leaving open the space between my right and the bluff, on which was the nearest battery.

At 1 o'clock the enemy opened from his right-center battery, which was soon followed by all his guns on his right and center, and the position occupied by my command was swept by a tempest of shot and shell from upward of one hundred guns for nearly three hours. When the cannonading subsided, the enemy's infantry debouched from the orchard and woods on his right center, and moved in two lines of battle across the fields toward the position I have described. Our skirmishers (from the Vermont brigade) fell back before them, and sought cover behind the breastworks on my left. The enemy came forward rapidly, and began firing as soon as they were within range of our men. When they had approached within about 200 feet of the bottom of the valley heretofore mentioned, the troops of my command opened a warm fire upon them. Almost immediately the first line faced by the left flank, and moved at a double-quick up the valley and toward Gettysburg. The second line followed the movement. Reaching a position opposite the bluff, they faced to the right, and moved forward rapidly in line of battle. Perceiving that their purpose was to gain the bluff, I moved my command by the right flank up to the foot of the bluff, delivering our fire as we marched, and keeping between the enemy and the object of his enterprise. He succeeded in reaching the fence at the foot of the bluff, but with ranks broken and his men evidently disheartened. Some succeeded in getting over the fence into the slashing, from which and behind the fence they kept up a murderous fire. The men were now within quarter pistol-range, and, as the fence and fallen trees gave the enemy considerable cover, I ordered the Twentieth New York State Militia and the One hundred and fifty-first Pennsylvania Volunteers to advance to the fence, which they did, cheering, and in gallant style, and poured a volley into the enemy at very short range, who now completely broke, and those who did not seek to escape by flight threw down their arms. Very few of those who fled reached their own lines. Many turned after having run several rods and surrendered themselves. We took a large number of prisoners, and the ground in front of us was strewn with their dead and wounded. During the latter part of this struggle, and after it ceased, the enemy's batteries played upon friend and foe alike. The troops engaged with us were Pickett's division, of Longstreet's Corps.

Among the killed and wounded in my immediate front was Colonel [J. H.] Hodges, Fourteenth Virginia, and several line officers. Two colors were left upon the ground by the enemy. Thus terminated the final and main attack upon our left center.

4. Colonel Norman Hall of the 7th Michigan commanded the brigade directly south of the copse of trees and north of Harrow's men. He saw the Confederates looking irresistible as they came across, but the rifles of his men, along with the others, proved deadly. The "follow the parade" movement of Hall's and Harrow's men caused chaos, but also bunched their rifles together

for greater firepower. **Report of Col. Norman J. Hall, Seventh Michigan Infantry, July 17, 1863, *OR*, 1, 27, 1, 437-441.**

. . . Nothing more than occasional skirmishing occurred until the afternoon of the 3d. At 1 o'clock the enemy opened with artillery upon that portion of the line between the cemetery and the right of the Fifth Corps, several hundred yards from Round Top. The number of pieces which concentrated their fire upon this line is said to have been about one hundred and fifty. The object was evidently to destroy our batteries and drive the infantry from the slight crest which marked the line of battle, while the concentration of fire upon the hill occupied by the Second and the right of the Third Brigades indicated where the real attack was to be made. The experience of the terrible grandeur of that rain of missiles and that chaos of strange and terror-spreading sounds, unexampled, perhaps, in history, must ever remain undescribed, but can never be forgotten by those who survived it.

I cannot suffer this opportunity to pass without paying just tribute to the noble service of the officers and men of the batteries that were served within my sight. Never before during this war were so many batteries subjected to so terrible a test. Horses, men, and carriages were piled together, but the fire scarcely slackened for an instant so long as the guns were standing.

Lieutenant Cushing, of Battery A, Fourth U. S. Artillery, challenged the admiration of all who saw him. Three of his limbers were blown up and changed with the caisson limbers under fire. Several wheels were shot off his guns and replaced, till at last, severely wounded himself, his officers all killed or wounded, and with but cannoneers enough to man a section, he pushed his gun to the fence in front, and was killed while serving his last canister into the ranks of the advancing enemy.

Knowing that the enemy's infantry would attack soon, I sent Lieutenant [William R.] Driver, acting assistant adjutant-general, to the Artillery Reserve for batteries, with orders to conduct them to the crest, if they were granted, with all possible speed. He arrived with one, which, though too late for service in arresting the advance of the enemy, yet had the opportunity to do him much damage.

At 3 o'clock exactly the fire of the enemy slackened, and his first line of battle advanced from the woods in front in beautiful order. About 100 yards in rear came a second line, and opposite the main point of attack was what appeared to be a column of battalions.

The accompanying diagram will illustrate the disposition of the troops of my own command. This sketch does not pretend to accuracy in distances or angles.

The conformation of the ground enabled the enemy, after advancing near the lines, to obtain cover. Arrived at this point, one

battalion continued to move toward the point A, occupied by the
Second and Third Brigades of the Second division. The other
battalions moved by the flank until completely masked by the
preceding one, when they moved by the flank again, thus forming
a column of regiments The few pieces of artillery still in position
were directed upon this column, while the rebel cannon again
opened with shell firing over their own troops.

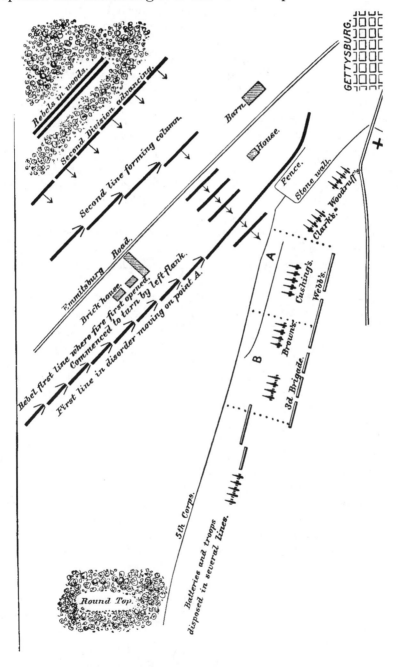

The perfect order and steady but rapid advance of the enemy called forth praise from our troops, but gave their line an appearance of being fearfully irresistible. My line was single, the only support (the Seventy-second Pennsylvania Volunteers) having been called away by General Webb before the action had fairly commenced. There was a disposition in the men to reserve their fire for close quarters, but when I observed the movement the enemy was endeavoring to execute, I caused the Seventh Michigan and Twentieth Massachusetts Volunteers to open fire at about 200 yards. The deadly aim of the former regiment was attested by the line of slain within its range. This had a great effect upon the result, for it caused the enemy to move rapidly at one point and consequently to crowd in front — being occasioned at the point where his column was forming, he did not recover from this disorder. The remainder of our line reserved its fire until within 100 yards, some regiments waiting even until but 50 paces intervened between them and the enemy.

There was but a moment of doubtful contest in front of the position of this brigade. The enemy halted to deliver his fire, wavered and fled, while the line of the fallen perfectly marked the limit of his advance. The troops were pouring into the ranks of the fleeing enemy that rapid and accurate fire, the delivery of which victorious lines always so much enjoy, when I saw that a portion of the line of General Webb on my right had given way, and many men were making to the rear as fast as possible, while the enemy was pouring over the rails that had been a slight cover for the troops.

Having gained this apparent advantage, the enemy seemed to turn again and re-engage my whole line. Going to the left, I found two regiments that could be spared from some command there, and endeavored to move them by the right flank to the break, but, coming under a warm fire, they crowded to the slight cover of the rail fence, mixing with the troops already there. Finding it impossible to draw them out and reform, and seeing no unengaged troops within reach, I was forced to order my own brigade back from the line, and move it by the flank under a heavy fire. The enemy was rapidly gaining a foothold; organization was mostly lost; in the confusion commands were useless, while a disposition on the part of the men to fall back a pace or two each time to load, gave the line a retiring direction. With the officers of my staff and a few others, who seemed to comprehend what was required, the head of the line, still slowly moving by the flank, was crowded closer to the enemy and the men obliged to load in their places. I did not see any man of my command who appeared disposed to run away, but the confusion first caused by the two regiments above spoken of so destroyed the formation in two ranks that in some places the line was several files deep.

. . . During this time, the Fifteenth Massachusetts Volunteers, First Minnesota, and Nineteenth Maine Volunteers, from the first Brigade of this division, had joined the line, and are entitled to a full share in the credit of the final repulse.

The line remained in this way for about ten minutes, rather giving way than advancing, when, by a simultaneous effort upon the part of all the officers I could instruct, aided by the general advance of many of the colors, the line closed with the enemy, and, after a few minutes of desperate, often hand-to-hand fighting, the crowd—for such had become that part of the enemy's column that had passed the fence threw down their arms and were taken prisoners of war, while the remainder broke and fled in great disorder. The Second Brigade had again joined the right of my line, which now occupied the position originally held by that command.

Generals Garnett and Armistead were picked up near this point, together with many colonels and officers of other grades.

Twenty battle-flags were captured in a space of 100 yards square. Several colors were stolen or taken with violence by officers of high rank from brave soldiers who had rushed forward and honestly captured them from the enemy, and were probably turned in as taken by commands which were not within 100 yards of the point of attack. Death is too light a punishment for such a dastardly offense.

To the efforts of a few officers and the courage and good discipline of the men is due the great result of the final repulse of the enemy. Conspicuous acts of individual bravery were unusually frequent. Colors were captured with clubbed muskets, and many men of both our own and the enemy had their clothes blown off for a large space around their wounds by the close discharge.

Between 1,000 and 2,000 prisoners were captured at the point of attack, where the First, Second, and Third Brigades were equally present. Piles of dead and thousands of wounded upon both sides attested the desperation of assailants and defenders.

The services of many officers of my command would, under ordinary circumstances, claim particular notice and reward, but so great was the necessity for every possible exertion that all who saw their duty I believe did it, forgetting all question of danger.

I cannot omit speaking in the highest terms of the magnificent conduct of Lieutenant Haskell, of General Gibbon's staff, in bringing forward regiments and in nerving the troops to their work by word and fearless example. Lieutenant-Colonel Steele, of the Seventh Michigan Volunteers, behaved most gallantly, and was killed in the line of his regiment urging men forward. Every regimental commander did his whole duty nobly. Three of them were killed or have since died of their wounds, viz: Colonel Revere, of the Twentieth Massachusetts Volunteers-Lieutenant-Colonel Thoman, Fifty-ninth New York Volunteers, and Lieutenant Colonel Steele, Seventh Michigan Volunteers. Lieutenant-Colonel Macy,

Twentieth Massachusetts; Lieutenant-Colonel Wass and Major Rice, Nineteenth Massachusetts Volunteers, were severely wounded. Captains [S. Newell] Smith and [George W.] Leach and Lieutenant [Vellum E.] Barrows, of my staff, were most conspicuous in closing the ranks, maintaining the lines, and pressing them against the enemy, while Lieutenant Driver, acting assistant adjutant-general twice ran the gauntlet of the terrific artillery fire in bringing fresh artillery.

I have been thus particular in describing the parts taken by the troops of this and other commands near by because I feel bound in justice to the men of my command, and those who assisted them on that day at that point, to claim for them what fortune gave them an opportunity to do and what their arms accomplished. While the attack was general and was repulsed along the whole line, still, the tremendous effort of the rebel chief was against the point which happened to be occupied by the Second and Third Brigades of the Second Division, Second Corps. It was fully repulsed in front of the Third Brigade, which then fell upon the partially successful enemy on the line of the Second Brigade, and, with the assistance before mentioned, drove him back, finishing the day there and completing the destruction of his splendid division and many of its supports. The attack was afterward renewed upon the left of the line, near Round Top, but without the vigor and desperation that characterized the previous effort.

In claiming for my brigade and a few other troops the turning point of the battle of July 3, I do not forget how liable inferior commanders are to regard only what takes place in their own front, or how extended a view it must require to judge of the relative importance of different points of the line of battle. The decision of the rebel commander was upon that point; the concentration of artillery fire was upon that point; the din of battle developed in a column of attack upon that point; the greatest effort and greatest carnage was at that point; and the victory was at that point.

No other inducement than the desire to do justice to troops who so nobly and at so dear a rate accomplished such a result, though their presence was primarily a matter of chance, would make me place myself in a position to defend an assertion generally so difficult to establish.

5. Colonel Arthur Devereux, commanding the 19th Massachusetts infantry in Hall's brigade, was in the thick of the fighting in the copse of trees and witnessed the surrender of a large number of Confederates. Report of Col. Arthur F. Devereux, Nineteenth

Massachusetts Infantry, July 7, 1863, *OR*, 1, 27, 1, 442-444.

Everything remained quiet on our front until 1 p. m., when, at a signal of a gun fired to our left, a most terrific cannonade commenced on the batteries and the troops in the center of our line, a portion of which was held by our brigade. It was the most terrific cannonading of the war. I have been told that one hundred and ten pieces of the enemy were firing upon our center at once. The men lay quiet and steady, and I am sure none of my regiment left the position where I ordered them to lie down. The cannonade lasted two hours.

The battery behind which we lay was disabled in the first hour's cannonading. The captain of it asked me if my men would volunteer to assist in manning his battery. I told him yes, and sent immediately 6 men to carry ammunition, and at a further call shortly after, 20 more to assist in working the pieces.

I desire here to mention the gallant conduct of Second Lieut. Moses Shackley, who insisted on joining the volunteers, walking from piece to piece, encouraging and assisting the men, although I told him that it was not required of him, and advised him to lie down with the regiment for shelter.

Just about 3 o'clock the enemy's cannonade slackened, and columns of attack appeared emerging from the woods across the open field in our front. They advanced gallantly upon our position, which was held firmly excepting immediately upon the right of our brigade line, at which point the left of the next brigade of our line seemed to give way in some confusion. Just then Major-General Hancock appeared on the left of my regiment. I ran to him, and asked permission to advance it to the point needed. Receiving it, I marched my regiment with all speed, obliquing to the right through the battery, and reached the desired point directly behind Colonel Mallon's regiment, which, being on my right when we started, had reached there first.

There was considerable confusion here, from the men running to the rear from the first line, and the two mentioned regiments coming up on a short space closely following each other, joined also by the Twentieth Massachusetts, having repulsed the enemy from their immediate front, but who still strongly pressed the attack at this point where our lines had given way. For an instant it seemed to hang in the balance whether we should drive the enemy out of our works, which they had entered, or they succeed in carrying the position; but I firmly believe that the extraordinary exertions of a few officers, among whom were conspicuous the brigade commander and staff, Lieutenant Haskell, of the division staff, Colonel Mallon, and some officers of my own regiment whom I saw, the line was carried back to the rifle-pits, driving the enemy out.

Just at this moment the enemy, as if actuated by one instinct, threw down their arms in a body, burst into our lines by hundreds, delivering themselves up as prisoners, and the battle was won, very few of the enemy attempting to retreat across the field to their own lines.

We must have killed, wounded, and captured the entire attacking column, with comparatively few exceptions. I might add here that when the enemy first broke our lines, and our men rallied to retrieve the lost ground, the enemy's artillery again opened on our troops collecting at that point, and continued to fire after the position was retaken, seemingly intended for their own troops, who had delivered themselves up in such numbers.

During the obstinate fight at this place, the two lines being actually hand to hand, my regiment captured four regimental colors from the enemy — one by Corpl. Joseph H. De Castro, Company I; another by Private John Robinson, Company I; another by Corpl. Benjamin F. Falls, Company A, and another by Private Benjamin H. Jellison, Company A.

A fifth one was handed to me by a sergeant of my regiment, but on representations from General Webb that he took the colors and gave them to my sergeant for safe-keeping, it has been delivered over to him. Three of the four taken by my regiment were taken from the hands of the rebel color-bearers, the fourth picked up beyond the stone wall. Three of these (the Fourteenth, Nineteenth, and Fifty-seventh Virginia, and marked with the numbers of their regiments, respectively) have been turned over to the brigade commander. The fourth I am unable positively to account for but have been informed was probably carried off the field by Major Rice when wounded, and by him taken home. That four were taken by my regiment, as above stated, I am sure, as I have minute statements in each case from company commanders whom I called on for a report.

It would be difficult to distinguish further than I have the individual officers and men under my command. The field and line officers universally and the men under my command behaved as steadily and as gallantly as men could do. I have but one instance of failure to report, that of Corporal [E. Augustus] Nichols, Company C, who was brought back, going to the rear, during the infantry fight.

6. Colonel James Mallon commanded the 42nd New York in Hall's brigade. He tells the story of his regiment and notes the courage of one individual in particular, a color-bearer. Report of Col. James E. Mallon, 42nd New York, July 16, 1863, *OR*, 1, 27, 1, 451-452.

. . . On the afternoon of the 3rd instant, about 1 o'clock, the enemy opened with a destructive artillery fire, which will ever be remembered by those subjected to its fury. After this fire, which lasted about four hours, had considerably slackened, the infantry of the enemy debouched from the woods to our front for the grand attack of the battle. This regiment was posted about 100 yards in rear of the front line. When those of the enemy who approached our brigade front had been successfully disposed of, and when those who had with great energy and persistence penetrated that portion of our line to our right, near the corps batteries, I caused the regiment to be formed in line facing the decisive point.

The line was but fairly established, and but just started in the direction of the contested point, when Colonel Hall, with words of encouragement, cheered us forward. With the impetus conveyed by these words, the regiment vigorously advanced, and in that charge which rescued our batteries from the hands of our foe, which saved our army from disaster and defeat, which gave to us glorious, triumphant success, this regiment was foremost and its flag in the advance.

The color-bearer, Sergt. Michael Cuddy, who established his great and superior courage in the first Fredericksburg battle, on this occasion displayed the most heroic bravery. When he fell, mortally wounded, he rose by a convulsive effort, and triumphantly waived in the face of the rebels, not 10 yards distant, that flag he loved so dearly, of which he was so proud, and for which his valuable life, without a murmur, was freely given up.

7. **Lieutenant Colonel Freeman McGilvery is one of the unsung Federal heroes of Gettysburg. His work with the 39 (or more) guns south of the copse of trees concentrated an enormous fire on Kemper's undefended men passing within easy range in front of them. He also describes his effective counter-battery fire. Also note that his estimate of 35,000 men in the charge is grossly inaccurate. Report of Lieut. Col. Freeman McGilvery, 1st Maine Light Artillery, Cmdg. First Volunteer Brigade, —, —, 1863, *OR*, 1, 27, 1, 883-884.**

. . . The line of batteries under my command, commencing on the left, which rested on an oak wood, occupied by our infantry, were, in numbers and kind of guns, as follows: Ames' battery, six light 12 pounders; Dow's Sixth Maine Battery, four light 12-pounders; a New Jersey battery, six 3-inch guns, one section New York [Pennsylvania] Artillery, Lieutenant Rock [Captain Rank], two 3-inch guns; First [Second] Connecticut, four James rifled and two howitzers; Hart's Fifteenth New York Independent Battery, four light 12-pounders; Phillips' Fifth Massachusetts, six 3-inch rifled guns; Thompson's battery, F and C, consolidated Pennsylvania Artillery, five 3-inch rifled guns; total, thirty-nine guns. In front of these guns I had a slight earthwork thrown up, which proved sufficient to resist all the projectiles which struck it, and the commanders of batteries were repeatedly ordered that, in the event of the enemy opening a cannonading upon our lines to cover their men as much as possible, and not return the fire until ordered.

. . . At about 3 p. m. a line of battle of about 3,000 or 4,000 men appeared, advancing directly upon our front, which was completely broken up and scattered by our fire before coming within musket range of our lines. Immediately after, appeared three extended lines of battle, of at least 35,000 men, advancing upon our center. These three lines of battle presented an oblique front to the guns under my command, and by training the whole line of guns obliquely to the right, we had a raking fire through all three of these lines. The execution of the fire must have been terrible, as it was over a level plain and the effect was plain to be seen. In a few minutes, instead of a well-ordered line of battle, there were broken and confused masses, and fugitives fleeing in every direction. This ended the operations of the batteries under my command at the battle of Gettysburg.

8. **Major Walter A. Van Rensselaer was part of Colonel Theodore Gates' 80th New York; he describes "following the parade" as well as a capture of a Confederate battle flag. Diary of Walter A. Van Rensselaer, Gettysburg National Military Park.**

Friday, July 3, 1863. Cloudy and warm. Very quiet during the morning. About 1 P. M. Johnny opened on us with 115 pieces of artillery — our Batteries replied — for four hours they poured on us a perfect shower of shell and solid shot, etc. The roar of the guns was almost deafening never witnessed anything of the kind that equaled it — 5 P. M. The enemy advanced a heavy line of skirmishers closely followed by long lines of Infantry. They steadily advanced obliquing to the left, forming two lines on their right. We followed up along the fence pouring in a tremendous fire. The old 20th took the lead. When near a slash of timber, I discovered a Rebel flag behind the fence in the hands of an officer — I demanded its surrender — he replied "not by a d__d sight!" and fired at me with his revolver, wounding me in the small of the back. I lunged at him with my sabre when he fired again, the ball striking my sabre scabbard — five or six of my boys came to the rescue and he

surrendered, followed by his whole regiment. — they came over the
fence like a flock of sheep — think we captured, at least, 1500
prisoners. Soon after a shell burst directly over and very near my
head knocking me senseless. I was taken to the 12th Corps Hospital
and placed under Dr. Tuthill's charge, who took excellent care of me.
Col. Gates and Lieut. Col. Hardenburgh behaved splendidly; they
led the whole of our forces.

**9. Like many of the troops on both sides, the 7th Michigan
had made a long, hot, and exhausting march before reaching
Gettysburg, and had not had anything to eat since the morning of
July 1st. Yet they fixed bayonets and engaged in hand-to-hand
combat along the wall and in the copse of trees. Report of Major
Sylvanus W. Curtis, Seventh Michigan Infantry, August 6, 1863.
OR, 1, 27, 1, 449-450.**

About 10.30 all firing ceased until 1 p. m, when the enemy
fired a signal gun from the right of their line, which was instantly
followed by the roar of all their artillery, which had been massed in
the edge of the woods opposite our line in such a manner as to bring
this regiment nearly in the center of their fire. Owing to our peculiar
situation in regard to their fire, not as much damage was done us
as would naturally be expected from such a storm of missiles.
Nearly all the shot and shell struck in front and ricocheted over us,
or passed over us and burst in our rear. This continued until 4 p.
m., when their infantry columns were advancing. Orders were given
the men to reserve their fire until the enemy were within short range.
They soon came within a very short distance, and our fire was
opened upon them with terrible effect, mowing them down by
scores. Still they came on till within a few yards of us, when the order
was given to fix bayonets. The men expressed a determination to
hold their works at all hazards. Many of the enemy at this time
crawled on their hands and feet under the sheet of fire, and, coming
up to our lines, surrendered themselves prisoners. The enemy, soon
finding our fire too hot for them, moved by the left flank, and joined
in the assault upon the crest of the hill, driving our line from its
position.

At this time Colonel Steele received an order to form the
regiment nearly at right angles to its then position, with the
intention of attacking the enemy's right flank, which had become
exposed. Owing to the great noise, the order was not understood by
any excepting those nearest Colonel Steele. The rest of the officers
seeing the men, as they supposed, retreating, made all efforts to
rally them. A part of them came back; the remainder kept on with

Colonel Steele, who advanced with them to the crest of the hill, when he fell, instantly killed by a bullet through his brain. The greater part of the regiment remained in their works and did great execution by a well directed fire upon the flanks of the enemy. The field was soon won and the enemy fleeing in great disorder. A great number of prisoners were taken, and a large amount of small-arms, ammunition was left upon the field.

The men by this time had become very much exhausted from previous long marches, constant watchfulness, and having been destitute of food nearly two days; yet all were cheerful, and worked during the night to improve their breastworks in anticipation of an attack next morning. Though but one spade could be obtained, the rails were nearly covered with earth by daylight.

Most of the men worked till late in the night in bringing in and caring for the wounded.

Our loss was 12 killed and 34 wounded, making the loss in both actions 21 killed and 44 wounded. The disproportionate number of killed arose from the fact that the men were partially protected by the breastwork of rails, and the greater part of them were consequently hit in the head and upper part of the body.

The 4th was spent in burying the dead, gathering up the arms left on the field, and taking care of the wounded.

Too much cannot be said in praise of the conduct of both officers and men. Where all did their duty to the fullest extent it would seem invidious to particularize. One instance deserves mention, not only for the bravery of the soldier but for the dastardly conduct of the officer concerned. Private William Deming, of Company F, during the assault on the crest of the hill, had shot a rebel color-bearer and taken the color from him. While loading his piece, with the flag by his side, a colonel rode up to him, and, menacing him with his saber, forced the color from him; even threatening to cut him down if he did not give it up. I regret to say that it was impossible to identify the officer alluded to. The act was witnessed by several who stood near.

10. Harrow's and Hall's brigades wheeled right, ran up the line of the stone wall and into the copse of trees, where desperate, face-to-face fighting occurred. Men on both sides were killed by friendly fire as Confederate artillery and Federal soldiers fired into the mass. Maj. Edmund Rice, "Repelling Lee's Last Blow At Gettysburg," *Battles and Leaders of the Civil War*, III, 387-390.

From the opposite ridge, three-fourths of a mile away, a line of skirmishers sprang lightly forward out of the woods, and with intervals well kept moved rapidly down into the open fields, closely followed by a line of battle, then by another, and by yet a third. Both sides watched this never-to-be-forgotten scene,—the grandeur of attack of so many thousand men. Gibbon's division, which was to stand the brunt of the assault, looked with admiration on the different lines of Confederates, marching forward with easy, swinging step, and the men were heard to exclaim: "Here they come!" "Here they come!" "Here comes the infantry!"

Soon little puffs of smoke issued from the skirmish line, as it came dashing forward, firing in reply to our own skirmishers in the plain below, and with this faint rattle of musketry the stillness was broken; never hesitating for an instant, but driving our men before it, or knocking them over by a biting fire as they rose up to run in, their skirmish line reached the fences of the Emmitsburg road. This was Pickett's advance, which carried a front of five hundred yards or more. I was just in rear of the right of the brigade, standing upon a large bowlder, in front of my regiment, the 19th Massachusetts, where, from the configuration of the ground, I had an excellent view of the advancing lines, and could see the entire formation of the attacking column. Pickett's separate brigade lines lost their formation as they swept across the Emmitsburg road, carrying with them their chain of skirmishers. They pushed on toward the crest, and merged into one crowding, rushing line many ranks deep. As they crossed the road, Webb's infantry, on the right of the trees, commenced an irregular, hesitating fire, gradually increasing to a rapid file firing, while the shrapnel and canister from the batteries tore gaps through those splendid Virginia battalions.

The men of our brigade, with their muskets at the ready, lay in waiting. One could plainly hear the orders of the officers as they commanded, "steady, men, steady! Don't fire!" and not a shot was fired at the advancing hostile line, now getting closer every moment. The heavy file firing on the right in Webb's brigade continued.

By an undulation of the surface of the ground to the left of the trees, the rapid advance of the dense line of Confederates was for a moment lost to view; an instant after they seemed to rise out of the earth, and so near that the expression on their faces was distinctly seen. Now our men knew that the time had come, and could wait no longer. Aiming low, they opened a deadly concentrated discharge upon the moving mass in their front. Nothing human could stand it. Staggered by the storm of lead, the charging line hesitated, answered with some wild firing which soon increased to a crashing roll of musketry, running down the whole length of their front, and then all that portion of Pickett's division which came within the zone of this terrible close musketry fire appeared to melt and drift away in the powder-smoke of both sides. At his juncture some one behind me gave the quick, impatient order: "Forward, men! Forward! Now is your chance!"

I turned and saw that it was General Hancock, who was passing the left of the regiment. He checked his horse and pointed toward the clump of trees to our right and front. I construed this into an order for both regiments—the 19th Massachusetts and the 42nd New York—to run for the trees, to prevent the enemy from breaking through. The men on the left of our regiment heard the command, and were up and on the run forward before the 42nd New York, which did not hear Hancock's order until Colonel Devereux repeated it, had a chance to rise. The line formation of the two regiments was partially broken, and the left of the 19th Massachusetts was brought forward, as though it had executed a right half-wheel. All the men who were now on their feet could see, to the right and front, Webb's wounded men with a few stragglers and several limbers leaving the line, as the battle-flags of Pickett's division were carried over it. With a cheer the two regiments left their position in rear of Hall's right, and made an impetuous dash, racing diagonally forward for the clump of trees. Many of Webb's men were still lying down in their paces in ranks, and firing at those who followed Pickett's advance, which, in the meantime, had passed over them. This could be determined by the puffs of smoke issuing from their muskets, as the first few men in gray sprang past them toward the cannon, only a few yards away. But for a few moments only could such a fire continue, for Pickett's disorganized mass rolled over, bent down, and smothered it.

One battle-flag after another, supported by Pickett's infantry, appeared along the edge of the trees, until the whole copse seemed literally crammed with men. As the 19th and 42nd passed along the brigade line, on our left, we could see the men prone in their places, unshaken, and firing steadily to their front, beating back the enemy. I saw one leader try several times to jump his horse over the line. He was shot by some of the men near me.

The two regiments, in a disorganized state, were now almost at right angles with the remainder of the brigade,—the left of the 19th Massachusetts being but a few yards distant,—and the officers and men were falling fast from the enfilading fire of the hostile line in front, and from the direct fire of those who were crowded in among the trees. The advance of the two regiments became so thinned that for a moment there was a pause. Captain Farrell, of the 1st Minnesota, with his company, came in on my left. As we greeted each other he received his death-wound, and fell in front of his men, who now began firing. As I looked back I could see our men, intermixed with those who were driven out of the clump of trees a few moments before, coming rapidly forward, firing, some trying to shoot through the intervals and past those who were in front.

The gap in the line seemed to widen, for the enemy in front, being once more driven by a terrible musketry in their very faces, left to join those who had effected an entrance through Webb's line.

The men now suffered from the enfilading fire of the enemy who were in the copse. Seeing no longer an enemy in front, and annoyed by this galling fire from the flank, the 7th Michigan and 59th New York, followed directly by the 20th Massachusetts and the regiments of Harrow's brigade, left their line, faced to the right, and in groups, without regimental or other organization, joined in the rush with those already at the edge of the clump of trees, all cheering and yelling, "Hurrah! for the white Trefoil!" (the badge of Gibbon's division—the Second, of the Second Corps—was a white trefoil.— Editors)

This was one of those periods in action which are measurable by seconds. The men near seemed to fire very slowly. Those in the rear, though coming up at a run, seemed to drag their feet. Many were firing through the intervals of those in front, in their eagerness to injure the enemy. This manner of firing, although efficacious, sometimes tells on friend instead of foe. A sergeant at my side received a ball to the back of his neck by this fire. All the time the crush toward the enemy in the copse was becoming greater. The men in gray were doing all that was possible to keep off the mixed bodies of men who were moving upon them swiftly and without hesitation, keeping up so close and continuous a fire that at last its effects became terrible. I could feel the touch of the men to my right and left, as we neared the edge of the copse. The grove was fairly jammed with Pickett's men, in all positions, lying and kneeling. Back from the edge were many standing and firing over those in front. By the side of several who were firing, lying down or kneeling, were others with their hands up, in token of surrender. I particular I noticed two men, not a musket-length away, one aiming so that I could look into his musket-barrel; the other, lying on his back, coolly ramming home a cartridge. A little farther on was one on his knees waving something white in both hands. Every foot of ground was occupied by men engaged in mortal combat, who were in every possible position which can be taken while under arms, or lying wounded or dead.

A Confederate battery, near the Peach Orchard, commenced firing, probably at the sight of Harrow's men leaving their line and closing to the right upon Pickett's column. A cannon-shot tore a horrible passage through the dense crowd of men in blue, who were gathering outside the trees; instantly another shot followed , and fairly cut a road through the mass. My thoughts were now to bring the men forward; it was but a few steps to the front, where they could at once extinguish that destructive musketry and be out of the line of the deadly artillery fire. Voices were lost in the uproar; so I turned partly toward them, and motioned to advance. They surged forward, and just then, as I was stepping backward with my face to the men, urging them on, I felt a sharp blow as a shot struck me, then another; I whirled round, my sword torn from my hand by a bullet or shell splinter. My visor saved my face, but the shock stunned me. As I went down our men rushed forward past me, capturing battleflags and making prisoners.

Pickett's division lost nearly six-sevenths of its officers and men. Gibbon's division, with its leader wounded, and with a loss of half its strength, still held the crest.

11. The discipline, spirit, and bravery of the Federal troops is highlighted in this report by the commander of the 20th Massachusetts in Hall's brigade. The Civil War soldier expected and honored the type of bravery described in Captain Henry Abbott's narration of the behavior of Lieutenant Henry Ropes. Report of Capt. Henry L. Abbott, Twentieth Massachusetts Infantry, July 16, 1863, *OR*, 1, 27, 1, 446-47.

After the repulse of the enemy on this night (the 2d), the regiment was moved up into the front line, where, during the night, with a single shovel, they threw up a slight rifle-pit, a foot deep and a foot high.

On the next day the regiment retained the same position.

About 2 p. m. the enemy opened a terrific cannonade, lasting perhaps two hours. The regiment lost only 4 or 5 men by this fire, being sheltered more by the slight depression in the ground where the pit was dug than by the earth thrown up, which was too thin to stop anything more than a spent ball.

After the cessation of the enemy's artillery fire, their infantry advanced in large force. The men were kept lying on their bellies, without firing a shot, until orders to fire came from Colonel Hall, commanding the brigade, the enemy having got within 3 or 4 rods of us, when the regiment rose up and delivered two or three volleys, which broke the rebel regiment opposite us entirely to pieces, leaving only scattered groups. When the enemy's advance was first checked by our fire, they tried to return it, but with little effect, hitting only 4 or 5 men.

We were feeling all the enthusiasm of victory, the men shouting out, "Fredericksburg," imagining the victory as complete everywhere else as it was in front of the Third Brigade, when Colonel Macy drew my attention to a spot some rods to the right of us, near a clump of trees, where the enemy seemed to have broken in. The regiment immediately got orders to face to the right and to file to the right, with the intention of forming a line at right angles with the original one; in other words, changing front to the right. The noise was such, however, that it was impossible to make any order heard. An order having been given, though it could not be heard, was naturally interpreted to be an order to retire and form a new line not outflanked by the enemy. The regiment accordingly retired some rods, but in the most perfect order. Perceiving, however, that an example could be seen, though words could not be heard, all the officers of the regiment rushed to the front, and without further formalities the regiment was hurried to the important spot. When they arrived there, there was a very thin line contending with the enemy, who was behind a rail fence, with the exception of a small number that climbed over, who were speedily dispatched. The enemy poured in a severe musketry fire, and at the clump of trees they burst also several shells, so that our loss was very heavy, more than half the enlisted men of the regiment being killed or disabled, while there remained but 3 out of 13 officers. Moreover, the contest round this important spot was very confused, every man fighting on his own hook, different regiments being mixed together, and half a dozen colors in a bunch, it being impossible to preserve a regimental line.

Notwithstanding these adverse circumstances, the men of this command kept so well together that after the contest near the trees, which lasted half an hour or so, was ended, I was enabled to collect, with the assistance of Lieutenant Summerhayes and Lieutenant Perkins, in an incredibly short period, nearly all the surviving men of the regiment and returned them to their original place in the pits. At the suggestion of Lieutenant Haskell, on the division staff I prepared to move back to the trees again, having 100 men collected together. This order was, however, countermanded by Colonel Devereux, commanding the left wing of the brigade, because of the second and last advance of the enemy on our extreme left, which happened only a very short time after the completion of our own success at the clump of trees. Without meaning to reflect on other regiments at all, I think it but fair to this command to state that I observed at the time that very few other regiments had even settled on a rendezvous for their scattered members.

It seems to me that great praise is due the enlisted men of this regiment for the speed with which they reorganized, for the discipline and *esprit de corps* which made them stick together in such a scene of confusion, where organization had been so completely broken up for the time. All the officers of the regiment behaved with the greatest gallantry, but I am enabled to select two, as their position or occupation made them more conspicuous than the rest. One of these (Captain Patten) I have already mentioned.

The other is First Lieut. Henry Ropes, who was shot dead. Never before has this regiment, in the death of any officer received one-half so heavy a blow. His conduct in this action, as in all previous ones, was perfectly brave, but not with the bravery of excitement that nerves common men. He was in battle absolutely cool and collected, apparently unconscious of the existence of such a reeling as personal danger, the slight impetuosity and excitability natural to him at ordinary times being sobered down into the utmost self-possession, giving him an eye that noticed every circumstance, no matter how thick the shot and shell; a judgment that suggested in every case the proper measures, and a decision that made the application instantaneous. It is impossible for me to conceive of a man more perfectly master of himself; more completely noting and remembering every circumstance in times when the ordinary brave man sees nothing but a tumult and remembers after it is over nothing but a whirl of events which he is unable to separate. Lieutenant Ropes' behavior in this battle was more conspicuous for coolness and absolute disregard of personal danger than I have ever witnessed in any other man. He entered the service remained in it until his death from the purest patriotism; not a single ambitious or selfish motive mingled with it. He would have made the noblest sacrifice where he knew that no man would even hear it as readily as if the eyes of the whole world were fixed upon him. Such perfect purity of sentiment deserves this distinguished mention; which Lieutenant Ropes himself would have been the last to expect.

I find it impossible to discriminate among the enlisted men, as all behaved so well (there being but 4 missing), and particularly as 7 company commanders, the only proper persons to report the behavior of their men, are absent, killed or wounded.

12.   Captain Patrick Hart commanded a battery in McGilvery's line. He describes the confusion over the correct tactics to be employed. Should they hold their fire and use their ammunition on the infantry when it charged, as Hunt wanted, or use it during the cannonade to boost the morale of the Federal forces, as Hancock wanted to do? He also describes his battery's work during the charge. Report of Capt. Patrick Hart, 15th New York Battery, August 2, 1863, *OR*, 1, 27, 1, 888.

Early on the morning of the 3d, I received orders by Major McGilvery's orderly to proceed to the front, which order I immediately obeyed. When I reached the front, not being able to find Major

McGilvery, I reported to Captain Thompson. He told me to come into position anywhere on his left, so as to leave room for Captain Phillips. I took position accordingly. A short time after, General Hunt, passing along the line, told me to hold my position and not to return the enemy's fire unless I saw his infantry advancing; then to open fire to the best advantage. This order was afterward repeated to me by Major McGilvery, which I obeyed, until ordered by General Hancock to open on the enemy's batteries. I obeyed this order, but after firing a few rounds Major McGilvery ordered me to cease firing. After the enemy opened with all of his batteries, I was ordered by Major McGilvery to return their fire which I did.

At this time Second Lieut. E. M. Knox and I were wounded; Lieutenant Knox severely and myself slightly. First Lieut. A. R. McMahon being at the rear in arrest, and in having no officer to place in charge of the right section, I placed ____ ____ in charge of it, and Sergt. William Sheehy in charge of the left. The conduct of the latter during that terrific day's fight is deserving of the highest praise.

While firing at the enemy's batteries I used solid shot and shell but when his infantry commenced to advance, I fired shell and shrapnel until the right of his first column came within about 500 yards of me, when I opened with canister, which took good effect. His second line appeared to be coming direct for my battery. I turned all my guns on this line, every piece loaded with two canisters. I continued this dreadful fire on this line until there was not a man of them to be seen.

At this time the enemy opened a battery on his right, in front of a barn, his projectiles killing many of my horses. I directed my fire on this battery and on his caissons which were partly covered by the barn. I candidly believe it was I who caused his caissons to explode and set the barn on fire. Immediately afterward he brought a section to bear on me. I brought all the guns of my battery to bear on this section. The first gun that I fired exploded one of his limbers. Corporal Hammond with the next shot dismounted, I believe, one of his guns. Sergt. William Sheehy, I believe, followed with equal success. There was not a gun fired or a man to be seen at this section afterward, until late in the evening, they sent down horses and took away one limber. My battery remained in position until near noon on the 4th, when I was ordered to the rear.

13. During the charge, the 5th Massachusetts Battery had a spectacular view of Kemper's men, who passed directly in front of them on their way north to the Angle. The enfilading fire from

McGilvery's line did massive injury to Kemper's men. Charles
Phillips, *History of the Fifth Massachusetts Battery*, 652-661.

This charge was made on our right, so that the rebels, in
crossing the fields, exposed their right flank to an enfilading fire
from our position.

As soon as the rebel line appeared, our cannoneers sprang
to their guns, and our *silenced* batteries poured in a rain of shot and
shell, which must have sickened the rebels of their work. I never saw
artillery so ably handled, or productive of such decisive results. It
was far superior even to Malvern Hill. For half an hour our line was
one continuous roar of artillery, and the shot ploughed through the
rebel ranks most terrifically. Then our infantry went in and repulsed
the rebels, taking a great many prisoners.

During this charge an event took place, which must have
convinced the rebel artillery officers that they had something to
learn. They advanced a 12 pdr. battery about 200 yards on our left,
and blazed away. We let them get well at work, and then the Major
turned four batteries on them, and in less than ten minutes not a
cannoneer was left to work the guns: all were dead or had
"skedaddled." The guns stood out in the field till late in the
afternoon, when we allowed the rebels to take them off, as it cost too
much ammunition to keep them off, and they could have removed
them after dark any way.

FROM NOTES OF CORPORAL SHACKLEY, 1863
THE WOUNDING OF JOHN M. CANTY

After the enemy had shelled our lines, and had begun their
advance, we commenced firing. John Canty was driver of the pole
team of the 1st caisson—the limber of the Gun was left on the field
on the previous day,—and was kneeling on his right knee, his right
arm behind the horse's left fore leg, his left hand holding the bridle
rein. Corporal Shackley, assisting No. 5 to serve ammunition, had
a Schenkle combination shell on the ground, between his knees,
trying to turn the cap to set the time-fuze, when a shell came and
took off the horse's leg above the knee, Canty's arm off above the
elbow, and the horse's right hind foot off above the ankle with such
force as to tear the shoe clear of the foot, and the shoe struck the
Corporal on his left wrist, and made him lame for nearly a week. The
skin was not broken, but turned very dark, the sleeve of his blouse
having protected it to some extent. The shell fell to the ground under
the Corporal's nose and he picked it up, and threw it away. Canty
died of his wound. The shell did not explode.

14. **Lieutenant Edwin Dow, commanding a battery in McGilvery's line south of the copse of trees, describes his guns' limited role but effective counter-battery fire during the charge. Report of Lieut. Edwin B. Dow, 6th Maine Battery, July 17, 1863, *OR*, 1, 27, 1, 898.**

After repairing damages and getting a new supply of ammunition, I reported to Major McGilvery on the morning of the 3d, and was ordered into position between the Second Connecticut Battery and Ames' (First New York) battery, supported by a brigade of the Second Corps. I built earthworks in front of my guns.

Nothing of importance occurred until about 11 o'clock, when, at a signal of one gun, the whole rebel line opened a most terrific fire upon our position. Case shot and shell filled the air. The men were ordered to cease firing and take refuge behind their earthworks. This fire lasted without much abatement about one hour and a half, when we discovered the enemy advancing under cover of the artillery. A light 12-pounder battery of four guns ran some 400 or 500 yards in front of the enemy's line, so as to enfilade the batteries on our right. We opened with solid shot and shell upon this battery, and succeeded in dismounting one gun, disabling the second, and compelled the battery to leave the field minus one caisson and several horses.

I deem it due to Major McGilvery to say that he was ever present, riding up and down the line in the thickest of the fire, encouraging the men by his words and dashing example his horse receiving eight wounds, of which he has since died, the gallant major himself receiving only a few scratches.

The enemy fired mostly case shot and shell at our position, nearly all of which passed over our line of artillery and supports and exploded in the woods behind, covering the road with their fragments. Our loss this day was only 5 men wounded and 5 horses killed.

Owing to an injunction from General Hunt not to reply to the enemy's fire, but save our ammunition, we expended only 13 rounds. In the two days' action we did not lose a gun or carriage, but reported for duty again as soon as our stock of ammunition was replenished. I was ably seconded by Lieutenant Rogers, to whom we owe much of our success.

15. **In combat, the individual often ceased to be part of a large unit and fought on his own, as Sergeant John Plummer recalls. John Plummer, *Rebellion Record*, 1861-1865, 179-181.**

Well, after firing about two hours and a half, they slackened up, and soon the order came "be ready for they are running," (their infantry.) We had expected it, and it was not many seconds before every man had on his armor, and was anxiously awaiting the coming of the foe. They had to advance more than half a mile across open fields. They came out of the woods in three lines, and advanced in good order till they got more than half way to us, and in good range of our muskets, which of course we used, as did the battery pour grape and canister, when they closed in to their left, and massed together for a charge, on the part of the line held by the Second Philadelphia brigade of our division. As they closed together, we (our brigade) marched by flank to confound them, firing at them continually, pouring most of our shot into their flank, where every shot must tell. The Second brigade gave way before the rebels got to them, and commenced to fall back. Our brigade was hurried up, and the Third were brought up to the rescue, and with the Second, which soon rallied again, we charged the rebels just as they had planted one of their colors on one of our guns. A Vermont brigade was sent out to flank them, which they did handsomely. The rebels, now seeing the position they had got in, threw away their guns and gave themselves up by hundreds, and thus ended the great assault of Lee on the third. Not enough went back of Pickett's division to make a good line of skirmishers. Another line came out on the left shortly afterwards, but they were repulsed as completely at the first, and with the exception of a little artillery firing, was the last of the fighting at Gettysburg.

During the assault the rebels poured into us lots of shell and grape from their batteries, but we scarce paid any attention to it, having all we could attend to in the infantry. Our boys felt bully during all the fight of the third, and no one thought of running or of the danger, except the Second brigade; and some of these regiments, Baxter Zouaves, for instance, never were known to stand fire. We took revenge for what they had done to our poor fellows the day before, and we never had had such a chance before. Most of us fired over twenty rounds, and at close range enough to do splendid execution; and if we didn't kill some Secesh in that battle we never did, and I fear never will during the war.

During the fight of the third, it might be said, almost, that every man fought on his own hook, for our division had been so used up the day before, that few officers were left. Generals Hancock and Gibbon were wounded early. Each man acted as though he felt what was at stake in the contest, and did all in their power to drive the enemy, without regard to officers, or whether there were any or not. Regiments all mixed up together, and in the last charge nearly all the flags of the division were together in a corner where the rebels got a hold. The flags of the rebel division were about the same, and when the assault was fully repulsed, they laid them on the ground in front of us, for anybody to get who chose, and, as might be expected, the brave men of the Second brigade were on hand to pick them up when there was no danger, and claim all the honor. They are welcome, though, to all they can get, for among those who knew them and saw them in the fight, they will have to show something besides flags to establish their bravery on that field. The sights on the battlefield were horrible, by far the worst of any field we have seen; but I have not the time or disposition to describe them. Never before were our batteries so used up. Some of them had not men, and horses enough for two guns, and the four batteries of our corps had to be consolidated into two before leaving the field.

16. **Battery B of the 1st Rhode Island artillery was devastated during the cannonade and pulled out of their position south of the copse of trees just as the charge began. Lance Corporal John Rhodes describes their journey through the chaos that existed just behind the Federal lines. John H. Rhodes, *The History of Battery B, First Regiment Rhode Island Light Artillery in the War to Preserve the Union, 1861-1865* (Providence: Snow and Farnham, 1894), 204-205.**

. . . As the battery was limbering up and retiring, the enemy's line of battle could be seen advancing from the woods on Seminary Ridge, three-fourths of a mile away. A line of their skirmishers sprang forward into the open field, closely followed first by one line of battle, then by a second, and then by a third line.

General Gibbon's division, which was to stand the brunt of the assault, looked with eager gaze upon their foe marching forward with easy swinging step, and along the Union line the men were heard to exclaim: "Here they come! Here comes the Johnnies!" Soon little puffs of smoke issued from the skirmish line, as it came dashing forward, firing in reply to our own skirmishers; it never hesitated for an instant but drove our men before it or knocked them over, by a biting fire, as they rose up to run in.

This was Pickett's advance, which carried a front of five hundred yards or more on that memorable charge of the Confederates against the Union centre. The repulse was one of the turning points against the Confederates, and helped to break the backbone of the Rebellion.

As Battery B was leaving the line of battle, the field in rear of its position was being swept by the enemy's shot and bursting shell. The gun detachments and drivers, in order to avoid this field, went with three pieces to the right (as they were facing to the rear) diagonally toward the Taneytown road. The other piece, of which the writer was lead driver at that time, instead of following the first three went to the left, down a cart-path, toward the same road.

We had not proceeded far when a rebel shell exploded on our right, and a piece of it struck the wheel driver, Charles G. Sprague on the forehead, cutting a gash from which the blood flowed copiously down his face, blinding him so that he could not manage his horses. He got on his horse, saying, "I cannot ride but will try to lead them." I asked the swing driver, Clark L. Woodmansee, to take the wheel horses and let his swing horses go alone. He did so, thus relieving Sprague. Then we started down the path again. The flash of the bursting shell, and the screeching of solid shot, which were flying thick and fast around us, caused the swing horses, now that they had no driver, to plunge frantically from one side to the other and then backward, entangling themselves in their traces and interfering greatly with our progress. Looking to my left I saw one of our cannoneers, a detached man from the One Hundred and Fortieth Pennsylvania Regiment, Joseph Brackell, lying beside a large boulder rock. I called to him to come and drive the swing horses as we could not get along. He came, and, after clearing the horses from their traces, mounted. This somewhat calmed the horses, and we started for the road again. When within a few rods of the road, where the path descended, a shell at our right exploded, and a piece cut through the bowels of the off wheel horse, another piece struck the nigh swing horse, which Brackell was riding, on the gambrel joint breaking the on leg. Still another piece swept across the saddle of my off horse cutting the feed-bags loose, whereby I lost my cooking utensils and extra rations. Whipping up my horses I shouted to the other drivers? "Let's get into the road!" We continued and finally swung around into the road, which was three feet lower than the field. Here the wheel horse dropped dead, and we could go no further. Having, cleared the horses from the piece, we were about changing the harnesses from the dead and wounded horses to the uninjured swing horse, when a shot struck the gun-wheel taking out a spoke, and then went screeching into the woods. This was followed by a shell exploding in the woods in our rear. The horses were frightened, and Woodmansee's ran down the road, me after him. Brackell, who had changed the saddles from his crippled horse to a sound one, now mounted and followed Woodmansee. The poor crippled horse, seeing his mate going off, hobbled on trying hard to keep up. Being thus left alone I could do nothing, so mounted and, leaving the piece where it was, went down the road hoping to find the battery. I found the road anything but pleasant to travel, for shot and shell were flying about quite lively.

On reaching a barn, on the west side of the road, used as the headquarters of the Artillery Brigade of the Second Corps, and also as a hospital, I found behind it several staff officers, aides, and some cavalry, and asked them for Battery B. They pointed down the road. Meeting Woodmansee we kept on together. We had not gone far before we heard a crash and report, and, on looking back, saw men and horses, which were back of the above mentioned barn, scattering in all directions. A shell struck a corner of the barn and exploded. Not far from the barn, in an opening among the woods on the east side of the Taneytown road, and about a mile from our position on the battle-field, we found Battery B parked and the men in bivouac, some already having the shelter tents up. I reported that one of our pieces was left up in the road near General Meade's headquarters.

17. Men fought on their own; no commanders were necessary, according to Daniel Bond, a private in the 1st Minnesota. As part of Harrow's brigade, they were south of Hall's brigade, but rushed over to the copse of trees with the rest. Daniel Bond, "Bonds Recollection," Minnesota Historical Society.

. . . We rose to our feet moved for each a few paces to where there was a sort of stone fence which was only a little above the ground but on top of which we had pulled rails which had however been displaced in many places by the rebel artillery. They were coming directly towards us, and having some extra cartridges which I had picked up on the field I laid them on the ground before me and kneeled behind the fence rested my gun across a rail and waited their approach. Never in my life have I felt so strong as I did at that minute as I looked along our lines and saw that the whole fences was bristling with guns. And that at the soldiers were calmly waiting the onset. I stole a glance at the countenances of those who were next to me I saw there nothing but a determination to do or to die. Here was the old 2nd Corps not over 2000 strong. Waiting patiently the approach of 30,000 of the best troops in the rebel army and as good soldiers as the world ever saw. (but we had the advantage of position) When they had reached a point about 300 yards distant one of our boys fired at them. Lieutenant Ball spoke out commanding us not to fire yet. "They are not close enough" I took a look at them and turned to the Lieutenant and said "We can throw our balls through their ranks every shot from here." "Fire away then" It seemed that the whole corps had come to the same conclusion for the entire line fired at once. They were coming at double quick time if not on the run. They changed their course and moved to our right directing their attack against Cemetery Hill where was posted Battery A, 4th U.S. Art. and Battery I, 1st U.S. (Ricketts, formerly

Magruders celebrated in time of the Mexican War) We wanted no command but moved to our right to meet them sending bullets into their ranks as fast as we could load and fire. They rushed up with such [impetuousness?] that they planted their colors on two pieces of Battery A. There they had seemed to mass on that point and we had [?] them with a thin semicircle. They could never lift their colors from these guns so deadly was our fire. Every man fighting on his own hook. Gibbon and Hancock both fell severely wounded. But we had no more need for a commander for we would now have achieved the victory had we been left without an officer for we could see every movement of the enemy and know how to defend our hills. In short we did the rest of the commanding ourselves. About this time a bullet passed through the leg of my pants. I soon after passed by Hezekiah he was laying down resting and loading his gun. I saw a spot of blood on his pants leg and asked him if he was wounded he said not. I told him I guessed he was and rushed on towards the enemy's flags 2 of which I was very anxious to secure a specimen to shake in Lieut. Ball's face. But I was not to be so highly favored. When I approached within a few steps of their flags I saw our old friend H. J. W. Brown firing as if his whole soul were bound up in the distruction of the rebel army. Close by was Jackson of Co. G. Covered with dust and dirt and blacked with powder fighting like he might have been a descendant of the *Hero* of the same name. My own gun had become so heated that I could hardly hold it in fact I had a bullet part way down but could not push it on. Jackson yelled "why don't you shoot?" this was sound advice but I was too much interested in securing a flag to heed it. I pushed on and reached the wall just a little to the left of where the flag was. Directly[?] behind there was twenty rebels jumped up without their guns. Holloring don't shoot. Do not take this to that I mean to say that twenty men surrendered to me. (I am not that kind of hero and God forbid that I ever should be.) But I was on this occasion the first one to the wall and the rebels knew when I appeared that our men would not fire on them should they spring up and surrender. We never attempted to guard them to the rear, but just told them to run back being the duty of the collecting for the provost guards. But to the right of the flags the rebels were still fighting and I saw one loading his gun with his eye fixed on the particular flag which was nearest to me. And I stopped put my ramrod against the stone wall and pushed the bullet home capped my gun and raised my eyes the rebels to the right of the flag were all passing through our lines minus their guns. And Marshall Sherman of Co. C had my prize. The rest of the flags were gobbled up by other soldiers so that out of the 28 stands which were taken by our corps I did not get a rag. Two more men had been wounded with our own colors. The staff of our flag had been shot in two. We had lost half the men in our corps and had taken more prisoners then there was of us and had killed and wounded more than we had taken. We had left the artillery on our left without protection in order to repel this fierce assault And now a division of rebels made a dash at it but we run down and before I could get there running my best those which were nearer had repulsed and captured. . . .

18. As the Federal troops south of the copse of trees moved north, they used bayonets, cobble stones, and any other weapons they could to stop the Confederate drive to break their lines. William Lochran, "Narrative of the First Regiment," *Minnesota in the Civil and Indian Wars* (n.p.: n.p, n.d.), 36-38.

On the morning of July 3d we were joined by company F, and by all men of the regiment who were detailed about brigade, division or corps headquarters, and Capt. Nathan S. Messick was in command. The morning opened bright and beautiful, with firing near the Little Round Top, and with a sharp fight on the right near Culp's Hill, where the enemy was forced back from positions gained the evening before. Soon after sunrise we were moved to our place in our brigade in the front line, passing Stannard's new brigade of Vermont troops as it was taking position to the left of our division under a sharp artillery fire from the enemy, which was turned on us also. The Vermont Brigade consisted of full regiments in new uniforms, and was therefore noticeable in contrast with the thinned regiments, in dusty garments, of the Second Corps. Reaching our place in the line, we made a slight barricade of stones, fence rails and knapsacks filled with dirt a little over knee-high, and, lying down behind it, many were soon asleep. During the forenoon there was a slight skirmish in our front in which some buildings used for cover by Confederate sharpshooters were burned. But suddenly, about one o'clock, a tremendous artillery fire opened along Seminary Ridge, all converging upon the position of the Second Division of the Second Corps. It was at once responded to by our artillery, whose position was on ground a little higher to the rear of our position. About one hundred and fifty pieces on each side were in action, firing with great rapidity, the missiles from both sides passing over us, except those of the enemy, which struck or burst at or in front of our line. We had been in many battles, and thought ourselves familiar with the roar of artillery, and with the striking and bursting of its missiles, but nothing approaching this cannonade had ever greeted our ears. In the storm of shells passing over us to the position of our artillery, where caissons were struck and burst every few moments, it did not seem that anything could live at that place. But our own artillery was served as rapidly, and we had the satisfaction of detecting the sound of bursting caissons on the enemy's side very frequently. Men will grow accustomed to anything; and before the two hours of this furious cannonade were ended some of the most weary of our men were sleeping. At length our artillery ceased to reply. We were surprised at this, thinking that we excelled the enemy in this arm. The Confederate fire appeared to increase in volume and rapidity for a few minutes, and then stopped at once. We well knew what was to follow, and were all alert in a moment, every man straining his eyes toward the wood, three-fourths of a mile distant, from which the Confederate infantry began to emerge in heavy force, forming two strong lines, with a supporting force in rear of each flank. We then estimated the force as over 20,000 men, though Confederate accounts reduce the number to 15,000. Moving directly for our position, with firm step and in perfect order, our artillery soon opened upon them with terrible effect, but without causing any pause, and we could not repress feelings and expressions of admiration at the steady, resolute style in which they came on, breasting that storm of shell and grape, which was plainly thinning their ranks. When about sixty rods distant from our line our division opened with musketry, and the slaughter was very great; but instead of hesitating, the step was changed to double-quick, and they rushed to the charge. But whether because Hancock here wheeled Stannard's Vermont Brigade to enfilade their right flank in passing, or from some other cause, their front opened at this time, and perhaps one-fourth of the force on Pickett's right here deflected further to their right, and were met and disposed of by the gallant Vermonters. The remainder of the charging force at the same time diverged or changed its direction to its left, and, passing from our front diagonally, under our fire and that of Hall's Brigade to our right, charged the position held by Webb's Second Brigade of our division, forcing back the Sixty-ninth and Seventy-first Pennsylvania regiments, and capturing Cushing's Battery, which had swept them with canister. But as soon as Pickett's force had passed our front, our brigade (Harrow' s) ran to the right for the threatened point, passing in rear of Hall's Brigade, which, as soon as uncovered, wheeled to the right to strike the enemy's flank. So that, by the time the Confederates had captured Cushing's Battery, our brigade, mingled with Webb's, was in front of it in a strong, though confused, line at a few rods distance. Just here we were joined by Capt. Farrell with Company C of our regiment, the division provost guard, who had promptly obeyed Gibbon's order to join the regiment in resisting this attack. The fire from both sides, so near to each other, was most deadly while it lasted. Corp. Dehn, the last of our color guard, then carrying our tattered flag, was here shot through the hand, and the flagstaff cut in two. Corp. Henry D. O'Brien of Company E instantly seized the flag by the remnant of the staff. Whether the command to charge was given by any general officer I do not know. My impression then was that it came as a spontaneous outburst from the men, and instantly the line precipitated itself upon the enemy. O'Brien, who then had the broken staff and tatters of our battle flag, with his characteristic bravery and impetuosity sprang with it to the front at the first sound of the word charge, and rushed right up to the enemy's line, keeping it noticeably in advance of every other color. My feeling at the instant blamed his rashness in so risking its capture. But the effect was electrical. Every man of the First Minnesota sprang to protect its flag, and the rest rushed with them upon the enemy. The bayonet was used for a few minutes, and cobble stones, with which the ground was well covered, filled the air, being thrown by those in the rear over the heads of their comrades. The struggle, desperate and deadly while it lasted, was soon over. Most of the Confederates remaining threw down their arms and surrendered, a very few escaping. Marshall Sherman of Company C here captured the colors of the Twenty-eighth Virginia Regiment. Our men were at once most kind and attentive to the three or four thousand captured Confederates, giving them refreshments from canteens and haversacks. Our loss in killed and wounded in this day's fight was seventeen. Among the killed was Capt. Nathan S. Messick, our commander; also Capt. Wilson B. Farrell, who succeeded to the command on the fall of Capt. Messick, both most gallant and capable officers. Our color guard had suffered severely in the battle. When the charge on July 2d was ordered, Sergt. Ellett P. Perkins, who had seized the colors at Antietam when Sam Bloomer was wounded, and had borne them bravely through every intermediate battle, still carried them. He and two corporals of the color guard succeeding him in carrying the colors were struck down in that charge. Corp. Dehn, the last of the color guard, carried the flag; that night, and in the repelling of Pickett's charge, until wounded in the hand when the flagstaff was cut in two as stated. Corp. O'Brien, who then seized the flag, received two wounds in the final *melee* at the moment of victory; but the flag was grasped by Corp. W. N. Irvine of Company D. The staff was spliced by the staff of a Confederate flag on the battlefield, and so carried till the regiment was mustered out, and still remains with the same splice in the capitol at St. Paul. With the repulse of Pickett's charge the serious fighting of the battle of Gettysburg ended.

19. The counter-charge by Stannard's Vermont brigade on Kemper's right wrecked havoc and undoubtedly played a key role in the repulse of the charge. Private Ralph Sturtevant of the 13th Vermont recalls the tense expectations before the charge, the sight of Kemper's men coming over the hill in their front and the orders to hold their fire yelled by Federal commanders. The immensely destructive volleys let loose at a range of 60 yards becomes less impersonal as Sturtevant records the argument over who killed Garnett. Finally, Sturtevant describes the incredible situation of the front line firing into Pickett's ranks while the back line faces about and fires at Wilcox and Lang in their rear. R. O. Sturtevant, *Pictorial History of the 13th Regiment Vermont Volunteers* (Burlington: The Self-Appointed Committee of Three, 1911), 259-264.

Two mighty armies numbering 100,000 each, composed of the best, most intelligent and the flower of the grandest and most progressive civilized nation of the world equipped with every known appliance of destruction spread out over an open country of cultivated fields as far as the eye could see. The whole battlefield could be plainly viewed from Round Top to Cemetery Hill, and much of the preparation for the final and desperate struggle on the last day was in plain view of the 13th regiment of Stannard's brigade. General Stannard's brigade saw and heard and were in the midst of the very center of the fiercest struggle, and witnessed and realized that which no person can possibly describe so as to paint and convey the awful scenes of the closing hours of that great battle. . . .

The left flank of General Stannard's brigade was well down on the low flat ground of Plum Run behind a thick copse that lined its banks and mostly out of sight of the enemy, and therefore suffered but little from Longstreet's artillery. . . .

The two long hours of cannonading was so appalling and fraught with constant apprehension, that the passing of each minute seemed a life time. We of the 13th now realized the value of the low breastwork of rails that protected us during the deadly storm and were grateful to Lieutenant Albert Clark and Sergeant George H. Scott and their associates for their foresight and timely efforts. Suddenly the cannon ceased on Cemetery Hill and from battery to battery all along our lines until every Federal gun was silent followed in a few moments with complete suspension of Confederate cannonading. We knew the time had come for the final charge and eagerly gazed and watched the crest of Seminary Ridge across the valley expecting each moment to see the long lines of gray with tilted bayonets glistening in the sunshine rapidly approaching. Every eye was scanning the open fields directly in front of Stannard's brigade beyond the Emmetsburg Road as if momentarily expecting to see moving columns pressing forward in the final charge. Commanding officers with their staffs and aides on elevated positions with field glasses to their eyes were intently looking westward along the crest of Seminary Ridge to catch the first glimpse of the expected foe. . .

. . . It was now about 3:30 o'clock in the afternoon comparative silence prevailed over the field and the Union army was intently watching and waiting the expected charge. The dread spell of silence suddenly gave way to excitement and activity from Cemetery Hill to Round Top and like the rush of a mighty wind the word came down our lines "See they are coming." Involuntarily every eye was quickly turned to the undulating crest of the low ridge across the valley that extended from west of Gettysburg village around to Big Round Top nearly parallel to Cemetery Ridge and between the two ridges the low valley of Plum Run distant from ridge to ridge three fourths of a mile. There all that was still and motionless before was now animated with excitement and hurrying to and fro on every part of the field. Hurried orders came from commanders and almost at the same moment the officers and the rank and file were told of the approaching charge before it could be seen only by those on Cemetery Hill and Round Top. Not one of the many thousands that wore the blue but what were ready and anxious for the mortal combat (knowing it must come) to commence that it might be settled then and there, who should be crowned with victory.

The long day of suspense was terrible and all longed to see the charging columns attempt to cross the open field which we believed to be an impassable gulf in the face of one hundred cannon belching forth solid shot, exploding shells and grape and canister, and the solid lines of infantry thickly massed on the slopes from crest to valley prepared to mow down General Lee's approaching battle lines when in range of musket ball.

We saw them first as they reached the crest of Seminary Ridge a full half mile away, at first horse and rider, then glistening bayonets and then flags and banners waving and fluttering in the sultry air could be seen.

Suddenly a battery opened on Cemetery Hill with deafening roar, and sent hurling across the valley into the approaching columns the first complimentary salute that warned them that all of our guns had not been silenced by their hundred and fifty guns during the early hours of the afternoon, but on they come regardless of exploding shells hurled against them, turning not to the right or left climbing the fences and walls, quickly reached the Emmitsburg Road, passed on both sides of the Cadora House and other buildings in that locality making momentary openings in their lines as they fast and the front line hesitated, moved slowly and melted away, could not advance against such a curious and steady storm of bullets in their faces and the raking fire of McGilvery's batteries against their flank and midst this, unexpected fusillade of bullets, grape and canister they halted and quickly in good order massed in columns to our right uncovering the immediate front of Stannard's brigade and with an awful menacing yell dashed forward with the evident purpose of carrying the crest of Cemetery Ridge at our right and rear.

Pickett's massing of columns and merging to his left and our right opened a clear field in front of Stannard's brigade, furnishing a golden opportunity for a flank advance attack against General Pickett's advancing battle lines.

General Stannard ordered the 13th and 16th regiments of his brigade to move forward (the 14th to remain in position in support) toward the enemy, and these two regiments the 13th and 16th, advanced about one hundred yards in quick time, the 13th on the double-quick and moved first, the 16th being at the left of the brigade did not receive the order as soon by some minutes as the 13th, and this advance movement while the 13th was still in motion was quickly followed by a more important order which was given first to the 13th regiment. As General Stannard looked over the field his quick eye discovered the salient angle, and like a flash of lightning came the inspired thought that evolved the famous and now historic order (unique in maneuvering in the midst of battle) "Change front forward on first company."

Colonel Randall repeated this order to Captain Lonergan of Company A and sent it along the line. Captain Lonergan on receiving the order halted his which was the right of the line placed First Sergeant James B. Scully in position and quickly swung his company around into position and thus each company was brought into line facing the right flank of General Pickett's advancing heroes and each company as it faced into line saw in their immediate front not sixty yards away General Pickett's command charging forward up the slope and at once opened a deadly fire on their flank which surprised and disconcerted officers and rank and file alike some turned about and returned our fire but knowing their objective point moved on. This was at short range and the concentrated fire of the 13th into the moving flank before them thickly covered the ground with the dead and wounded until General Pickett's command had lost most of its distinguished officers and a large per cent. of its rank and file. It was while our regiment was firing into Pickett's flank that brave General Garnet fell from his horse pierced with a minnie ball and General Armistead too as he scaled the wall fell into the ranks of the blue with cap on his sword urging his men to follow.

Not until the dead and wounded covered the ground so as to

passed. They crossed the road, reached the open field before them, moved rapidly forward in solid columns the first and second divisions in advance, and then the third in support in short echelon as they moved down the slope into the valley from the Emmitsburg Road. The charging columns were now in plain sight and range of our guns from Round Top to Ziegler's Grove which with an infilading fire made numerous gaps in their lines which were quickly closed, but on they came as if impelled by some unresistless force, paying no attention to the grape and canister that made gory swaths through their battle lines. This was the animated opportunity for our artillery and with a flash and roar they improved it. We of Stannard's brigade against whom the right wing of General Pickett's chargers seemed to be pointed for, wondered if it would be possible for any to pass through the iron storm that assailed them. They were now in plain view, but we only knew that they were the selected veteran heroes of General Lee's great army. We soon learned that these serried columns coming down the slope into the valley of slaughter and death were the gallant warriors that on many a sanguinary field had made the charge that secured victory, now being led by General George E. Pickett, the one of all the veteran officers of the great army of Northern Virginia personally selected by General Lee to command and lead the flower of his army in whom was centered all his hopes on this field,—they were to him like Napoleon's body guard at Waterloo. . . .

Pettigrew and Trimble's . . . with steady step and undaunted courage boldly pushed forward down the slope across the valley into the very mouths of belching cannon, leaped the wall among the cannoneers and mingled with gunners and infantry men of the blue with sword, pistol, musket and bayonet in a life and death struggle for vantage ground. . . .

No such sight in all the history of battles had ever been seen. On they came regardless of the carnage among them, nearer and nearer until horse and rider, officer and private, standards and banners waving in the lead were plainly seen, and almost within musket range, the right wing now face to face with the right wing of Stannard's brigade. Down the line of the 13th regiment comes the order from company to company "Steady boys, hold your position, don't fire until the word is given, keep cool, lie low till order is given to fire, make ready, take good aim, fire low." Then like an electric flash came down the line the order from Colonel Randall quickly repeated by every officer in the line "Fire," up rose the Green Mountain Boys, 3,000 strong as if by magic with forms erect took deliberate aim and with a simultaneous flash and roar fired into the compact ranks of the desperate foe and again and again in quick succession until a dozen or more volleys had been discharged with deadly effect. We saw at every volley the grey uniforms fall quick and make progress almost impossible did they seem to realize their awful situation and then they waved handkerchiefs and threw up their hands as evidence of surrender. It was at this juncture that Colonel Randall at risk of his own life from the muskets of his own regiment passed rapidly down the line and shouted "Stop firing." Then we advanced and captured nearly all that still survived of Pickett's old division. It is claimed that of all the field officers in Pickett's division only one (a Major) came out without injury. ... The numbers we here captured were so large that Colonel Randall detailed Companies G and I to take the prisoners to the rear.

From the moment General Pickett's command crossed the Emmitsburg Road and started on its perilous charge to the time we of the 13th returned to our position just in the rear of the breastwork of rails full two hours must have passed. Every moment was so appalling and the horrid scenes all about us so dreadful we took no thought of swift passing time. The carnage was terrible but wonderful and glorious the results.

As the 13th charged forward from its last position where it had been pouring in volley after volley at short range from musket and pistol (the officers of the line now had an opportunity to use their pistols with deadly effect and right well they improved it and many of them were skilled and accurate marksmen) realizing (though many had indicated their willingness and anxiety to surrender) that some of the more revengeful and desperate continued to fire in our faces as we advanced. We opened fire again and then rushed up against them With bayonets pushed forward revengefully determined to slay the very last man unless they would heed their proffered offer of surrender. Bayonets were crossed and the desperate thrusts exchanged and the hand to hand struggle followed. Many fell wounded and bleeding pierced with bayonet sword and pistol and musket balls. This was the final struggle and was soon over. We were now in their front and rear and escape was impossible. The crouching rose up and all the living including the slightly wounded hurriedly and anxiously passed through our ranks to the rear turning over their guns pistols and sabres as they passed on. The author was there and fully alive to duty and self preservation and saw for himself the dreadful havoc before him. If there was any spot on that great field of battle that approximated more nearly than any other the maelstrom of destruction this was the place. They lay one upon the other clutched in death side by side. The dead dying and horribly wounded some had on the blue but nearly all wore the gray for on a few square rods one could hardly step so thickly lay the dead. A thousand could have been counted on less than two acres of ground. This was indeed the great slaughter pen on the field of Gettysburg and in it lay hundreds of the brave heroes who an hour before buoyed up with hope and ambition were being led by the brave and intrepid General Pickett against solid phalanxes of infantry and a hundred belching cannon and the strong bulwarks of their foe as they fully believed to victory.

Brave General Garnett who was shot from his horse while leading his brigade fell only a few paces in the rear of the stone wall where General Armistead was shot and no doubt from bullets fired from the 13th Vermont Regiment who at that moment was on Pickett's flank firing at short range in that direction. First Corporal Londas S. Terrill of Company F claims the honor (if it be an honor to shoot so brave a soldier) of firing the bullet that so suddenly ended the brilliant career of this young Rebel officer. Corporal Terrill says he took deliberate aim fired and Garnet fell. It was as likely Terrill's gun as any but no man could possibly tell whether the gun he fired fell the person aimed at or not. Seven hundred rifles in the skillful hands of the 13th regiment were sending a continuous rain of bullets in the same direction. Private Oliver Pariso of Company K (and there was no better shot in the regiment) claimed that he too about the same time took aim at a mounted officer and saw him fall while looking along the sight of his gun barrel, Pariso's honesty and. veracity was never questioned, and it may be true that his deadly aim reached the very mark, but the surroundings and flying bullets that filled the air removes every probability of certainty.

Private Cadmus S. Gates of Company K also was confident because of peculiar situation that one officer fell as the result of his careful aim. Indeed many of the boys claimed just after the battle they had fell their man and some a half a dozen or more. The author also took good aim and saw many a poor fellow fall, and the bullets he fired into the solid ranks of General Pickett's brave boys may have killed one or more, but he has ever since been happy in the thought that he could not tell the result of his firing; eternity alone can reveal the fact. It is enough to know that hundreds fell by the hands of boys that fought in the ranks of the gallant 13th on that memorable charge. Quite a number of the boys brought from the field pistols, sabres and guns and other mementos recovered in the charge or scattered over the field, but all to no particular purpose excepting in the case of Lieutenant Stephen F. Brown of Company K who was armed up to the end of this charge with only a common camp hatchet (having been relieved of his sword while on the march some days before, the particulars of which are mentioned elsewhere in this book) and he wanted a sword, and as one of General Pickett's Lieutenants approached and was about to pass as a prisoner within our lines, Lieutenant Brown demanded his sword. The officer in gray hesitated, saw the upraised hatchet as it glistened in the sun and then quickly unbuckled his belt and passed belt, sword and scabbard and pistol to Lieutenant Brown, said not a word and passed on. Lieutenant Brown buckled on the belt, dropped the hatchet and took the sword and thereafter carried it until mustered out. The author was near and saw this singular and timely capture of sword and pistol and exchange of an aboriginal implement of warfare (a hatchet) for the more modern and less savage, a sword.

Marvelous and unusual incidents occurred in connection with General Pickett's charge, one of which was General Stannard's original and famous order "Change front forward on first company" has already been mentioned, and I call attention to a more unique and strange Occurrence while out on General Pickett's flank. . . . Very soon after the 16th passed in the immediate rear of the 13th into position there appeared some four hundred yards to the rear having just crossed the Emmitsburg Road and moving rapidly down into the valley charging forward in the direction of Cemetery Ridge a large body of soldiers who we at once recognized by the uniforms they wore and the flags and banners they carried and the yell they made as the enemy exposing their left flank to our view in passing. At this juncture the unheard of happened namely those standing in the rear rank of the 13th and 16th regiments who had been firing into General Pickett's flanks as they turned half way around to load their guns discovered the passing Rebel column in the rear and without orders faced square to the rear and opened fire causing dismay and confusion and hesitancy and thus it was with the front ranks of the 13th and 16th were sending bullets thick and fast into General Pickett's right flank causing fearful slaughter because of good aim and short range the rear ranks of the 13th and 16th regiments at the same time were facing in an opposite direction and with steady aim firing as rapidly into the charging left flank of the belated columns that had come in support of General Pickett's right flank with equal effect. For a time the 13th and 16th stood in line in double ranks across Plum Run valley extending from near the base of Cemetery Ridge to within a few rods of the Emmitsburg Road the front rank facing northerly towards Gettysburg village and firing into Pickett's huddled struggling ranks and the rear rank facing southerly towards Peach Orchard Devil's Den Big Round Top deliberately and steadily firing into the left flank of what proved to be General Wilcox's brigade and command. This was an accidental situation but who were inborn fighters would have so suddenly taken advantage of so good an opportunity and made use of it as an expected duty. Yet, as once before said the boys of the Second Vermont Brigade who carried guns in that memorable charge inherited the same intuitive ability and prowess as shown on that field by their beloved and highly respected commander General George J. Stannard.

Section VI

"The Colors Were Planted On The Works":

The Charge Of Pettigrew's And Trimble's Divisions

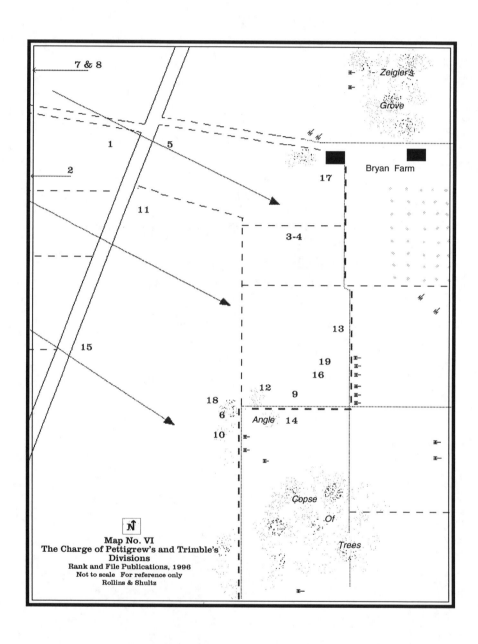

7 & 8

Zeigler's

Grove

1

5

2

17

Bryan Farm

11

3-4

13

19

16

15

12

18

9

6

Angle

14

10

N

Copse

Map No. VI
The Charge of Pettigrew's and Trimble's
Divisions
Rank and File Publications, 1996
Not to scale   For reference only
Rollins & Shultz

Of

Trees

1. Major General Isaac Trimble, at 61 years one of the oldest men at Gettysburg, had been wounded in 1862 and just returned to the army. Thus, he had marched to Gettysburg a Major General with no command. When he heard that two divisions had lost their commanders on the 2nd, he asked Lee for one. Lee gave him the division formerly led by Major General William Dorsey Pender. He recorded the events in his diary, including his wounding close to the stone wall. Isaac R. Trimble, "Civil War Diary of I. R. Trimble," *Maryland Historical Magazine*, XVII(1922), 1-2.

On Thursday Longstreet got up & gained considerable advantage over the enemy's left and drove them. Johnson's and Early's div. attempted on the evening to drive the enemy from his position on his right, but found him too strongly defended by triple lines. Friday it was decided that Longstreet should make a vigorous assault on the enemy's left. after a furious cannonade of 2 hours this attack was made, our troops marching over open fields (exposed at every step to a most destructive fire) for a mile. This distance broke down the men and exhausted & ranks thinned, they only reached the enemy's line in small numbers and were repulsed — The error was in charging over so broad a space. Had the troops marched at night to 1/2 mile of the works & charged vigorously by day break we must have carried the lines on the enemy's left — Hill's corps was not engaged on Friday. The enemy were so shattered that any show of an attack on Saturday would have compelled Meade to fall back. As it was Genl. Lee, decided to fall back & cross the Potomac which was done, without any interruption — no doubt Genl. Meade did not wish to attack him.

[July 2nd {3rd?}] I heard that Genl. Heth & Pender were wounded & applied to Genl. Lee for one of the Div. He promptly put me in command of Penders. I took command at 12, went into the fight on the extreme left at 12 30; after the terrible artillery fire ceased at 2 made the charge on the batteries. I took in 2 N. C. Brigades, Prince's & Lanes, as the supporting force. We marched 3/4 mile under a terrible fire passed the first line & reached a point some 200 yards from the breast works — here the men broke down from exhaustion & the fatal fire & went no further but walked sullenly back to their entrenchments. It was a mistake to charge batteries & lines over so great a distance every yard exposed to a hot fire. Had we marched at night to 1/2 mile of the works it is I think certain we could have carrie[sic] them. It was the enemy admit they "Shook in their shoes." I was shot through the left leg on horse back near the close of the fight my fine mare after taking me off the field died of the same shot — Poor Jinny, noble horse, I grieve to part thus with you.

My leg was amputated by Drs. McGuire, Black & Hays Saturday but the surgeons saying my leg would become inflamed by moving in the ambulance & erysipolas ensue — I decided to fall a prisoner — was taken to Mr. McCardy's house in Gettysburg & treated with the most tender kindness for two weeks when I was removed by *orders* to the Seminary Hos. 1/2 mile west of town.

2. Major General Richard Anderson commanded a division in Lt. Gen. A. P. Hill's Corps, including the brigades led by Cadmus Wilcox, A.R. Wright, Carnot Posey, William Mahone and David Lang. His role was to prepare his men to support the charge when success became evident. As he reports here, he had two brigades ready to follow up, and had them in motion when Longstreet ordered him to stop them. Report of Major General Richard H. Anderson, Commanding Division, August 7, 1863, *OR*, 1, 27, 2, 614-615.

On July 3, nothing of consequence occurred along that portion of the line occupied by my division until the afternoon, when at 3.30 o'clock a great number of pieces of our artillery, massed against the enemy's center, opened upon it, and were replied to with equal force and fury. After about an hour's continuance of this conflict, enemy's fire seemed to subside, and the troops of Longstreet's corps were advanced to the assault of the enemy's center. I received order to hold my division in readiness to move up in support, if it should become necessary. The same success at first, and the same repulse, attended this assault as that made by my division on the preceding evening. The troops advanced gallantly under the galling and destructive storm of missiles of every description; gained the first ridge; were unable to hold it; gave way, and fell back, their support giving way at the same time.

Wilcox's and Perry's brigades had been moved forward, so as to be in position to render assistance, or to take advantage of any success gained by the assaulting column, and, at what I supposed to be the proper time, I was about to move forward Wright's and Posey's brigades, when Lieutenant - General Longstreet directed me to stop the movement, adding that it was useless, and would only involve unnecessary loss, the assault having failed. I then caused the troops to resume their places in line, to afford a rallying point to those retiring and to oppose the enemy should he follow our retreating forces. No attempt at pursuit was made, and our troops resumed their line of battle.

3. Brigadier General James Lane describes the pounding of the artillery from the right, and the Federal infantry on the left, during the charge. Report of Brig. Gen. James Lane, August 13, 1863, *OR*, 1, 27, 2, 666-667.

Next morning, the skirmishing was very heavy in front of Thomas and Perrin, requiring at times whole regiments to be deployed to resist the enemy and drive them back, which was always most gallantly done. While this was going on, I was ordered by General Hill, through Captain [F. To.] Hill, to move in person to the right, with the two brigades forming my second line, and to report to General Longstreet as a support to Pettigrew. General Longstreet ordered me to form in rear of the right of Heth's division, commanded by General Pettigrew. Soon after I had executed this order, putting Lowrance on the right, I was relieved of the command of the division by Major-General Trimble, who acted under the same orders that I had received. Heth's division was much larger than Lowrance's brigade and my own, which were its only support, and there was consequently no second line in rear of its left.

Now in command of my own brigade, I moved forward to the support of Pettigrew's right, through the woods in which our batteries were planted, and through an open field about a mile, in full view of the enemy's fortified position, and under a murderous artillery and infantry fire.

As soon as Pettigrew's command gave back, Lowrance's brigade and my own, without ever having halted, took position on the left of the troops which were still contesting the ground with the enemy. My command never moved forward more handsomely. The men reserved their fire, in accordance with orders, until within good range of the enemy, and then opened with telling effect, repeatedly driving the cannoneers from their pieces, completely silencing the guns in our immediate front, and breaking the line of infantry which was formed on the crest of the hill. We advanced to within a few yards of the stone wall, exposed all the while to a heavy raking artillery fire from the right. My left was here very much exposed, and a column of the enemy's infantry was thrown forward in that direction, which enfiladed my whole line. This forced me to withdraw my brigade, the troops on my right having already done so. We fell back as well as could be expected, reformed immediately in rear of the artillery, as directed by General Trimble, and remained there until the following morning.

I cannot speak in too high terms of the behavior of my brigade in this bloody engagement. Both officers and men moved forward with a heroism unsurpassed, giving the brigade inspector and his rear guard nothing to do.

4. By 1877 the verbal war between Virginians and North Carolinians over who had failed on July 3rd had escalated. The Raleigh *Observer* sent a questionnaire to veterans asking for answers to a series of questions designed to elicit testimony about the charge. In this letter to the Editor of the *Observer*, Lane describes the movement of his brigade from the second to the first line, and reports getting an order from Longstreet as he approached the stone wall, and the destructive fire from the left. James Lane to the Raleigh *Observer*, September 7, 1877.

My position in rear of Pettigrew's command was such as to prevent my seeing the first movement of the front line as there was an intervening strip of woods, but Brig. Gen. Edward L. Thomas, who could see from his position in the road everything that was going on the left, informed me that next day, that Brockenbrough's brigade, which was on the left of Pettigrew's (Heth's) division, did not advance beyond the road; and that Davis' brigade, which was next to it, pushed forward in advance of the general line, with too much impetuosity and was driven back. The remaining brigades of this division were Pettigrew's and Archer's, but the greater part of Archer's brigade and [Brig.] Gen. [James J.] Archer himself, had been captured in the first day's fight. When Gen. Trimble ordered us forward, we gained distance or obliqued to the left as we advanced, and took position in the front line on the left of Pettigrew's brigade, and when the right of my command was within a short distance of the stone fence used by the enemy as a breastwork, one of Gen. Longstreet's staff officers came dashing through a hot fire with orders from Gen. Longstreet to move by brigade rapidly to the left, as the enemy had thrown out a flanking force in that direction—this force was already pouring a destructive fire into us. As soon as I could dismount from my wounded and plunging horse, I ordered Col. [C. M.] Avery in command of my left regiment [33d N.C.], to move to meet the force above referred to, when he quickly replied, "My God General, do you intend rushing your men into such a place unsupported, when the troops on the right are falling back[?]" Seeing it was useless to sacrifice my brave men, I ordered my brigade back, and formed in rear of the artillery as directed by Gen. Trimble. Perhaps this last statement may serve to explain the "APPARENT" echelon movement of Pettigrew's division to those who witnessed the fight at a distance.

5. Brigadier General Joseph Davis' brigade of Mississippi and North Carolina troops in A. P. Hill's Corps had taken heavy

casualties on July 1st, and suffered again on the 3rd. The heavy losses he describes among the field officers crippled the Army of Northern Virginia throughout the rest of the war. Report of Brig. Gen. Joseph Davis, 22 August 1863, *OR*, 1, 27, 2, 650-651.

Headquarters, Davis' Brigade
August 22, 1863.

MAJOR:

Early on the morning of the 3d, the enemy threw some shells at the artillery in our front, from which a few casualties occurred in one of the brigades. About 9 a. m. the division was moved to the left about a quarter of a mile, and in the same order of battle was formed in the rear of Major Pegram's battalion of artillery, which was posted on the crest of a high hill, the ground between us and the enemy being like that of our first position.

About 1 p. m. the artillery along our entire line opened on the enemy, and was promptly replied to. For two hours the fire was heavy and incessant. Being immediately in the rear of our batteries, and having had no time to prepare means of protection, we suffered some losses.

Davis' brigade, 2 men were killed and 21 wounded. The order had been given that when the artillery in our front ceased firing, the division would attack the enemy's battle lines, keeping dressed to the right, and moving in line with Major-General Pickett's division, who was on our right, and march obliquely to the left.

The artillery ceased firing at 3 o'clock, and the order to move forward was given and promptly obeyed. The division moved off in line, and, passing the wooded crest of the hill, descended to the open fields that lay between us and the enemy. Not a gun was fired at us until we reached a strong post and rail fence about three-quarter of a mile from the enemy's position, when we were met by a heavy fire of grape, canister, and shell, which told sadly upon our ranks. Under this destructive fire, which commanded our front and left with fatal effect, the troops displayed great coolness, were well in hand, and moved steadily forward, regularly closing up the gaps made in their ranks. Our advance across the fields was interrupted by other fences of a similar character, in crossing which the alignment became more or less deranged. This was in each case promptly rectified, and though its ranks were growing thinner at every step, this division moved steadily on in line with the troops on the right. When within musket-range, we encountered a heavy fire of small-arms, from which we suffered severely; but this did not for a moment check the advance.

The right of the division, owing to the conformation of the ridge on which the enemy was posted, having a shorter distance to pass over to reach his first line of defense, encountered him first in close conflict; but the whole division dashed up to his first line of defense: a stone wall — behind which the opposing infantry was strongly posted. Here we were subjected to a most galling fire of musketry and artillery, that so reduced the already thinned ranks that any further effort to carry the position was hopeless, and there was nothing left but to retire to the position originally held, which was done in more or less confusion. About 4 p. m. the division reached the line held in the morning, and remained there thirty hours, expecting an attack from the enemy. No demonstration was made on any part of our line during that or the following day, on the night of which we began our retreat to Hagerstown.

In the assault upon the enemy's position, the coolness and courage of officers and men are worthy of high commendation, and I regret that the names of the gallant men who fell distinguished on that bloody field have not been more fully reported.

In this assault, we are called upon to mourn the loss of many brave officers and men. Col. B. D. Fry, Thirteenth Alabama, commanding Archer's brigade, and Col. James K. Marshall, of the Fifty-second North Carolina, commanding Pettigrew's, were wounded and taken prisoners while gallantly leading their brigades. The number killed and wounded was very great, and in officers unusually so, as may be seen from the fact that in Archer's brigade but two field officers escaped, in Pettigrew's but one, and in Davis' all were killed or wounded. Brigadier-General Pettigrew had his horse killed, and received a slight wound in the hand.

Not having commanded the division in this engagement, and having been exclusively occupied by the operations of my own brigade this report is necessarily imperfect, and I regret that I am unable to do full justice to the division.

6. Much of Archer's brigade had been captured on July 1st, and the remainder was commanded by Colonel Birkett D. Fry. He had been wounded in the cannonade, but started across the field anyway. He fell near the stone wall. B. D. Fry, "Pettigrew's Charge At Gettysburg," *SHSP*, VII(1879), 93.

During the forenoon of the 3d, while our division was resting in line behind the ridge and skirt of woods which masked us from the enemy, Generals Lee, Longstreet and A.P. Hill rode up, and, dismounting, seated themselves on the trunk of a fallen tree some fifty or sixty paces from where I sat on my horse at the right of our division. After an apparently careful examination of a map, and a consultation of some length, they remounted and rode away. Staff officers and couriers began to move briskly about, and a few minutes after General Pettigrew rode up and informed me that after a heavy cannonade we would assault the position in our front, and added: "They will of course return the fire with all the guns they have; we must shelter the men as best we can, and make them lie down." At the same time he directed me to see General Pickett at once and have an understanding as to the dress in the advance. I rode to General Pickett, whose division was formed on the right of and in line with ours. He appeared to be in excellent spirits, and, after a cordial greeting and a pleasant reference to our having been together in work of that kind at Chapultipec, expressed great confidence in the ability of our troops to drive the enemy after they had been "demoralized" by our artillery. General Garnett, who commanded his left brigade, having joined us, it was agreed that he would dress on my command. I immediately returned and informed General Pettigrew of this agreement. It was then understood that my command should be considered the centre, and that in the assault both divisions should align themselves by it. Soon after the two divisions moved forward about a hundred paces, and the men lay down behind our lines of batteries. The cannonade which followed has been often and justly described as the most terrible of the war. In it my command suffered a considerable loss. Several officers were killed and wounded, with a number of the rank and file. I received a painful wound on the right shoulder from a fragment of shell. After lying inactive under that deadly storm of hissing and exploding missiles, it seemed a relief to go forward to the desperate assault. At a signal from Pettigrew I called my command to attention. The men sprang up with cheerful alacrity, and the long line advanced. "Stormed at with shot and shell," it moved steadily on, and even when grape, canister, and musket balls began to rain upon it the gaps were quickly closed and the alignment preserved. Strong as was the position of the enemy, it seemed that such determination could not fail. I heard Garnett give a command to his men which, amid the rattle of musketry, I could not distinguish. Seeing my look or gesture of inquiry, he called out, "I am dressing on you!" A few seconds after he fell dead. A moment later — and after Captain Williams and Colonel George had been wounded by my side — a shot through the thigh prostrated me. I was so confident of victory that to some of my men who ran up to carry me off I shouted, "Go on: it will not last five minutes longer!" The men rushed forward into the smoke, which soon became so dense that I could see little of what was going on before me. But a moment later I heard General Pettigrew, behind me, calling to some of his staff to "rally them on the left." The roll of musketry was then incessant, and I believe that the Federal troops — probably blinded by the smoke — continued a rapid fire for some minutes after none but dead and wounded remained in their front. At length the firing ceased, and cheer after cheer from the enemy announced the failure of our attack. I was of course left a prisoner.

As evidence of how close was the fighting at that part of the line, I saw a Federal soldier with an ugly wound in his shoulder, which he told me he received from the spear on the end of one of my regimental colors; and I remembered having that morning observed and laughingly commented on the fact that the color-bearer of the Thirteenth Alabama had attached to his staff a formidible-looking lance head. All of the five regimental colors of my command reached the line of the enemy's works, and many of my men and officers were killed or wounded after passing over it. I believe the same was true of other brigades in General Pettigrew's command.

7. The brigade of Virginia troops commanded by Colonel John M. Brockenbrough stepped off on the far left of the Confederate line. Colonel W. S. Christian, commanding the 55th Virginia, writes that the attack was disorganized from the beginning. W. S. Christian to John Daniels, October 24, 1904, Daniels Papers, University of Virginia.

Soon after we heard that we were to make the charge. Colonel Brockenbrough came to me and said that he intended to divide the brigade, and said that the 55th and 47th would move only at the orders of Colonel Mayo of the 47th, and that I must consider myself under the command temporarily of Colonel Mayo. When the movement commenced and we saw Colonel Brockenbrough move forward with the Fortieth and 32nd Lieutenant Colonel John Lyle of the 47th and myself me for consultation, each inquiring; "Where is Colonel Mayo?" We remained there sometime as we had orders not to move until Colonel Mayo said so. Finding that he did not come, and Colonel Lyle suggesting that he might possibly have been killed by the Artillery fire, these two regiments, the 47th and the 55th Virginia moved forward. We were a long ways behind and had to run to catch up with the rest of the Brigade. Even when on a run down that slope, I could see that disaster had befallen the right of our lines. We caught up with the two regiments commanded by Colonel Brockenbrough, and advanced a considerable distance beyond General Pettigrew's left. (I mean Pettigrew's Brigade, for Pettigrew commanded the Division that day, Heath having been wounded on the first day of July.)

We remained out in that field until all the troops on our right had fallen back. We saw that the whole attack had miscarried. Some officer that I did not know, some aide perhaps, rode down the line to my regiment, and begged us to stand firm, that efforts were being made to rally the forces and to renew the charge. We stood there to be shot at, and that was about all that we did, and did not retire until after the retreat had become general. I remember that after being filled by Yankee bullets, which were first being concentrated upon our small and thin command, I told my men to scatter and to get back to the same position as before the charge, as I felt sure that the Yankees would now charge us.

Being lame from severe wounds received in the Seven Days fight around Richmond, I retreated slowly, with the Color bearer my only attendant. The Color bearer was severely wounded by a shell while we were retiring, and I had to bear him and the Colors to a place of safety, where I found other men who took him back to the rear. That Color bearer is still living. We remained in position the whole of the nest day, the fourth, expecting an attack.

8.   The official post-battle report for Brockenbrough's brigade was filed by Colonel Robert Mayo of the 47th Virginia. It does nothing to explain what happened to prevent them from completing the charge. Report of Col. R. M. Mayo, 47th Va. Regt., Aug. 14, 1863, Henry Heth Collection, Eleanor S. Brockenbrough Library, Museum of the Confederacy.

Having suffered quite severely in the first days fight we now number not more than 500 muskets, and consequently, being engaged by ten times our number, we were obliged to extend our line until it was nothing more than a line of skirmishers, we succeeded however in holding the Enemy in check until everything on our right had given way. Our Brigade was the last to leave the field, the flag of the 47th Va. having been shot down, after the flags of every other Brigade had disappeared. We halted, at Gen. Thomas' Brigade which during the entire fight, had occupied a position, about midway between our line and the Enemy's, and waited to see if the yankees would pursue us, but they did not follow us one hundred yards. The Brigade on both of these Occassions[sic] was managed with remarkable Skill, Coolness, and Gallantry.

9.   Lieutenant Colonel Shepard of the 7th Tennessee, Archer's brigade, describes the march from Seminary Ridge, closing the gaps caused by the Federal artillery shells, and entering the Federal works. Report of Lieut. Col. S. G. Shepard, Seventh Tennessee Infantry, of operations of Archer's brigade, August 10, 1863, *OR*, 1, 27, 2, 647-648.

. . . In the engagement of the 3d, the brigade was on the right of our division, in the following order: First Tennessee on the right; on its left, Thirteenth Alabama; next, Fourteenth Tennessee; on its left, Seventh Tennessee, and on the left, Fifth Alabama Battalion. There was a space of a few hundred yards between the right of Archer's brigade and the left of General Pickett's division gradually approached each other, so that by the time we had advanced a little over half of the way, the right of Archer's touched and connected with Pickett's left.

The command was then passed down the line by the officers, "Guide right;" and we advanced our right, guiding by General Pickett's left. The enemy held their fire until we were in fine range, and opened upon us a terrible and well-directed fire. Within 180 or 200 yards of his works, we came to a lane inclosed by two stout post and plank fences. This was a very great obstruction to us, but the men rushed over as rapidly as they could, and advanced directly upon the enemy's works, the first line of which was composed of rough stones. The enemy abandoned this, but just in rear was massed a heavy force. By the time we had reached this work, our lines all along, as far as I could see, had become very much weakened; indeed, the line both right and left, as far as I could observe, seemed to melt away until there was but little of it left. Those who remained at the works saw that it was a hopeless case, and fell back. Archer's brigade remained at the works fighting as long as any other troops either on their right or left, so far as I could observe.

Every flag in the brigade excepting one was captured at or within the works of the enemy. The First Tennessee had 3 color-bearers shot down, the last of whom was at the works, and the flag captured. The Thirteenth Alabama lost 3 in the same way, the last of whom was shot down at the works. The Fourteenth Tennessee had 4 shot down, the last of whom was at the enemy's works. The Seventh Tennessee lost 3 color-bearers, the last of whom was at the enemy's works, and the flag was only saved by Captain [A. D.] Norris tearing it away from the staff and bringing it out beneath his coat. The Fifth Alabama Battalion also lost their flag at the enemy's works.

10.   Major McLeod Turner of the 7th North Carolina describes the flight of some of Brockenbrough's brigade early in the charge and the mid-field maneuvers of his line. The fence along the Emmitsburg Road posed a considerable obstacle to the men of Pettigrew's and Trimble's command, as Turner indicates.   J. McLeod Turner to the Editor, Raleigh *Observer*, October 10, 1877.

MESSRS. EDITORS: In reply to yours of the 17th ultimo, I

will give you my recollections of the part taken by my command on the 3rd day of the battle of Gettysburg; also of the conduct of the troops that acted with and near us.

I was at that time Major, commanding the 7th N. C. troops, Lane's brigade, Pender's division, A. P. Hill's corps.

Sometime after midday, we were ordered to a position in the woods and formed the second line of battle, supporting Heth's division, then commanded by Gen. Pettigrew; my regiment being the right of our brigade, with Scales' brigade on our right. We were confronted by that part of the enemy's line known as [Cemetery Ridge]. We remained in this position during the cannonading, which preceded the general advance of that day. During a slight cessation of the firing we were ordered forward. As we emerged from the woods and had cleared the artillery, (Maj. William T. Poague's battalion) we were met by crowds of stragglers coming to the rear, and in such numbers that I ordered my men to charge bayonets in order to compel them to go around the flanks of our regiment to prevent their breaking our line; these men were from Brockenbrough's brigade. On looking to our front, I saw the remainder of Pettigrew's division advancing in fine style, good order and unbroken. We pressed rapidly forward and in spite of the numerous obstacles, such as fences, ditches, &c., the whole line remained unbroken until we had passed over a least two thirds of the distance from the woods to the enemy's line, when there was a parting of the line, some distance to the right of my regiment, which was due to the fact that the left of our brigade understood the "guide" to be "left," whilst on the right the order was "guide right." This opening was but slight and the only material disadvantage was the crowding and lapping of our right on Scales' brigade. Thus far the line of battle was as good as I ever saw; our loss up to within a few yards of the road had been very slight, as I think the enfilading fire from the enemy's guns on the right had been directed to those in our front.

As we neared the road we suffered severely from the artillery fire. When we were in about one hundred yards of the enemy's works, it being a stone wall in our front, I saw the enemy leave their works and retreat precipitately over the hill in their rear, their works being about thirty (30) yards from the top of the ridge. I called the attention of the men to this fact, and the whole line rushed forward with increased vigor, but before they had entirely disappeared, their reinforcements came rapidly over the ridge and reoccupied the works before we had time to reach the road, here running nearly parallel to both lines of battle — on our right the enemies line approached nearer the road. This road known as the Emmettsburg Pike, had a post and rail fence on either side; the first, I ordered the men to rush against and push down, which they did, but having to run up out of the road they did not succeed in a like attempt on the second, and seeing that we were losing time, I climbed over on the right and my men were following me rapidly. I had advanced ten yards or more towards the works when I was shot down; the men who had gotten over returned to and laid down in the Pike, as did the entire regiment. The wound received proved to be a contusion on the instep of my foot, laming me and giving me great pain, in a little while I made my way back and over the fence to the left where Capt. Harris, the next officer in rank to myself, was. I had scarcely turned over the command when I was shot through the waist, the ball striking the spinal column, instantly paralyzing the part below. For some moments I was insensible, but in a little while became fully conscious and was perfectly aware of everything transpiring around me.

Not up to this time, nor was there afterwards, any attempt of the enemy to come over their works in our front, and it was not until the expiration of nearly, if not quite, half an hour, after we had reached the Pike, that Captain Harris and others came to me and said that they were compelled to fall back as the enemy were coming in on the right, and wanted to carry me to the rear, but as I had made an examination of my wound, and thought I could only live a short while, and that they would only endanger themselves the more in attempting to carry me off, I declined and insisted on being left where I was: After the lapse of some minutes my attention was attracted to our right and I succeeded in sitting up, when I saw crowds of the enemy advancing from that direction with some prisoners, and assisting the slightly wounded off of the field, one of my old company coming by, bleeding profusely from a wound above the ankle, I took a tourniquet from my pocket, and adjusted it to his leg, so as to stop the hemorrhage completely. I mention these minor facts to show that I had sufficiently recovered my faculties to be able to form a correct understanding of what had been and was transpiring around me.

I was removed by two of the enemy from a ditch by the roadside to the field on our side of the road. Our loss in this vicinity was fearful, the dead and wounded lying in great numbers both in the field and road. I conversed with the wounded near me and found that they were, in addition to my own command from the 11th and 26th North Carolina troops of Pettigrew's brigade, and that they as a command had been compelled to stop at the road, by reason of the heavy loss inflicted by the enemy's guns on our right, and I am positive there was no attempt made by those who survived to go to the rear, and as for my own division commanded by Gen. Trimble, there was neither faltering nor falling back of any part of it that came under my observation. As I was climbing the second fence before alluded to I saw Gen. Trimble riding only a few yards in my rear giving an order to an aide. In conversation with Gen. Trimble since, he told me that he never saw a better line of battle or men conduct themselves better than those of his command that day.

11. With no field officers left in Trimble's (Pender's) division, a staff officer filed the official report. He describes the change of command, the maneuvers on the field, and the point at which they began to retreat. Report of Major Joseph H. Englehard, Asst. Adjutant General, Pender's Division, November 4, 1863, *OR*, 1, 27, 2, 659-660.

During the morning of the 3d, General Lane received an order from Lieutenant-General Hill to report in person with the two brigades forming his second line to the right of Lieutenant-General Longstreet, as a support to Pettigrew. General Longstreet ordered him to form in rear of the right of Heth's division, commanded by General Pettigrew.

Having executed this order, General Lane was relieved of the command by Maj. Gen. I. R. Trimble, who acted under the same orders given to General Lane.

The two brigades, thus formed as a support to Pettigrew, with Lowrance on the right, after suffering no little from the two hours' exposure to the heavy artillery fire which preceded the attack on the 3d, advanced in close support distance of Pettigrew's line, General Trimble, with portions of his own and General Pender's staff, being with and taking immediate command of the movement. The line moved forward through the woods into the open field about 1 mile, in full view of the fortified position of the enemy, exposed to a murderous artillery and infantry fire in front, a severe artillery fire from the right, and an enfilade fire of musketry from the left. The brigade moved forward handsomely and firmly. The division in front gaining ground to the right, uncovered the left of Lane's brigade, which caused it to advance more rapidly than the rest of the line, which was checked by an order from General Trimble.

When within a few hundred yards of the enemy's works, the line in front being entirely gone, the division moved rapidly up, connecting with the troops on the right, still stubbornly contesting the ground with the enemy, reserving their fire until within easy range, and then opening with telling effect, driving the artillerists from their guns, completely silencing them, and breaking the line of infantry supports formed on the crest of the hill. All the guns in the immediate front of the division were silenced, and the infantry had fallen behind their second and third lines of defense, when the division, advancing in an oblique direction, the extreme right of which had reached the works, was compelled to fall back, the troops on the right having already gone, exposing the line to a very deadly fire from that direction immediately on the flank, and, a large column of infantry appearing on the left, that flank also became exposed. The two extreme left regiments of Lane's brigade, under Colonel Avery and [J. D.] Barr, advanced some minutes after the whole line had given way, and fell back, under direct orders.

12. **Archer's brigade, now commanded by Birkett D. Fry, formed the right flank of the Pettigrew--Trimble line. The plan called for its right and the left of Garnett and Armistead to merge and attack the center of the line, and that did occur. Captain J. B. Turney of the 1st Tennessee describes the bayonet charge at the double-quick, penetration of the Angle with Armistead, and their reasons for surrendering. Capt. J. B. Turney, "The First Tennessee at Gettysburg," _CV_, VII(1900), 535-537.**

. . . For three miles from right to left we charged in unbroken line, across the fields; through ravines over-fences — on we went, bent on victory or death. The lead rained; the gallant Colonel George, of the First Tennessee fell wounded; thirty steps farther, and Colonel Fry was checked by an enemy bullet -- wounded in the leg. He called to me and asked for Colonel Georg, and, when informed of his wound, said to me: "Captain, take command of the regiment. Proceed with the charge, but don't stop to fire a gun." By the time I reached my line it was to the first plank fence that inclosed the Emmettsburg road. How like hail upon a roof sounded the patter of the enemy's bullets upon that fence! Onward swept the columns, thinned now and weakened, the dead behind, the foe in front, and no thought of quarter. The second fence was reached and scaled, now no impediment, save the deadly fire of ten thousand rifles that barred our head — long charge. It was one hundred and fifty yards now of open field. Who would live to reach the goal? In wonderful order, at double-quick time, we continued the charge; and not until we were within about fifteen steps of the stone wall did I give the command to fire. The volley confused the enemy.   I then ordered a charge with bayonets, and on moved our gallant boys. Another instant, and we were engaged in a desperate hand-to-hand conflict for the possession of the fragile wall of masonry that held out as the sole barrier between the combatants. Each man seemed to pick his foe, and it fell my lot to struggle with a stalwart Federal officer, who made a vicious thrust at my brest.[sic] I parried it just in time. Thus for a few moments the contest settled as for a death struggle, and one triumphant shout was given as the Federals in our immediate front and to our right yielded and fled in confusion to a point just back of the crest of the hill, abandoning their artillery. Having given no heed to our lines to the right or to the left after crossing the Emmettsburg road, I now mounted the rock wall and found everything successful to my right, while the center and left of Archer's Brigade had failed. From my position to the right the works were ours, but to the left the enemy was still in possession. Thus the First Tennessee, constituting the right of Archer's Brigade, occupied a most important position. I decided to throw a column beyond the works and enfilade the lines to my left, and succeeded in taking with me my own company and parts of others.

The volleys we fired were effective, and created confusion, enabling Capt. J. H. Moore, and possibly others, of the Seventh Tennessee, and Captain Taylor, of the Thirteenth Alabama, to lead their companies over the works. A few of the Fifth Alabama Battalion also crossed. By this time, at a distance of only about thirty yards, and behind the crest of the hill, I noted the re-forming of the Federal lines. This necessitated a withdrawal to a position behind the stone wall, and there we joined the balance of the First Tennessee. After a desperate, but unsuccessful, effort to dislodge us, the enemy again retired over the crest of the hill. I then made a second effort to cross the works and enfilade, but by this time our lines, from my position to the left, were being beaten back by a most destructive fire; and as our opposition melted in their front, the enemy turned a deadly fire upon the unprotected squad of First Tennesseeans, who, together with a few of Garnett's Virginians, had the second time crossed the works. The artillery as well as the musketry belched forth destruction to our little band, and we were forced to drop back behind the wall. By this time General Armistead had noted the importance of the position held by the First Tennessee, and was obliquing to his left to reach us. A few moments of waiting brought his recruits to our aid. The General was on foot at the head of his column. I shall ever have a distinct remembrance of the dash and fire that was in him. He threw his hat on his saber, called for the command to follow, and scaled the stone wall. I kept by his side, and with us went the colors of the First Tennessee. Armistead's purpose was to enfilade, as I had attempted. Again we became the targets for the concentrated fire of the enemy's guns of all sizes and all positions. At the first volley I noticed General Armistead drop his saber, on which still hung his hat, and grast[sic] with his right hand his left arm and stagger as if he were about to fall. I caught and supported him. He was wounded in the left arm, and his men bore him behind the stone wall for protection. Seeing the impossibility of effective work from behind the wall and the shattered condition of our lines, I hastily called the captains of my regiment for conference. Captains Thompson, Hawkins, Arnold, and Alexander responded. While we were conferring, a courier arrived, and, calling for the officer in charge, told me General Lee's orders were to hold my position, as Ewell had broken the lines on the extreme left. These orders, settled the question, and brought us face to face with the critical moments of that decisive battle. To the left of the First Tennessee our lines had entirely given way, thus enabling the enemy to concentrate its fire — not only from our center, but from our left — directly upon my command. The heavy artillery on the ridge and that massed on Little Round Top poured destruction into our ranks. Some of the Virginians to our right had already yielded. For ten minutes still we remained the target, and each minute perceptible weakened our gallant band and made less possible our chance of retreat. All realized that our was a hopeless chance, yet General Lee desired that we remain, and that was sufficient.

Retreat across the open was now impossible, and a white flag was reluctantly hoisted by a Virginia regiment to my right; and thus it was that those of the First Tennessee who survived the struggle and had not escaped yielded themselves as prisoners. Within an hour all firing had ceased, and the great battle was at an end. . . . Except a flesh wound in my neck and a number of bullet holes in my clothes, I was unharmed.

13. Captain A. S. Haynes, 11th North Carolina, recalls being shot down just short of the wall, and that he was "dead awhile." It took him nearly 8 hours to crawl back to the lines along Seminary Ridge. A. S. Haynes to the Editor, Raleigh *Observer*, October 8, 1877.

MESSRS. EDITORS: Yours of the 3d inst. to hand with circular and in reply I beg leave to state that in the fight on the third day at Gettysburg I was Captain of Company I, 11th North Carolina, in Pettigrew's Brigade.

I was shot down near the cemetery wall and was insensible for a time. When I recovered our line was gone; when shot we were in line going towards the cemetery wall having crossed the last fence. I crawled through their lines to our own; could not walk; got through at 11 o'clock at night; I was on the field all the evening; I thought everyone had been shot down.

. . . All that went in on the third day were cut down. The orders came along our line to dress our line under that galling fire, which was done twice; were going too fast for the right and left of the long line and drawing a very heavy fire. When we dressed the line I did not see one falter; this was taken for wavering, when it required more courage to dress a line under fire than to continue the charge.

I was in about fifty yards (I think nearer) of the wall when I was shot down, so says Lieut. O. A. Ramsour who saw me fall. He with about 150 men of our Regiment went on to the wall or to a fence at or near the wall. He bears witness to the giving way on our left and says we dressed our lines under that galling fire. I was dead awhile. After this was shot down again and I cannot tell much as I was so used up that I did not know much.

I had no one in my company to fall back; up to the time I feel no one fell back from our Regiment that I saw. We were all cut down — no one but wounded left in my company save two.

14. Captain June Kimble of the 14th Tennessee was one of those who crossed the wall. He discusses his own emotional preparation for the charge, then describes his experiences with less detail than we would like. June Kimble, "Tennesseeans at Gettysburg — The Retreat," *CV*, XVIII(1910), 460-461.

During the lull, already oppressive, I walked out alone to the edge of the open some fifty yards in advance of the line then lying in the timber, and there deliberately surveyed the field from Round Top Mountain on our right to the suburbs and spires of Gettysburg on the left. I sought to locate the point on Cemetery Ridge about which our brigade and regiment would strike the enemy, provided our advance be made in a straight line. Realizing just what was before me and the brave boys with me, and at one of the most serious moments in life, I asked aloud the question: "June Kimble, are you going to do your duty to-day?" The audible answer was "I'll do it, so help me God." I turned and walked back to the line. "How does it look, June?" said Lieutenant Waters. I replied: "Boys, if we have to go, it will be hot for us, and we will have to do our best." When I responded to my own question as to doing my duty, a change of feeling immediately took possession of me; all dread even passed away, and from that moment to the close of that disastrous struggle I retained my nerve, and my action was as calm and deliberate as if upon dress parade. It was different from all other experiences, many and various, in my four years of unbroken service.

At about one o'clock a solitary signal shot was fired far to our right by Longstreet's command. Instantly every battery upon the Confederate line opened on its mission of death and destruction, and was as promptly responded to by every battery, I presume, on the Federal line, and the third and last day of the battle of Gettysburg was on.

For about one hour an artillery duel, the equal of which was never fought on this earth, followed this signal gun. The rear and crash of five hundred booming cannon, screaming and bursting shells, and the swish of crashing solid shot brought forth a veritable pandemonium. The very earth shook as from a mighty quake. So intense were its vibrations that loose grass, leaves, and twigs arose from six to eight inches above the ground, hovered and quivered as birds about to drop until the mighty roar ceased. And it did cease almost as suddenly as it began.

Another ominous lull, and each veteran drew a long breath of relief; then sharply "Attention!" rang out clear along the line. Instantly fourteen thousand veterans sprang to their feet and awaited the word "Forward!" which they knew was coming. From Pickett's Division of three brigades came at intervals the command, "Dress on the left," and from Heth's or Pettigrew's, six brigades came, "Dress to the right," Archer's Brigade being near the center and the guiding brigade of the assaulting column. It emerged into the open field silent save for the tramp, tramp of the veterans in solid line, with steady nerve and determined mien. In my admiration and enthusiasm I rushed some ten paces in advance and cast my eyes right and left. It was magnificent! When observed by the enemy, the vicious roar of artillery began its deadly work. Soon shot and shell were plowing through the Confederate ranks; but on, steadily on the line moved without a waver or break save as gaps were rent by solid shot or exploding shell. The first fence was soon reached and quickly toppled over by hand and upon the points of bayonets. No check, but on we moved. The second fence shared the fate of the first, and without a halt the column went forward as if to victory. The third obstacle appeared, a strong, well-built post or slab fence, too strong to be quickly torn away. Realizing this, over the fence the Confederates sprang, thus pausing for a moment in some confusion; but re-forming quickly the line, still unbroken but terribly punished, rushed forward undismayed.

It was here that I again sprang in advance, looked up and down that line, and became an eyewitness of the most vivid and stupendous battle scene doubtless that ever fell to mortal. As far as I could see this same line seemed to move as close and steady as upon the start. On it advanced until, having reached close range of the enemy's protected infantry, withering volleys of musketry, grape, double-charged canister, shot and shell shattered and mutilated as fine as body of Southern heroes as ever trod a battlefield. Still, after practical annihilation, the remnant of these glorious Confederates kept going forward, until they silenced the guns and stood in the works of the enemy. Those of the enemy who remained in the works were prostrated at our feet, practically prisoners, with their arms upon the ground, not firing a shot.

For five, perhaps ten, minutes we held our ground and looked back for and prayed for support. It came not, and we knew that the battle of Gettysburg was ended. Many of this brave remnant chose to surrender rather than run the gauntlet of the enemy's fire. Among others, I refused to yield, and made a break for my liberty in the face of their guns. For about one hundred yards I broke the lightening speed record. Suddenly I realized that I was a good target for those yelling Yankees, and, having a horror of being shot in the back, I faced about and backed out of range, and all without so much as a scratch. I stopped at our rifle pits that had been dug in advance of our original line on Seminary Ridge. Four men could occupy each of these pits, and I found about four men in each, but I joined them. Anticipating that the enemy would follow up our discomfiture, I made inquiry for an officer. Not one could be found. I then suggested that we constitute ourselves a line of skirmishers. To my joy every man readily responded, and all agreed to stand together.

15. Captain James Harris kept a daily memorandum of his experiences in the 7th North Carolina infantry throughout the war. He recorded much about the charge, including mid-field maneuvers. James Harris, *Historical Sketches* (Mooresville, N.C.: n.p., n.p., 1893), 35-36.

Friday July 3. Learned that our division commander General Pender was badly wounded by a fragment of shell last evening, that Brigadier General Lane is in command of Pender's division, and that Col. C. M. Avery of the Thirty third regiment is in command of Lane's brigade. In our immediate front the skirmishing was heavy all morning and the wounded, at times, come out in squads. Thomas and McGowan's brigades were advanced last night to take part in the contemplated night attack, and they still occupy their advanced positions. At 12m. Lane's and Scale's brigades (the latter under Col. W. L. Lowrance, 34th N.C.T.) marched to the right in rear of the main line on Seminary Ridge about one mile, and formed line of battle in an open woods, and under cover of the rising ground in front. Scale's brigade having preceded Lane's in the meeting with Scales' extended the line to the line to the left. These two brigades were the only troops on the second line so far as we could see, and were some 150 yards in rear of the right of Heth's division, then commanded by General Pettigrew, and awaiting orders to advance on the enemy's strong hold, Cemetery Hill. By 1 o'clock p. m. the lines were established, and company commanders were instructed to inform their men of the magnitude of the task assigned to them, and also to caution their men to keep cool, preserve the alignment, press steadily to the front, and gain the enemy's works.

At a given signal, the confederate artillery previously posted on Seminary Ridge, (75 guns on Longstreets, and 63 on Hills front — so stated at the time), opened fire, and they were immediately responded to, gun answering gun, for nearly two hours, as fast as men hurried by passion and excitement could load and discharge them. When this fearful cannonade was at its heighth[sic], a fox, doubtless alarmed for its safety came at full speed from the direction of the enemy's line, and in its attempt to pass our line was surrounded, and Major Turner despatched it with his sword. This incident is thrown in to show the make up on the confederate soldier, and that no danger however great deterred him from the enjoyment of a little sport.

About this time, Major General Trimble accompanied by members of his staff rode up, and upon his application, the command of Pender's division (Lane's and Scales' brigades), was accordingly given him, General Lane resuming command of his brigade, and Col. Avery, his regiment.

At length, the fire of the Federal batteries some what slackened, and the forward movement began. The distance to be traversed, was nearly one mile, over a field intersected by several straight (post and rail) fences, running some what parallel to our line of battle. From the top of Seminary Ridge, the ground gradually sloped to the intervening valley below, and from thence, to the top of Cemetery Hill it was much steeper. As the second line [Lane and Scales], passed over the top of Seminary Ridge into the open field, a staff officer [unknown to the writer], rode back from the front, and cautioned us not to fire into, nor pass the front line unless it wavered and he added with an apparent feeling of pride, "the men in front never waver." For the first hundred yards we were screened from the enemys' view by the smoke of the cannonade which had settled over the field, but as our batteries ceased firing it was blown away, and we were instantly subjected to a withering fire of shot and shell. Looking in that direction, it was evident that the right wing of the front line was much nearer on starting, and directing its march on the projecting angle of the Federal line, would necessarily reach that point, while the troops on the left, marching with equal celerity, but approaching the receding part of the same line, would be distant there from several hundred yards and this advantage was still further increased by the "left oblique" direction of the march.

To the beholders, it must have been a grand and inspiring sight, as our veteran troops in "quicktime," so cheerfully and gallantly passed over that storm swept field of strife and blood for never did men confront danger with more determined purpose to succeed. When the second line [Lane and Scales], was two thirds of the way across the field, the remnants of Pettigrew's commands immediately in Lane's front, that escaped destruction from the tempest of iron and lead hurled at them closed to the right, and a glance in that direction revealed the fact that our troops on the right were in possession of the "projecting angle" of the Federal line but unfortunately they were too weak and too much disorganized to long maintain the position, or advance with any hope of success. This movement of Pettigrew's uncovered Lane's brigade, and it there by became the left and front of the assaulting column, — its left regiments having an open field sooner, advanced more rapidly, and gained ground to the right to lap on Scales' left. This was speedily remedied by Lanes brigade changing direction to the left, and as Scale's brigade continued to "dress to the right," the two commands became separated by about 150 yards.

The Seventh Regiment, having reserved its fire in accordance with orders previously given, now began cheering for the "Old North State" with such volume, of voice as to be heard above the din of battle; meanwhile advancing with more than its customary gallantry to the Emmitsburg road, all the while delivering into the enemy's ranks such a well directed fire as to clear the first line of works immediately in front, and compel the cannoneers to abandon their guns. On either side of the road there was a straight rail fence supported by posts firmly set in the embankment of the ditches, the first of which was thrown down, but the second one was not so easily disposed of, and Major Turner climbed over and advanced towards the stone wall, closely followed by his men. Perceiving however, that the advance of the other regiments was not general beyond the road, Maj. Turner ordered his men to recross, and they availed themselves of such protection as was afforded by the ditch and fence.

An additional source of danger that now confronted us, was the enemy's flanking party in the open field to our left, and their fire raked our already thin line, while their batteries swept the field on either side. Our troops on the right had by this time abandoned the contest and were falling back, and our position was one of extreme peril.

To remain and be captured, or run the gauntlet of the enemy's batteries and escape, was our only alternative and the latter, (the bravest act of the day), was resorted to, every man going to the rear as fast as his well nigh exhausted nature would admit, spurred onward by dangers which the heroic courage of the day failed to surmount.

16. Along with other members of the 38th North Carolina, Lieutenant Henry Moore ran into the Emmitsburg Road fences.

That caused the attack to slow as they momentarily took shelter from the storm of lead coming at them. The battery in front of the Federal works was probably part of Arnold's battery. Moore says there was a "cut" behind the works, but that was the worn down farm lane. H. C. Moore to the Editor, Raleigh *Observer*, November 6, 1877.

I was a Lieutenant in Company A, 38th N. C. Regiment, Scales' Brigade, and was that day acting as Adjutant of the Regiment. After the artillery duel had ceased on the evening of the third day we were ordered forward. As we emerged from the skirt of woods into the open field a grand sight met our view. The Federal lines were, I think, nearly or quite three-fourths of a mile from our line. We could see about a mile from our line. We could see about a mile of the enemy' s works. Other troops were in advance of us. I was told since the battle that Pickett's division was on our right. They appeared to be on a line with the troops in front of Scales' brigade. We suffered very little from the enemy' s fire until about half way across the field. We came to a strong fence running diagonally across the field and as we had it to climb it deranged our line very much. We were now greeted with heavy doses of . . . canister. Our men were falling in every direction but we managed to struggle on with a tolerably good line as we had rearranged it the best we could. We were now about 200 yards from the enemy's line and were exposed to a severe musketry fire. Our first line was now retreating and the men passed through our line. They had suffered a heavy loss as the men were lying thick on our front.

About 150 yards from the enemy a part of our line struck another fence which confused us considerably. The fire from the enemy's artillery and infantry was now terrible, and we were reduced to a mere skirmish line. We reached another fence, which was on the side of the road. Here we halted and endeavored to reform our line with the men who had become mixed up from different commands. I spoke to Captain A. S. Cloud, who was that day in command of the 16th North Carolina regiment, and asked him what we should do. He replied "we will hold on here until we get help." I looked back and saw some of our troops apparently moving in our direction but they were some distance in the rear. They finally disappeared and I suppose they were ordered back. Our men kept up a weak fire through the plank fence. The enemy's fire slackened and we climbed the fence and attempted to advance. They rushed out from their works to meet us, and we were then fired on by a flanking party on our left who closed in upon us and compelled us to surrender.

We were then at an abandoned battery a few feet in front of their infantry lines. I now perceived that they had been protected by a cut in the rear which seemed to run parallel with the road we had crossed and I supposed forked off from it. Some of our men attempted to escape but were shot down. We had heard no order to retreat, and I don't think any such order was given. After our party was captured there was a lull in the firing along the whole line; a shell would be thrown occasionally. We had not been in the enemy's line more than five or ten minutes before a courier came galloping down from the enemy's left and spoke to an officer, (a Federal General) and said: "General, we are all right." Judging from this the whole Confederate line was then repulsed. There was then no firing of small arms at all within hearing. The last I saw of the troops on our right they were moving forward and within a few yards of the enemy's line, but they were then wavering somewhat. I perceived that they had been much less exposed than our rear portion of the line, as they had a much shorter distance to go across the field. The ground on the right was also undulating, which was some protection to them as they advanced. I knew no commands in that charge, then except Scales' and Lane's brigades. I know nothing of the number of men in Pettigrew's brigade, or their position on that day. If they were in our front they certainly lost many men, as the field was dotted with the dead and wounded. . . . The 38th N. C. regiment, I have understood, numbered only forty men after the third day's fight, and was commanded by a first lieutenant. I saw every man in my company shot down before we surrendered, except Lieut. A. J. Brown, who surrendered with me. Adjutant D. M. McIntire, who was that day acting as Brigade Adjutant General of Scales' Brigade, was one of the few who managed to make his escape. There was not a more gallant officer in the Confederate army than he was.

. . . Had there been no fence in the way in the third day's fight at Gettysburg I think Scales', Lane's and Pettigrew's brigades would have driven the Federals from their line. I found a few Confederate soldiers prisoners in the enemy's line when I surrendered, also one dead man. Where these prisoners came from or how they got that I never ascertained. My opinion, I suppose, is not worth much, as I occupied a very subordinate position on that day, but as you have asked me for it I cheerfully give it.

17. Lieutenant William Peel of the 11th Mississippi tells of the importance of the battle flag to his men. What was left of the 11th reached the Brian Barn about 20 feet in front of the stone wall and then surrendered. "Diary of Lieutenant William Peel," Mississippi State Archives.

About 3 Oclock the artillery firing ceased. A momentary

[lull], of the men resuming their places in line, and silence — a silence almost as awful as the thunder of the minute before had been — settled itself around us. All ears were strung for the command we knew full well must follow soon. "Attention" rang loud & clear, along the line. In an instant all hands were upon their feet, and the line was dressed.

The ashen hue that lingered upon every cheek, showed the a[c]curacy with which the magnitude of the task before us was estimated, while the firm grasp that fixed itself upon every musket, & the look of steady determination that lurked in every eye, bespoke an unflinching resolution to "do or die." Alas! how truly was that resolve sustained. "Forward" now resounded along the line, from right to left.

Moving forward a few yards, we passed our line of artillery, & a little further on, we crossed a low stone fence & found ourselves in a large open field, extending far to the right, left & front, rising with a gradual slope in the latter direction.

Far over the field to the front, at the distance of perhaps a little less than a mile, & near the top of the ascent, there lay a long dark line, parallel with our advancing front, which a stranger would probably not have understood, but which we recognized as a stone fence—something very common in this section of country. Nor were we blind to another important fact: that behind this fence was sheltered a line of Yankee infantry. Just in rear of this fence, on the more elevated knolls, was ranged the enemy's scowling artillery.

The peaceful contemplation of the scene, however, was destined to be short lived. Our debut into the field was greeted with a broad-side from the long line of artillery that sent a storm of screaming, howling shells, across the field, that burst & tore the timber behind us in frightful manner. Volley after volley resounded, as broadsides were [sent] forth, until they subsided into one unbroken roar, louder than the thunder-peals of Heaven. Shells, screaming & bursting around us, scattered their fragments & projectiles in every direction. "Steady boys" — "& slow" — "Don't break yourselves down by running." Alas! that such commands should ever have found their way into the mouths of Confederate officers.

We were now advancing in the face of a perfect tempest of maddened shells that ploughed our line & made sad havock in our ranks. As we moved onward we were greeted, as we came successively within range of these less farreaching, but far more destructive projectiles, with showers of . . . canister, &, at the distance of about two hundred yards the infantry opened on us from behind the stone fence. Pressing onward, we returned the fire. Our line was now melting away with an alarming rapidity. It was already reduced to a mere skeleton to the line of one hour ago. Still on it pushed, with a determination that must ever be a credit to the Confederate soldiery.

Four brave men had already fallen under the colors of our Reg't, & now the fifth bore them aloft, & rushed boldly forward, to embrace, if need be, the fate of the other four. The flag staff was now cut in two midway the flag, but without one moment's pause, the never-flinching little Irishman (Geo. Kidd) [Joseph Marable], his flag now dangling in graceless confusion, from one corner, still pushed fearlessly, upon the stone fence. Thirteen of our Reg't had concentrated upon the colors, as if to constitute ourselves its guard. We were some yards in advance of the line, & now found ourselves within about thirty yards of the stone fence. Immediately before us was a small framed house [the Brian barn] — about twenty feet square — the farther end of which joined the fence. Springing forward, we secured its shelter, gaining at the same time, a position, within twenty five feet of the Yankees behind the fence. The boys betook themselves to the work before them in good earnest.

A number of shots were fired, which must have proven very fatal, as the distance was so small. Thinking the line rather a long time coming up, I looked to the rear.

The state of my feelings may be imagined, but not described, upon seeing the line broken, & flying in full disorder, at the distance of about one hundred & fifty yards from us. What was to be done? A momentary consultation decided. Lt. R. A. McDowell and I were the only officers with the party. I being the senior, the responsibility, if indeed there were any, devolved upon me. There were but two alternatives: to surrender, or become the "flying target" of a thousand muskets. We preferred the former, & in a moment more a white flag floated from behind the corner, around which the moment before, our ac[c]urately aimed muskets had belched their deadly contents into the ranks of the enemy. An old serg't came out & took charge of us, and ordered us through the gate that was open on the left of the [barn]. As [we] passed through, all unarmed of course, a Yankee soldier brought down his musket, &, with its muzzle right at the breast of one of our party, was on the point of firing. I cringed for the safety of my brave comrade, and shuddered at the thought of seeing him thus butchered, but just at this critical juncture, our serg't sprang forward, knocked up the musket, &, with a word of reproach, asked the soldier if he did not see that these men had surrendered. In passing the line, we were surrounded by a crowd of soldiers, all of whom were anxious to take charge of us. (It is a mighty good thing to get to take prisoners to the rear, especially when the front is well heated up as that at Gettysburg was.) We were hurried on under a strong guard. Our retreating line had, in the mean time, repassed our line of artillery, which immediately resumed its fire. Shells came screaming through the air, & began to burst around us. They flew thicker, & faster as the greater number of pieces opened, and I saw several very narrow escapes . . .

For half a mile we were thus exposed to the fire of our own guns. Hobbling along as best we were able—most of us wounded—hurried at every step by our impatient guard, we at length reached the Baltimore pike, where we found the second line of battle.

18. With Brigadier General Johnston Pettigrew in command of Major General Henry Heth's division, Pettigrew's brigade was commanded by Colonel James K. Marshall of the 52nd North Carolina. Louis Young, Pettigrew's aide-de-camp, briefly describes their approach to the Angle. Louis S. Young to Major William J. Baker, February 10, 1864, Francis Winston Papers, North Carolina State Archives and History.

In the alignment of the Division, Pettigrew's Brigade, under Col. Marshall, was second from the right, and with Archer's, advanced promptly and in good order, in continuation of Pickett's line. The distance over which we had to advance may be estimated when I state that the fuses for the shell used by the artillery stationed immediately in our front, were cut for one and a quarter miles. The ground over which we had to pass was perfectly open and numerous fences, some parallel and others oblique to our line of battle, were formidable impediments in our way. The position of the enemy was all he could desire. From the crest upon which he was intrenched, the hill sloped gradually forming a natural glacis; and the configuration of the ground was such, that when the left of our line approached his works, it must come within the arc of a circle, from which a direct, oblique and enfilade fire could be and was concentrated upon it. Under this fire from artillery and musketry, the Brigade on our left, reduced almost to a line of skirmishers; gave way. Pettigrew's and Archer's Brigades advanced a little further, and in perfect continuation of Pickett's line, which arrived at the works before we did, only because they jutted out in their front, and because they had to move over a considerably shorter distance. The right of the line formed by Archer's and Pettigrew's Brigades rested on the works, while the left was of course further removed, say forty to sixty yards. Subjected to a fire even more fatal than that which had driven back the Brigades on our left, and the men listening in vain for the cheering commands of officers, who had fallen, our Brigade gave way likewise, and *simultaneously* with it, the whole line. The supports under Maj. Gen. Trimble did not advance as far as we had. This repulse, to judge from results, was fatal to our campaign in Pennsylvania, and the troops engaged in the charge of the 3rd of July are blameable for having retired without orders; but you will perceive that they had to pass through a most trying ordeal; and it must remain always a sealed question, whether or not Cemetery Hill could have been taken with the forces engaged.

19. The 26th North Carolina, commanded by 20-year-old Colonel Henry Burgwyn, had been in the thick of the fighting on July 1st and had suffered heavy casualties. An unidentified soldier in the 26th North Carolina recorded the words spoken by Brigadier General Johnston Pettigrew as the charge began. Today a monument to the 26th stands about 20 yards west of the stone wall. Quoted in G. C. Underwood, *The History of the Twentieth-Sixth Regiment of the North Carolina Troops* (Goldsboro, N.C.: Hall, 1901), 365-366.

As soon as the fire of the artillery ceased, General Pettigrew, his face lit up with the bright look it always wore when in battle, rode up to Colonel Marshall, in command of the brigade, and said: "Now Colonel, for the honor of the good Old North State. Forward." Colonel Marshall promptly repeated the command, which taken up by the regimental commanders, the Twenty-sixth marched down the hill into the valley between the two lines. As the forward march continued, our artillery would occasionally fire a shot over the heads of the troops to assure them that they had friends in the rear.

The brigade had not advanced far when the noble Marshall fell, and the command of the brigade devolved on Major Jones, of the Twenty-sixth, while that of the regiment on Captain S. W. Brewer, of Company E, a man who proved on that day as he has often since, that he was thoroughly qualified to lead.

The Confederate line was yet unbroken and still perfect, when about half a mile from their works the enemy's artillery opened fire, sweeping the field with grape and canister; but the line crossed the lane (Emmettsburg Road) in good order. When about 300 yards from their works the musketry of the enemy opened on us, but nothing daunted the brave men of the Twenty-sixth who pressed quickly forward and when the regiment reached within about forty yards of the enemy's works, it had been reduced to a skirmish line. But the brave remnant still pressed ahead and the colors were triumphantly planted on the works by J. M. Brooks and Daniel Thomas, of Company E, when a cry came from the left, and it was seen that the entire left of the line had been swept away.

The Twenty-sixth now exposed to a front and enfilade fire, there was no alternative but to retreat, and the order was accordingly given. Captain Cureton, of Company B, and others, attempted to form the shattered remnants of the regiment in the lane (Emmettsburg road) but pressed by the enemy, the attempt was abandoned.

General Pettigrew had his horse shot under him during the charge, and though wounded (bones of his left hand shattered by a grape shot) he was one of the last men of his division to leave, and was assisted off the field by Captain Cureton, whom he ordered to rally and form Heth's division behind the guns for their support. Pettigrew's brigade promptly responded and formed when told where to go.

By night a very good skirmish line had been collected and the gallant old Twentieth-sixth had 67 privates and 3 officers present on the night of 3 July 1863, out of 800 who went into battle on the morning of 1 July. In this enumeration the cooks and extra duty men and others who had been armed are not counted. These 70 officers and men remained to support the artillery that night and all next day.

Section VII

"Our Artillery . . . Saved The Day
And Won The Victory":

The Federal Right

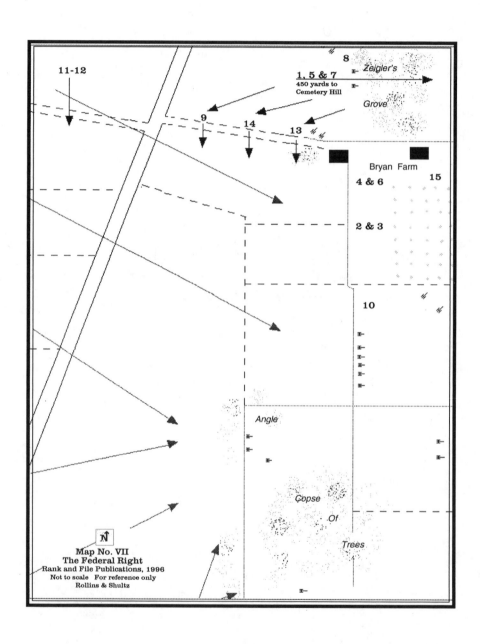

8

11-12

1, 5 & 7
450 yards to
Cemetery Hill

Zeigler's

9

14

13

Grove

Bryan Farm

4 & 6

15

2 & 3

10

Angle

Copse

.Of

Trees

N

Map No. VII
The Federal Right
Rank and File Publications, 1996
Not to scale   For reference only
Rollins & Shultz

1. Major General Oliver O. Howard, in command of the 11th Corps on Cemetery Hill, watched the cannonade and charge from that vantage point. Report of Maj. Gen. O. O. Howard, August 31, 1863, *OR*, 1, 27, 1, 706.

July 3, at 5 a. m., heavy infantry firing commenced on the right. It continued with more or less severity until after 10 a. m. Neither the artillery nor infantry of the Eleventh corps were much engaged. Occasionally an attempt was made by the enemy to put batteries in position, and some shots were fired. He always received a prompt reply from our batteries, and failed to receive any advantage.

At about 1 p. m. a terrific cannonade opened upon us from the west, northwest, north, and northeast, hurling into the cemetery grounds missiles of every description. Shells burst in the air, in the ground to the right and left, killing horses, exploding caissons, overturning tombstones, and smashing fences. There was no place of safety. In one regiment 27 were killed and wounded by one shell, and yet the regiments of this corps did not move excepting when ordered.

At 2.30 p. m. we ceased our artillery fire. Soon after, the enemy's artillery also ceased, when a line of his infantry appeared, emerging from the woods upon Seminary Ridge, his left nearly opposite our front, and the line extending far to the left. Our batteries again opened fire, using shells at first. The gaps made by them seemed to have no effect in checking the onward progress of the enemy. Still his line advanced steadily, gaining ground gradually toward his right. When near our line of skirmishers, the batteries opened upon them with grape and canister from the hill. The infantry also commenced firing. The enemy's lines were broken, and the plain in our front was covered with fugitives running in every direction. Colonel Smith's brigade, of General Steinwehr's division, was pushed to the left and front, to the support of the First corps, moving forward. This time great numbers of prisoners were taken, in which this portion of the Second Division bore a part.

2. Brigadier General Alexander Hays had taken command of the 3rd Division, 2nd Corps, just two weeks before the battle. He saw the first volley from his line break the charge of the Confederate left wing. Report of Brig. Gen. Alexander Hays, July 8, 1863, *OR*, 1, 27, 1, 454-455.

About 11 a. m. an entire lull occurred, which was continued until nearly 2 p. m. Anticipating the movement of the enemy, I caused the house and barn in our front, which interrupted the fire of our artillery, to be burned. At the hour last named, they opened upon our front the most terrific and uninterrupted fire from artillery. I cannot believe there were less than eighty pieces bearing on us within good range. It was continued uninterruptedly until 4:30 o'clock, when a heavy column of the enemy moved forward in three lines, preceded by a strong line of skirmishers, debouched from the wood opposite our line. Their march was as steady as if impelled by machinery, unbroken by our artillery, which played upon them a storm of missiles. When within 100 yards of our line of infantry, the fire of our men could no longer be restrained. Four lines rose from behind our stone wall, and before the smoke of our first volley had cleared away, the enemy, in dismay and consternation, were seeking safety in flight. Every attempt by their officers to rally them was vain. In less time than I can recount it, they were throwing away their arms and appealing most piteously for mercy. The angel of death alone can produce such a field as was presented.

3. A soldier-correspondent from a Buffalo, N.Y., newspaper filed a story about Hays during and after the battle. G. T. Fleming, ed., *Life and Letters of General Alexander Hays* (Pittsburgh: n.p., 1919), 424-425.

. . .I wish you could have seen the picture, just at the close of last friday's battle on the left of our center, of which his splendid figure formed such a prominent part. Our little brigade, which had been lying on Cemetery Hill, was ordered over to the position that was so valiantly but unsuccessfully charged by Pickett's Rebel Division. We hurried there through shot and shell, but only arrived in time to see the grand finale, the *tableau vivants*, and alas! *morants*, at the close of the drama. The enemy's batteries were still playing briskly, and their sharpshooters kept up a lively fire, but their infantry, slain, wounded and routed, were pouring, as prisoners, into our lines throughout their whole extent. Then enters Alexander Hays, brigadier general, United States Volunteers, the brave American soldier. Six feet or more in height, erect and smiling, lightly holding in hand his horse — the third within an hour — a noble animal, his flanks bespattered with blood, tied to his streaming tail a Rebel flag that drags ignominiously in the mud, he dashes along our lines, now rushing out into the open field, a mark for a hundred sharpshooters, but never touched, now quietly cantering back to our lines to be welcomed with a storm of cheers. I reckon him the grandest view of my life. I bar not Niagara. It was the arch-spirit of glorious victory triumphing wildly over the fallen foe. It was not my good fortune to be personally acquainted with this General Alexander Hays, but I wish every one, as far as I can effect it, to honor him as the bravest of soldiers and love him as the best hearted of men. A true chevalier he must be, *sans peur et sans reproche*. It seems miraculous that General Hays escaped unharmed. His division stood upon the broad open field, joining Webb's Brigade, and only shielded from the death storm which swept its ranks by the slight stone wall perched upon the brow of a shelving ledge, but which could be no protection to an officer on horseback.

4. The 12th New Jersey, part of Colonel Thomas Smyth's 2nd Brigade in Hays' division, was posted behind the stone wall just south of the Brian farm. An officer tells of the 12th's unusual armaments and their actions in the repulse of the charge. Address of Colonel William E. Potter, 6 May 1888, at the dedication of the monument to the 12th New Jersey at Gettysburg, quoted in Samuel Toombs, *New Jersey Troops in the Gettysburg Campaign* (Orange, N.J.: The Evening Mail Publishing House, 1898), 284-304.

The brigade of Smyth, now about to receive this tremendous attack, was still posted as I have heretofore stated. Our own regiment (the Twelfth New Jersey) was its proper right. The strength of the latter, as shown at the muster of June 30th, three days before, was twenty-five officers and five hundred and seven enlisted men present for duty, or a total of five hundred and thirty-two. Despite the casualties thus far it probably then had in line four hundred men. It was armed with the Springfield smooth-bore musket, calibre 69—a terrible weapon at close range. The usual cartridge carried a large ball and three buckshot, but many of the men, while awaiting the enemy's advance, had opened their boxes and prepared special cartridges of from ten to twenty-five buckshot alone. It was the only regiment in the division bearing the arm mentioned, and I doubt whether anywhere upon that field a more destructive fire was encountered than at the proper time blazed forth from its front.

The men were young, well disciplined, of respectable parentage, in comfortable circumstances and almost solely of native birth. In the entire regiment, as originally mustered, there were but seventy-two men of foreign nativity, and these were almost without exception faithful soldiers. The men had the confidence of their officers, who were in turn very generally trusted and respected by their men. Of very much the same stock were the One Hundred and Eighth New York, Fourteenth Connecticut and First Delaware, as they then stood.

The skirmishers along our front fell back before the enemy's advance, and taking position in the Emmetsburg road, fire with destructive effect; they are, however, soon driven in.

The enemy's column first comes in contact with the Eighth Ohio Volunteers, under command of Lieutenant-Colonel Franklin Sawyer, who, with four companies, deployed as skirmishers, supported them with the remainder of the regiment as a reserve, to the front of and somewhat to the right of Woodruff's battery. Under the stringent orders of Colonel Carroll to hold their position to the last man, they had maintained their post without relief since 4 p. m., of the second of July; having lost from their small numbers, up to noon of the third, 4 men killed, and 1 Captain, 1 Lieutenant, the Sergeant-Major and 38 men wounded.

As the enemy's column came on, according to Colonel Sawyer's report, now deployed in mass with a regiment in line upon its flank, that officer exhibits brilliant soldiership. Instead of retiring his skirmishers, he advances his reserve to their support, and dispersing the enemy's regiment advancing in line, he changes front forward upon his tenth company, closes down upon the column itself, and opens a fierce fire directly upon its flank. Though smitten deep, the force of Sawyer was too light to stay the progress of the heavy column, which swept onward with majestic impetus to attack Smyth's brigade. The Eighth Ohio, however, captured a large number of prisoners and three stands of colors, and its total loss during the action was 101 killed and wounded; including 1 officer killed, and 9 officers, the sergeant-major, 2 orderly sergeants and 2 duty sergeants wounded.

In our main line, to use the language of the official report of General Hancock, the "men evinced a striking disposition to withhold their fire." In our own regiment they did so under the orders of Major Hill, enforced by their company officers. The enemy now reached the Emmetsburg road, the fences fall before their pressure, and as they emerge into the broad turnpike, Smyth's brigade rising to its feet pours a terrific sheet of musketry into the column before which the whole front line seems to go down. The masses in rear press on, but vainly strive to pass the line of death marked by the road. The blazing line of Smyth's brigade is in their front; the Eighth Ohio presses upon their left; the guns of Woodruff firing double charges of canister upon their flank, sweep down whole ranks at once. To advance is annihilation, to retreat is death. In vain do they make the most strenuous exertions to regain their lost momentum; in vain do their leaders, officers, colorbearers, strong men, spring to the front and endeavor to move the column forward or cause it to deploy to fire. These are instantly shot down; and in less time than I have taken to tell the story the whole of the six brigades to the left of Pickett are either prone upon the ground, or fleeing in disordered groups northward and westward to escape the fire and to regain Seminary Ridge.

Just at the critical moment General Hays brought forward

from the rear the Third Brigade and formed it in rear of the Twelfth New Jersey. These troops did not, however, open fire, though they suffered considerable loss, and one shell, it is said, exploding near the colors of the One Hundred and Eleventh New York, killed 7 men.

In the height of the fight Lieutenant Richard H. Townsend, of Cape May county, fell shot through the heart. Promoted from the Tenth Regiment New Jersey Volunteers, he had been able to join his new command only three days before, and thus died in his first battle.

At least 2,000 prisoners and fifteen colors were taken by Hays' division.   Of the latter Smyth's brigade took nine; the Fourteenth Connecticut capturing four, the First Delaware three and the Twelfth New Jersey two. The aggregate loss of the brigade in the action was 366. The loss of the Twelfth New Jersey was: killed, 2 officers and 21 men; wounded, 4 officers and 79 men; missing, 9 men; an aggregate of 115, about one-fourth of its total strength.

5. Major Thomas Osborn, commander of the 11th Corps artillery, details the artillery tactics used during the charge, including the use of different types of shells at various distances. Thomas Osborn, "Experiences at the Battle of Gettysburg," in Crumb, ed., *The Papers of Major Thomas Osborn*, 29-45.

. . . We had but a few minutes to wait after the artillery ceased firing for developments. I think it was not more than ten minutes before the enemy's line of battle showed itself coming over Seminary Ridge at the point where we supposed Lee's troops were massed. As the line of battle came into view, it appeared to be about three-fourths of a mile in length and was moving in perfect line. The moment that line appeared coming down the slope of Seminary Ridge, every battery on Meade's line opened on it. Lee believed that he had silenced all our batteries while, with the exception of one or two a couple of hundred yards beyond my left, none had been so seriously injured that they were not able to continue their fire. The enemy's artillery kept up their fire on our line, but none of our batteries paid any further attention to it. They devoted their attention exclusively to the advancing line of battle.

From the very first minute our guns created sad havoc in that line. Lee's first line of battle had advanced about two hundred yards, after it came within sight, when another line in every way similar followed. These two lines of battle, nearly a mile distant, were then the sole object of fire of all the guns which could be made to bear upon them. The effects of this fire could very soon be seen.

At first the distance was so great that only solid shot from the brass guns and percussion shells from the rifled guns could be effectively used. The artillerymen endeavored to roll the solid shot through the ranks and explode the percussion shells in front of the lines. This method was effective to a large degree, as we would see the ranks thinned at many points and here and there a wide gap made as from two to a dozen men were taken out by the men being shot down. All this made no impression on the movement of the double line of battle. The men moved as steadily as if on dress parade. The entire field was open, and the movement was in plain view on a nearly level plain.

As the lines advanced, both the rifled and smooth bore guns used time shells upon the advancing lines and the killing and wounding was proportionately more severe. When they had covered about one third of the distance from Seminary Ridge to our line, their ranks had been a good deal cut out. They halted and closed their ranks from the right and left on the center and dressed their lines, which were materially shortened. This was done under a fearful artillery fire which was cutting them down by the hundreds every minute. They then moved forward as before, but the nearer they approached the more severe was their loss from our guns and the more seriously were the lines thinned. Still there was no hesitation or irregularity in the movement. The steady and firm step of the veteran soldiers continued.

Again they made another third of the distance and were just within the long range of cannister by the artillery and musketry by the infantry when the lines again halted, closed up and dressed, still more depleted than before. The lines were then very materially shortened in comparison with what they were when they first came into view.

After leaving Seminary Ridge, the lines had moved at a quick step, not double quick. From this second halt, the charge proper was made at a double quick. From that point to about half the distance to Hancock's line, Lee's lines passed out of range of my guns as an elevation of ground cut them off from my sight. I then turned my guns to answer the enemy's artillery which had not ceased playing upon the hill.

The remainder of the charge upon Hancock's front was made upon the double quick over about an eighth of a mile and of course occupied but a very few minutes. In that few minutes they received the full shock of the musketry and cannister of our line in their front, as the guns on the flanks could no longer reach them. Still they were so rapidly cut down that the regular lines of battle could not be maintained. As they approached Hancock's line, as is always the case in such charges, they took advantage of the slight irregularities of the ground, formed themselves into wedge shape and made a dash in this form to break Hancock's line. They struck that line about a fourth of a mile to my left. They did break the line, and a little more than three thousand men passed through it and were immediately captured. The remainder were driven back or killed or wounded.

The break made in Hancock's line was open only long enough for the men captured to pass through and was then closed from the right and left while they were still passing. All not carried through by the momentum of the movement were turned back. Those who had gone through were immediately surrounded and captured. No other break was made in the line.

The repulse of this column of the 15,000 men commanded by Major General Pickett was completed. All that was left of Pickett's command hurried back to Seminary Ridge. No order was preserved in the retreat, as indeed none was possible. No two men remained together, but each one ran back as rapidly as he could to Lee's line. As the men were retreating in disorder over the plain, all of Meade's batteries again opened upon them and did them considerable damage, but of course not so much as when they were in a well organized line of battle. When the greater part of these men reached Lee's line, he ordered his artillery to cease firing. Ours immediately ceased, and the Battle of Gettysburg was finished. Meade had won the fight.

6. **The diary of Captain George Bowen of the 12th New Jersey records the release of tension that men on both sides felt when the charge began. A "file closer" was a company-level officer who took a place behind the infantry line to make sure no men retreated without orders. As such, he had a good view of the fight. Diary of Captain George D. Bowen, 12th Regiment New Jersey Volunteers, *The Valley Forge Journal*, Vol. II, No. 1 (June 1884), 132-135.**

Friday July 3rd. 1863. Gettysburg. We are still behind the stone fence. Have been annoyed by the firing of the confederate sharpshooters, they are continually dropping shot in among us, but they are so far away that we can do nothing in reply as our guns will not carry so far. They became such a nuisance that 4 other companies of this Regt. were detailed to charge the Bliss house and barn and dislodge them. These 4 companies started across this field of nearly or quite of a mile under a very severe fire from the enemy all the way over. They reached the house and barn, they burned the barn. They were not strong enough to hold them, they retired in good order. They met a very severe loss. This charge is said to have been one of the finest of the war. This charge relieved us of the constant fire of their sharpshooters. After this things were comparatively quiet in our front. Many of the boys started foraging for some thing to eat, as we were entirely out of rations. Sergt. Morton of my company went into a small house only a few yards in our rear and went to bed in a feather bed in the house.

At one o'clock there was a single confederate gun sent a shot across to us, we heard it and tumbled out of bed just as a shot ploughed through the bed on which he had been lying. This appeared to be a signal. Their guns were trained on us, at once they opened on us with apparently all the artillery they have, they threw every kind of shot and shell. . . . We lay under this fire for 2 long hours, hugging the earth as close as we could. Finally our guns quit firing and the confederate fire slackened and at last quit. Looking up we saw them advancing out of the woods across the field, coming in three lines of battle, their bayonets fixed, lines dressed as if on parade, as they advanced the skirmish line advanced in front of them. As soon as they were within range of our artillery they [our artillery] opened on them with Spherical Case Shot, Shrapnel and round shot and shell, moving great swaths through their lines, they closed up the gaps only to have them again cut down. There was no hurry, no confusion as our shot was poured into them. They came as steady and regular as if on a dress parade, our guns pouring the shot into them. As before mentioned we were armed with smooth bore muskets that shot one ball and buck shot, no good at long range but very effective at short. We waited until they were in the Emmitsburg road, a distance of not over 100 yards from us. Then we opened fire, pouring in the most deadly kind of fire, they fell like wheat before the garner, but still on they came until they were within a dozen feet of us when those that were left threw down their guns and surrendered.   In passing a small house that stood on the opposite side of the Emmittsburg road, they broke into the movement known as "obstacle" breaking to the right and left, on passing this they filed back into line again as finely as if on dress parade. One man came up and got behind a small barn, not over 15 feet square that stood at the right of the Regt. I had just emptied my gun, he was pointing his gun right at me it seemed, Lieut. Acton was beside me shooting, I called his attention to him and said shoot him, he shot and the man fell, Acton said if he hit him it was in the head. Later saw him with a bullet through the center of his forehead. During this fight, I fired 30 or 40 loads, though a file closer and not supposed to fire my gun, used several guns to do it as they got so full that I could not get a load down them. Being in the line of File Closers, that is behind the line, had to set on one knee and one foot, extending my gun as far to the front as I could reach, this only brought the muzzle near the ears of the men in front line, each time I fired they looked back and told me I would shoot them, swearing about it, I told them they need not fear. Really think there was little danger as I was as cool as I ever was in my life. Was scared and that badly during the cannonading but as soon as [I] saw them come out to charge us it all faded away. Just at the left of the Regt. was a battery of steel rifled cannon, here the enemy got over the fence and to the battery. Here I saw a confederate jump on one of the guns, wave his flag and give a cheer, a gunner brained him with a sponge staff, or rammer.

7. **Captain Frederick Edgell reports the effectiveness of Federal artillery fire against the brigades of Brockenbrough and Davis. Report of Capt. Frederick M. Edgell, First New Hampshire Battery, Third Volunteer Brigade, July 6, 1863, _OR_, 1, 27, 1, 893-894.**

As the morning of the 3d began to dawn, the firing became more rapid, and did not cease until about 11 a. m.

At about 1:30 p. m. the enemy opened a rapid artillery fire on our center and left. Their batteries, in a semicircle about the point, swept the hill with a terrible cross-fire. The battery was now much exposed to the plunging shots of the enemy, which fell continually among my pieces, but fortunately without doing much damage.

At 2.30 p. m. I was ordered to take up my old position on Cemetery Hill, relieving Captain Huntington's Ohio battery. I commenced again to throw shell at the enemy's batteries, and also at some bodies of troops, apparently picket reserves, which caused them to break and retreat to the woods. The firing of the enemy's artillery was now very inaccurate most of the shots being too high, and by the direction of General Meade the firing was discontinued by the batteries on the hill, as the men were ordered to lie down.

Soon after at about 4. p. m. a grand attack was made by the enemy on our left, and commenced a rapid fire of caseshot on his advancing lines. I fired obliquely from my position upon the left of the attacking column with destructive effect, as that wing was broken and fled across the field to the woods. I next saw what appeared to be the remainder of the attacking force come into our lines prisoners. There was no firing by my battery after this.

I expended this day 248 rounds of shell and case shot, making 353 total expended. The Hotchkiss time shell and Schenkl percussion worked well, but the Schenkl combination case seldom exploded. From what experience I have had with this fuse, I think it is not reliable.

The casualties in my battery were 3 men wounded (only 1 seriously). I also lost 3 horses killed, and a wheel and axle broken. The latter were replaced during the night of the 4th from the field.

I am happy to state that the officers and men of the New Hampshire battery behaved nobly. Although for forty-eight hours under fire, and a part of that time exposed to a terrific cannonade, not a man left his post or wavered, and, by their steadiness and precision of fire in the afternoon of the 3d, I believe contributed much toward repulsing the enemy's attack. For confirmation of this, I would respectfully refer to Major Osborn, chief of artillery, Eleventh Corps, under whose direction my battery was placed during the action of the 2d and 3d.

8.   Lieutenant Tully McCrea, with Woodruff's battery behind Hays' division, north of the Brian farm, moved down the slope to better enfilade the Confederate advance. The effectiveness of the guns, and the slaughter they inflicted, did not deter the Confederates from firing back, causing serious losses among the artillerymen. Tully McCrea to John Bachelder, 30 March 1904, GNMP.

This Artillery fire of the enemy, which I have since learned lasted two hours, but which seemed to me to have lasted two days, suddenly ceased, and we were all on the *Qui Vive* to see what was to happen next. We had not long to wait before the men in gray began to pour out of the woods on Seminary Hill opposite our position, and they continued to come until there were eighteen thousand of them. . . .

When I saw this mass of men, in three long lines, approaching our position, and knowing that we had but one thin line of infantry to oppose them, I thought that our chances for Kingdom Come, or Libby Prison were very good. Now this is where our Artillery came in, saved the day, and won the battle. I have always been of the opinion that the Artillery has never received the credit which was its due for this battle.

As the enemy started across the field in such splendid array, every rifled battery from Cemetery Hill to Round Top was brought to bear upon their line. We, with the smooth bores, loaded with cannister, and bided our time. When they arrived within five hundred yards we commenced to fire, and the slaughter was dreadful. Never was there such a splendid target for Light Artillery.

As their men were killed or wounded, the others would close toward the centre, and by the time they reached our lines it was a mass of men without organization. But they did reach it, through all of that terrible cannonade, and at one place penetrated it, but there were so few left that they were too weak to be effective, and were captured. It was the splendid work of the Artillery that saved the day and gave us the victory.

When the enemy's Artillery fire ceased and we saw his infantry preparing to charge our position, Woodruff had his guns run to the crest of the hill, and gave the necessary orders to prepare for the struggle which was coming. He would not fire a shot until the enemy got in close range where our cannister would be most effective. At the command "Commence firing" everybody worked with a will and two rounds of cannister per minute was delivered from each gun. The slaughter was fearful, and great gaps were made in the mass of the enemy upon each discharge.

After it all ended, as it did in a few minutes after we commenced firing, I had a chance to look around me. I found that we had only four of the six guns left, and I was the only officer. In the thickest of it, Egan, who had the left platoon, had been ordered to change to another position further to the left. I was so intently attending to my duties with the right platoon that I did not know that he was gone.

Woodruff had been wounded and disabled and the men had placed him behind a tree to protect him from being further wounded. It was a sad sight for us to see his life coming to this untimely end, for we knew it was the end from the nature of the wound. We removed him to the little stone school-house in rear of the line of battle, where he remained until he died the next day. Everything was done that could be done with our limited means to make him as comfortable as possible. He died on July fourth, was buried behind the school-house, and his grave so marked that it could be identified.

His suffering, from the nature of the wound, must have been great, but not a murmur or groan escaped him. His nerve and courage continued to the end.

9. As Pettigrew's and Trimble's men crossed the Emmitsburg Road and moved up the slope, Hays ordered several of his units to make a left wheel from their positions along the line, ending up as a flanking movement that put the Confederates in a cross fire. Lieutenant L. E. Bicknall and the 1st Massachusetts Sharpshooters were in the Emmitsburg Road and could see both wings of the Confederate line. Bicknall and his men had a perfect line of fire and did their work well. Letter of Lieut. L. E. Bicknall, 1st Massachusetts Sharpshooters, n.d., 1883, quoted in *Life and Letters of Hays*, 438-439.

I found a monument in Ziegler's Grove to the 88th Pennsylvania Volunteers which marks the spot where our infantry were being rapidly cut down by the enemy's sharpshooters on the morning of July 3rd. In fact, when, with twenty of the 1st

Massachusetts Sharpshooters, I entered the grove our infantry were virtually driven from it. We held the grove to the right and left of the 88th's monument until the heavy cannonading checked sharp-shooting. A shattered remnant of some regiment, perhaps the one that had suffered so in front of and in the grove, lay along the remains of a stone wall in our rear, and during the heavy cannon-ading which preceded the enemy's assault, with many others, sought the seeming shelter of the grove.

Just before the grand charge, at the request of General Alexander Hays, who commanded the Third Division of the Second Crops, I gathered up all these men that lay in the grove and General Hays formed them in line to the right of the Bryan house, which is the house to the left of the monument on the line of battle as you go towards Round Top. At the time of the battle the grove extended to this house. I took position with the remainder of my squad of sharpshooters on the right of this line.

While the enemy were advancing to the Emmittsburg Road, General Hays drilled the line in the manual of arms, allowing them to fire left oblique while the enemy were closing with our line to the left of the Bryan house, then swung them down by a left wheel to the lane which then ran from the house to the Emmittsburg Road; across the lane they then fired. The moment chosen for the left wheel or flanking movement was just as the last division of the enemy's charging column was crossing the Emmittsburg Road, moving directly for Ziegler's Grove. As the entire front of the Second Corps to the left of the Bryan house was already covered and in many places penetrated, this fresh division would probably have forced our line back and gained the shelter of the grove had it not been subjected to our flank fire, which destroyed its formation and sent its shattered and disordered masses along the other side of the lane and in front of the Third Division of the Second Corps.

I finally drew back our line a little from the fence to prevent our rear being gained by the enemy moving north on the Emmittsburg Road, and also to uncover a gun [or two guns] which had during the melee been got into position at the head of the lane near the Bryan house, and as the enemy crowded forward into the lane the fire of these guns ended the contest.

I have not yet learned what regiments or fragments of regiments composed the line swung down, but they were strangers to me, and I have just learned the 39th, 111th, 125th and 126th New York Regiments were added to the Third Division on the march to Gettysburg. I left the army soon after the battle and had no opportunity to learn afterwards.

10. Charles Page of the 14th Connecticut describes the
sounds of the charge. Some in his regiment fired their Sharps
breechloading rifles so fast that the barrels grew hot and had to be
cooled with water. The Sharps gave them the firepower of several
regiments of men with muzzleloaders. Like many Confederates,
most Federals felt that this moment was of extreme importance,
both for themselves and for the Union cause. Page underscores
this when he describes their preparation during the last few
moments as the Confederates approached within rifle range.
Charles D. Page, *History of the Fourteenth Regiment, Connecticut
Volunteer Infantry* (Meridian, Conn.: The Horton Printing Co.,
1906), 142-156.

Deducting the two companies that were acting as skirmishers at the front and the killed and wounded in the destroying of the
Bliss buildings, the regiment now numbered about one hundred
men. To occupy the space at the wall left vacant by the disrupted
battery, it was necessary for the regiment to stretch out, leaving only
one line.

All eyes were turned upon the front to catch the first sight of
the advancing foe. Slowly it emerged from the woods, and such a
column! Eleven brigades of Pickett's division advancing obliquely
upon the Second division of the Second Corps, Heth's four brigades,
commanded by General Pettigrew, in front, while that of Lane and
Scales formed in their rear. There were three lines, and a portion of
a fourth line, extending a mile or more. It was, indeed, a scene of
unsurpassed grandeur and majesty. It is no wonder that Major Ellis
in his official report said "It was magnificent." As far as eye could
reach could be seen the advancing troops, their gay war flags
fluttering in the gentle summer breeze, while their sabers and
bayonets flashed and glistened in the midday sun. Step by step they
came, the music and rhythm of their tread resounding upon the
rock-ribbed earth. Every movement expressed determination and
resolute defiance, the line moving forward like a victorious giant,
confident of power and victory. If one listened, he might hear the
voice of the commander, "Steady men, steady." There is no swaying
of the line, no faltering of the step. The advance seems as resistless
as the incoming tide. It was the last throw of the dice in this supreme
moment of the great game of war. On, on, they come and slowly
approach the fence that skirts the Emmettsburg road. Watchful
eyes are peering through the loosely built stone wall. Anxious hearts
are crouched behind this rude redoubt. Hardly can the men be
restrained from firing although positive orders had been given that
not a gun should be fired until the enemy reached the Emmettsburg
road. It was, indeed, an anxious moment. One you can see is

looking at the far off home he will never see again. Another is looking at his little ones, as he mechanically empties his cartridge-box on the ground before him, that he may load more quickly, determined to part with life as dearly as possible. Others are communing with Him before whom so many will shortly have to appear.

The skirmishers are driven in, but not in confusion, and some lines about face to return the Confederate skirmish fire, and thus gain time to bring in the killed and wounded.

Slowly the great line moved forward until it reached the fence. The men mounted to cross when the word fire! fire! ran along the Union line, crack! crack! spoke out the musketry, and the men dropped from the fence as if swept by a gigantic sickle swung by some powerful force of nature. Great gaps were formed in the line, the number of slain and wounded could not be estimated by numbers, but must be measured by yards. Yet on came the second line in full face of the awful carnage. No longer could the measured tread be heard, no longer were the orders of the commanding officers audible for the shrieks of the wounded and groans of the dying filled the air, but on they came, meeting with the same fate as their comrades. The third line wavered and faltered, even their courage forbidding them to face such a storm of musketry. The color-bearers now advanced, apparently in obedience to previous orders, and, attended by their color-guards, planted their battle flags in the ground much nearer. Then the firing being too hot for them, lay down, waiting for their men to advance and rally around them. One of them in particular was in advance of the others and planted his flag not more than ten rods distant from and in front of the center of the Fourteenth.

The men of the regiment still actively continued firing. Several of the men were fortunate in having two breech-loaders for while one was loading the other was firing. So rapid was this firing that the barrels became so hot that it was almost impossible to use them, some using the precious water in their canteens to pour upon the overworked guns. Accounts seem to agree that the Confederate line broke quicker in the immediate front of the Fourteenth than any where else, and seeing this a shout went up from the regiment, which was taken up and echoed and reechoed along the whole Union line. In vain did the Confederate commanders attempt to reform their broken columns, colors were dropped and the men fled in confusion. Major Ellis gave the order to the regiment to fire left oblique to dislodge some of the Confederates who had come uncomfortably near the front of an adjoining battery. The regiment had just turned when a daring and audacious Confederate jumped upon the gun of a battery which had been left about two rods in front, when the battery withdrew for want of horses, and waved his hat in his hand for his comrades to follow. He did not remain there an instant, but fell riddled through. With the help of the regiment's crossfire, the rebels in front of the neighboring battery were soon in full retreat.

Another incident connected with this remarkable record of the Fourteenth was the capture of a flag by Major Hincks. Confederate color planted about ten rods in front of the center of the regiment still stood. There were no rebels standing near it, but several were lying down, waiting for the men to advance. Major Ellis called for volunteers to capture the flag and instantly Major Hincks, Major Broatch and Lieutenant Brigham leaped the wall. Brigham was shot down by a retreating rebel, but the other two sped on, Hincks finally outstripping Broatch ran straight and swift for the color, amid a storm of shot. Swinging his saber over the prostrate Confederates and uttering a terrific yell, he seized the flag and hastily returned to the line. He was the object of all eyes and the men cheered him heartily as he reached the ranks. It was the flag of the Fourteenth Tennessee Regiment and had inscribed upon it the twelve battles in which the regiment had participated, VIZ.:—"Seven Pines, Mechanicsville, Cold Harbor, Shepardstown, Fredericksburg, Chancellorsville, Oxhill, Harper's Ferry, Sharpsburg, Frazier's Farm, Cedar Run and Manassas."

11. Private Thomas Galway of the 8th Ohio, though wounded during the cannonade, described the attack on the left of the Pettigrew-Trimble line. Galway, *The Valiant Hours*, 114-122.

We stepped out of the ditch and moved up on the roadside bank. For a minute we saw nothing but the smoke of our skirmishers in front. Then came a distant murmur from the front, followed by a renewal of our artillery fire, which had slackened for a few minutes. All at once the murmur increased into a prolonged yell, and we saw the enemy with colors flying advancing in columns in mass, to the left of where the barn had been burnt in the morning. I had often read of battles and of charges; had been in not a few myself; but until this moment I had not gazed upon so grand a sight as was presented by that beautiful mass of gray, with its small, square colors, as it came on in serried array, cheering their peculiar cheer, right towards the crest of the hill which we and our batteries were to defend. We went forward to the fence line at a run; and now against us moved a large force of the enemy who were formed to the north of the *column in mass.* Later in the day I learned that the massed column was Pickett's division of Longstreet's corps; the troops north of them, who were assaulting us, were Pender's and Pettigrew's divisions of Hill's corps. They were in two lines of battle, with their batteries in the intervals of the line, advancing at a gallop.

Our artillery fire that now opened upon the advancing Confederates was such as nothing but the heroic could endure. Before the lines moving against us were come within close range, we watched and very anxiously too, that beautiful, terrible mass coming toward our left shoulders. At its head was a mounted officer who rode like a demigod and was worthy by his courage to lead those brave men who followed. We now heard the fearful din of the artillery, the savage, threatening yells of the advancing and now seemingly invincible enemy, of the insulting taunts of the enemy's old skirmish line in our front, who had now risen to their feet and were pouring a destructive fire into us. We stood all alone out in that open field, waving our colors; in spite of all the threatening advance we took time to praise the valor of that Confederate officer who rode ahead, a conspicuous mark for sixty cannon and thousands of muskets.

A few seconds, and a cheer rises to the west of us. Now Pender's line, with colors flying, issues from the trees that cover the crest of the low ridge to our front, and comes right towards us. But from the first it was easy to see the difference between the mettle of these men and those of Pickett's glorious column. Two or three times Pender's line hesitated, whether obliged to reform, because of the irregularity of the ground, or whether owing to a disposition to give way before the effect of our artillery shells exploding right in front of them. These bursts, which occasionally hid them in smoke from us, were now actually tearing their ranks to pieces. The enemy came as far as the fence opposite us, where the Confederate skirmishers had been from the first of the battle, and here they lay down.

Had they continued their advance with the same spirit shown by their comrades in Pickett's column, God knows how many days might have been added to this war! But down they lay, though only for a few minutes. We so galled them with our fire that a panic soon took hold of them and they fled, back to the low ridge.

I must say something about the anomalous position of our regiment, sent out to the Emmitsburg pike to skirmish with the advance of the enemy's assaulting troops. We found ourselves, a single regiment of less than three hundred men, two hundred yards in front of the main Federal position. Seemingly a forlorn position for us but, as it turned out, destined to play an unexpectedly vital part in the defense of the salient angle which Meade's line of battle made just behind us.

Pender's advance being so soon checked, every shot was turned on Pickett. On and on came his column, the mounted officer still conspicuous at its head. From time to time the smoke of bursting shells would envelop them for a few seconds, but when the smoke lifted, the gray mass was still coming on, still compact, still orderly, ever and anon raising one of those piercing yelps which had been so terrifying for our new troops to hear. They have ascended the last slope and now have nothing between them and the crest of the heights but the blueclad men who, at one part of the line, are behind a stone wall. Now they are almost at the turnpike, to the left of our regiment. The blood goes fast through the veins now; the light of battle shines in the eye; the heart becomes, for the time, steeled; goodness and mercy and all the softer emotions that, at other times, influence a man's action, are dormant. This is the moment and the circumstance of which poets have sung, which historians have narrated, which even painters have endeavored to depict; but which none can understand, who have not seen, heard, or felt the crisis of a great battle. The enemy column has now approached the turnpike just to the south of us. They seem to pay no attention to us, who are a mere handful. Yet the fire which we pour into their left flank is a deadly one and tells visibly upon them. They are now over the turnpike and begin to ascend the rise to the stone wall. We have entirely recovered from the momentary doubt that had seized us and, with the fresh ammunition which a short time ago was issued us, play havoc with them. Still brave and cheering, they ascend the stone wall. Our men up there break and disappear beyond the crest of the ridge which at that point is not as high as it is just behind us. For a few seconds things look dubious; the enemy has taken Griffin's battery and are beginning to train its guns on our own line. Then in the nick of time Major Rorty of Hancock's staff, rallying a portion of the 29th New York, charges them and recovers the battery. The enemy, now broken and disorganized and far from any support, begin to retire. The retreat is, almost at once, turned into a flight! From our position on their flank we and other troops off on the Confederate right (south) flank, have not ceased to pour a devastating fire into their masses. Now at last they begin to melt. They had gained the crest of the ridge, almost had victory in their grasp, when now, unfortunate men, they are forced to turn their charge into a disastrous flight. They threw away everything — cartridge boxes, waist-belts, and haversacks — in their stampede. We dashed in amongst them, taking prisoners by droves. One man of my company, a corporal, took fifteen prisoners including two officers as well as a stand of colors. As far the eye could reach, the ground was covered with flying Confederates. They all seemed to extend their arms in their flight, as if to assist their speed. From the time when the enemy's signal gun was fired, at ten minutes to one, until the moment when the magnificent troops of Pickett's column had disappeared over the low ridge, a mere mass of fugitives, was about seventy minutes.

Our own loss was severe. I myself was hit three times between the opening of the cannonade and the rout of the enemy. The First and Second Sergeants of my company each lost a leg. Old

John Burke, who had served twenty one years in the 18th Royal Irish, of the British Army, before entering ours, also lost the use of a leg. Lelievre, who was an old French sailor, was also crippled in the leg. Wilson was killed outright, as was Corporal Barney McGuire, a brave, humorous fellow; and Private William Brown died before dark. Out of the two hundred and sixteen men that our regiment took into battle, we lost one hundred and three in killed and severely wounded. As for the slightly wounded, almost every man was hit. In other words, we suffered nearly 100 percent casualties. As Pickett's column was running we had dashed amongst them, and our one hundred and fifty men captured about the same number of prisoners. When we had reached the ditch of the Emmitsburg Pike on our way back, we beheld a sorry sight. Many of the wounded had been carried back to it during the fight. Others had hobbled and crawled into it, some dying after reaching it. It was full of pools of blood, and the grass for some distance in front was saturated with blood. In the ditch along with many others in like condition, lay two of our sergeants, Fairchild (Orderly) and Kelly (Second) Sergeant; each with the lower part of the leg hanging by a piece of flesh to the rest of the limb. This brought the tears to my eyes, for they were both good men, brave soldiers, and favorites with everyone.

12.   Another private in the 8th Ohio, T. S. Potter, also recalled the magnificent sight of the Confederate battle lines, as well as the destructive power of their rifles. T .S. Potter, "The Battle of Gettysburg," *National Tribune*, August 5, 1882.

. . . The morning of the 3d broke calm and beautiful. Oh! how many saw the sun rise for the last time, and ere it should sink behind those blue hills to the westward they would receive their final muster out. After we had eaten our breakfast of coffee and hard-tack we gathered in groups to discuss the situation.

"Boys!" said our first lieutenant, "to-day will probably decide the battle. We have held them pretty well so far, and to -day we must whip them; yes, I say we *must* whip them. I would rather be killed right here, than that they should whip us."

Poor fellow. Were his words prophetic? Before night he was killed. At noon, Company H, with others, relieved pickets. We were farther to the left than the line we occupied the day before; we were deployed along a gentle rise of ground that ran parallel with Cemetery Ridge; we took our stations along a board fence; we were near the little white house that all will remember who were in the battle of the 3d. We had orders not to fire on the picket line, so everything was quiet along our part of the line; but to our left were some Germans, who kept up a continuous fusillade. An order came from the general to our captain (who was officer of the pickets for the day) to have that firing stopped. He sent a sergeant to enforce the order. 'Nix! nix!' and they would point to the dead bodies lying along the fence, and blaze away again. They could not understand the logic of not answering the rebel fire, and so the sergeant came back from his fruitless errand. One o'clock. How the sun blazed and scorched, hardly a breath of air, the water in our canteens too warm to quench our thirst. Why were the rebs so quiet? We strained our eyes looking for some movements to denote what they were up to, but we could see nothing suspicious. Suddenly two shots ring out, and two shells come shrieking and howling over us; then all the woods in our front, a half mile away, blaze out. Boom! whiz! bang! whir - r - r, the air appears to be filled with the missiles of death. Shells burst all around us. Solid shot come ricochetting along the ground. A rebel battery comes rushing down the opposite hill and unlimbers almost in range of our rifles. Our batteries are replying. Rickett's battery of Napoleons are immediately in our rear. He fires slow and deliberate, and we are sure every shot goes home, but the rebel batteries concentrate on him and his guns cease firing, one by one, until only one was left, but that kept up, responding to the rebel fire until the order was given to all the batteries to cease firing and let the guns cool — a wise precaution, as the sequel showed. After about a half hour more the rebel batteries ceased suddenly, as their guns had become so heated they could fire no longer. Soon we began to see the glint of bayonets among the trees; then a line of battle detached itself and came moving across the valley. I should judge by the looks that the line was about one mile in length by three lines of battle deep. As they came sweeping towards us the left of their line came opposite Company H's position on the skirmish line. It was a magnificent sight, their well-dressed lines and colors flying. Their general was mounted on a white horse. As soon as they had got into plain view our batteries opened upon them. We could see the huge gaps torn through their ranks, but they came steadily on, faster and faster; the artillery fired, men went down by scores, until the lines had to oblique to the centre to close up the ranks. Soon they came within range of the skirmish line. "Now, boys, look out for the general," was the word passed along the line; but he kept moving rapidly up and down the line encouraging his men; so we could not hit him, but many a poor fellow in the ranks received the bullet that was intended for him. We fell back slowly, loading at a trail arms, then facing about and firing. We found the reserve standing to arms in the sunken road, and we took our proper place in the regiment. Our line of battle had now opened, and musketry and artillery roared in unison. Captain Miller, of Company H, was the first man to spring up the bank, shouting "come on, boys!" He was immediately followed by the whole regiment and a part of a New York regiment that had been on the skirmish line with us. What a sight met us. As we raised the bank, a dozen rods away to our left was a board fence that ran north from the road. Beyond the fence was a large field; it appeared to be nearly filled with rebels getting badly demoralized. The slaughter among them was fearful. Rifle-balls, canister, shrapnel, and shells were pouring into their doomed ranks. I saw shells burst among them and men were thrown twenty feet into the air by the explosion. They struggled and fought bravely, but it was of no avail. In a very brief time the firing ceased, and our bugle blew the assembly. We had captured three battle-flags and a large number of prisoners, but we had lost fearfully — 107 killed and wounded — within the two days. All the commissioned officers of Company H were killed or wounded. First Lieutenant Hayden killed in the last charge, Captain _____ shot through the shoulder with a rifle-ball nearly at the same time; the second lieutenant was hit with a piece of shell. . . .

13. An unidentified private in the 108th New York writes home to his father. Quoted in G. T. Fleming, ed., *Life and Letters of Alexander Hays*, 442-443.

Battlefield at Gettysburg, Pa., July 4th, 1863

Dear Father — Another great battle has been fought and won. Wednesday night we arrived here from Taneytown, and Thursday morning our regiment was ordered to the front to support the First Regular Battery. During the day we were shelled occasionally and a few of our men were wounded. Yesterday forenoon they opened on us again, but were soon silenced by our brass twelve-pounders. The enemy could be seen building breastworks, or abatis work, for protection from our shot and shells. In the forenoon Companies A & C were sent out as skirmishers and had three killed and four wounded. At noon or near that hour they were relieved and came in. About 2 o'clock the enemy opened fire from their batteries, thus getting a partial cross-fire on us. Our guns replied in good time and order. Our regiment was immediately in their rear and laid down, but very many of them suffered severely; indeed, it was the hardest fire the 108th ever experienced — perfectly awful, murderous. Not a second but a shell shot or ball flew over, or by us. Large limbs were torn from the trunks of the oak trees under which we lay and precipitated down upon our heads. One shell came shrieking and tearing through the trees with the velocity of lightning, striking a caisson, causing it to explode, wounding several. Three or four men started to their feet to leave the spot, but Lieut. Card drew his sword and commanded them to go back and lay down in their places, which they did. Small trees were cut down and large ones shattered almost to pieces. Five different cannon-balls struck a large oak three feet in diameter, which stood not five feet from where I lay, and one of them passed entirely through it. A shell struck right at my feet, killing Sergeant Maurice Welch and Private John Fitzner. This destructive and murderous fire continued to pour in upon us for more than an hour — in fact, until they silenced our batteries, or rather until we had exhausted our ammunition. Very many of our cannoneers were killed or wounded and the most of the horses. Some of our regiment had to help them run their pieces back by hand. General French having taken command of the Third Corps, Brigadier General Hays had command of our division, and I must say I think he is the bravest division general I ever saw in the saddle. Most of the time he was riding up and down the line in front of us, exhorting the "boy" to stand fast and fight like men. Shell, shot, nor the bullets of the Rebel sharpshooters seemed to intimidate him in the least; in fact, he paid not the least attention to them, nor did his staff officers. Once he rode by and said, "Boys, don't let 'em touch these pieces," and in a few moments he rode back again, laughing, and sung out, "Hurrah! boys, we're giving them h—ll" and he dashed up to the brow of the hill and cheered our skirmishers, who were driving the Rebs before them. Soon after our pieces ceased firing, the Rebels slackened theirs also, and then advanced in three lines of infantry from the woods and across the fields. I never saw troops march out with more military precision. Their lines were straight and unbroken and they looked in the distance like statues. On they came, steady, firm, moving like so many automatons. Our brigade now formed in line to receive them, the skirmishers coming in at the same time. The 108th was taken out of the grove, drawn up in line of battle and then told to kneel down until the word to fire. The 12th New Jersey was on our left and the 126th New York on our right. Two pieces of the First Battery were brought up by hand, and when the Rebs had advanced about half way across the field a deadly fire of grape and canister was thrown into them, mowing them down like chaff. But still on they came. When within musket range the infantry rose up and gave them a withering shower and the gray lines melted away.

14. The 125th New York, part of Colonel George Willard's 3rd Brigade of Hays' division, had been captured by Stonewall Jackson in September 1862 at Harper's Ferry. The New Yorkers had been exchanged, but had not lived down the embarrassment. They set out to prove themselves at Gettysburg, they had been in

the thick of the fight on July 2nd. Chaplain Ezra Simons watched the flanking movement of part of the regiment, and the work of the rest behind the wall. Ezra D. Simons, *A Regimental History: The One Hundred and Twenty-Fifth New York State Volunteers* (New York: Ezra D. Simons, 1888), 136-138.

But, what of the regiment? Some of its number had been on the skirmish line all day. Lieutenant Merritt Miller, with others, had served in command of the skirmishers during the morning; and another of our officers, Captain Samuel C. Armstrong, was in charge of the brigade pickets, from before the cannonading and under its fierce progress. During the morning the men hugged the ground, for the firing was hot, the rebels pouring in a flank fire on the picket-line, from the houses of Gettysburg, killing and wounding some of our men. About noon, Captain Armstrong withdrew the line for rest to the reserve station on the Emmettsburg road; and at this point they were under the artillery fire which preceded Pickett's charge. The shot and shell from both sides passed over their heads. Noticing a lull in the cannonading, Captain Armstrong looked around and saw the Confederate lines marching grandly down the slope towards our men. He immediately ordered the entire picket-reserve and all whom he could muster — about seventy-five all told — to fall in, and led them on the "doublequick" about three hundred yards down the Emmettsburg road, to get at the enemy in flank.

Finding a rail fence at right angle to their advancing line, some sixty or seventy yards from their extreme left, he posted his men along the rail fence. They took position unflinchingly; and, resting their rifles on the top of the fence, took deliberate aim and poured a murderous fire into the rebel flank, comprising Pettigrew's men. The Confederate leader afterwards confessed surprise that this part of the charging line should have been the first to break. To the Eighth Ohio has been given the credit for the flank fire which contributed efficiently to this result. But, distinct record should go into general history of Captain Armstrong's brave and skillful part at that important point of the battle. From Captain Armstrong's position the Confederate dead could be seen lying in heaps. Hundreds of the charging line prostrated themselves on their backs in the Emmettsburg road, and waved their hats and handkerchiefs in token of surrender. Some of the bravest rushed close to the main Union line, and fell a few yards away. Of the five officers who served with Captain Armstrong in his brave action, which aided in the great victory secured, he was the only survivor. As he remembers, the first Confederate line near his position was nearly all shot down or captured; the second line did not support the first efficiently; and the third did not get at all into the thick of the fight.

The position of the One Hundred and Twenty-fifth during

Pickett's charge was immediately behind the stone wall at the place occupied by the regiment during the second day and before the charge made in the swale, where Colonel Willard was killed. The position was directly to the left of the Bryan barn. Some one not connected with the regiment has located the position on a second line some yards to the rear of the stone wall. This error will be corrected when a monument marks — as it soon will — the true ground. Other troops were mingled with our regiment at the crucial point. when the rebel line broke, our color-sergeant, Harrison Clark, sprang over the wall and bore the flag proudly down the slope to the fence skirting the Emmettsburg road. In the shelling that preceded the charge, among others killed as John W. Deforest, a near relative of the writer; one who had passed with his brother and his captain, Ephraim Wood of H Company, through the rebel lines investing Harper's Ferry.

Bravely standing behind that historic stone wall was the captain just named, who scorned the defense of even a low field-marking fence; and with needless boldness faced death.

And death came. A bullet pierced his abdomen, and he was borne from the field to the hospital at Rock Creek, there — the next day — to die. Willard D. Green, of H Company, saw him the moment he was struck. Sergeant Jacob Houch and the writer kneeled at the brave dying man's side, who, after intense suffering, passed away, speaking with last breath the name of his wife.

15. Assistant Surgeon Francis Moses Wafer of the 108th New York watched the repulse from behind the lines. Diary of Francis Moses Wafer, Queen's University Library, Kingston, Ontario, Canada.

. . . The enemy fire somewhat slackened about 3 p.m. & a line of battle appeared emerging from the woods immediately in front of the 2nd Corps. It was their first Corps, Longstreet's. On they came in solemn grandeur formed in several lines deep, their lines gay with battle flags, across the open plain more than half a mile of which was fully exposed to the fire of our artillery. Their guns now opened over the heads of their charging lines as they advanced like men who expected but trifling opposition

The ground over which this charge was made was level and exposed, yet their line did not suffer much from our guns until it came so near that it became necessary for their gunners to slacken their fire — lest they should injure their infantry — & elevate their pieces so that as to aid their attack somewhat by throwing shells over the heads of both combatants. The line maintained the most perfect order until reaching the Emmetsburg road, although our guns were now all opened upon them with canister shot. This road was bounded on both sides, in our front, by straight rail fence, the double posts of which were firmly planted in the earth. These could not be thrown down without taking them slowly to pieces — consequently they had to climb those two fences & reform in the open field which gently sloped up to our position. Our line of infantry which had lain flat under what slight cover some piles of rails & stones gathered from the fields afforded, in order to escape observation & to avoid as much as possible the storm of iron poured up on them, now simultaneously rose to their feet — reminding one of the British guards at Waterloo, & indeed Brig. Genl. Alex Hayes commanding our Division used the Duke's expression — modified by saying to his men "Up Vols. & at them!" The musketry at once broke into a crashing roll that drownded [sic] for the time the fearful whizz of the canister, but through all this Longstreet's Corps still essayed to advance & return the fire. They did not disturb the line of our Division at any point although some of their dead were found within 15 yds of our line, but succeeded for a moment in penetrating the 2nd Division stuck some of their battleflags in the gun carriages & attempted in one case at least to drag off a gun & were actually rolling it down the slope. But the infantry promptly rallied & reformed behind the guns & finally repulsed them. Their officers now made many superhuman efforts to reform their lines & compel their men to advance & capture the artillery. Their determination was evident in their frequent attempts to advance against Woodruff's battery. As before mentioned the ammunition of the battery being expended to some rounds of canister & the guns rolled back out of view. A portion of the guns were now again placed in position by hand, some men of the 108th assisting for [?] . . . his remaining rounds of canister with terrible energy, & just as this, too, was about expended, this noble artillery officer fell mortally wounded, an irreparable loss to his country & the military profession. The rebel officers after making forlorn & desperate attempts to rally their men found all their efforts in vain, for the men opposed to them stood immovable & resolute as the ground on which they fought. The line began to break into hopeless & despairing squads of men, many of whom ran in & surrendered. The enemy commanders, seeing this, now reopened their artillery indiscriminately upon friend & foe. Whether this was done in a clumsy attempt to cover the retreat or to punish their men who surrendered remains to be explained. The latter suspicion has been aroused by some of the prisoners stating that they were threatened to be fired upon by artillery if they broke. But this course probably prevented our line in making any counter-charge & permitted more of their men to escape from the field. But the day was won. The *elite* of the Confederacy, the finest Corps of their principal army — their hope & pride — led by their best lieutenant & under the eye of their *first* chieftain, drifted broken & hopeless across the fields, artillery thundering in their ears mingled with the cheers of the victors. No attempt at pursuit was made. There were no reserve force in sufficient force to undertake it, besides the enemy's batteries had opened generally & none of our officers knew how soon an attack might be made at some other point, & prepared themselves accordingly until the day was too far spent to attack. The 108th here suffered terribly which was chiefly owing to their exposure to all the artillery fire directed at the battery which they supported for two whole days. Sixteen of their number died on the field & upwards of 70 wounded, making the casualties more than on third of the whole number went into action. . . .

Section VIII

"Let Them Come Up Close Before You Fire":

The Angle

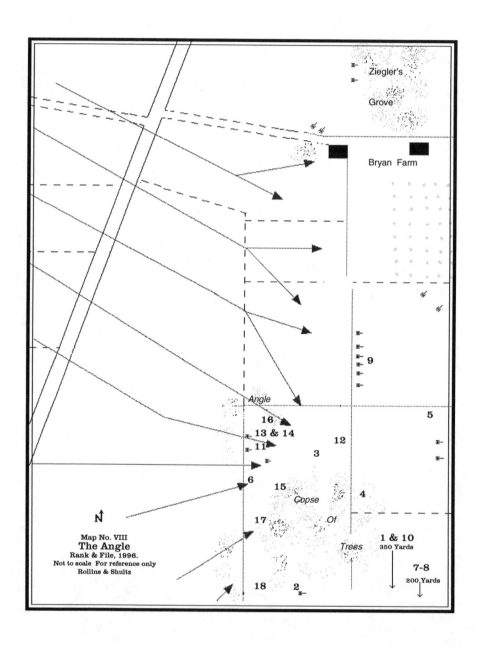

Ziegler's

Grove

Bryan Farm

9

Angle

16

13 & 14

11

5

12

3

6

15

Copse

4

N

17

Of

1 & 10
350 Yards

Map No. VIII
The Angle
Rank & File, 1996.
Not to scale For reference only
Rollins & Shultz

Trees

7-8

18

2

200 Yards

1. Major General Winfield Scott Hancock moved along the Federal line before being wounded while on the left flank. His official report is an excellent overview of the Federal defense of the line. Report of Maj. Gen. Winfield Scott Hancock, ___, ____, 1863, *OR*, 1, 27, 1, 372-374.

The corps had been so weakened by its losses on the 2d, that on the 3d instant it required every available man in the line of battle to cover the ground held the previous day. Colonel Carroll's brigade, of General Hays' division, was retained by General Howard, and, with the exception of the Eighth Ohio, was not engaged with the Second Corps during the day.

The early morning passed in comparative quiet along our front, but the heavy and continued firing on the right indicated that the efforts of the enemy were being directed on the Twelfth corps. Trifling affairs occurred at intervals between the enemy's skirmishers and our own, and the artillery of the corps was frequently and successfully engaged with that of the enemy.

From 11 a. m. until 1 p. m. there was an ominous stillness. About 1 o'clock, apparently by a given signal, the enemy opened upon our front with the heaviest artillery fire I have ever known. Their guns were in position at an average distance of about 1,400 yards from my line, and ran in a semicircle from the town of Gettysburg to a point opposite Round Top Mountain. Their number is variously estimated at from one hundred and fifteen to one hundred and fifty. The air was filled with projectiles, there being scarcely an instant but that several were seen bursting at once. No irregularity of ground afforded much protection, and the plain in rear of the line of battle was soon swept of everything movable. The infantry troops maintained their position with great steadiness, covering themselves as best they might by the temporary but trifling defenses they had erected and the accidents of the ground. Scarcely a straggler was seen, but all waited the cessation of the fierce cannonade, knowing well what it foreshadowed. The artillery of the corps, imperfectly supplied with ammunition, replied to the enemy most gallantly, maintaining the unequal contest in a manner that reflected the highest honor on this arm of the service. Brown's battery (B, First Rhode Island), which had suffered severely on the 2d, and expended all of its canister on that day, retired before the cannonading ceased, not being effective for further service. The remaining batteries continued their fire until only canister remained to them, and then ceased.

After an hour and forty-five minutes, the fire of the enemy became less furious, and immediately their infantry was seen in the woods beyond the Emmitsburg road, preparing for the assault. A strong line of skirmishers soon advanced, (followed by two deployed lines of battle), supported at different points by small columns of infantry. Their lines were formed with a precision and steadiness that extorted the admiration of the witnesses of that memorable scene. The left of the enemy extended slightly beyond the right of General Alexander Hays' division, the right being about opposite the left of General Gibbon's. Their line of battle thus covered a front of not more than two of the small and incomplete divisions of the corps. The whole attacking force is estimated to have exceeded 15,000 men.

No attempt was made to check the advance of the enemy until the first line had arrived within about 700 yards of our position, when a feeble fire of artillery was opened upon it, but with no material effect, and without delaying for a moment its determined advance. The column pressed on, coming within musketry range without receiving immediately our fire, our men evincing a striking disposition to withhold it until it could be delivered with deadly effect.

Two regiments of Stannard's Vermont Brigade (of the First Corps), which had been posted in a little grove in front of and at a considerable angle with the main line, first opened with an oblique fire upon the right of the enemy's column, which had the effect to make the troops on that flank double in a little toward their left. They still pressed on, however, without halting to return the fire. The rifled guns of our artillery, having fired away all their canister, were now withdrawn, or left on the ground inactive, to await the issue of the struggle between the opposing infantry. Arrived at between 200 and 300 yards, the troops of the enemy were met by a destructive fire from the divisions of Gibbon and Hays, which they promptly returned, and the fight at once became fierce and general. In front of Hays' division it was not of very long duration. Mowed down by canister from Woodruff's battery, and by the fire from two regiments judiciously posted by General Hays in his extreme front and right, and by the fire of different lines in the rear, the enemy broke in great disorder, leaving fifteen colors and nearly 2,000 prisoners in the hands of this division. Those of the enemy's troops who did not fall into disorder in front of the Third Division were moved to the right, and re-enforced the line attacking Gibbon's division. The right of the attacking line having been repulsed by Hall's and Harrow's brigades, of the latter division, assisted by the fire of the Vermont regiments before referred to, doubled to its left and also re-enforced the center, and thus the attack was in its fullest strength opposite the brigade of General Webb. This brigade was disposed in two lines. Two regiments of the brigade, the Sixty-ninth and Seventy-first Pennsylvania Volunteers, were behind a low stone wall and a slight breastwork hastily constructed by them, the remainder of the brigade being behind the crest some 60 paces to the rear, and so disposed as to fire over the heads of those in front. When the enemy's line had nearly reached the stone wall, led by General Armistead, the most of that part of Webb's brigade posted here abandoned their position, but fortunately did not retreat entirely. They were, by the personal bravery of General Webb and his officers, immediately formed behind the crest before referred to, which was occupied by the remnant of the brigade.

Emboldened by seeing this indication of weakness, the enemy pushed forward more pertinaciously, numbers of them crossing over the breastwork abandoned by the troops. The fight here became very close and deadly. The enemy's battle-flags were soon seen waving on the stone wall. Passing at this time, Colonel Devereux, commanding the Nineteenth Massachusetts Volunteers, anxious to be in the right place, applied to me for permission to move his regiment to the right and to the front, where the line had been broken. Glranted it, and his regiment and Colonel Mallon's (Forty-second New York Volunteers, on his right) proceeded there at once; but the enemy having left Colonel Hall's front, as described before, this officer promptly moved his command by the right flank to still further re-enforce the position of General Webb, and was immediately followed by Harrow's brigade. The movement was executed, but not without confusion, owing to many men leaving their ranks to fire at the enemy from the breastwork. The situation was now very peculiar. The men of all the brigades had in some measure lost their regimental organization, but individually they were firm. The ambition of individual commanders to promptly cover the point penetrated by the enemy, the smoke of battle, and the intensity of the close engagement, caused this confusion. The point, however, was now covered. In regular formation our line would have stood four ranks deep.

The colors of the different regiments were now advanced, waving in defiance of the long line of battle-flags presented by the enemy. The men pressed firmly after them, under the energetic commands and example of their officers, and after a few moments of desperate fighting the enemy's troops were repulsed, threw down their arms and sought safety in flight or by throwing themselves on the ground to escape our fire. The battle-flags were ours and the victory was won.

Gibbon's division secured 12 stand of colors and prisoners enough to swell the number captured by the corps to about 4,000.

While the enemy was still in front of Gibbon's division, I directed Colonel [General] Stannard to send two regiments of his Vermont Brigade, First Corps, to a point which would strike the enemy on the right flank. I cannot report on the execution of this order, as Colonel [General] Stannard's report has not passed through my hands; but from the good conduct of these troops during the action I have no doubt the service was promptly performed. Just in time to increase the panic of the fleeing fugitives, Battery K, Fifth U. S. Artillery, Lieutenant Kinzie commanding, and Fitzhugh's New York battery arrived, and opened on them. The enemy's attack was feebly renewed immediately after his first repulse. A single line of battle, with its left running nearly along the line followed by the right of the preceding lines, and numbering about 3,000 men, advanced, but it was utterly broken by the fire of the batteries on my left before it arrived within musketry range. A large number of the enemy came in and gave themselves up as soon as their line was broken, and 2 stand of colors fell into our hands.

Toward the close of the main contest, I had the misfortune to lose the valuable services of a distinguished officer, Brig. Gen. John Gibbon, commanding Second Division, who was severely wounded. A short time afterward I was myself wounded, but was enabled to remain on the field until the action was entirely over, when I transferred the command to Brigadier-General Caldwell.

. . . To speak of the conduct of the troops would seem to be unnecessary, but still it may be justly remarked that this corps sustained its well-earned reputation on many fields, and that the boast of its gallant first commander, the late Maj. Gen. E. V. Sumner, that the Second Corps had "never given to the enemy a gun or color," holds good now as it did under the command of my predecessor, Major General Couch. To attest to its good conduct and the perils through which it has passed, it may be stated that its losses in battle have been greater than those of any other corps in the Army of the Potomac, or probably in the service, notwithstanding it has usually been numerically weakest.

2. Brigadier General Henry Hunt's orders to fire slowly and accurately, and harbor ammunition until the Confederates got close, were designed to use the Army's artillery in the most efficient manner possible. However Maj. Gen. W. S. Hancock, an infantryman's infantryman, ordered the guns to keep firing to provide a boost in morale. The result, in Hunt's eyes, allowed the Confederates a much better possibility of breaching the Federal line than would have occurred had his orders been followed. His comments about Col. A. L. Long again point out the connections between the officers of both armies. His explanations for the lack of counter-attack make Meade's hesitancy understandable. Henry J. Hunt, "The Third Day At Gettysburg," *Battles and Leaders of the Civil War*, Vol. III, 369-376.

. . . Meantime the enemy had advanced, and McGilvery

opened a destructive oblique fire, reenforced by that of Rittenhouse's six rifle-guns from Round Top, which were served with remarkable accuracy, enfilading Pickett's lines. The Confederate approach was magnificent, and excited our admiration but the story of that charge is so well known that I need not dwell upon it further than as it concerns my own command. The steady fire from McGilvery and Rittenhouse, on their right caused Pickett's men to "drift" in the opposite direction, so that the weight of the assault fell upon the positions occupied by Hazard's batteries. I had counted on the artillery cross-fire that would stop it before it reached our lines, but, except a few shots here and there, Hazard's batteries were silent until the enemy came within canister range. They had unfortunately exhausted their long range projectiles during the cannonade, under the orders of their corps commander, and it was too late to replace them. Had my instructions been followed here, they as they were by McGilvery, I do not believe that Pickett's division would have reached our line. We lost not only the fire of one-third of our guns, but the resulting cross-fire, which would have doubled its value. The prime fault was in the obscurity of our army regulations as to the artillery, and the absence of all regulations as to the proper relations of the different arms of service to one another. On this occasion it cost us much blood, many lives, and for a moment endangered the integrity of our line if not the success of the battle. Soon after Pickett's repulse, Wilcox's, Wright's, and Perry's brigades were moved forward, but under the fire of the fresh batteries in Gibbon's front of McGilvery's and Rittenhouse's guns and the advance of two regiments of Stannard's Vermont brigade, they soon fell back. The losses in the batteries of the Second Corps were very heavy. Of the five battery commanders and their successors on the field, Rorty, Cushing, and Woodruff were killed, and Milne was mortally and Sheldon severely wounded at their guns. So great was the destruction of men and horses, that Cushing's and Woodruff's United States, and Brown's and Arnold's Rhode Island batteries were consolidated to form two serviceable ones.

The advance of the confederate brigades to cover Pickett's retreat showed that the enemy's line opposite Cemetery Ridge was occupied by infantry. Our own line on the ridge was in more or less disorder, as the result of the conflict, and in no condition to advance a sufficient force for a counter-assault. The largest bodies of organized troops available were on the left, and General Meade now proceeded to Round Top and pushed out skirmishers to feel the enemy in its front. An advance to the Plum Run line, of the troops behind it, would have brought them directly in front of the numerous batteries which crowned the Emmitsburg Ridge, commanding that line and all the intervening ground; a farther advance, to the attack, would have brought them under additional heavy flank fires.

McCandless's brigade, supported by Nevin's, was, however, pushed forward, under cover of the woods, which protected them from the fire of all these batteries; it crossed the Wheat-field, cleared the woods, and had an encounter with a portion of Benning's brigade, which was retiring. Hood's and McLaw's divisions were falling back under Longstreet's orders to their strong position, resting on Peach Orchard and covering Hill's line. It needs but a moment's examination of the official map to see that our troops on the left were locked up. As to the center, Pickett's and Pettigrew's assaulting divisions had formed no part of A. P. Hill's line, which was virtually intact. The idea that there must have been "a gap of at least a mile" in that line, made by throwing forward these divisions, and that a prompt advance of it, was a delusion. A prompt counter-charge after a combat between two small bodies of men is one thing; the change from the defensive to the offensive of an army, after an engagement at a single *point*, is quite another. *This* was not a "Waterloo defeat" with a fresh army to follow it up, and to have made no provision against a reverse, would have been rash in the extreme. An advance of 20,000 men from Cemetery Ridge in the face of the 140 guns then in position would have been stark madness; an immediate advance from any point, in force, was simply impracticable, and before due preparation could have been made for a change to the offensive, the favorable moment — had any resulted from the repulse — would have passed away.

3.   **The Philadelphia Brigade, commanded by Brigadier General Alexander Webb, defended the Angle. In the 1880s, the veterans of one of his regiments, the 72nd Pennsylvania infantry, wanted to place their monument at the stone wall. The Gettysburg Monument Commission decided to place it on the crest, behind the copse of trees because they believed the 72nd had not fought at the wall. The veterans sued, and their case eventually wound up in the Pennsylvania Supreme Court; they won. In this testimony taken from the trial, Webb reports the placement of his regiments and recalls their actions during the charge. Testimony of Alexander Webb,** *Supreme Court of Pennsylvania. Middle District. May Term, 1891, Nos. 20 and 30. Appeal of the Gettysburg Battlefield Memorial Association From the Decree of the Court of Common Pleas of Adams County.* **(Hereafter cited as** *Supreme Court Pennsylvania***), 159-161. The court reporter often left out adjectives and other parts of the testimony.**

I reside in New York city, and my age is fifty-four. I am president of the College of the City of New York for twenty years. I was educated at West Point, graduated in 1855. I was an instructor

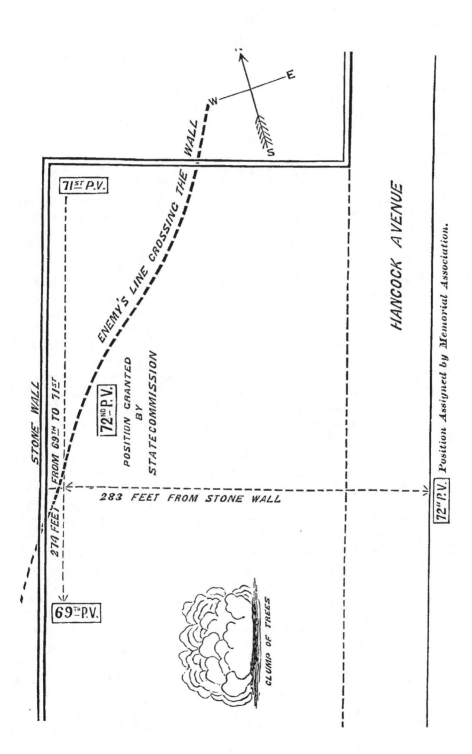

STONE WALL

71ST P.V.

ENEMY'S LINE CROSSING THE WALL

W
E
S

72ND P.V.

POSITION GRANTED BY STATE COMMISSION

274 FEET FROM 69TH TO 71ST

283 FEET FROM STONE WALL

69TH P.V.

CLUMP OF TREES

HANCOCK AVENUE

72ND P.V. Position Assigned by Memorial Association.

at West Point and in the army when the war broke out. I was through the war as an officer. After the close of the war was again an instructor at West Point. My highest rank during the war was brigadier general and brevet major general. I was in the battle of Gettysburg and held the rank of brigadier general in that battle. I commanded the Second brigade, Second division, Second corps. That brigade was commonly known as the Philadelphia brigade. I was in command of that brigade one day before the battle of Gettysburg. It was from the time of General Meade's promotion; it was probably two days. The Sixty-ninth, Seventy-first, Seventy-second and One Hundred and Sixth Pennsylvania regiments composed that brigade. On the left joining the brigade of Hall was the Sixty-ninth Pennsylvania regiment, two companies of the One Hundred and Sixth Pennsylvania regiment out on picket, and the remaining of that regiment were over with Howard, all of the Seventy-first Pennsylvania regiment, along the stone wall, to the right and front of Cushing's Battery, save two behind the angle, the Seventy-second regiment in reserve to the left and rear of the center of the brigade, the two companies of the Seventy-first regiment to the north and rear angle. The Sixty-ninth regiment, in reference to the copse of trees, were in front of it at the stone wall, and the Seventy-first to the right and up the angle with a space in between them. The Seventy-second regiment was behind the copse of trees, some yards, I don't remember that exact distance, but to the best of my recollection it was under cover of the crest of the hill. Cushing's Battery was in that locality, as I remember it; it was on the line which would join the angle with the rear portion of the clump of trees. The cannonading commenced about one o'clock, I believe, and that was the position of Cushing's Battery at that time. There was one regiment in reserve to cover up the space the battery held in case it should be destroyed, and this was the Seventy-second regiment. Cannonading lasted from an hour to an hour and a half. Cushing's Battery was destroyed, leaving but one or two pieces that could be manned, and at half-past one, or about that time, the enemy formed in line and emerged from the woods, showing that an infantry attack was about to take place. The concentration of the artillery fired from the rebel side upon the ground about the clump of trees had made known to us that there was to be the point of attack. The Seventy-second regiment was therefore sent for to be brought up to cover the space vacated by the battery, and was brought from the left to the right and took that position, covering that space and the unoccupied stone wall in its immediate rear angle, and its left a little advanced; the enemy at that time must have been trying to cross the road running oblique in our immediate front, the Emmittsburg road. When the enemy's infantry had driven in our skirmishers and was advancing to the stone wall, our skirmishers of the One Hundred and Sixth Pennsylvania regiment joined these troops that then formed a broken line, the Sixty-ninth regiment not joining the left of the Seventy-second regiment. When they advanced and crowded on the stone wall forcing back the detached portion of the line composing the Seventy-first regiment, I thought it time to advance the Seventy-second regiment to the wall to take advantage of the halt and confusion, and I went to their front and center and gave an order for them to move down, but not their commanding officers. They failed to move with me at that time and I passed to the left, to the right of the Sixty-ninth regiment, to prevent that regiment from being forced back into the clump of trees if possible. From that point I saw that the enemy had in some numbers crossed the wall and required the right of the Sixty-ninth regiment to break and fall to their right and rear and fire upon these troops. At this time, Hall, who was on my left, had, during these few minutes, advanced his regiments in reserve, I hear, to assist our line and had adjoined on to this curve line of battle from the rear, his troops *en masse*. The general melee or push took place at this moment and from the raising of their hands on the part of the rebels and dropping of their hands I saw that the charge had failed and the field was ours. I suppose the Seventy-second regiment during this melee or push was with the whole crowd, the Seventy-second regiment had first fired from the crest, or what I would call a little in advance of the crest. They were in the most exposed position in which they could be placed; they had remained in that exposed condition because they had not gone down to the wall. The color bearer and myself stood together, I holding on to the staff and he did not move forward with me. I ordered him forward; this was the color bearer of the Seventy-second regiment. I know of no words said when I ordered him forward, he moved in his place but did not carry the colors out of the regimental line. My adjutant at the time, was Adjutant, now Colonel, Charles H. Banes. I cannot now recall whether I urged him to have the Seventy-second go forward. The position of the Seventy-second in line of battle was from the Seventy-first regiment to near the copse of trees, about one hundred and fifty to one hundred and sixty feet from the front stonewall, maybe more.

[At this point Webb reads part of a letter he wrote to his wife from Gettysburg on July 6, 1863:]

"I ordered my few guns to fire and we opened great gaps in them and steadily they advanced in four solid lines right up to my works and fences, and shot my men with their muskets touching their breasts; seeing two companies driven out, all my artillery in their hands, I ordered up my reserve right and led it up myself. General Armistead, an old army officer, led his men, came over my fences and passed me with four of his men. He fell mortally wounded. I got but one shot, grazing my thigh. I stood but thirty-nine paces from them. Their officers pointed me out, but God preserved me. As soon as I got my regiment up to the wall, the enemy was whipped for good and all. When they came over the fences, the army of the Potomac was nearer being whipped than it was at any time of the battle. When my men fell back I almost wished to get killed. I was almost disgraced but Hall (Colonel) on my left saw it all and brought up two regiment to help me. . . ."

4. Brigadier General John Gibbon, commanding the division that lined the stone wall south of the angle, had a good overall view of the development of the charge until taken out of action with a serious wound. He discusses the difficulty of executing maneuvers amidst the noise and chaos of battle, and notes that some Federal troops did retreat in the face of the Confederate advance. John Gibbon, *Recollections*, 150-153.

The fire on both sides had now considerably slackened and only a few shells were coming from the enemy's guns. As we walked towards the right, a staff officer with an orderly leading my horse met me with the information that the enemy was coming in force. I hurriedly mounted and rode to the top of the hill where a magnificent sight met my eyes. The enemy in a long grey line was marching towards us over the rolling ground in our front, their flags fluttering in the air and serving as guides to their line of battle. In front was a heavy skirmish line which was driving ours in on a run. Behind the front line another appeared and finally a third and the whole came on like a great wave of men, steadily and stolidly. Hastily telling Haskell to ride to Gen. Meade and tell him the enemy was coming upon us in force and we should need all the help he could send us, I directed the guns of Arnold's Battery to be run forward to the wall loaded with double rounds of canister and then rode down my line and cautioned the men not to fire until the first line crossed the Emmetsburg road. By this time the bullets were flying pretty thickly along the line and the batteries from other portions of the field had opened fire upon the moving mass in front of us. The front line reached the Emmetsburg road and hastily springing over the two fences, paused a moment to reform and then started up the slope. My division, up to this time, had fired but little but now from the low stone wall on each side of the angle every gun along it sent forth the most terrific fire. From my position on the left I could see the terrible effect of this. Mounted officers in the rear were seen to go down before it and as the rear lines came up and clambered over the fences, men fell from the top rails, but the mass still moved on up to our very guns and the stone wall in front. I noticed after all three lines were closed up, that the men on the right of the assaulting force were continually closing in to their left, evidently to fill the gaps made by our fire, and that the right of their line was hesitating behind the clump of bushes where I had stood during the cannonade. To our left of this point was a regiment of the Division, and desirous of aiding in the desperate struggle now taking place on the hill to the right I endeavored to get this regiment to swing out to the front, by a change front forward on the right company, take the enemy's line in flank to sweep up along the front of our line. But in the noise and turmoil of the conflict it was difficult to get my orders understood. Few unacquainted with the rigid requirements of discipline and of how an efficient military organization *must* necessarily be a machine which works by the will of one man, as completely as a locomotive obeys the will of the engineer not in all things, but in every thing which the locomotive was *built* to obey, can appreciate the importance of drill and discipline in a crisis like the one now facing us.

In my eagerness to get the regiment to swing out and do what I wanted, I spurred my horse in front of it and waved forward the left flank. I was suddenly recalled to the absurd position I had assumed by the whole regiment opening fire. I got to the rear as soon as possible. Looking to my left to see if I could find troops there likely to be induced to follow out my orders I saw a command lying behind a small breastwork I had, myself, caused to be erected the day before and putting spurs to my horse, I rode towards it. Just before I reached the position to my amazement, the men commenced to break to the rear, though there was no fire whatever to amount to anything on their front. With some difficulty I induced the command to return to their breastwork, calling the attention of the officers and men to the large numbers falling back from the assaulting party which could be plainly seen from where we were and then, satisfied that I could derive no benefit from that command, I galloped back to my own division and again attempted to get the left of that to swing out. Whilst so engaged, I felt a stinging blow apparently behind the left shoulder.

I soon began to grow faint from the loss of blood which was trickling from my left hand. I directed Lt. Moale, my aide, to turn over the command of the Division to Gen. Harrow and in company with another staff officer, Capt. Francis Wessells, 106th Penn., Division J.A. left the field, the sounds of the conflict on the hill still ringing in my ears.

5.   Captain John Hazard, Chief of Artillery, 2nd Corps, sketches the condition of the artillery near the Angle after the cannonade, the replacement of some guns with reinforcements from the Artillery Reserve, and their actions during the charge. Report of Capt. Jno. G. Hazard, August 1, 1863, *OR*, 1, 27, 1, 477-481.

The morning of July 3 was quiet until about 8 o'clock, when the enemy suddenly opened fire upon our position, exploding three limbers of Battery A, 4th U. S. Artillery, but otherwise causing little loss. Little reply was made, save by Light Company I, First U. S. Artillery, which battery during the forenoon had eight separate engagements with the enemy.

At 1 p. m. the artillery of the enemy opened along the whole line, and for an hour and a quarter we were subjected to a very warm artillery fire. The batteries did not at first reply, till the fire of the enemy becoming too terrible, they returned it till all their ammunition, excepting canister, had been exploded; they then waited for the anticipated infantry attack of the enemy. Battery B, First New York Artillery, was entirely exhausted; its ammunition expended; its horses and men killed and disabled; the commanding officer, Capt. J. M. Rorty, killed, and senior First Lieut. A. S. Sheldon severely wounded. The other batteries were in similar condition; still, they bided the attack. The rebel lines advanced slowly but surely; half the valley had been passed over by them before the guns dared expend a round of the precious ammunition remaining on hand. The enemy steadily approached, and, when within deadly range, canister was thrown with terrible effect into their ranks. Battery A, First Rhode Island Light Artillery, had expended every round, and the lines of the enemy still advanced. Cushing was killed; Milne had fallen, mortally wounded; their battery was exhausted, their ammunition gone, and it was feared the guns would be lost if not withdrawn.

At this trying moment the two batteries were taken away; but Woodruff still remained in the grove, and poured death and destruction into the rebel lines. They had gained the crest, and but few shots remained. All seemed lost, and the enemy, exultant, rushed on. But on reaching the crest they found our infantry, fresh and waiting on the opposite side. The tide turned; backward and downward rushed the rebel line, shattered and broken, and the victory was gained. Woodruff, who had gallantly commanded the battery through the action of July 2 and 3, fell, mortally wounded, at the very moment of victory. The command of the battery devolved upon Second Lieut. Tully McCrea, First U. S. Artillery.

Batteries from the Artillery Reserve of the army immediately occupied the positions vacated by the exhausted batteries of the brigade, and immediate efforts were made to recuperate and restore them to serviceable condition. So great was the loss in officers, men, and horses, that it was found necessary to consolidate Light Company I, First U. S. Artillery, Battery A, Fourth U. S. Artillery, and Batteries A and B, First Rhode Island Light Artillery, thus reducing the five batteries that entered the fight to three.

The greatest praise is due to the gallantry and courage of the officers and men of the brigade, of whom one-third were either killed or wounded. The fire under which they fought on the afternoon of July 3 was most severe and terrible, as the inclosed list of killed, wounded, and missing will sufficiently testify.

In the death of Capt. J. M. Rorty the brigade has lost a worthy officer, a gallant soldier, and an estimable man. He had enjoyed his new position but one day, having assumed command of Battery B, First New York Artillery, on July 2, as it was about to engage the enemy.

First Lieut. A. H. Cushing, commanding Battery A, Fourth U. S. Artillery, fell on July 3, mortally wounded by a musket-shot. He especially distinguished himself for his extreme gallantry and bravery, his courage and ability, and his love for his profession. His untimely death and the loss of such a promise as his youth cherished are sincerely mourned.

First Lieut. George A. Woodruff, commanding Light Company I, First U. S. Artillery, fell, mortally wounded, on July 3, while the rebel lines, after a most successful and daring advance, were being pushed back in destruction and defeat. To the manner in which the guns of his battery were served and his unflinching courage and determination may be due the pertinacity with which this part of the line was so gallantly held under a most severe attack. Lieutenant Woodruff was an able soldier, distinguished for his excellent judgment and firmness in execution, and his loss is one which cannot be easily replaced. He expired on July 4, and, at his own request, was buried on the field on which he had yielded his life to his country.

Second Lieut. Joseph S. Milne, First Rhode Island Light Artillery, was mortally wounded on the afternoon of July 3 by a musket-shot through the lungs. He survived his wound one week, and breathed his last at Gettysburg on July 10. In his regiment he was noted for his bravery and willingness to encounter death in any guise, while his modesty and manliness gained for him the ready esteem of his many comrades. His death is a loss to all, and we cannot but mourn that so bright a life should thus suddenly be veiled in death. At the time of his decease he was attached to Battery A, Fourth U. S. Artillery, with which battery he had served during the campaign. Every officer in this battery was either killed or wounded.

6.   Captain Robert McBride of the 71st Pennsylvania captured a flag near the wall. Testimony of Robert McBride, *Supreme Court of Pennsylvania*, 125-127.

I was with my company; I was to the right of the colors; the colors were right on our left. . . .   I lay to the rear of clump of trees with my company previous to the cannonading, on the rise of the hill, on a little crest of the hill in the rear of the clump of trees, at about the line along the avenue. After the cannonading we moved by the flank, oblique to the right . . . that's as near as I can get it. The enemy was coming over the wall, were inside the wall, then we commenced our fire; speaking of what I saw in my immediate front. We fired some time there and then we charged right down to the wall through the battery; we charged right to the wall, and right there I captured the colors of a rebel standard and drove him to the rear; that was right at the wall; I took them from him; grabbed them out of his hands(witness marks on the diagram the place where he took the colors at the letter "m" in "from"); that's as near as I can get it. We fought our way down to the wall; nothing but rebels had charge of the wall, behind and over it. I saw some of my men fall there; I had one of the men of my company fall there with the colors, his name was William H. Bortman; he was killed not less than ten feet from the wall. He was picked up by one of the men of my company. A number of my men were killed there, I can't recall exactly how many. I can't give exact number killed and wounded. . . .   We went down not in a straight line, but we fought down to the wall, saw other members of regiment down at the wall, plenty of them. I saw a good many of the dead of the regiment piled up at the wall. They were piled up inside the wall close to the wall.

7.   As part of the Artillery Reserve of the Army of the Potomac, Lieutenant Augustin Parsons commanded a battery of six 10-pound Parrott rifles. In his post-battle report, he tells of moving into position just behind the copse of trees. Report of Lieut. Augustin N. Parsons, Battery A, New Jersey Light Artillery, July 17, 1863, *OR*, 1, 27, 1, 899-900.

I have the honor to report that on the 3d instant, about 3 p. m., I received orders from General Hunt to move the battery to the front as quickly as possible. I at once obeyed the order, and soon had the battery in position about one-fourth of a mile south of

Gettysburg Cemetery and near the Second Division, Second Corps, Captain Fitzhugh's battery following immediately after me and taking position on my right. At this time the enemy's infantry were advancing very rapidly. I at once opened fire upon them with case shot, and fired about 120 rounds with good effect. As soon as they fell back, I opened fire upon one of the enemy's batteries (which by this time had gotten an exact range of my position) with shell, and used 80 rounds, when I received orders from General Hunt to cease firing. My shell were telling upon the enemy's battery, and I believe that I could have completely silenced it in five minutes more.

During the action I lost 2 men killed and 7 wounded. I also lost 3 horses killed and 2 wounded, which have since died.

8. In a letter written after the war, Parsons recalls the details of the two deaths in his battery during the charge. Augustin N. Parsons to ?, June 2, 1889, Gettysburg National Military Park.

. . . We arrived near Gettysburg early in the morning, and it being uncertain where General Lee's lines were, we were moved two or three times. In the meantime Captain Fitzhugh and myself rode down to Round Top, or near there, and from there we could see the Confederate cavalry away to the north. We then rode back to our batteries, and I was ordered to take position behind a stone wall and some large rocks, which was about a quarter of a mile in the rear of what afterwards proved to be the fighting ground, with order to move at a moment's notice. Capt. Rigby, of the First Maryland Artillery, from Baltimore, occupied a rocky point a short distance north of me. I think that Gen. Slocum's command was in front of Rigby's battery. About the time the ball opened there were heard heavy volleys of musketry in front of Rigby, and he was ordered to shell the woods beyond the Federal lines. Rigby's battery was twelve-pound rifled guns. About the second shot he fired the recoil of the gun broke an axletree. I happened up about that time (Gen. Meade was there), and told Capt. Rigby to have his gun dragged down into the hollow, where my battery was, bring his traveling forge alongside of mine, behind a big rock, and with the two fires and the two smiths we could mend that axletree directly. It was done; the men welded that axletree while the shells from the enemy's batteries went screaming over their heads like wild geese in a storm. In less than one hour that axle was mended, the gun remounted, hauled back into position, and blazed away as though nothing had happened; and all this was done during an incessant roar of artillery. About this time an Aide from Gen. Hunt came with orders for me to get to the front as quickly as possible. I moved at a sharp trot, the men running beside the guns. The Aide-de-Camp pointed out the place, which was an open space on the ridge between Fitzhugh's and McGilvery's batteries. I got into position, unlimbered and got to work in less time that it takes me to write this. Pickett's division was then advancing. . . . As soon as I got into position the drivers all dismounted, save one. He rode the lead team on the first gun, which was a the right. I sat upon my horse, moving back and forward. The shell from the enemy's guns were bursting over us and all around us. Meanwhile the German driver sat in his saddle as cooly as he would at a table drinking a glass of lager and nibbling a piece of limberger, when a piece of a shell struck him in the side, about the pocket. I was looking right at him at the time. When struck, he raised in the saddle at least six inches, then settled back, dismounted and stood on his feet for about a second, and then fell. I at once ordered the Sergeant of his detachment to carry him to a tree that was a few yards to the rear and right, and get back to his gun as quickly as possible. The Sergeant did so, but said that the would like to take him to an old house a few rods farther to the rear and right, one that had been used as a hospital in the early part of the day, but at that time fragments of shell and bullets were rattling on the roof like hailstones. I told the Sergeant to take three men and a blanket, carry the wounded man to the house, and do it as quickly as possible and get back to his gun. I do not think the Sergeant and his men were gone more than ten minutes, when he returned and told me that the man was dead, and showed me his pocketbook, dripping with blood, which had been driven by the broken shell partly into his bowels. I opened the book, and as near as I remember there was $20 in bills, which were all stained with blood. The Sergeant told me that the man said that he had no relatives in this country, and that he wanted the Sergeant to take the money and divide it equally among the men of his detachment. I returned the pocketbook to the Sergeant and told him to get to his gun at once. The next was at the left gun. I thought the men were working the gun a little slow and rode up pretty close to it, when a shell from the enemy's battery burst in front and slightly above us. A small piece struck my horse, but did no harm. A piece struck an old German soldier, who was number two at the gun. He wheeled around on one foot and fell flat on his back. I jumped from my horse, bent down by him, called him by name. The only audible reply was, "water." I called for a canteen, placed it to his lips. He took one swallow and was dead. I mounted my horse and ordered the dead man carried to the stone wall (which, as near as I can remember, was not more than 100 feet from my left gun), and covered with a blanket. This is the stone wall that you had reference to in your letter. My battery was on the north side of that, the wall being on my left. The old German soldier that I have just mentioned used to take care of my horses. He was a faithful and good man, and I was truly sorry to see him killed. Just before nightfall, and after the cannonading had ceased, I got the men to dig a grave on the north side of that stone wall. We wrapped the old soldier in his blanket and buried him as tenderly as we could, under the circumstances. It was not more than five minutes after the old German soldier was killed before a shrapnel burst over our heads and knocked down five men. None were killed. They were taken to the rear, and finally down to a barn under the hill, used as a hospital. One of the men was struck by a shrapnel bullet near the nose and just under the eye, which was torn out, the ball passing out near the ear. I considered him as good as dead, for to look at him (covered in blood as he was) one would think half his head was blown away. Now comes the funny part of the story. This same man was sent to the hospital in Philadelphia. He got well, but of course was discharged from the service on account of disability. In due course of time I received a letter from the surgeon in charge, saying that the government furnished false eyes, but it was necessary that the applicant have a certificate from his commanding officer, stating that he lost his eye while in discharge of his duty. I at once forwarded the papers. He got the glass eye and his discharge, and was a free man once more. In about three months I received another letter, asking for a duplicate of the original certificate. I sent the second certificate, but never learned whether he ever got the second glass eye.

9. Captain Gulian Weir brought his battery into the area north of the Angle from the Artillery Reserve. He probably pulled in when Arnold pulled out. Gulian V. Weir, "Recollections of the 3d day at Gettysburg with Battery C." Gettysburg National Military Park.

Between 1 and 2 o'clock p.m., on July 3d, 1863 at Gettysburg (I believe it to have been on the 3d day, but this part is immaterial,) a small group of artillery officers, (myself included) from the reserve artillery Camp were on the ridge, above the camp, (in Thomas battery, I think,) talking and looking over the quiet country, beyond, it was the calm before the storm, suddenly three guns were fired. As we were in a conspicuous place, it was thought, at the time, that the enemy were practicing it. Either knowing, or feeling, that something would happen some-where, we all scattered and joined our separate commands. My battery was in the Reserve Camp.

(I think directly in the rear of Thomas') Before very long there was a terrible cannonading going on along the whole front, of our line, from Cemetery Hill to Round Top. Shells bursting directly over and very close to the Reserve's Batteries, orders were given to move our batteries, and get out of the way far as possible. In my battery, in mounting drivers, Lt. Baldwin called to me that he was struck by a piece of shell in the back. I called upon some men to go to Lt. Baldwin's assistance. When moving out, or shortly after, I received an order to report to Gen. Newton, and passed in towards the left, (from where I was, I do not know how far,) when drawn up in front of a woods, where I had been told I would find Gen. Newton.

Upon reporting to him I was informed that rifle guns were wanted. Not eight but 12 (Napoleons?) I felt better, and immediately withdrew, and was on my way back, (to the Reserve Camp) in column of "pieces" (now called "sections") when I met Col. Warner, 3d Arty who said to me "Weir, every battery is ordered to the front, an aide, a somebody)[sic] who will show you where to go," I said "all right come along," took up the trot, went across fields, in rear of the ridge (heavy artillery firing going on all the time) until I approached a hill, rather more steep than others near it. At the foot of this hill, the aide (or somebody) said to me, "go right up there, pointing in the direction of up the hill, and you will come in on their flank, and mow them down." I replied "all right," then moved to the left, and pushed my horse up the hill, ahead of the battery. Now what kind of ground I was coming on, I saw before me a small plain, lines of our troops on right and left, were to the front several guns lying to the left, an open space, (gap) in front, and beyond this gap, (as it appeared to me) a dense body of the enemy, (a great big black mass)[.] My leading piece was now well up the hill, near the top. I motioned it to keep well to the right, near a wall, then turned and moved my hand to show the rear carriage what direction to take, coming up the hill. (The battery executed, forward with battery, left oblique), my motion was seen and the movement commenced, when my horse was shot, in the breast, and began to plunge. I dismounted as best I could (got a tumble) ran ahead, halted caissons of right pieces, and motioned pieces, to go "in battery" "action front" (I think was executed) It was all quickly done, and no mishaps.

Opened with canister, the other pieces doing so, as they successively arrived on the ground. In a short time, our infantry then went forward, and the enemy was driven back. I followed up with case, and the solid shot. Numbers of the enemy came up in front of, and through the battery, to give themselves up, throwing themselves on the ground, as my guns in their front were fired. One came up to me and said "where can I go to get out of this Hellish fire?" I pointed back and said "go down there," I believe I added "I wish I could go with you." The artillery fire of the enemy burst all around and about us, but with little effect. The musketry fire was slow, and I can distinctly remember hearing shots striking the bodies of the wounded, and dead which lay about me. The only casualties I can recall on this day, were, Sergt. Whitwell, (whom I was standing near) lost a leg by explosion of shell which struck the axle of his (left) piece, and my own horse, killed. No other officer or 1st Sergt. of the battery with me on this afternoon.

After the battle was over, I remember going over to the left to see Gen. Webb, who, I think was slightly wounded, and was resting in the ground, close to and directly in rear of this lines. I remained on the ground until I was assured there was no possibility of another attack, and then, asked to go back to the Reserve Artillery Camp.

> Respectfully submitted,
> G. V. Weir
> Capt. 5th Arty.

10. Lieutenant William Wheeler commanded the 13th New York Battery on Cemetery Hill in Major Osborn's line. He moved his guns into the middle of the 2nd Corps line near the copse of trees. Petit's battery, to whom he refers, was commanded by Captain James Rorty. Hancock was wounded shortly after he showed Wheeler where to go, so it was probably well before 4:00 when that event took place. Report of Lieut. William Wheeler, Thirteenth New York Battery, July 29, 1863, *OR*, 1, 27, 1, 753.

At about 4 p. m. I received an order from you to go to assist the Second Corps, upon which a very heavy attack was being made. I immediately reported to General Hancock, who showed me my position. Upon coming into battery, I found the enemy not more than 400 yards off, marching in heavy column by a flank to attack Petit's Battery, which was on my right and somewhat in advance of me. This gave me a fine opportunity to enfilade their column with canister, which threw them into great disorder, and brought them to a halt three times. The charge was finally repulsed, and most of the enemy taken prisoners. I then returned to the corps at Cemetery Hill.

11. Lieutenant Henry Russell of the 72nd Pennsylvania led his company with fixed bayonets down to the stone wall. Henry Russell, *Supreme Court of Pennsylvania*, 97-102.

Company A covered over part of that woods when we were firing. General Webb was near to me at the time, and I told General

Webb that I couldn't fire because there were men in front of me I was afraid of hurting them, and he gave a command by the right flank but it couldn't be heard. I had to go and force the men up past this clump of trees, so they could fire . . .

. . . We were firing and fighting, and General Webb gave the command to charge bayonets. It couldn't be heard, I don't suppose ten feet away. . . .

. . . I heard it distinctly, and was the first one to give the command to my company to fix bayonets. They did fix bayonets, and the balance of the regiment took it up. From my company fixing their bayonets the balance took it up, and then we charged down to the enemy that were down over this wall, and drove them over that wall and captured them, and I went directly to that wall . . . the reason I know I got down there, there was a wounded rebel laying across that wall with his head towards us. He asked me if I wouldn't pull him down and I caught him under the shoulders and pulled him on to the level ground.

12. Several officers, including Hancock and Gibbon, would laud the performance of Lieutenant Frank Haskell on this day. As a staff officer in Gibbon's division, Haskell was in the thick of the fight, and made the most of it. Frank Haskell, "Gettysburg."

The Artillery fight over, men began to breathe more freely, and to ask: — "What next I wonder?" The Battery men were among their guns, some leaning to rest, and wipe the sweat from their sooty faces, — some were handling ammunition boxes, and replenishing those that were empty. Some Batteries from the Artillery Reserve were moving up to take the places of the disabled ones: — the smoke was clearing from the crests. — There was a pause between acts, with the curtain down, soon to rise upon the great final act, and catastrophe of Gettysburg. We had passed by the left of the 2nd Division, coming from the 1st, — when we crossed the crest, the enemy was not in sight, and all was still, — we walked slowly along in rear of the troops, by the ridge cut off now from a view of the enemy, or his position, and were returning to the spot where we had left our horses. Gnl. Gibbon had just said that he inclined to the belief that the enemy was falling back, and that the cannonade was only one of his noisy modes of covering the movement. I said that I thought that fifteen minutes would show that, by all his bowling, the Rebel did not mean retreat. We were near our horses when we noticed Brig. Gnl. [Henry J.] Hunt, Chief of Artillery of the Army, near Woodruff's Battery, swiftly moving about on horseback, and apparently in a rapid manner giving some orders about the guns. Thought we, what could this mean! In a moment afterwards we met Capt. Wessels, and the orderlies who had our horses, — they were on foot leading the horses. — Capt. Wessels was pale, and he said, excited: "General, they say the enemy's infantry is advancing." We sprang into our saddles — a score of bounds brought us upon the all-seeing crest. To say that none grew pale and held their breath at what we and they there saw, would not be true. Might not six thousand men be brave and without shade of fear, and yet, before a hostile eighteen thousand, armed, and not five minutes' march away, turn ashy white?

None on that crest now need be told that *the enemy is advancing.* Every eye could see his legions, an overwhelming, resistless tide of an ocean of armed men, sweeping upon us!

Regiment after Regiment, and Brigade after Brigade, move from the woods, and rapidly take their places in the lines forming the assault. Pickett's proud Division, with some additional troops, hold their right; Pettigrew's, (Heth's) their left. The first line at short interval, is followed by a second, and that a third succeeds; and columns between support the lines. More than half a mile their front extends; — more than a thousand yards the dull gray masses deploy, man touching man, rank pressing rank, and line supporting line. Their red flags wave; their horsemen gallop up and down; the arms of eighteen thousand men, barrel and bayonet, gleam in the sun, a sloping forrest of flashing steel. Right on they move, as with one soul, in perfect order, without impediment of ditch, or wall, or stream, over ridge and slope, through orchard, and meadow, and cornfield, magnificent, grim, irresistible. All was orderly and still upon our crest, — no noise, and no confusion. The men had little need of commands, for the survivors of a dozen battles knew well enough what this array in front portended; and already in their places, they would be prepared to act when the right time should come.

The click of the locks as each man raised the hammer, to feel with his finger that the cap was on the nipple; the sharp jar as a musket touched a stone upon the wall when thrust, in aiming, over it; and the clinking of the iron axles, as the guns were rolled up by hand a little further to the front, were quite all the sounds that could be heard. Cap-boxes were slid around to the front of the body; — cartridge-boxes opened; — officers opened their pistol holsters. Such preparation, little more, was needed. The trefoil flags, colors of the Brigades and Divisions, moved to their places in rear; but along the lines in front, the grand old ensign that first waved in battle at Saratoga, in 1777, and which these people coming would rob of half its stars, stood up, and the west-wind kissed it as the sergeants sloped its lance towards the enemy. I believe that not one above whom it then waved, but blessed his God that he was loyal to it, and whose heart did not swell with pride towards it, as the emblem of the Republic, before that treason's flaunting rag in front. — Gnl. Gibbon rode down the lines, cool and calm, and in an unimpassioned voice he said to the men: "Do not hurry, men, and fire too fast; — let them come up close before you fire, and then aim low, and steadily." The coolness of their General was reflected in the faces of his men. Five minutes had elapsed since first the enemy had emerged from the woods, — no great space of time, surely, if measured by the usual standards by which men estimate duration, — but it was long enough for us to note and weigh some of the elements of mighty moment, that surrounded us: the disparity of numbers between the assailants and the assailed; — that few as were our numbers, we could not be supported or reinforced until support would not be needed, or would be too late; — that upon the ability of the two trefoil Divisions to hold the crest, and repel the assault, depended not only their own safety or destruction, but also the honor of the Army of the Potomac, and defeat or victory at Gettysburg. — Should these advancing men pierce our line, and become the entering wedge, driven home, that would sever our army asunder, what hope would there be afterwards, and where the blood-earned fruits of yesterday? — It was long enough for the Rebel storm to drift across more than half the space that had at first separated it from us. None, or all, of these considerations either depressed or elevated us — they might have done the former had we been timid, the latter, had we been confident and vain, — but, we were there waiting, and ready to do our duty; — that done, results could not dishonor us.

Our skirmishers open a spattering fire along the front, and, fighting, retire upon the main line, — the first drops, the heralds of the storm, sounding on our windows. Then the thunders of our guns, first Arnold's then Cushing's, and Woodruff's and the rest, shake and reverberate again through the air, and their sounding shells smite the enemy. — The General said I had better go and tell General Meade of this advance; — to gallop to Gnl. Meade's Head Quarters, — to learn there that he had changed them to another part of the field, — to dispatch to him, by the Signal Corps, in Gnl. Gibbon's name the message: "The enemy is advancing his infantry in force upon my front," — and to be again upon the crest, were but the work of a minute. All our available guns are now active, and from the fire of shells, as the range grows shorter and shorter, they change to shrapnel, and from shrapnel to canister; but in spite of shells, and shrapnel, and canister, without wavering or halt, the hardy lines of the enemy continue to move on. The Rebel guns make no reply to ours; and no charging shout rings out to-day, as is the Rebel wont; but the courage of these silent men amid our shot, seems not to need the stimulus of other noise. The enemy's right flank sweeps near Stannard's bushy crest, and his concealed Vermonters rake it with a well delivered fire of musketry; — the gray lines do not halt or reply, but withdrawing a little from that extreme, they still move on. And so across all that broad open ground they have come, nearer and nearer, nearly half the way with our guns bellowing in their faces, until now a hundred yards, no more, divide our ready left, from their advancing right. The eager men there are impatient to begin. Let them. — First Harrow's breast-works flame, — then Hall's, — then Webb's. As if our bullets were the fire-coals that touched off their muskets, the enemy in front halts, and his countless level barrels blaze back upon us. — The 2nd Division is struggling in battle; the rattling storm soon spreads to the right, and the blue trefoils are vieing with the white. All along each hostile front, a thousand yards, with narrowest space between, the volleys blaze and roll; as thick the sound as when a summer hailstorm pelts the city roofs; as thick the fire as when the incessant lightning fringes a summer cloud. — When the Rebel Infantry had opened fire, our Batteries soon became silent; and this without their fault, for they were fouled by long previous use, they were the targets of the concentrated Rebel bullets, and some of them had expended all their canister. But they were not silent before Rhorty [sic] was killed, Woodruff had fallen mortally wounded, and Cushing, firing almost his last canister, had dropped dead among his guns, shot through the head by a bullet. The conflict is left to the infantry alone. Unable to find my General when I had returned to the crest after transmitting his message to Genl. Meade, and while riding in the search, having witnessed the development of the fight, from the first fire upon the left, by the main lines, until all of the two Divisions were furiously engaged, I gave up hunting as useless, — I was convinced Gnl. Gibbon could not be on the field, — I left him mounted, — I could easily have found him now had he so remained, — but now, save myself there was not a mounted officer near the engaged lines, — and I was riding towards the right of the 2nd Division with purpose to stop there, as the most eligible position to watch the further progress of the battle, there to be ready to take part, according to my own notions, whenever and wherever occasion was presented. The conflict was tremendous, but I had seen no wavering in all our line. Wondering how long the Rebel ranks, deep though they were, could stand our sheltered volleys had come near my destination, when — Great Heaven! — were my senses mad! — the larger portion of Webb's Brigade, — my God, it was true — there by the group of trees, and the angles of the wall, was breaking from the cover of their works, and without orders or reason, with no hand lifted to check them, was falling back a fear-stricken flock of confusion! The fate of Gettysburg hung upon a spider's single thread! — A great magnificent passion came on me at the instant, not one that overpowers and confounds, but one that blanches the face, and sublimes every sense and faculty. My sword that had always hung idle by my side, the sign of rank only, in every battle, I drew bright and gleaming, the symbol of command. Was not that a fit occasion, and these fugitives the men on whom, to try the temper of the Solingen steel? All rules and proprieties were forgotten all considerations of person, and danger, and safety, despised; for as I met the tide of these rabbits, the damned red flags of the rebellion began to thicken and flaunt along the wall they had just deserted, and one was already waving over one of the guns of the dead Cushing. I ordered these men to *"halt,"* and *"face about,"* and *"fire,"* and they heard my voice, and gathered my meaning, and obeyed my commands. On some unpatriotic backs, of those not quick of comprehension, the flat of my sabre fell, not lightly; and at its touch their love of country returned; and with a look at me as if I were the destroying angel, as I might have become theirs, they again faced the enemy. Genl. Webb soon came to my assistance. He was on foot, but he was active, and did all that one could do to repair the breach, or to avert its calamity. The men that had fallen back, facing the enemy soon regained confidence in themselves, and became steady. This portion of the wall was lost to us, and the enemy had gained the cover of the reverse side, where he now stormed with fire; but Webb's men, with their bodies in part protected by the abruptness of the crest, now sent back in the enemy's faces as fierce a storm. Some scores of venturesome Rebels, that in their first push at the wall, had dared to cross at the further angle, and those that had desecrated Cushing's guns, were promptly shot down, and speedy death met him who should raise his body to cross it again. At this point little could be seen of the enemy, by reason of his cover, and the smoke, except the flash of his muskets, and his waving flags. Those red flags were accumulating at the wall every moment, and they maddened us as the same color does the bull. Webb's men are falling fast, and he is among them to direct and encourage; but however well they may now do, with that walled enemy in front, with more than a dozen flags to Webb's three, it soon becomes apparent that in not many minutes they will be overpowered, or that there will be none alive for the enemy to overpower. Webb has but three Regiments, all small, the 69th, 71st, and 72nd Penn. — the 106th Penn. except two companies, is not here to day, — and he must have speedy assistance, or this crest will be lost. Oh, where is Gibbon, — where is Hancock, — some General — any body, with the power and the will to support that wasting, melting line? No general came, and no succor I thought of Hays upon the right; but from the smoke and war along his front, it was evident that he had enough upon his hands, if he staid the in rolling tide of the Rebels there.— Doubleday upon the left, was too far off, and too slow, and on another occasion I had begged him to send his idle Regiments to support another line, battling with thrice its numbers, and this *"Old Sumpter Hero"* had declined. As a last resort I resolved to see if Hall and Harrow could not send some of their commands to reinforce Webb. I galloped to the left in the execution of my purpose, and as I attained the rear of Hall's line, from the nature of the ground there, and the position of the enemy, it was easy to discover the reason and the manner of this gathering of Rebel flags in front of Webb. The enemy, emboldened by his success in gaining our line by the group of trees and the angle of the wall, was concentrating all his right against, and was further pressing, that point. There was the stress of his assault, — there would he drive his fiery wedge to split our line. In front of Harrow's and Hall's Brigades he had been able to advance no nearer than where he first halted to deliver fire: and these commands had not yielded an inch. To effect the concentration before Webb, the enemy would march the regiment on his extreme right of each of his lines, by the left flank, to the rear of the troops, still halted and facing to the front, and so continuing to draw in his right, when they were all massed in the position desired, he would again face them to the front, and advance to the storming. This was the way he made the wall before Webb's line blaze red with his battle flags; and such was the purpose there of his thick-crowding battalions. Not a moment must be lost. Col. Hall I found just in rear of his line, sword in hand, cool, vigilant, noting all that passed, and directing the battle of his Brigade. The fire was constantly diminishing now in his front, in the manner by the movement of the enemy, that I have mentioned: — drifting to the right. "How is it going?," — Col. Hall asked me as I rode up. "Well, but Webb is hotly pressed, and must have support, or he will be overpowered. Can you assist him?" — "Yes." — "You cannot be too quick." — "I will move my Brigade at once." — "Good." — He gave the order, and in briefest time I saw five friendly colors hurrying to the aid of the imperiled three; and each color represented true, battle-tried men, that had not turned back from Rebel fire that day nor yesterday, though their ranks were sadly thinned. To Webb's Brigade, pressed back, as it had been from the wall, the distance was not great, from Hall's right. — The Regiments marched by the right flank. Col. Hall superintended the movement in person. Col. Devereux cooly commanded the 19th Mass. — his Major, [Edmund] Rice, had already been wounded and carried off. — Lieut. Col. [George N.] Macy of the 20th Mass. had just had his left hand shot off, and so Capt. [Henry L.] Abbott gallantly led over this fine Regiment; — the 42nd N.Y. followed their excellent Colonel, [James E.] Mallon; — Lieut. Col. [Amos E.] Steele, 7th Mich. had just been killed, and this Regiment, and the handful of the 59th N.Y. followed their colors. The movement, as it did, attracting the enemy's fire, and executed in haste, as it must be, was difficult; but in reasonable time, and in order that is serviceable, if not regular, Hall's men are fighting gallantly side by side with Webb's, before the all-important point. I did not stop to see all this movement of Hall's; but from him I went at once further to the left, to the 1st Brigade. — Gnl. Harrow I did not see, but his fighting men would answer my purpose as well. The 19th Me., the 15th Mass., the 82nd N.Y., and the shattered old thunderbolt, the 1st Minn. — poor Farrell was dying there upon the ground, where he had fallen, — all men that I could find, I took over to the right at the *double quick*. As we were moving to, and near, the other Brigades of the Division, from my position on horseback, I could see that the enemy's right, under Hall's fire was beginning to stagger and to break. "See," I said to the men, "see the *'chivalry,'* See the gray-backs run!" The men saw, and as they swept to their places by the side of Hall's and opened fire, they roared; and this in a manner that said more plainly than words, — for the deaf could have seen it in their faces, and the blind could have heard it in their voices, — *the crest is safe.*

The whole Division concentrated, and changes of position, and new phases, as well on our part, as on that of the enemy, having as indicated occurred, for the purpose of showing the exact present posture of affairs, some further description is necessary. Before the 2nd Division the enemy is massed, the main bulk of his force covered by the ground that slopes to his rear, with his front at the stone wall. Between his front and us extends the very apex of the crest. All there are left of the White Trefoil Division, — yesterday morning there were three thousand eight hundred; — this morning there were less than three thousand; — at this moment there are somewhat over two thousand; — twelve Regiments in three Brigades, are below, or behind the crest, in such a position that by the exposure of the head and upper part of the body, above the crest, they can deliver their fire in the enemy's faces along the top of the wall. By reason of the disorganization incidental, in Webb's Brigade, to his men's having broken and fallen back, as mentioned, in the two other Brigades, to their rapid and difficult change of position under fire, and in all the Division, in part, to severe and continuous battle, formation of Companies, and Regiments in regular ranks is lost; but commands, Companies, Regiments, and Brigades, are blended and intermixed, — an irregular, extended mass, — men enough, if in order, to form a line of four or five ranks along the whole front of the Division. The twelve flags of the Regiments wave defiantly at intervals along the front; at the stone wall, at unequal distances from ours, of forty, fifty, or sixty yards, stream nearly double this number of the battle flags of the enemy. These changes accomplished on either side, and the concentration complete, although no cessation or abatement in the general din of conflict since the commencement had at any time been appreciable, now it was as if a new battle, deadlier, stormier than before had sprung from the body of the old, — a young Phenix of Combat, whose eyes stream lightning, shaking his arrowy wings over the yet glowing ashes of his progenitor. The jostling swaying lines on either side boil, and roar, and dash their flamy spray, two hostile billows of a fiery ocean. Thick flashes stream from the wall; — thick volleys answer from the crest. No threats or expostulation now; — only example and encouragement. All depths of passion are stirred, and all combative fire, down to their deep foundations. Individuality is drowned in a sea of clamor; and timid men, breathing the breath of the multitude, are brave. The frequent dead and wounded lie where they stagger and fall; — there is no humanity for them now, and none can be spared to care for them. The men do not cheer, or shout, — they growl; and over that uneasy sea, heard with the roar of musketry, sweeps the muttered thunder of a storm of growls. Webb, Hall, Devereux, Mallon, Abbott, among the men where all are heroes, are doing deeds of note. Now the loyal wave rolls up as if it would overleap its barrier, the crest, — pistols flash with the muskets. — "Forward to the wall," is answered by the Rebel counter-command, "Steady, men," — and the wave swings back. — Again it surges, and again it sinks. These men of Pennsylvania, on the soil of their own homesteads, the first and only to flee the wall, must be the first to storm it. "Major — lead your men over the crest, — they will follow." "By the tactics I understand my place is in rear of the men." "Your pardon, sir; I see your place is in rear of the men. I thought you were fit to lead." — "Capt. Suplee come on with your men." "Let me first stop this fire in the rear, or we shall be hit by our own men." "Never mind the fire in the rear; let us take care of this in front first." — "Sergeant forward with your color. Let the Rebels see it close to their eyes once more before they die." The Color Sergeant of the 72 Pa. grasping the stump of the severed lance in both his hands, waved the flag above his head, and rushed towards the wall. — "Will you see your color storm the wall alone!" One man only starts to follow. Almost half way to the wall, down go color bearer and color to the ground, — the gallant Sergeant is dead. — The line springs, — the crest of the solid ground, with a great roar, heaves forward its maddened load, men, arms, smoke, fire, a fighting mass; — it rolls to the wall; — flash meets flash; — the wall is crossed; — a moment ensues of thrusts, yells, blows, shots, and undistinguishable conflict, followed by a shout, universal, that makes the welkin ring again; and — the last and bloodiest fight of the great battle of Gettysburg is ended and won.

Many things cannot be described by pen or pencil, — such a fight is one. Some hints and incidents may be given but a description, a picture, never. From what is told, the imagination may for itself construct the scene; otherwise he who never saw, can have no adequate idea of what such a battle is.

When the vortex of battle passion had subsided, hopes, fears, rage, joy, of which the maddest and the noisiest was the last, and we were calm enough to look about us, we saw, that as with us, the fight with the 3d Division was ended; and that in that Division was a repetition of the scenes immediately about us. In that moment the judgment almost refused to credit the senses. Are these abject wretches about us, whom our men are now disarming and driving together in flocks, the jaunty men of Pickett's Division, whose sturdy lines and flashing arms, but a few moments, since, came sweeping up the slope to destroy us? Are these red cloths that our men toss about in derision, the "fiery Southern crosses," thrice ardent, the battle-flags of the rebellion, that waved defiance at the wall? We know, but so sudden has been the transition, we yet can scarce believe.

13. **Lieutenant Alonzo Cushing commanded the battery closest to the Angle. Cushing became one of the Federal heroes because of bravery, and his sergeant, Frederick Fuger (the court reporter misspelled it Huger), describes how and why. Testimony of Frederick Fuger, *Supreme Court of Pennsylvania*, 127-130.**

. . . I remember the positions occupied by our guns when the cannonading first commenced . . . the distance from one gun to another fourteen yards, the distance from the stone wall to that line of guns was about one hundred feet, to the best of my recollection, now the second line represents the timbers[sic], and they are direct in the rear of the guns and measure about seven yards from the trail of the handspikes to the head of the lead horses, in the rear of that is the line of caissons, they are directly in rear of timbers, the distance from rear of timbers to the heads of horses is about ten yards; that's the battle line of the battle. By the back of my hand I can describe the land, the guns were on the highest point of the ridge called the extension of the Cemetery Ridge. Now our caissons were in the rear of that over that ridge.... That was the position occupied by the guns when the cannonading commenced. I think the Seventy-first Regiment Pennsylvania was right over to the corner of the angle to the right of the battery. There was nothing in front of the battery, except the enemy; the Sixty-ninth Regiment Pennsylvania was to the left of the battery. The four regiments constituted what was called the Philadelphia brigade; don't know what was to the rear of the battery. The artillery firing commenced about one o'clock and lasted nearly an hour and a half or three-fourths. When the artillery firing ceased General Webb came up to Lieutenant

Cushing. Cushing was about between the third and fourth piece. . , and remarked to Cushing that this is going to be a hot place. Cushing then said, wouldn't it be better to move the guns by hand to the front and right up to the stone wall. What reply General Webb made I cannot tell exactly, but Lieutenant Cushing turned around to me and ordered me to move all six guns to the stone wall, which order I obeyed. He then ordered me to bring all the canister alongside of each No. 2 post, which order I obeyed. There was really left room enough between muzzle of gun and stone wall for cannoneers No. 1 and 2 to work. . . . When the enemy advanced and got within four hundred and five hundred rods of the battery we commenced firing single charges of canister and about that time Lieutenant Cushing was wounded in the shoulder, when they got nearer within three hundred yards we used double charges, and about that time Lieutenant Cushing was wounded in the testicles. When they got within two hundred yards, Cushing was shot through the mouth, instantly killed, and the time he was shot through the mouth I was to his right about three feet and about a foot in advance of him. When he fell, he fell in my right arm. I turned around and he fell on that arm, and if I recollect right, I called up a man of my battery, by name Wright, to take Cushing's body to the rear. Just as soon as Cushing was killed, Lieutenant Milne, an officer attached to our battery from the volunteers announced to the men that he was in command and to obey him. He had hardly said that word when he was killed, and that placed me in command of the battery. We continued firing canister until all the ammunition was fired. The enemy were, after we ceased firing, to the best of my recollection, to within thirty or forty yards of the stone wall. We hadn't anything to do then, but I noticed infantry troops moving toward our right, which I recognized to be the Seventy-second regiment Pennsylvania volunteers. They moved, it appeared to me, in an oblique direction and came directly in rear of four pieces or three and a fraction over. When they came right close to the stone wall and uncovered the artillery men, they commenced firing and moving towards the stone wall. The enemy gained some points towards the stone wall by coming over (as marked in red across the angle); the heaviest fighting took place right here in the angle, as indicated by red mark, and all those men from the enemy. When the enemy came to the stone wall they were not formed to a solid line, they came up in groups of fifty or a hundred. There were various groups of them, and of all those rebels that came over the stone wall not one got back. They were all killed, or wounded or taken prisoners by the Seventy-second regiment. It was all over in a few minutes. I refer to the group that came over the wall into the angle. I saw the killed and wounded in the angle, seventy-five or a hundred of them. On the union side, they were all men belonging to the Seventy-second regiment with part of their clothing burned, which was caused by discharge of muskets at close range. That shows that it was close fighting at close distances. The bodies of the Seventy-second regiment I saw were between the wall and five, six or eight feet, right along the front wall, between the first gun and the angle and twenty feet in the rear. They fell right in their track, advancing. We were not doing anything in particular, we were standing up with hand spikes, and rocks and anything we could get our hands on for fighting. . . . They looked to me as if they moved in columns of divisions, and oblique direction, and as they got within forty feet of the guns they seemed to deploy; the first gun, in describing position of guns at stone wall, was about forty or thirty-five feet from the angle at the stone wall; the other guns extended to the left along the stone wall, about fourteen yards apart from each other; the muzzles were about two to three feet from the wall(witness numbers the gun in ink from right to left)(witness marks on diagram the post where Cushing fell, writing over it "Cushing"). Cushing fell at the right of the trail handspike of No. 3 gun, and within two feet to the right. I did not know Armistead; I saw him come over but did not know who he was then but found out afterwards that it was Armistead; I saw him fall near the point in advance of where Cushing fell. . . . I fired at Armistead with my pistol; if he was hit by it I do not know. I was about ten feet from where Armistead fell when I shot at him, in rear of gun No. 3. I was about six or seven feet from where Cushing fell, and Armistead fell between Cushing and the wall. At time Armistead fell Gen. Webb was right up on the stone wall to the left of the battery. . . . Gen. Webb was with Cushing when he was killed and moved off to the left . . . I didn't see anything in the hand of Gen. Armistead when he came over the wall. I think he was hatless when he came over. I think he was hatless when he came over; before he came over he put his hands on gun No. 3 and jumped over. I noticed the killed and wounded of my own command to the left of No. 3 gun; I don't think any of the Seventy-second regiment were among them. I don't think they extended to the third piece. I saw the colors come up here with them when they obliqued to the right from the rear. I recollect distinctly the national color. I did not see any Massachusetts or New York regiments or any other down where the Seventy-second regiment was fighting. None came there while I was there during the fighting. I saw a good many troops come up after the fighting in an irregular way.

14. The desperate fighting at the Angle included the use of any piece of metal available in Cushing's guns, as a sergeant-major in the 71st Pennsylvania tells us. Some of the 71st were captured, but got away when the Confederates were too busy fighting from behind the wall to take them back to Seminary Ridge. Testimony of William S. Stockton, *Supreme Court of Pennsylvania,* 243-4.

Q. What orders had you?

A. To go forward, and we went over to the front wall; a portion, two companies, stepped on the rear wall at the north-east angle. Before we started I was in the rear of the regiment a little towards the right wing, and as we went forward we took one of Cushing's guns. The men of our regiment had been manning Cushing's guns and had handled for some time, and, when we moved forward, we took the gun with us, although I do not think that was done by orders. They ran the gun down into the angle of the lower wall to about the position where the Seventy-first's monument now stands.

Q. What was done with it?

A. It was loaded up to the muzzle with all sorts of things they even put a bayonet in it, and while we were there a non-commissioned officer of Cushing's Battery came up and told us to sight it along the Emmittsburg road. There was none of Cushing's men at that gun, it was manned entirely by men of the Seventy-first.

Q. Was there another gun of Cushing's Battery?

A. I understood that there was.

Q. Did you go down to the wall?

A. Yes, sir. I was there and I watched the enemy as they came across the plain. I saw them come to the road and just as they got to the road the gun was fired and after they passed the fence they came on with a great rush. I saw one or two of our men start for the rear and I must say that, at the time, I thought it was rather cowardly. The gun was right here in the corner of the angle (explaining by map). The men who were with me stood and fought, and the enemy came in in great numbers, and, as I remember it, there was a great boulder which formed a sort of stepping stone and made it easy to get over the wall, and they appeared to mass at this place, I suppose on account of it being easier to get over, and came over the wall in overwhelming numbers. They came with such force that they seemed to rebound and go back, like a wave receding from the shore, and as they went back they took us with them. When we got on the other side of the wall they ordered us to the rear, but I told the men to stay where they were. Then, a non-commissioned officer was ordered to take us back but he didn't do it.

Q. Where did you lie?

A. Just outside of the wall, from our own side. We laid there along that boulder and the rebels knelt along the wall as far as I could see to our left; kneeling down, firing over the wall. While we were lying there, the five of us agreed among ourselves to escape if we got the opportunity. I was to give the word, which would be the signal, and we were to jump altogether and get over the wall, it being impossible to have done so singly. Previous to that a number of balls were striking the wall all around our heads while we were on the other side of it; the balls came from the rear and we supposed it was some of our troops. I raised my head to see where they came from and over to the extreme left I saw some of our troops, on their left, and I then found that our men had gotten to their rear and on their flank, and then I gave the order to jump and we all jumped over the wall and ran in a body and we were met in the rush by our regiment and another and we immediately commenced taking the rebels prisoners.

15. Some men in the Philadelphia Brigade, like Corporal Robert Whittick of the 69th Pennsylvania, increased their fire-power in preparation for the charge by picking up rifles from the field. He also describes the hand-to-hand combat near the wall. Testimony of Robert Whittick, *Supreme Court of Pennsylvania*, 79-81.

. . . When they opened up the artillery on us in the morning, they ordered us to lay down. We laid there I suppose until one or two o'clock, somewheres there, and they advanced in three lines on us, and after the second day's fight we went out on the battle-field and gathered up all the guns and loaded them. I suppose each man had some six, or eight, or ten, or twelve, all laying aside of them, and as the enemy advanced, the first line, we gave it to them. Our orders were not to fire until we saw the whites of their eyes. I believe that was the order General Webb gave us. Finally the first line wavered, and then the second line came up, and when the third line came up, that was the time there was a breakup on the right of us, and then the enemy came in on our rear, and came down by those bushes that we cut down, a lot of trees in our rear were cut down, and they got into us there. That is the time our men commenced clubbing one another, just about the time the Seventy-second came in. . . . Our line kind of wavered, swung around like . . . our colors retreated back about six or eight feet, probably, maybe, a little further; we could not go beyond these woods, because it was all cut down, and there was more danger tramping over the trees in the position we had there than if we stood still. Then as near as I can judge, all hands were together. . . . The Seventy-second came from the rear kind of oblique like towards us, and mobbed in with us, and just a few minutes before that a fellow was taken in with me and I knocked him over and took him prisoner, and took him in over the stone wall. Then part of our regiment, company K, company G — part of company G, I think it was, and D, I think, and C, were all together there, and company H — all in this mob while this shooting was going on. Some of them had their muskets reversed clubbing one another.

16. **A private in the 72nd Pennsylvania describes how the regiment got to the Angle and the fighting there. Testimony of William H. Good, *Supreme Court of Pennsylvania*, 34-37.**

WILLIAM H. GOOD, having been duly sworn, was examined as follows:

By Mr. Ker :

Q. Where do you reside?

A. No. 161 Fontaine Street, Manayunk.

Q. You are now employed in the mint, are you not?

A. Yes, sir.

Q. Were you a member of the Seventy-second Pennsylvania on July 3, 1863?

A. Yes, sir.

Q. What were you?

A. A private in company K.

Q Were you there at the time of the advance of the enemy across the wall ?

A. Yes, sir;

Q. Whereabouts was company K in relation to the colors? was it on the right or on the left?

A. Company K was the left color company.

Q. What was the right color company?

A. Company E, I believe, was the right color company.

Q. I show you diagram Exhibit C in the bill of complaint.

A. I will have to ask some information about this.

Q. Look at that piece of paper. Do you recognize that diagram as in any way a description of the stone fence?

A. This is supposed to be the clump of trees.

Q. Do you recognize the diagram?

A. As I understand the diagram, this is supposed to be the stone wall, but I don't exactly understand this. The stone wall did not run up this way. The stone wall only ran a piece in this direction. There is a fence runs on this angle — a rail fence — or was at that time.

Q. Where?

A. On this angle here. On the upper end of this angle there was a rail fence. There was a stone wall run along the front, and we lay.

Q. Never mind where you lay. I am asking you about that paper.

A. I understand the stone wall as run on that angle. A portion of the Seventy-first Pennsylvania lay on that angle. The Seventy-first continued along this line from this angle.

Q. What portion of the Seventy-first lay on the front angle?

A. Two companies. I do not know exactly the two companies, but there was a certain portion of them.

Q. What lay over here to the left?

A. Sixty-ninth lay on the left in front of the woods.

Q. Between the Sixty-ninth and Seventy-first there was a battery?

A. Fronting on the wall.

Q. Up at the wall?

A. Yes, sir; right at the wall. When the engagement started there was a battery. In our front. We supported a battery.

Q. Was that occupied by troops?

A. No, sir; it was not. There was an opening there.

Q. The battery was where?

A. Supposed to be about here. The batteries were in front of the stone fence between the Seventy-first and Sixty-ninth.

Q. Be careful in your words; you call that front. Do you mean that for the front or for the rear?

A. We were certainly to the front here. We were front of that stone wall; anything that was back of that stone wall we would face.

Q. On which side was the enemy?

A. On the front.

Q. You mean the stone wall was in front of you?

A. The stone wall was directly in front of us.

Q. Between you and the enemy?

A. Yes, sir.

Q. When the enemy advanced over the wall what took place?

A. When the enemy advanced — at least come up to the stone wall or pretty close to the stone wall at that time, we were laying right close behind these woods, extending here right down to the battery. After the firing had got pretty well advanced, General Webb made a whole lot of motions, or sword motions, and we advanced them to our right. That would be towards the Seventy-first, and then as soon as we advanced along to the Seventy-first he commenced to pull his sword this way (illustrating). He might have said something but it would very hard for anybody to hear what he did say. He might have said a great many things, but I can't tell what he said. It was all done by motions.

Q. Because of the noise?

A. Yes! sir. Then we started down on the front and we ran within about sixteen or eighteen feet I think of the stone wall and we come into it pretty sharp there. Company E and K advanced over the stone wall. On the other side of the stone wall from us, when we advanced over, we found a lot of blue rocks running on a pitch slanting that way. When we jumped over that some of us slid down quick. I did myself. It got so warm on that side of the stone fence that some were shooting this way and some were shooting the other, and it got to be a regular jumble. It was a rough and tumble fight after the firing chiefly ceased, in line — after we charged over stone wall.

Q. In going down you say you went through the guns?

A. Rode between the guns.

Q. Was your company with you and were you in line?

A. The company was with us.

Q. When you got down near the stone fence, what did you find; any opposition?

A. Yes, sir.

Q. What was it?

A. The rebels; some of them on this side of the stone fence and some on the other.

Q. What did you do?

A. We advanced right over the stone fence.

Q. Where did they meet the enemy? Were they in front of you?

A. Some were on the right of us and some of them were on the left of us.

Q. You went through them?

A. We went right through them. As we went over the fence our company E and K that is company E at the right of us, and K that I belonged to, I was, I guess about seven or eight feet from the colors, not more than that, as I used to be what they call "the pony," but as we got thinned down in ranks my right fetched me more to the right of the company.

Q. You closed in what direction?

A. To the right.

Q. Towards whom?

A. Towards the colors.

Q. Then you went across the wall, where were the colors?

A. The colors were right with us, at the wall and over.

Q. Went over the wall?

A. Yes, sir. If I am not mistaken, the man that carried the colors a very little while was a man by the name of Murphy. He is a red-headed man. I have seen him once or twice in Philadelphia, but not for a year.

Q. When you started in how many men had you in your company?

A. Thirty-five.

Q. How many had you when you came out?

A. Ten.

Q. Subsequent to that, after it was over, were you detailed to bury the dead?

A. Yes, sir. We commenced to bury the dead on towards evening.

Q. You were one of those detailed to bury the dead?

A. Yes, sir. We buried them that night. I buried my cousin there.

Q. Where did you find the bodies in the angle; I mean of the Seventy-second people in the angle?

A. The most I can remember was one by the name of Metz belonging to my company — him and me were great chums — He fell across the stone wall. He fell crossways across the stone wall.

Q. At about what distance from the Sixty-ninth, or between the Sixty — ninth and the Seventy-first?

A. I should say it would be perhaps — it is hard to take measurements — but perhaps two hundred feet, or two hundred and fifty-feet to the right of the Sixty-ninth. It might two hundred and thirty-feet. In a place of that kind you cannot take measurement close.

17. A nineteen year old private in the 69th Pennsylvania, Anthony McDermott, was at the center of the storm. In this remarkable letter to John Bachelder, the historian at Gettysburg from the time of the battle until the early twentieth century, McDermott gives a perceptive and informative description of the action at the Angle. He draws striking vignettes of Cushing and the men in his unit. His commander's orders not to fire until they saw the whites of their enemy's eyes echoed the words shouted at Bunker Hill in 1775. McDermott's account of the right of his line buckling, the Confederates yelling at the Federals to surrender, Armistead's death, and of men being killed by "friendly fire," all add up to make this a most vivid and evocative essay. Anthony McDermott to J. Bachelder, n.d., New Hampshire Historical Society.

69th Regt. Penn. Vols.
Col. J. B. Bachelor[sic],
Supt. of Monuments and Inscriptions,
of Gettysburg Battlefield.

Dear Sir:

. . . Before sunset Gen. Webb had informed us that if we would hold our position until 4 o'clock, on the following afternoon, Gen. McClelland[sic] would be in the rear of the Rebels with 30,000 troops, and their defeat would be easily accomplished. I don't not know exactly why he made those representations to us, unless that it was because of the fierce attack made upon Culps Hill (12th Corps front) by Ewell's corps of the enemy, and not knowing that our line curved to our rear at that point, we supposed the enemy had managed to gain our rear, and for a time was pressing close upon us, as the sound of his musketry fire seemed to be near. But at the time the sun was sinking from sight the firing grew more distant and the cheering of our troops (for we could always tell the difference between the "Rebel Yell" and the "Union Cheer"), assured us that the darkness set in for that day with the victory at all points for our army.

The morning of the 3d passed off quietly, except the usual picket firing; sometimes very brisk and again all quiet until about noon. The troops had all finished eating their stew, or sipping their coffee, when a death like stillness prevailed throughout the army. The sun was shining in all its glory, giving forth a heat almost stifling and not a breath of air came to cause the slightest quiver to the most delicate leaf, or blade of grass. Of that stillness you have often heard, no language of mine could cause you to imagine its reality, such a stillness I had never before experienced nor since, and I have borne part in every engagement of the Army of the Potomac. The sound of a Whitworth gun was the first to break that stillness, it came from the Rebel lines and its shots passed high over our heads, a minute or two elapsed, then there was opened a volley of artillery, shot and shell, that ploughed through the air around and over our heads. You are already much more familiar with this terrible cannonade, than any statement of mine could make you. I cannot state with any precision the duration of time; this fire was kept up until the lines of battle made their appearance. It may have been but half an hour, but it certainly seemed over an hour before the fire slackened, and the infantry appeared in three lines of battle, and a skirmish line until our skirmishers had retired, and after the infantry cleared the woods, their artillery appeared. No holiday display seemed more imposing, nor troops on parade more regular, then this division of Pickett's Rebels. They came steadily arms at a trail. Their appearance was truly a relief from that terrible fire of their artillery; not that it was so destructive, but the dread it occasioned, the range seemed so low and the air so thick with flying missiles that we did not enjoy any space of relief from the dread of being ploughed into shreds, until the appearance of the infantry when the fire slackened. Cushing had already ordered two pieces from the crest down to the wall, and were placed in our line of battle, with company "I" the right flanking company of the regiment, and of which I was a private at that time. These pieces done more harm in that position to us than they did the enemy, as they only fired two or three rounds when their ammunition gave out, and one of those rounds blew the heads off two privates of the company, who were on one knee, at the time, besides these pieces drew upon us more than our share of fire from the battery that followed Pickett from the woods opposite to us, the gunners left us leaving their guns behind, hence they were useless. Poor Cushing was struck in the thighs, just previous to the arrival of those two guns on our line. During all that terrible storm of artillery, Cushing stood at the wall with one Co. Glass in hands, watching the effect of each shot from his own guns, all his commands were distinctly heard by our men. He would shout back to his men to elevate or depress their pieces so many degrees, his last command, that we heard was, "that[sic] excellent, keep that range." a [sic] few moments after we were rising from the ground to receive the advancing infantry, one of our men called out "that artillery officer has his legs knocked from under him." thus[sic] ended the life of a cool and brave an officer as the army was possessed of.

      After getting to our feet, our Col. O'Kane, gave us orders not to fire a shot until the enemy came so close to us, that we could distinguish the white of their eyes, he also reminded us that we were upon the soil of our own state, and that the enemy would probably make a desperate assault upon us, but as he knew we were at least as brave as they were, he did not fear but that we would render an account of ourselves this day, that would bring upon us the plaudits of our country, and that should any man among us flinch in our duty, he asked that the man nearest him would kill him on the spot. He went along the line speaking encouragement to all the companies, Gen. Webb, had also addressed our men on the centre and left in an similar manner, and gave them all the encouragement in his power. These addresses were not necessary as I do not believe there was a soldier in the regiment, that did not feel that he had more courage to meet the enemy at Gettysburg, than upon any field of battle in which we had as yet been engaged. The stimulus being the fact that we were upon the soil of our own State. When about two thirds of the field, that lay between the stone-wall and the Emmittsburg pike, had been crossed the enemy changed his direction to an oblique march to his left, and kept this direction in as good order, as when marching directly to the front, when within about 200 yards of us we received the command to fire, our first round was fired with deliberation and simultaneously, and threw their front line into confusion, from which they quickly rallied and opened their fire upon us. The troops on our right abandoned their position which left a blank space, that Armistead was quick to take advantage of, seeing it, he rushed through his ranks, taking off his hat, and putting it upon the point of his sword, he raised it for a standard, waving it, he ran along our front to a point near the angle and crossed the wall, his men following him, he continued in a direction towards the clump of trees in our rear, and close to where Gen. Webb stood when he was trying to get the 72d to come up to our assistance, the first three companies were now ordered to change their front to protect our right and rear, these were "I" "A" and "F" the enemy in our front was pouring in their shot, and Armistead's followers were giving it to us from our right flank, Co. "I" and "A" quickly changed and moved back to the crest to get between Armistead and Cushing's four misces.(sic) Co. "F" seemed to either not have received the order in time or had no desire to leave the wall hence an opening was left which left the enemy get between them, and our two flanking Co's. they[sic] rushed in on the rear of our main line, and it looked as though our regiment would be annihilated, the contest here became a hand to hand affair. Company "F" completely hustled over the stone-wall into the enemy's ranks, and all were captured, their Capt. Geo. Thompson being killed, and their Lt's wounded, and prisoners. I believe this company had no representation with the Regt. except those who had been on extra duty, and convalescents returned from the hospital, many of the enemy were here mingled with our own men some so close that while they struck at each other with the barrels of their rifles, they could not inflict any disabling injury. Gen. Kemper who as commanding the enemy on our left and centre, I suppose saw the shuffling on the right of our regiment rushed to the front and pressed his men upon our colors, the fighting here at close quarters was more desperate than at any other part of our line and involved Co. "C" "D" "H" "G" "E". What took place here I could not see, my range of vision only took in what was on my front, but seeing the enemy rushing into the gap between Co. "A" and "F" caused me to look at their movement, when I then saw the dangers that beset the regiment, or that part of it at the stone-wall. I then cast my eyes on Webb, who was not far from me, and saw him giving his fruitless command, by shouting for the 72d to come up the hill to our assistance, it was in vain. Kemper's men, some of them I believe used their musket butts as clubs as well as some of our own men, as an instance, Corpl. Bradley of Co. "D" who was quite a savage sort of a fellow, wielded his piece, striking right and left, and was killed in the hell by having his skull crushed by a musket in the hands of a rebel, and Private Donnelly of some Co. used his piece as a club, and when called upon to surrender replied tauntingly. "I surrender" at the same time striking his would be captor to the ground. I cite these two instances because they seem to have been particularly noticed by their comrades and spoken of by many of the men of the above mentioned Co. as well as of Co.'s "F" had been spoken of being struck, but not sufficiently to send them to the hospital. The fighting here continued until Gen. Kemper fell, seriously wounded near our colors: his men kept repeatedly calling upon our men to surrender, they only succeeded in making prisoners of two men apart from Co. "F". With Kemper's fall the enemy here surrendered. All this time the fighting was still kept up by Co's "T" and "A". We poured our fire upon him (the enemy) until Armistead received his mortal wound; he swerved from the way in which he winced, as though he was struck in the stomach, after wincing or bending like a person with cramp, he pressed his left hand on his stomach, his sword and hat (a slouch) fell to the ground. He then made two or three staggering steps, reached out his hands trying to grasp at the suzzle [sic] of what was then the 1st [sic] piece of Cushing's battery, and fell. I was at the time the nearest person, to him. At the time he was struck his fall was much about the same time that Kemper fell. His men (Armistead's) threw down their arms, most of them ran back to the stone-wall and lay down behind it. Some of them lay down between us and the wall, to which we now returned, we sent all that surrendered to our rear, unarmed leaving the troops behind to take charge of them. As soon as Armistead fell I turned round to Gen. Webb. Who was still calling upon the 72d to come up, to our assistance[.] I tapped him on the shoulder and told him their leader had fallen, and the rebels are running, he turned his head in the direction of the enemy and saw that what I said was true. He then cried out to Baxter (or the 72d) "Yes boys the enemy is running, come up, come up," then the 72d came up, but the fight was over, at the same time, Halls brigade came upon the scene in an oblique direction from our left and rear. I do not think they done any firing, if they did then they fired either upon our regiment, or the unarmed rebels who were sent to the rear, if the fighting was not over when Hall's brigade came upon the scene how could they fire upon the enemy without shooting us when our men were mingled with the enemy and Hall's men did not at any time come to the stone-wall except as individuals after the fight was over, when they came to view the field. It is said that the 72d are claiming, some, that their position was on the crest of Cemetery ridge in rear of Cushing's battery, and by others a claim is being made for them that they occupied the angle of the stone wall which they term the "bloody angle" now if they occupied either one of those positions how happened it that Armistead crossed the wall close by that angle, and when did they relieve the 71st Regt. from that position. Did they run from there and 1st [sic] Armistead over the wall, and again did they run from the crest, to let Armistead get to Cushing's guns, also how did they get at the foot of the ridge near the Taneytown road when Webb turned to urge them to come and Capt. Banes Asst. Adjt. Gen. of the brigade was riding up and down their line urging or trying to drive them up. The extreme left of the Regt. Co. "B" and "I" were hotly engaged but the enemy did not get so close to the wall at the centre. . . .

At the time of the battle I was a private of Co. "I" which was always the 1st Co. of the Regt., but was detailed as clerk to the Adjt. By the advice of Maj. Palmer who was on the Division staff as Inspector, the Adjt. took from me my rifle and accoutrements so that I could not go into battle, his object was that if the Adjt. and his clerk were both disabled it would be a different matter to transact the business of the Regt. properly for sometimes afterwards. I always disregarded these instructions and at Gettysburg I filled my pockets with cartridges, and before noon of the 2d I got a rifle from a wounded picket and endeavored to discharge my duty as a soldier, and as an American. I was then in my nineteenth year.

18. Private John Buckley, 69th Pennsylvania, testifies to the "friendly fire" from Cowan's battery. Testimony of John Buckley, *Supreme Court of Pennsylvania*, 135.

There was no infantry firing behind the copse of trees there was a battery there firing, directly in rear of the left companies of the Sixty-ninth regiment. I didn't know what battery that was at the time. They were firing grape and canister over, and it killed some of our men. It sometimes threw up stones. I was hit by a stone; got a lump from it. I found out afterwards it was Cowan's Battery. The battery disappeared as quick as it come. It didn't stay there until the end of the firing. My position at the stone wall was taken on the morning of the 2d at about 8 o'clock. I was in the one position except on night of 2d, when I took my comrade back with both eyes shot out of him. I was absent from there about twenty minutes.

Section IX

"The Fault Is Entirely My Own":

Afterwords

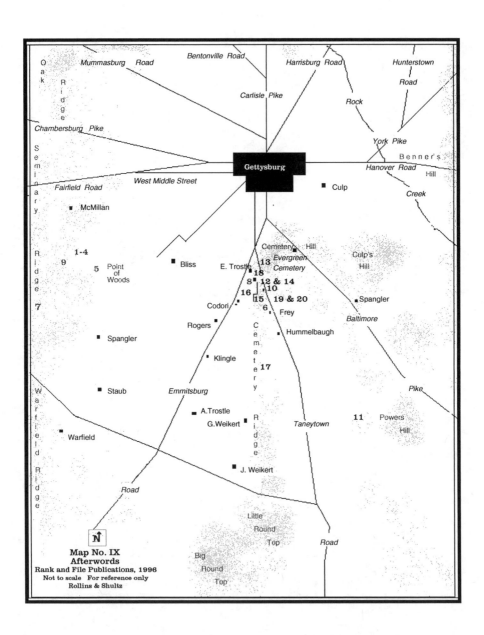

Oak Ridge

Mummasburg Road

Bentonville Road

Harrisburg Road

Hunterstown Road

Carlisle Pike

Rock

Chambersburg Pike

York Pike

Benner's Hill

Seminary

Gettysburg

Hanover Road

Fairfield Road

West Middle Street

Culp

Creek

McMillan

Ridge

Cemetery Hill

Culp's Hill

1-4

Evergreen Cemetery

9

Bliss

E. Trostle

13

5

Point of Woods

18

8

12 & 14

10

7

16

15

19 & 20

Codori

6

Spangler

Rogers

Frey

Baltimore

Cemetery

Hummelbaugh

Spangler

Klingle

17

Warfield Ridge

Staub

Emmitsburg

Pike

A.Trostle

11

Powers Hill

G.Weikert

Ridge

Taneytown

Warfield

J. Weikert

Road

N

Little Round Top

Road

Map No. IX
Afterwords
Rank and File Publications, 1996
Not to scale   For reference only
Rollins & Shultz

Big Round Top

1. The burden of failure weighed heavily on Robert E. Lee.
As he said numerous times on July 3rd, Lee genuinely considered
the failure of Pickett's Charge as his fault. Many in the South
agreed, and criticism of the failure of the Pennsylvania campaign
was widespread. Yet Lee apparently still did not see Longstreet's
idea as a significantly better alternative. Robert E. Lee to Jefferson Davis, July 31, 1863, in Clifford Dowdey and Louis Manarin,
eds., *The Wartime Papers of Robert E. Lee* (Boston: Little Brown,
1961), 565.

. . . No blame can be attached to the army for its failure to
accomplish what was projected by me, nor should it be censured for
the unreasonable expectations of the public. . . . But with the
knowledge I then had, & in the circumstances I was then placed, I
do not know what better course I could have pursued. With my
present knowledge, & could I have foreseen that the attack on the
last day would have failed to drive the enemy from his position, I
should certainly have tried some other course. What the ultimate
result would have been is not so clear to me.

**2. Lee had said going into Pennsylvania that the key to the
campaign was finding officers to carry out his orders, and he had
failed to find them and to get his ideas implemented. He had also
admitted his supreme confidence in his men, "as gallant and brave
an army as ever existed," but on July 3rd had asked them to do
more than they were capable of, and he knew it. With retreat to
Virginia, his army would never again be an offensive threat,
spending the next 21 months fighting a defensive holding action,
one they could not win. Lee saw the hand of Providence in this
defeat; he was also sick, and thus on August 8th he wrote to
President Jefferson Davis and asked to be replaced. Robert E. Lee
to Jefferson Davis, August 8, 1863, *The Robert E. Lee Reader*
Edited by Stanley F. Horn (Indianapolis: The Bobbs-Merrill
Company, 1961), 337-338.**

Mr. President:
Your letters of July 28th and August 2nd have been received,
and I have waited for a leisure hour to reply, but I fear that will never
come. I am extremely obliged to you for the attention given to the
wants of this army and the efforts made to supply them. Our
absentees are returning, and I hope the earnest and beautiful
appeal made to the country in your proclamation may stir up the
whole people and that they may see their duty and perform it.
Nothing is wanted but that their fortitude should equal their bravery
to insure the success of our cause. We must expect reverses, even
defeats. They are sent to teach us wisdom and prudence, to call forth

greater energies, and to prevent our falling into greater disasters. Our people have only to be true and united, to bear manfully the misfortunes incident to the war, and all will come right in the end.

I know how prone we are to censure and how ready to blame others for the non-fulfillment of our expectations. This is unbecoming in a generous people, and I grieve to see its expression. The general remedy for the want of success in a military commander is his removal. This is natural, and in many instances proper. For no matter what may be the ability of the officer, if he loses the confidence of his troops disaster must sooner or later ensue.

I have been prompted by these reflections more than once since my return from Pennsylvania to propose to your excellency the propriety of selecting another commander for this army. I have seen and heard of expressions of discontent in the public journals at the result of the expedition. I do not know how far this feeling extends in the army. My brother officers have been too kind to report it, and so far the troops have been too generous to exhibit it. It is fair, however, to suppose that it does exist, and success is so necessary to us that nothing should be risked to secure it.

I therefore, in all sincerity, request Your Excellency to take measures to supply my place. I do this with the more earnestness because no one is more aware than myself of my inability for the duties of my position. I cannot even accomplish what I myself desire. How can I fulfill the expectations of others? In addition, I sensibly feel the growing failure of my bodily strength. I have not yet recovered from the attack I experienced last spring. I am becoming more and more incapable of exertion, and am thus prevented from making the personal supervision of the operations in the field which I feel to be necessary. I am so dull that in making use of the eyes of others I am frequently misled.

Everything, therefore, points to the advantages to be derived from a new commander, and I the more anxiously urge the matter upon Your Excellency from the belief that a younger and abler man than myself can readily be obtained. I know that he will have as gallant and brave an army as ever existed to second his efforts, and it would be the happiest day of my life to see at its head a worthy leader, one that would accomplish more than I could perform and all that I have wished. I hope Your Excellency will attribute my request to the true reason, the desire to serve my country and do all in my power to insure the success of her righteous cause.

I have no complaints to make of any one but myself. I have received nothing but kindness from those above me, and the most considerate attention from my comrades and companions in arms. To Your Excellency I am especially indebted for uniform kindness and consideration. You have done everything in your power to aid me in the work committed to my charge, without omitting anything to promote the general welfare. I pray that your efforts may at length be crowned with success, and that you may live long to enjoy the thanks of a grateful people.

3. This is the "earnest and beautiful appeal" Lee spoke of in his letter to Davis. While it is unclear exactly who put these words on paper, it is clear that Lee shared these sentiments. One can't help but read here his critical evaluation of his own performance on July 3rd. Capt. Robert E. Lee, *Recollections and Letters of General Robert E. Lee* (Garden City, N.J.: Garden City Publishing, 1924), 105-106.

HEADQUARTERS, ARMY NORTHERN VIRGINIA,
August 13, 1863.
The President of the Confederate States has, in the name of the people, appointed August 21st as a day of fasting, humiliation, and prayer. A strict observance of the day is enjoined upon the officers and soldiers of this army. All military duties, except such as are absolutely necessary, will be suspended. The commanding officer of brigades and regiments are requested to cause divine services, suitable to the occasion, to be performed in their respective commands. Soldiers! we have sinned against Almighty God. We have forgotten His signal mercies, and have cultivated a revengeful, haughty, and boastful spirit. We have not remembered that the defenders of a just cause should be pure in His eyes; that "our times are in His hands," and we have relied too much on our own arms for the achievement of our independence. God is our only refuge and our strength. Let us humble ourselves before Him. Let us confess our many sins, and beseech Him to give us a higher courage, a purer patriotism, and more determined will; that He will convert the hearts of our enemies; that He will hasten the time when war, with its sorrows and sufferings, shall cease, and that He will give us a name and place among the nations of the earth.
R. E. LEE, General

4. Lee went home after the war, and then served as President of Washington College in Lexington until his death in 1870. He never got around to writing his memoirs, and was uninterested in rehashing battles and strategy. In 1868 he wrote a letter to a man who was intending to write a history of the war, and this is as close as he got to giving his view of the failure of Pickett's Charge, and the Pennsylvania campaign. Pickett's Charge was the "one determined and united blow . . . by our whole line" that he had planned and watched fail. Lee, *ed., Recollections*, 106.

As to the battle of Gettysburg, I must again refer you to the official accounts. Its loss was occasioned by a combination of circumstances. It was commenced in the absence of correct intelligence. It was continued in the effort to overcome the difficulties by which we were surrounded, and it would have been gained could one determined and united blow have been delivered by our whole line. As it was, victory trembled in the balance for three days, and the battle resulted in the infliction of as great an amount of injury as was received and in frustrating the Federal campaign for the season.

5. Major General George Pickett wrote several letters to Sallie after the battle. He poured out his innermost feelings about the cause of the failure of the charge — lack of support for his troops — as well as his personal feelings of depression, his belief that the war had reached a turning point, and that the South could no longer win. Pickett would remain bitter about the destruction of his division for the remainder of his life, and would, on at least one occasion, blame Lee for it. Inman, ed., *General Pickett's War Letters to His Wife*, 66-73.

My letter of yesterday, my darling, written before the battle, was full of hope and cheer; even though it told you of the long hours of waiting from four in the morning, when Gary's pistol rang out from the Federal lines signaling the attack upon Culp's Hill, to the solemn eight o'clock review of my men, who rose and stood silently lifting their hats in loving reverence as Marse Robert, Old Peter and your own soldier reviewed them — on then to the deadly stillness of the five hours following, when the men lay in the tall grass in the rear of the artillery line, the July sun pouring its scorching rays almost vertically down upon them, till one o'clock when the awful silence of the vast battlefield was broken by a cannon-shot which opened the greatest artillery duel of the world. The firing lasted two hours. When it ceased we took advantage of the blackened field and in the glowering darkness formed our attacking column just before the brow of Seminary Ridge.

I closed my letter to you a little before three o'clock and rode up to Old Peter for orders. I found him like a great lion at bay. I have never seen him so grave and troubled. For several minutes after I had saluted him he looked at me without speaking. Then in an agonized voice, the reserve all gone, he said:

"Pickett, I am being crucified at the thought of the sacrifice of life which this attack will make. I have instructed Alexander to watch the effect of our fire upon the enemy, and when it begins to tell he must take the responsibility and give you your orders, for I can't."

While he was yet speaking a note was brought to me from Alexander. After reading it I handed it to him, asking if I should obey and go forward. He looked at me for a moment, then held out his hand. Presently, clasping his other hand over mine without speaking he bowed his head upon his breast. I shall never forget the look in his face nor the clasp of his hand when I said "Then, General, I shall lead my Division on." I had ridden only a few paces when I remembered your letter and (forgive me) thoughtlessly scribbled in a corner of the envelope, "If Old Peter's nod means death then good by and God bless you, little one," turned back and asked the dear old chief if he would be good enough to mail it for me. As he took your letter from me, my darling, I saw tears glistening on his cheeks and beard. The stern old war — horse, God bless him, was weeping for his men and, I know, praying too that this cup might pass from them. I obeyed the silent assent of his bowed head, an assent given against his own convictions, — given in anguish and with reluctance.

My brave boys were full of hope and confident of victory as I led them forth, forming them in column of attack, and though officers and men alike knew what was before them, — knew the odds against them, — they eagerly offered up their lives on the altar of duty, having absolute faith in their ultimate success. Over on Cemetery Ridge the Federals beheld a scene never before witnessed on this continent, — a scene which has never previously been enacted and can never take place again — an army forming in line of battle in full view, under their very eyes — charging across a space nearly a mile in length over fields of waving grain and anon of stubble and then a smooth expanse — moving with the steadiness of a dress parade, the pride and glory soon to be crushed by an overwhelming heartbreak.

Well, it is all over now. The battle is lost, and many of us are prisoners, many are dead, many wounded, bleeding and dying. Your soldier lives and mourns and but for you, my darling, he would rather, a million times rather, be back there with his dead, to sleep for all time in an unknown grave.

Your sorrowing
Soldier

In camp, July 4, 1863

On the Fourth — far from a glorious Fourth to us or to any with love for his fellow-men — I wrote you just a line of heart-break. The sacrifice of life on that blood-soaked field on the fatal third was too awful for the heralding of victory, even for our victorious foe, who, I think, believe as we do, that it decided the fate of our cause.

No words can picture the anguish of that roll-call — the breathless waits between the responses. The "Here" of those who, by God's mercy, had miraculously escaped the awful rain of shot and shell was a sob — a gasp — a knell — for the unanswered name of his comrade called before his. There was no tone of thankfulness for having been spared to answer to their names, but rather a toll, and an unvoiced wish that they, too, had been among the missing.

But for the blight to your sweet young life, but for you, only you, my darling, your soldier would rather by far be out there, too, with his brave Virginians — dead —

Even now I can hear them cheering as I gave the order, "Forward"! I can feel their faith and trust in me and their love for our cause. I can feel the thrill of their joyous voices as they called out all along the line, "We'll follow you, Marse George. We'll follow you — we'll follow you." Oh, how faithfully they kept their word — following me on — on —to their death, and I, believing in the promised support, led them on — on — on — Oh, God!

I can't write you a love letter to-day, my Sallie, for with my great love for you and my gratitude to God for sparing my life to devote to you, comes the over-powering thought of those whose lives were sacrificed of the broken-hearted widows and mothers and orphans. The moans of my wounded boys, the sight of the dead, upturned faces, flood my soul with grief and here am I whom they trusted, whom they followed, leaving them on that field of carnage — leaving them to the mercy of and guarding four thousand prisoners across the river back to Winchester. Such a duty for men who a few hours ago covered themselves with glory eternal.

Well, my darling, I put the prisoners all on their honor and gave them equal liberties with my own soldier boys. My first command to them was to go and enjoy themselves the best they could, and they have obeyed my order. To-day a Dutchman and two of his comrades came up and told me that they were lost and besought me to help them find their commands. They had been with my men and had gotten separated from their own comrades. So I sent old Floyd off on St. Paul to find out where they belonged and deliver them.

This is too gloomy and too poor a letter for so beautiful a sweetheart, but it seems sacriligious, almost, to say I love you, with the hearts that are stilled to love on the field of battle.

Your Soldier

Headquarters, July 6, 1863

I have but one moment to tell my own darling how entirely my heart is hers. But for her and her love, I should not have cared to survive the conflict of the 3rd. My division is almost extinguished.

How any of us escaped is miraculous. More than a fourth of my division have been placed *hors du combat.* Two of my brigadiers were killed, and one wounded and a prisoner. Only two field officers out of the whole command came out of the fight unhurt.

I was ordered to take a height, which I did, under the most withering fire I have ever known, and I have seen many battles. But, alas, *no support came;* and my poor fellows who had gotten in were over-powered. My heart is very, very sad!

I am crossing the river to-day, guarding some four thousand prisoners back to Winchester, where I shall take command and recruit my wearied and cut up people.

You must write to me at that place. I received a letter from you dated the fourteenth of last month, immediately after you arrived at your home. I was delighted to learn of your mother's convalescence. Give her my best love, and tell her to take good care of my own, my precious.

Devotedly and forever,

Your Soldier

Just one month to-day since I parted from you it seems a year.

Williamsport, July 8, 1863

I am enclosing you a copy of General Lee's official letter of July 9th, in answer to mine of the 8th, the same day on which I wrote you (who deserved something brighter) that ghostly, woeful letter.

General Lee's letter has been published to the division in general orders, and has been received with appreciative satisfaction —for the soldiers, one and all, love and honor Lee, and his sympathy and praise are always very dear to them. Just after the order was published I heard one of the men, rather rough and uncouth and not, as are most of the men, to the manner born, say, as he wiped away the tears with the back of his hand: "Dag-gone him, dag-gone him, dag-gone his old soul, I'm blamed ef I wouldn't be dag-gone willin' to go right through it all and be killed again with them others to hear Marse Robert, dag- gone him, say over again as how he grieved bout'n we-all's losses and honored us for we-all's bravery! Darned ef I wouldn't!" Isn't that reverential adoration, my darling, to be willing to be "killed again" for a word of praise?

It seems selfish and inhuman to speak of love — haunted as I am with the unnecessary sacrifice of the lives of so many of my brave boys. I can't think of anything but the desolate homes in Virginia and the unknown dead in Pennsylvania. At the beginning of the fight I was so sanguine, so sure of success! Early in the morning I had been assured by Alexander that General Lee had ordered that every brigade in his command was to charge Cemetery Hill; so I had no fear of not being supported. Alexander also assured me of the support of his artillery, which would move ahead of my division in the advance. He told me that he had borrowed seven twelve-pound howitzers from Pendleton, Lee's Chief of Artillery, which he had put in reserve to accompany me.

In the morning I rode with him while he, by Longstreet's orders, selected the salient angle of the wood in which my line was formed, which line was just on the left of his seventy-five guns. At about a quarter to three o'clock, when his written order to make the charge was handed to me, and dear Old Peter after reading it in sorrow and fear reluctantly bowed his head in assent, I obeyed, leading my three brigades straight on the enemy's front, Kemper and Garnett in front and Armistead on Garnett's left. You never saw anything like it. They moved across that field of death as a battalion marches forward in line of battle upon drill, each commander in front of his command leading and cheering on his men. Two lines of the enemy's infantry were driven back; two lines of guns were taken—and no support came. Pendleton, without Alexander's knowledge, had sent four of the guns which he had loaned him to some other part of the field, and the other three guns could not be found. The two brigades which were to have followed me had, poor fellows, been seriously engaged in the fights of the two previous days. Both of their commanding officers had been killed, and while they had been replaced by gallant, competent officers, these new leaders were unknown to the men.

Ah, if I had only had my other two brigades, a different story would have been flashed to the world. It was too late to retreat; and to go on was death or capture. Poor old Dick Garnett did not dismount, as did the others of us, and he was killed instantly, falling from his horse. Kemper was desperately wounded; was brought from the field but was subsequently taken prisoner. Dear old Lewis Armistead, God bless him, was mortally wounded at the head of his command, after planting the flag of Virginia within the enemy's lines. Seven of my colonels, Hodges, Edmonds, Magruder, Williams, Patten, Allen, and Owens, were killed; and one, Stuart, was mortally wounded. Nine of my lieutenant colonels, Carrington, Otey, Richardson, Hunton, Terry, Garnett, Mayo, Phillips, and Aylett, were wounded; and three, Colcott, Wade, and Ellis, were killed. Only one field officer of my whole command, Colonel Cabell, was unhurt; and the loss of my company officers was in proportion.

I wonder, my dear, if in the light of the Great Eternity we shall any of us feel this was for the best and shall have learned to say, "Thy will be done."

No castles to-day, sweetheart. No, the bricks of happiness and the mortar of love must lie untouched in this lowering gloom.

Pray, dear, for the sorrowing ones—
    Faithfully and lovingly and forever,
    Your Soldier

Headquarters, July—, 1863
HEADQUARTERS, A. N. Va., July 9th, 1863.

General:
Your letter of the 8th has been received. It was with reluctance that I imposed upon your gallant division the duty of carrying prisoners to Staunton. I regretted to assign them to such a service, as well as to separate them from the Army, though temporarily, with which they have been so long and efficiently associated. Though small in numbers, their worth is not diminished, and I had supposed that the division itself would be loth to part from its comrades, at a time when the presence of every man is so essential.

No one grieves more than I do at the loss suffered by your noble division in the recent conflict, or honors it more for its bravery and gallantry. It will afford me hereafter satisfaction, when an opportunity occurs, to do all in my power to recruit its diminished ranks, and to recognize it in the most efficient manner.

    Very respectfully, your obedient servant,
    R. E. LEE, General.
Major Gen. G. E. Pickett, commanding,
Forwarded through Lieut. Gen. Longstreet.
C. MARSHALL, Major and A. D. C

6. Major John Timberlake, 3rd Virginia, recorded the feelings that many Southerners had after the battle: that the attack had failed and that Southern independence seemed a more remote possibility than it had been just a couple of hours earlier. John Timberlake, untitled essay, n.d., Timberlake Papers, Virginia Historical Society.

After I was captured & was being led to the enemy's rear, we passed by Genl Patrick the federal provost marshall, who noticing my rank by the star on my coat called, ordered the guard to bring me to him. Addressing my by my rank, said "I understand Major that Genl Pickett is killed; to which I replied, "No, sir, Genl. Pickett is safe." he then said ["]a few more men Major, and you would have gained your independence right here[.]"   I replied by saying "Yes, Genl., and right here we have lost it."

7. **Captain Henry T. Owen of the 18th Virginia describes the situation on Seminary Ridge after the charge, and by implication the impact of the defeat on the men. Henry T. Owen to Col. H. A. Carrington, January 27, 1878, Frank Yates Collection.**

. . . A Captain with a Palmetto tree upon his cap run up to me and asked me to assist him in rallying the stragglers. I agreed and we made the attempt but not a single man *non-officer* could we stop. We then agreed to try just in rear of the artillery and in passing through the artillery I lost my Captain and kept on to the road below. Here where the road made a short turn with bluff on one side and swamp on the other I thought a favourable point and tried again. I made all sorts of appeals, but not an officer did I succeed in stopping. I succeeded in rallying about 30 men all privates from various commands and with these thrown across the road presented a barrier to all straggling that way. Genl. Pickett came along (crying) and said "Capt. do not stop any of my men. Tell them to come to the camping ground we occupied last night." As soon as he passed every straggler we had in front claimed to belong to Pickett's Div. I opened the line and let them out. Closing up again Capt. Linthicum came by told me you were a prisoner Col. Hunton wounded Genls. Armistead, Garnet & Kemper killed etc. I began to wish I was somewhere else but saw no good excuse for it and held on for a while longer 'till I caught a few hundred more, then Major Charles Marshall came up from the direction Pickett had gone and arriving at the other end of my picket opposite to where I was asked "Whats this here?" A soldier replied "a picket" "who put it here" "that Captain yonder" Call him here? "Who is he" I came forward and these questions were repeated I answered that I had rallied the men and put them there as a picket to stop stragglers. He asked "By whose orders" I replied that I had no orders. He said he would give me orders which he did and sent me back to the creek where we deployed and as we collected the stragglers he marched them back to the battlefield. During the evening I saw only two 18th men that I knew to be such One was from Cumberland shot through the thighs and I saw him sent to field hospital. The other was Thackston of Farmville unhurt and I started him on to our camp as Gen. Pickett had directed but he deserted and was reported a prisoner.

8. **Lieutenant William Peel of the 11th Mississippi was captured at the wall, and tells the fate of the prisoners. William Peel, "Diary," Mississippi State Archives.**

We at length reached the point of concentration [for prisoners] for our part of the line.

Here we found about a thousand of our country-men, who had been captured during the day, or the two days previous. We were turned into the pen with the balance of the herd, & now found ourselves under guard in an open field.

There were small squads & large squads being constantly brought in, & by night-fall our number was increased to sixteen or eighteen hundred

[Brig. Gen. Marsena] Patrick, the Provost Marshal General [of the Army of the Potomac] came upon the ground at this time . . . and addressed us thus:

"Prisoners, you are here now in my charge; quite a large number of you; I guarantee to you the kindest treatment the nature of the case will permit, so long as you conduct yourselves in a becoming manner. If, however, there should be any attempt, upon your part to escape me, woe be unto you. My splendid cavalry is at hand, armed & ready for action, & in numbers almost equal to you own, & in case of any disturbances among you, they shall be ordered to charge you, cutting & slashing, right & left, indiscriminately."

9. Private Charles T. Loehr of the 1st Virginia survived the charge and described the Confederates after the repulse. He notes Pickett's emotional state, the continued reverence for Robert E. Lee, and less enthusiasm for the flag. Loehr, "The 'Old First' Virginia at Gettysburg," *SHSP,* **XXXII(1904), 33-34.**

After The Battle

In straggling groups the survivors of that charge gathered in rear of Seminary Ridge, near the point from which they set out to do or die. It was a sad sight. Most of them were bleeding; numbers of them were washing their wounds in a little creek which ran along the valley, making its clear water run red, which others used to quench their burning thirst. Some 300 or 400 men were there. General George E. Pickett was mounted, and was talking to the men here and there. Only two of the regiments had retained their colors, one of which was the 24th Virginia and the color bearer, a tall mountaineer, named Charles Belcher, was waving it, crying: "General, let us go at them again!" Just about then General James L. Kemper was carried into the crowd, and the latter came to a halt. Then General Lee was seen to ride up, and we, as was usual, wanted to know what he had to say, crowded around him.

General Pickett broke out into tears, while General Lee rode up to him, and they shook hands. General Lee spoke to General Pickett in a slow and distinct manner. Anyone could see that he, too, felt the repulse and slaughter of the division, whose remains he viewed.

Lee's Words

Of the remarks made to General Pickett by General Lee, we distinctly heard him say: "General Pickett, your men have done all that men could do; the fault is entirely my own." These words will never be forgotten.

Just then, he turned to General Kemper and remarked: "General Kemper, I hope you are not seriously hurt, can I do anything for you?" General Kemper looked up and replied: "General Lee, you can do nothing for me; I am mortally wounded, but see to it that full justice is done my men who made this charge." General Lee said: "I will," and rode off.

General Pickett turned to us, saying: "You can go back to the wagons and rest until you are wanted." The men then left for their wagon trains.

There was little or no organization among them. Night was coming on and the writer and several of his company slept in a mill, about half way to the wagon train, getting back with those of the survivors of the Old First on the morning of the 4th. The whole command numbered hardly thirty men, rank and file, and Captain B. F. Howard had charge of the squad.

About 10 o'clock the drum beat to fall in, and, as we took our places in rank, J. R. Polak came out with a set of colors, which he got from an ordinance wagon (the same had been left in our hands by Holecomb's Legion at Second Manassas) and, waving it, though he had his hand in a sling, and his nose was all bloody from the charge, but we declined to play color guard, and the flag was returned to the wagon.

10. Like Lee, George Meade saw the hand of Providence in the Union repulse of Pickett's Charge. As the Army of Northern Virginia started on its long road back to Virginia, and eventually to Appomattox, Meade issued this message to his men. The second paragraph so angered Abraham Lincoln that he wrote a caustic letter denouncing Meade's lack of aggressiveness. Meade had proven a capable defensive commander, but Lincoln wanted someone who would do more than drive an invader from Union soil. Ulysses S. Grant would be that man, and thus in a sense this message is the beginning of the final phase of the war. Quoted in Rhodes, *The History of Battery B*, 215.

Headquarters Army of the Potomac
Near Gettysburg,

July 4, 1863
General Orders, No. 63.

The commanding general, in behalf of the country, thanks the Army of the Potomac for the glorious result of the recent operations. Our enemy, superior in numbers, flushed with pride of successful invasion, attempted to overcome or destroy this army. Baffled and defeated, he has now withdrawn from the contest. The privations and fatigue the army has endured, and the heroic courage and gallantry it displayed, will be matters of history to be ever remembered.

Our task is not yet accomplished, and the commanding general looks to the army for greater efforts to drive from our soil every vestige of the presence of the invader.

It is right and proper that we should, on suitable occasions, return our grateful thanks to the Almighty Disposer of events, that in the goodness of His providence, He has thought fit to give victory to the cause of the just.

By command of
GEORGE B. MEADE, Maj. Gen. Commanding.

11. Immediately after the battle, Major General Winfield Scott Hancock wrote to General Meade from his hospital bed urging him to follow up the victory. Hancock said he was shot with a nail; in fact a bullet had passed through his saddle, and carried a nail from it into him. Hancock to General Meade, *OR*, 1, 27, 1, 366.

Headquarters Second Corps, July 3, 1863.

Although I repulsed a tremendous attack, yet on seeing it from my left and advancing to the right, I, much to my sorrow, found that the twelve guns on my salient had been removed by some one, whom I call upon you to hold accountable, as without them, with worse troops, I should certainly have lost the day. I arrived just in time to put a small battalion of infantry in the place occupied by those two batteries.

I have never seen a more formidible attack, and if the Sixth and Fifth Corps have pressed up, the enemy will be destroyed. The enemy must be short of ammunition, as I was shot with a tenpenny nail. I did not leave the field till the victory was entirely secured and the enemy no longer in sight. I am badly wounded, though I trust not seriously. I had to break the line to attack the enemy in flank on my right, where the enemy was most persistent after the front attack was repelled. Not a rebel was in sight upright when I left. The

line should be immediately restored and perfected. General Caldwell is in command of the corps, and I have directed him to restore
the line.

> Winf'd S. Hancock, Major-General,
> By A. N. Dougherty, Surgeon, and Medical Director Second
Corps.

12.   Colonel Clinton D. MacDougall, 111th New York Volunteers, remembers Brig. Gen. Alexander Hays' ride after the repulse and his brief career after Gettysburg. Hays was killed the following May. Clinton MacDougall to Mr. Gilbert A. Hays, 29 August 1909, quoted in Fleming, ed., *Life and Letters of Hays*, 433-434.

Just as this charge commenced a sharpshooter of the enemy
shot the lower bone of my left arm in two. I had it bound up and
remained with my command until the charge was repulsed, when
I went to the hospital to have the wound attended to. On my return
General Hays was lying under the fly of a tent in the orchard of the
Bryan house, just in the rear of my regiment. Seeing me passing
with my arm in a sling he called to me as was his wont, "Oh, Colonel
Mac." I sat on the ground in front of him. He asked about my injury,
was enthusiastic about our victory, our captures of prisoners and
colors. Beside his quarters lay a large pile of captured flags; he
asked me to count them, and I counted twenty-one, large and small.
We then engaged in general conversation about the battle and what
would probably occur next.

Soon a staff officer appeared and said General Webb pre-
sents his compliments and asks that General Hays send him some
battle flags he has, which were captured by him [Webb]. General
Hays replied with a good deal of warmth, "How in h—l did I get them
if he captured them?" and calling to his aide, Lieut. Shields, "Oh,
Dave!" pick out half a dozen flags and send them to General Webb
as a present, with my compliments; we have so many here we don't
know what to do with them and Webb needs them."

It is far from my disposition or intention to take one laurel
from the brow of any gallant soldier, but I am constrained to say that
medals of honor and brevets were showered upon others for
Gettysburg's victory that justly belonged to General Hays.

The Third Division served under General Hays at Bristoe and
all the other engagements of the division until the reorganization of
the army took place in the winter of 1864, and when General Hays
was taken from us we all felt we had lost our best friend, a

commander beloved by all, one whom we all know we would find where danger was the greatest, where the bullets flew the thickest, where the fighting was the fiercest, there we would always find General Hays, with the blue trefoil behind him and Captain Corts and Lieut. Shields at his side. No one could hang back with such a leader and such an example of bravery before them.

When Longstreet's charge [wrongly called Pickett's, who only commanded one of the three divisions making the charge] was broken, General Hays seized two captured flags by their staffs, and mounted on "Dan" rode up and down between the lines, trailing them in the dirt, a target for the enemy's artillery and sharpshooters. "Dan" was killed, but the general was unhurt.

13. Major Thomas Osborn speculated on the comparative significance of Pickett's Charge, then spent the next few days acquiring the horses needed to use his artillery. Thomas Osborn, "Experiences at the Battle of Gettysburg," in Crumb, ed., *The Papers of Major Thomas Osborn*, 29-45.

Pickett's charge at Gettysburg stands out by itself as the grandest charge made by any command during the war. I was in many great battles, but I never saw so superb and desperate a charge made and under conditions so favorable to view as that. The charges made by the several corps of Burnside's army at Fredericksburg were fully as desperate, but there was no chance of success. These charges were almost criminally foolish on Burnside's part. Lee's charge on Malvern Hill was worse and more foolish than was Burnside's at Fredericksburg. All these I saw from the best points of view, but there was no chance of success in either of them. Hazen's charge to carry Fort McAllister, near Savannah, was a splendid feat at arms. The fort was an immense fortification mounted with heavy and light guns and garrisoned with artillery and infantry troops. The earth walls were 20 feet high and the whole work surrounded by abatis and planted with torpedoes, and yet he carried it with an infantry charge.

Sherman's battle at Kennesaw Mountain was, in fact, a grand charge upon the enemy's works and up the steep side of a rugged mountain. I did not witness that. This, like Pickett's charge, had the chance of success in it and was worth the attempt. Sheridan's charge up the flank of Missionary Ridge, which I saw, was eminently successful. He lost heavily, but broke Bragg's line and cut his army in two. Hooker's charge up Lookout Mountain, which I also saw, was successful and a grand success of arms. At Dalton, in the same battle, he made a charge and while he won on the ground, his force was so crippled that he could not take advantage of his success. At that, I was not present. Taking it all in all, Pickett's charge, although a failure, was the grandest of them all. Although they were our enemies at the time, those men were Americans, of our own blood and our own kindred. It was the American spirit which carried them to the front and held them there to be slaughtered. Phenomenal bravery is admired by everyone, and that Pickett's men possessed.

The remainder of the afternoon and evening, Lee held his army in position to see if Meade would make a counter charge. This was not made, and in the night Lee commenced his retrograde movement towards the Potomac River and Virginia. Meade's army had suffered severely, and the next day after the battle, the Fourth of July, he rested it and hastened to put it into condition to follow Lee south. He rested two days before commencing the pursuit of Lee. So great a delay was unfortunate, if not an error. No matter how greatly we were worn, Lee's army was still more worn and exhausted, and for that reason we should have had an advantage in a pursuit. The day following the battle was raining. It was used to care for the wounded and to bury the dead, as we prepared to move again.

I lost in the battle about 100 horses. The government had no spare horses with the army or anywhere immediately available. Unless these horses were replaced, I should be compelled to dismount one battery, take its horses for the others and leave it. This was not advisable. I therefore asked General Howard for an order to send men into the country and gather up the horses required from the citizens, in other words, press them into service. This order he gave, and I sent out the quartermaster sergeants of all the batteries with instructions to take from the citizens the horses that each battery required and give memoranda receipts for them. The orders were carried out to the letter and much to the consternation of the farmers. The receipts were given, and the government soon after paid $125 for each horse without inquiring as to its market value. It was a good sale for some, a bad one for others.

After waiting two days, Meade undertook the pursuit of Lee. He overtook his rear guard at Hagerstown, while the body of his army was entrenched on the bank of the Potomac at Williamsport. The Army of the Potomac was brought up in front of Lee's Army, and Meade occupied a day in preparing to attack. In the night Lee crossed the Potomac into Virginia and for the time being was out of reach of the Army of the Potomac.

14. Captain George Bowen of the 12th New Jersey de-

scribes the battlefield after the repulse and his attempts to help the wounded. Diary of Captain George D. Bowen, *The Valley Forge Journal*, 132-135.

The field of battle is a sight never to be forgotten, the dead and wounded lay as thick as one ever saw sheaves of wheat in a harvest field, for a distance of a hundred yards or more in front and as far to the right and left as the eye can reach. Of all the thousands that started that day very few ever returned, those not killed or wounded were captured, they giving themselves up rather than risk again crossing that field. As soon as they attempted to retire we [were] out and after them capturing very many of them. Those of the wounded who we could get at were brought in and sent to our hospitals.

As soon as it was dark I with many others went out over the field, had my canteen filled with water before starting, giving a drink to such of the wounded that I found, soon it was empty, it was a long distance to go for more, so filled my canteen from a ditch beside the Emmittsburg road. This road was filled with their dead, the ditch was piled up with them. I did not think about the water being bloody, it was dark so could not see, knew it was muddy, but that kind of water I had frequently had to drink. I gave some of this to a wounded man, he said can't you get me some clear cool water that is so full of blood I cannot drink it. This is the first time we have had the privilege of going over a battlefield immediately after a fight, one time is enough, the sight and sound were terrible, no one can give an idea of what it is like, the pain and misery of those poor fellows whom we shot down only a few hours ago — it is a heart breaking sight. Our men went through their haversacks taking any food they could find, they were well supplied as they have been living off the country. It sounds bad to rob a dead man, but we had nothing to eat, they had plenty for a living man, they were dead and would never want it any more.

15. Lieutenant Frank Haskell was near the center of the Federal line at the end of the charge. His version of Armistead's words of remorse is hearsay, and questionable. He describes Meade's reaction to the repulse. Haskell, "Gettysburg."

Just as the fight was over, and the first outburst of victory had a little subsided, when all in front of the crest was noise, and confusion, — prisoners being collected, small parties in pursuit of them far down into the field, flags waving, officers giving quick, sharp commands to their men, — I stood apart for a few moments, upon the crest, by that group of trees which ought to be historic forever, a spectator of the thrilling scene around. Some few musket shots were still heard in the 3d Division; and the enemy's guns, almost silent since the advance of his Infantry, until the moment of his defeat, were dropping a few sullen shells among friend and foe upon the crest, — rebellion fosters such humanity. Near me, saddest sight, of the many of such a field, and not in keeping with all this noise, were mingled, alone the thick dead of Maine, and Minnesota, and Michigan, and Massachusetts, and the Empire and the Keystone states, who, not yet cold, with the blood still oozing from their death wounds, had given their lives to the country upon the stormy field, — so mingled upon that crest let their honored graves be. Look with me, about us. These dead have been avenged already. Where the long lines of the enemy's thousands so proudly advanced, see how thick the silent men of gray are scattered. It is not an hour since those legions were sweeping along so grandly, — now sixteen hundred of that fiery mass, are strewn among the trampled grass, dead as the clods they load; more than seven thousand, probably eight thousand, are wounded, some there with the dead, in our hands, some fugitive far towards the woods, — among them Generals Pettigrew, Garnett, Kemper, and Armistead the last three mortally, and the last one in our hands, — "Tell Gnl. Hancock," he said to Lieut. Mitchell, Hancock's Aide-de-Camp, to whom he handed his watch, "that I know I did my country a great wrong when I took up arms against her, for which I am sorry, but for which I cannot live to atone," four thousand wounded, are prisoners of war, — more in number of the captured, than the captors. Our men are still "gathering them in." Some hold up their hands, or a handkerchief, in sign of submission; some have hugged the ground to escape our bullets, and so are taken; few made resistance after the first moment of our crossing the wall; some yield submissively with good grace; some with grim, dogged aspect, showing that but for the other alternative, they could not submit to this. Colonels, and all less grades of officers, in the usual proportions, are among them, and all are being stripped of their arms. Such of them as escaped wounds and capture, are fleeing routed and panic-stricken, and disappearing in the woods. Small arms, more thousands than we can count, are in our hands, scattered over the field. And those defiant battle-flags, some inscribed with; "1st Manassas," the numerous battles of the Peninsula, "2nd Manassas," "South Mountain," "Sharpsburg," (our Antietam,) "Fredericksburg," "Chancellorsville," and many more names, our men have, and are showing about, *over thirty of them.*

     Such was really the closing scene of the grand drama of Gettysburg. After repeated assaults upon the right and the left, where, and in all of which repulse had been his only success, this persistent and presuming enemy forms his chosen troops, the flower of his army, for a grand assault upon our center. The manner and result of such assault have been told, — a loss to the enemy of from twelve thousand to fourteen thousand, killed, wounded, and prisoners, and of over thirty battle flags. This was accomplished by not over six thousand men, with a loss on our part of not over two thousand five hundred, killed and wounded.

Would to Heaven Gnls. Hancock and Gibbon could have stood there where I did, and have looked upon that field! It would have done two men, to whom the country owes much, good to have been with their men in that moment of victory, — to have seen the results of those dispositions which they had made, and of that splendid fighting which men schooled by their discipline, had executed. But they are both severely wounded, and have been carried from the field. One person did come then that I was glad to see there; and that was no less than Major General Meade, whom the Army of the Potomac was fortunate enough to have at that time to command it. See how a great General looked upon the field, and what he said and did, at the moment, and when he learned, of his great victory. To appreciate the incident I give, it should be borne in mind, that one coming up from the rear of the line, as did Gnl. Meade, could have seen very little of our own men, who had now crossed the crest, and although he could have heard the noise, he could not have told its occasion, or by whom made, until he had actually attained the crest. One who did not know results, so coming, would have been quite as likely to have supposed that our line there had been carried and captured by the enemy, so many gray Rebels were on the crest, as to have discovered the real truth. Such mistake was really made by one of our own officers, as I shall relate.

Gnl. Meade rode up, accompanied alone by his son, who is his Aide-de-Camp, an escort, if select, not large for a commander of such an army. The principal horseman was no bedizened hero of some holy day review, but he was a plain man, dressed in a serviceable summer suit of dark blue cloth, without badge or ornament, save the shoulder-straps of his grade, and a light, straight sword of a General, a General Staff officer. He wore heavy, high top-boots and buff gauntlets; and his soft black felt hat was slouched down over his eyes. His face was very white, not pale, and the lines were marked, and earnest, and full of care. As he arrived near me, coming up the hill, he asked in a sharp, eager voice: "How is it going here?" "I believe, General, the enemy's attack is repulsed," I answered. Still approaching, and a new light began to come in his face, of gratified surprise, with a touch of incredulity, of which his voice was also the medium, he further asked: *"What? is the assault entirely repulsed?"* — his voice quicker and more eager than before. "It is, Sir:" I replied. By this time he was on the crest; and when his eye had for an instant swept over the field, taking in just a glance of the whole, — the masses of prisoners, — the numerous captured flags, which the men were derisively flaunting about, — the fugitives of the routed enemy, disappearing with the speed of terror in the woods, — partly at what I had told him, partly at what he saw, he said impressively, and his face was lighted: *"Thank God."* And then his right hand moved as if it would have caught off his hat and waved it; but this gesture he suppressed, and instead he waved his hand, and said "Hur-rah." The son, with more youth in his blood, and less rank upon his shoulders, snatched off his cap, and roared out his three "hurrahs," right heartily. The general then surveyed the field, some minutes, in silence. He at length asked who was in command. He had heard that Hancock and Gibbon were wounded, — and I told him that Gnl. Caldwell was the senior officer of the Corps, and Gnl. Harrow, of the Division. He asked where they were, but before I had time to answer that I did not know, he resumed: "No matter; I will give my orders to you and you will see them executed." He then gave direction that the troops should be re-formed as soon as practicable, and kept in their places, as the enemy might be mad enough to attack again; to move back, when closer observation discovered that the gray backs that were coming had no arms, and then the truth flashed upon the minds of the observers. The same mistake was made by others.

In view of results of that day, — the successes of the arms of the country, would not the people of the whole country, standing then upon the crest with Gnl. Meade, have said, with him: "Thank God"?

I have no knowledge, and little notion, of how long a time elapsed from the moment the fire of the Infantry commenced, until the enemy was entirely repulsed, in this his grand assault. I judge, from the amount of fighting, and the changes of position that occurred, that probably the fight was of nearly an hour's duration — but I cannot tell, and I have seen none who knew. — The time seemed but a very few minutes, when the battle was over.

When the prisoners were cleared away, and order was again established upon our crest, where the conflict had impaired it, until between five and six o'clock, I remained upon the field, directing some troops to their positions, in conformity to the orders of Gnl. Meade. The enemy appeared no more in front of the 2nd Corps; but while I was engaged as I have mentioned, farther to our left some considerable force of the enemy moved out, and made show of attack. Our Artillery now in good order again, in due time opened fire, and the shells scattered the *Butternuts*, as clubs do the gray snow-birds of winter, before they came within range of our Infantry. This, save unimportant outpost firing, was the last of the battle.

16. **Artilleryman John Rhodes buried his friends and looked for his lost gun.** John H. Rhodes, *The History of Battery B*, 204-205.

On reaching a barn, on the west side of the road, used as the headquarters of the Artillery Brigade of the Second Corps, and also as a hospital, I found behind it several staff officers, aides, and some cavalry, and asked them for Battery B. They pointed down the road. Meeting Woodmansee we kept on together. We had not gone far before we heard a crash and report, and, on looking back, saw men and horses, which were back of the above-mentioned barn, scattering in all directions. A shell had struck a corner of the barn and exploded. Not far from the barn, in an opening among the woods on the east side of the Taneytown road and about a mile from our position on the battlefield, we found Battery B parked and the men in bivouac, some already having the shelter tents up. I reported that one of our pieces was left up in the road near General Meade's headquarters.

Late in the afternoon, after the firing had subsided and all was quiet along the lines, Lieutenant Perrin with a detail of men, the writer being one of the number, went back to the battle-field. Our troops had advanced from the position they occupied when the battery left, and the ground was strewn with torn haversacks, battered canteens, broken wheels of gun carriages, and piles of knapsacks and blankets overturned, silently telling of the destruction which had visited the place.

Our men, under Sergt. Albert Straight and Corp. Calvin L. Macomber, dug graves, near a clump of bushes at the left of the gap in the wall, and our dead, Alfred G. Gardner, William Jones, David B. King, Ira L. Bennett, and Michael Flynn, were buried, and a rough marker placed at the head of each dead comrade.

The men gathered such accouterments as belonged to the battery, and which had been left on the field when it withdrew. In returning to camp, by way of the cart-path, we reached the place where the third piece had been left. The dead horse lay beside the road, but the piece and harnesses were gone. We could get no information from any one near by as to who carried it off, or in what direction it went. We knew it could not have fallen into the hands of the enemy, being within our own lines, therefore it was evident that some battery, ordnance supply wagon had taken it to the rear, where all condemned ordnance was parked. As the number of the gun was unknown to the officers of the battery, it was not returned nor any information concerning it as far as the writer could learn.

17. The gruesome task of taking care of the wounded and burying the dead began nearly as soon as the charge was repelled. Phillips, *History of the Fifth Massachusetts Battery*, 652-661.

Martin J. Coleman was mortally wounded at Gettysburg and was brought to a temporary hospital where I was. I did not know that he was seriously wounded until I asked the surgeon how he was getting on, and he told me he could not live long. Soon after Coleman sent for me to write a letter for him. I could relate other instances to show the spirit and material of the old 5th Mass. Battery, but writing that letter was the most pathetic act I was called upon to perform while in service. He dictated this to me: -- "Dear Father: I have not long to live. I have tried to be a faithful soldier, and I die for the flag."

NOTES OF CORPORAL GRAHAM
FINDING THE BODIES

On the afternoon of the 4th Captain Phillips ordered a sergeant to go down on the centre of the field, out beyond our pickets, where the rebs had left one of their guns the day before. So he mounts a horse and starts down. When he got to the picket line his heart failed him, so he came back. Then the Captain came to me, and he says, "Graham, you go down on the field, and get me that pole-yoke from that limber." So I went out on the centre of the field, and tried to get it, but as I had no wrench, and there was none in the limber chest, I had to leave it. I walked from there in the centre of both picket lines, to the position we occupied on the second day. It was there where I found poor Henry Soule. He was the first one that I found. He was under a small apple tree. Fotheringham was nearer the position of the Battery.

From the field I went into the Trostle house, where I found John Hathaway and Coleman. They were both badly wounded. The rebels had stripped Hathaway of all his clothing. When I found him he was sitting in a chair underneath a mirror, and I saw him in the glass first, and he gave me quite a fright, for the only thing he had on was a white sheet. He looked more like a ghost than a man. I asked him if there were any other of the boys in the house, and he said he did not know, so I looked the house over from garret to cellar, and there, behind the chimney, found Coleman. I tried to get an ambulance to take them to the rear, but it was of no use. I went back to the Battery and reported to the Captain. He had the men make some stretchers, and had Hathaway and Coleman taken to the field hospital, where they died in a day or two. The last I saw of Henry Soule they were digging a grave under that apple tree, but I did not stay to see whether he was buried there or not. The last resting place of Henry W. Soule is in Oak Grove Cemetery, New Bedford, Mass.

18. Chaplain Ezra D. Simons of the 125th New York describes the suffering of the Federal wounded and the rain that came on the evening of the 3rd. Simons, *The One Hundred and Twenty-Fifth New York State Volunteers*, 146.

And at the rear were the dead, and the dying, and the suffering wounded. Barns and houses were crowded with wounded men. The outlying grounds were covered. On rude benches the surgeons wrought their needful, merciful work. The barn — on the Taneytown road, on the very battle-field — that served as a hospital for the men of the One Hundred and Twenty-fifth and of other regiments, after the fighting of the second day, was full of the wounded. The stalls were full of them; the loft was full the yard in front and rear was full. When, on the afternoon of the third day, the shelling opened, and the barn was found exposed, the surgeons were directed to Rock Creek, and the wounded who could walk went with the surgeons, but many wounded remained. One man — whom the writer has recently learned was Hiram D. Clark — was lying unconscious, with leg just amputated, on the operating bench, midway on the floor of the barn, as the storm of shell burst around the place. But he aroused from the effects of the chloroform administered, with a smile on his lips, and remained uncomplainingly all that fearful afternoon. Dreadful was the night which followed. The rain now fell as in torrents. The densest darkness filled the woods by the creek, as the sad cries — the very wailings of the wounded peopled the air with images of distress. That night, given to the care of hundreds of suffering men — Confederates and Union men mingled — remains a dark, dread memory. But, over against the darkness of the suffering was the brightness of victory; and the price paid in blood was none too great for the fruitage to the Nation and the world. Some things are evermore costly; and they are the more prized because their price is paid in blood and death. Rock Creek, in that night of storm, overflowed its banks, and the ground where the wounded were lying was flooded. The men were hastily moved, some of them being taken from a foot depth of water. The writer had opportunity then to witness the bravery of men whose valor was equally manifested in enduring suffering as on battlefield.

19. Virtually every major northern city had a newspaper reporter at Gettysburg. The New York *Tribune,* run by Republican stalwart Horace Greeley, put out numerous special editions between the 3rd and 6th of July. Unfortunately, much of the specific information about individuals turned out to be incorrect. Longstreet was not captured. Anderson was not directly involved in the charge; no Federal division commander named Hill was on the field (he probably meant Hays), and Doubleday was not hurt. New York *Tribune,* July 3 and 6, 1863.

> Special Dispatch to the N.Y. Tribune
> Hanover, Friday, July 3, 1863

The most terrific fight of the war has taken place. Our men never stood up so heroically. To-day was the most awful of all. The loss on both sides has been tremendous. We have Longstreet a prisoner sure. I left the battle-field at 6 1/2 o'clock, and reached here by relay of horses. We had the best of the fight to-day, and the General says if Couch arrives to-night, the victory is ours beyond a chance.

[July 6th]

On Friday morning the ball was opened by Gen. Geary, who moved upon the enemy to retake these rifle pits. Firing now became general, and continued without damage to us until eleven o'clock, the rifle-pits falling into our possession. From 11 till 1 o'clock the firing slackened, but as 1 o'clock arrived, there were indications of another clash of arms more bloody than the historian of the war has yet recorded. The Rebels under Gen. Ewell now made a concentration of all their artillery, and opened a terrible artillery fire on our left center. Battery after battery roared, shaking the surrounding hills, and shot and shell raised death and destruction upon our lines.

The Second Corps occupied the center, and the position which withstood the last convulsive attack of the Rebels was commanded by Gen. Hayes. The enemy followed their artillery with a tremendous infantry assault under the Rebel Gen. Anderson, coming up in masses, sometimes in close column by division. Our men stood like serried hosts, and on came the enemy, crowding, shouting, and rushing toward our guns like infuriated demons. There was no waver in our lines. On came the Rebels, while the canister from batteries told fearfully among their dying ranks. Now they are within twenty yards of our guns, and volley after volley of shot and shell and whizzing bullets go crashing down among them, dealing death and scattering the motley ranks to die or surrender.

The slaughter was fearful, and there were a few men of the enemy who did not find even a grave near our guns. The Third and Fifth Corps now joined in the fight. Gen. Hill's division alone took ten battle flags as this last move of the enemy burst upon our center. A panic seemed to seize them. Men laid down on the ground to escape our fire and lying there they supplicatingly held up white pieces of paper in token of surrender. In this repulse we took several thousand prisoners, and crowds of Rebel stragglers came into our lines giving themselves up in despair.

Gen. Hancock's corps now flanked the field, when crowds of disorganized Rebels threw up their arms and surrendered, while the field strewn with Rebel wounded, battle flags and arms fell into our possession.

The result amounted to a rout. Cavalry has been sent out to harvest the straggle[r]s. Gen. Hayes is said to have covered himself with glory. General Doubleday fell fighting gallantly, saying, as a ball pierced his head, "I'm killed! I'm killed!" Gen. Hancock thinks he is not killed, but seriously wounded. And thus night has drawn her mantle over another bloody day, but a day so bright with deeds of heroism and grand results, with patriotic devotion and sublime death, that the page of History shall glitter with that light.

20. Samuel Wilkeson, covering the Army of the Potomac for the New York *Times*, watched the battle from a point near Meade's headquarters directly behind the center of the Federal line. He had a unique perspective: his son, Lieutenant Bayard Wilkeson, commanding Battery G, 4th U. S. Artillery, had been killed earlier in the battle. His 19 year-old son had been hit in the leg by a Confederate shell on or near Barlow's Knoll on July 1st. He had severed his own leg with a pocketknife, and died. Despite the severe shock of his son's death, Wilkeson managed to file an interesting account of the third day. He made a few errors—Hill commanded a corps not a division, but got most of the essentials correct, and was one of the first to tell Cushing's story. His phrase describing the victory as a "new birth of Freedom in America" foreshadows Lincoln's famous words in the Gettysburg Address. New York *Times*, July 6, 1863.

Who can write the history of a battle whose eyes are immovably fastened upon a central figure of transcendingly absorbing interest—the dead body of an oldest born, crushed by a shell in a position where a battery should never have been sent, and abandoned to death in a building where surgeons dared not to stay?

The battle of Gettysburgh! I am told that it commenced, on the 1st of July, a mile north of the town, between two weak brigades of infantry and some doomed artillery and the whole force of the rebel army. Among other costs of this error was the death of Reynolds. Its value was priceless, however, though priceless was the young and the old blood with which it was bought. The error put us on the defensive, and gave us the choice of position. From the moment that our artillery and infantry rolled back through the main street of Gettysburgh and rolled out of the town to the circle of eminences south of it. We were not to attack but to be attacked. The risks, the difficulties and the advantages[?] of the coming battle were the enemy's. Our[s] were the heights for artillery; ours the short, inside lines for manoeuvering and reinforcing; ours the cover of stonewalls, fences and the crests of hills. The ground upon which we were driven to accept battle was wonderfully favorable to us. A popular description of it would be to say that it was in from an elongated and somewhat sharpened horseshoe, with the toe to Gettysburgh and the heel to the south.

Lee's plan of battle was simple. He manned his troops upon the east side of this shoe of position, and thundered on it obstinately to break it. The shelling of our batteries from the nearest overlooking hill, and the unflinching courage and complete discipline of the army of the Potomac repelled the attack. It was renewed at the point of of[sic] the shoe—renewed desperately at the southwest heel—renewed on the western side with an effort consecrated to success by Ewell's earnest oaths, and on which the fate of the invasion of Pennsylvania was fully put at stake. Only a perfect infantry and an artillery educated in the midst of charges of hostile brigades could possibly have sustained this assault. Hancock's corps did sustain it, and has covered itself with immortal honors by its constancy and courage. The total wreck of Cushing's battery—the list of its killed and wounded—the losses of officers, men and horses Cowen[sic] sustained—and the marvellous outspread upon the board of death of dead soldiers and dead animals—of dead soldiers in blue, and dead soldiers in gray—more marvellous to me than anything I have ever seen in war—are a ghastly and shocking testimony to the terrible fight of the Second corps that none will gainsay. That corps will ever have the distinction of breaking the pride and power of the rebel invasion.

For such details as I have the heart for. The battle commenced at daylight, on the side of the horse-shoe position, exactly opposite to that which Ewell had sworn to crash through. Musketry preceded the rising of the sun. A thick wood veiled this fight, but out of its leafy darkness arose the smoke and the surging and swelling of the fire, from intermittent to continuous, and crushing, told of the wise tactics of the rebels of attacking in force and changing their troops. Seemingly the attack of the day was to be made through that wood. The demonstration was protracted—it was absolutely preparative; there was no artillery fire accompanying the musketry, and shrewd officers in our western front mentioned, with the gravity due to the fact, that the rebels had felled trees at intervals upon the edge of the wood they occupied in face of our position. These were breastworks for the protection of artillery men.

Suddenly, and about 10 in the forenoon, the firing on the east side, and everywhere about our lines, ceased. A silence as of deep sleep fell upon the field of battle. Our army cooked, ate and slumbered. The rebel army moved 130 guns to the west, and massed there Longstreet's corps and Hill's corps, to hurl them upon the really weakest point of our entire position.

Eleven o'clock—twelve o'clock—one o'clock. In the shadow cast by the tiny farm house 10 by 20, which Gen. Meade had made his Headquarters, lay wearied staff officers and tired reporters. There was not wanting to the peacefulness of the scene the singing of a bird, which had a nest in a peach tree within the tiny yard of the whitewashed cottage. In the midst of its warbling, a shell screamed over the house, instantly followed by another, and another, and in a moment the air was full of the most complete artillery prelude to an infantry battle that was ever exhibited. Every size and form of shell known to British and to American gunnery shrieked, whirled, moaned, whistled and wrathfully fluttered over our ground. As many as six in a second, constantly two in a second, bursting and screaming over and around the headquarters, made a very hell of fire that amazed the oldest officers. They burst in the yard—burst next to the fence on both sides, garnished as usual with the hitched horses of aids[sic] and orderlies. The fastened animals reared and plunged with terror. Then one fell, then another—sixteen lay dead and mangled before the fire ceased., still fastened by their halters, which gave the expression of being wickedly tied up to die painfully. These brute victims of a cruel war touched all hearts. Through the midst of the storm of screaming and exploding shells, an ambulance, driven by its frenzied conductor at full speed, presented to all of us the marvelous spectacle of a horse going rapidly on three legs. A hinder one had been shot off at the hock. A shell tore up the little step of the Headquarters Cottage, and ripped bags of oats as with a knife. Another soon carried off one of the two pillars. Soon a spherical case burst opposite the open door—another ripped through the low garret. The remaining pillar went almost immediately to the howl of a fixed shot that Wentworth must have made. During this fire the houses at twenty and thirty feet distant, were receiving their death, and soldiers in Federal blue were torn to pieces in the road and died with the peculiar yells that blend the extorted cry of pain with horror and despair. Not an orderly—not an ambulance—not a straggler[sic] was to be seen upon the plain swept by this tempest of orchestral death thirty minutes after it commenced. Were not one hundred and twenty pieces of artillery, trying to out from the field every battery we had in position to resist their purposed infantry attack, and to sweep away the light defences behind which our infantry were waiting? Forty minutes—fifty minutes—counted on watches that ran! Oh so languidly. Shells through the two lower rooms. A shell into the chimney that daringly did not explode. Shells in the yard. The air thicker and fuller and more deafening with the howling and whirring of those infernal missiles. The chief of staff struck—Seth Williams—loved and respected through the army, separated from instant death by two inches of space vertically measured. An Aide bored with a fragment of iron through the bone of the arm. Another, out with an exploded piece. And the time measured on the sluggish watches was one hour and forty minutes.

Then there was a lull, and we knew that the rebel infantry was charging. And splendidly they did this work—the highest and severest test of the stuff that soldiers are made of. Hill's division, in line of battle, came first on the double-quick. Their muskets at the "right-shoulder-shift." Longstreet's came as the support, at the usual distance, with war cries and a savage insolence as yet untutored by defeat. They rushed in perfect order across the open field up to the very muzzles of the guns, which tore lanes through them as they came. But they met men who were their equals in spirit, and their superiors in tenacity. There never was better fighting since Thermopyalae than was done yesterday by our infantry and artillery. The rebels were over our defenses. They had cleaned cannoniers and horses from one of the guns, and were whirling it around to use upon us. The bayonet drove them back. But so hard pressed was this brave infantry that at one time, from the exhaustion of their ammunition, every battery upon the principal crest of attack was silent, except Crowen's.[sic] His service of grape and cannister was awful. It enabled our line, outnumbered two to one, first to beat back Longstreet, and then to charge upon him, and take a great number of his men and himself prisoners. Strange sight! So terrible was our musketry and artillery fire, that when Armistead's brigade was checked in its charge, and stood reeling, all of its men dropped their muskets and crawled on their hands and knees underneath the stream of shot till close to our troops, where they made signs of surrendering. They passed through our ranks scarcely noticed, and slowly went down the slope to the road in the rear.

Before they got there the grand charge of Ewell, solemnly sworn to and carefully prepared, had failed.

The rebels had retreated to their lines, and opened anew the storm of shell and shot from their 120 guns. Those who remained at the riddled headquarters will never [forget] the crouching, and dodging, and running, of the Butternut-colored captives when they got under this, their friends, fire. It was appalling to as good soldiers even as they were.

What remains to say of the fight? It staggled[sic] warily on the middle of the horse shoe on the west, grew big and angry on the heel at the southwest, lasted there till 8 o'clock in the evening, when the fighting Sixth corps went joyously by as a reinforcement through the wood, bright with coffee pots on the fire.

I leave details to my excellent friend and associate Mr. Henry. My pen is heavy. Oh, you dead, who at Gettysburgh have baptized with your blood the second birth of Freedom in America, how you are to be envied! I rise from a grave whose wet clay I have passionately kissed, and I look up and see Christ spanning this battlefield with his feet and reaching fraternal and lovingly up to heaven. His right hand opens the gate of Paradise—with his left he beckons to these mutilated, bloody, swollen forms to ascend.

Incidents of the Battle

Capt. CUSHING, Company A, Fourth regular artillery, was killed, and his battery suffered severely. The gallantry of this officer is beyond praise. Severely wounded early in the afternoon, he refused to leave his post beside his guns, but continued to pour grape and canister into the advancing columns of the rebels until they had reached the very muzzles of his pieces, and sure of their capture, were attempting to turn them upon our forces, when they were driven off by our infantry. At this moment Capt. Cushing received his death wound, and fell lifeless to the earth. Heaps of corpses and wounded in front of his battery this morning, told a terrible tale of the effectiveness of its fire.

None of the company were taken prisoners by the rebels. After the battle but one gun of this battery remained uninjured— the rest having been dismounted or destroyed by the terrible fire of the enemy was concentrated upon the batteries on this part of the field. In front of this position fell dead the rebel Gen. DICK GARNETT, who was courageously leading his men in this charge upon our batteries upon Crow Hill. The rebel Gen. ARMISTEAD[sic] was also wounded here while advancing at the head of his brigade.

About fifty yards in front of our batteries was a stone wall, running from our centre in a southwesterly direction, behind which laid several of our regiments, picking off the enemy as they advanced up the slope of the hill. Notwithstanding the terrible fire poured into their ranks from our guns, so impetuous was the charge of the rebels that they drove our men from their position, and were advancing upon our batteries, several of which they captured, but the capture was only temporary. Gen. Gibbon's division, composed of Gens. Webb's, Russell's and Hall's brigades, at the point of the bayonet, drove them back over the stone wall into the plain below.

Gen. Gibbon's division captured fourteen stand of colors

and a large number of prisoners. Twenty-eight stands of colors in all were captured by the Second crops.

Gen. ARMISTEAD, when taken prisoner, asked immediately for Gen. MEADE, who was his classmate at West Point.

Col. WARD, of the Fifteenth Massachusetts, was killed.

Corp. HAYDEN, of the First Minnesota, was captured—escaped, seized a musket and seized a rare opportunity, and actually made ten rebels surrender. While marching them to Gen. GIBBON'S quarters, a rebel behind a tree on the way drew a bead on him with his rifle. HAYDEN saw him in time to bring his piece to a level, and cry out, "Surrender." The fellow actually threw down his gun and joined the cavalcade, and HAYDEN came in with eleven captives.

Order of Battle, Pickett's Charge, July 3, 1863

This is an Order of Battle of troops intended to be used by readers to identify the units of individuals in this book. Time and space limitations prohibit a full explanation of the actions of each unit listed here. Infantry units are included if they actually participated in the Charge or fired against it. In addition, I have included those Confederate units, Wright's and Posey's brigades, that were planned as support troops, even though they did not engage. Artillery units on either side are included if they fired a minimum of 1 round either in support of the Charge or against it. If a Battalion is listed but not all the batteries fired, only those that actually participated are included.

I have placed an additional number (such as F1 or C1) at the end of the artillery listings indicating their position during the cannonade between 1 and 3 p.m. as marked on the map included in the section on the Cannonade. Those batteries with no * or number following them were engaged during or in support of the Charge, but not during the Cannonade. Those batteries marked with an * fired during the Cannonade, but not during or in support of the Charge.

Several of the batteries listed were only partially engaged. For example, a battery with 2 Howitzers and 2 Ordnance rifles might have engaged only the Ordnance rifles. I have not included this level of specificity because this book is about eyewitness accounts, not artillery, and so that must be left for another author.

All positions and times are as accurate as possible, but are nevertheless approximate and subject to revision. The commander listed is, as often as possible, the one in command at the beginning of the Charge.

Army of Northern Virginia
General Robert E. Lee

First Corps, Lieutenant General James Longstreet
Pickett's Division, Major General George E. Pickett

Armistead's Brigade, Brigadier Gen. Lewis Armistead
9th Virginia, Major H. C. Owens
14th Virginia, Colonel James G. Hodges
38th Virginia, Colonel E. C. Edmonds
53rd Virginia, Colonel W. R. Aylett
57th Virginia, Colonel John B. Magruder

Garnett's Brigade, Brigadier Gen. Richard B. Garnett

8th Virginia, Colonel Eppa Hunton
18th Virginia, Lieutenant Colonel H. A. Carrington
19th Virginia, Colonel Henry Gantt
28th Virginia, Colonel R. C. Allen
56th Virginia, Colonel W. D. Stuart

Kemper's Brigade, Brigadier General James Kemper
1st Virginia, Colonel Lewis B. Williams
3rd Virginia, Colonel Joseph Mayo, Jr.
7th Virginia, Colonel W. T. Patton
11th Virginia, Major Kirkwood Otey
24th Virginia, Colonel William R. Terry

Artillery, Major James Dearing
Fauquier Artillery, Captain R. M. Stribling (C12)
Hampden Artillery, Captain W. H. Caskie (C14)
Richmond Fayette Artillery, Captain M. C. Macon (C13)
Virginia Battery, Captain Joseph O. Blount (C15)

McLaw's Division, Colonel H. C. Cabell
1st N. C. Battery A, Captain B. C. Manly (C10)
Pulaski Artillery, Lieutenant W. J. Furlong
Troup Artillery, Captain H. H. Carleton (C17)

Hood's Division, Major M. W. Henry
Branch Artillery, Captain A. C. Latham (C2)
German Artillery, Captain W. K. Bachman
Palmetto Light Artillery, Captain H. R. Garden (C1)
Rowan Artillery, Captain James Reilly

Artillery Reserve, Colonel J. B. Walton
Alexander's Battalion, Colonel E. P. Alexander
Ashland Artillery, Captain P. Woolfolk, Jr. (C18)
Bedford Artillery, Captain T. C. Jordan (C6)
Brooks Artillery, Lieutenant S. C. Gilbert
Madison Light Artillery, Captain George Moody (C3)
Virginia Battery, Captain W. W. Parker (C5)
Virginia Battery, Captain O. B. Taylor (C7)

Washington Artillery, Major B. F. Eshelman
First Company, Captain C. W. Squires
Second Company, Captain J. B. Richardson (C11)
Third Company, Captain M. B. Miller (C8)
Fourth Company, Captain Joe Norcom (C9)

Second Corps, Lieutenant General Richard Ewell

Rodes' Division Artillery, Lieut. Colonel Thomas H. Carter
   Artillery Reserve, Colonel J. Thompson Brown
   Jeff Davis Artillery, Captain W. J. Reese (C36)
   King William Artillery, Captain W. P. Carter(C25)
   Morris Artillery, Captain R. C. M. Page
   Orange Artillery, Captain C. W. Fry

   First Virginia Battalion, Captain Willis Dance
   2nd Richmond Howitzers, Captain David Watson (C28)
   3d Richmond Howitzers, Captain B. H. Smith, Jr. (C30)
   Powhatan Artillery, Lieutenant John Cunningham (C24)
   Rockbridge Artillery, Captain A. Graham (C29)

   Nelson's Battalion, Lt. Colonel William Nelson
   Amherst Artillery, Captain T. J. Kirkpatrick (C45)
   Fluvanna Artillery, Captain J. L. Massie (C44)
   Georgia Battery, Captain John Milledge (46)

Third Corps, Lieutenant General Ambrose Powell Hill
   Anderson's Division, Major General Richard Anderson
   Wilcox's Brigade, Brigadier General Cadmus Wilcox
   8th Alabama, Lieutenant Colonel Hilary Herbert
   9th Alabama, Captain J. H. King
   10th Alabama, Lieutenant Colonel James Shelley
   11th Alabama, Lieutenant Colonel George Tayloe
   14th Alabama, Lieutenant Colonel James Broome

   Perry's Brigade, Colonel David Lang
   2nd Florida, Captain Seton Fleming
   5th Florida, Captain Hollyman
   8th Florida, Lieutenant Colonel Baya

   Wright's Brigade, Brigadier General Ambrose Wright
   3d Georgia, Colonel E. J. Walker
   22d Georgia, Captain B. C. McCurry
   48th Georgia, Captain M. R. Hall
   2nd Georgia Battalion, Captain Charles J. Moffett

   Posey's Brigade, Brigadier General Carnot Posey
   12th Mississippi, Colonel W. H. Taylor
   16th Mississippi, Colonel Samuel Baker
   19th Mississippi, Colonel Nathaniel Harris
   48th Mississippi, Colonel Joseph Jayne

Heth's Division, Brigadier Gen. Johnston J. Pettigrew
   Pettigrew's Brigade, Colonel J. K. Marshall

11th North Carolina, Lieutenant Colonel Martin
26th North Carolina, Captain H. C. Albright
47th North Carolina, Colonel G. H. Faribault
52nd North Carolina, Colonel J. K. Marshall

Archer's Brigade, Colonel Birkett D. Fry
13th Alabama, Colonel Birkett D. Fry
5th Alabama Battalion, Major A. S. Van de Graaff
1st Tennessee, Major Felix Buchanan
7th Tennessee, Lieutenant Colonel S. G. Shepard
14th Tennessee, Captain B. L. Phillips

Davis's Brigade, Brigadier General Joseph Davis
2nd Mississippi, Colonel J. M. Stone
11th Mississippi, Colonel F. M. Green
42nd Mississippi, Colonel H. R. Miller
55th North Carolina, Captain Gilreath

Brockenbrough's Brigade, Colonel Robert Mayo
47th Virginia, Colonel Robert Mayo
40th Virginia, Captain R. B. Davis
55th Virginia, Colonel W. S. Christian
22nd Virginia Battalion, Major John Bowles

Artillery, Lieutenant Colonel John Garnett
Donaldson Artillery, Captain V. Maurin
Huger Artillery, Captain Joseph Moore
Lewis Artillery, Captain John Lewis

Pender's Division, Major General Isaac R. Trimble
Lane's Brigade, Brigadier General James Lane
7th North Carolina, Major J. McLeod Turner
18th North Carolina, Colonel John Barry
33rd North Carolina, Colonel C. M. Avery
28th North Carolina, Lieutenant Colonel John Ashford
37th North Carolina, Colonel W. W. Barbour

Scale's Brigade, Colonel W. L. J. Lowrance
13th North Carolina, Lieutenant Colonel H. A. Rogers
16th North Carolina, Captain A. S. Cloud
22nd North Carolina, Colonel James Conner
34th North Carolina, Lieutenant Colonel G. T. Gordon
38th North Carolina, Lieutenant Colonel John Ashford

Artillery, Major William T. Poague
Albemarle Artillery, Captain James W. Wyatt (C20)

Charlotte Artillery, Captain Joseph Graham
Madison Light Artillery, Captain George Ward (C19)
Virginia Battery, Captain J. V. Brooke

Artillery Reserve, Colonel R. Lindsay Walker
McIntosh's Battalion, Major D. G. McIntosh
Danville Artillery, Captain R. S. Rice (C31)
Hardaway Artillery, Captain W. B. Hurt (C38)
2nd Rockbridge Artillery, Lt. Samuel Wallace (C32)
Virginia Battery, Captain M. Johnson

Pegram's Battalion, Major W. J. Pegram
Richmond Artillery, Crenshaw Battery, Capt. Johnson
Fredericksburg Artillery, Captain E. A. Marye (C23)
Letcher Artillery, Captain T. A. Brander (C27)
Pee Dee Artillery, Lieut. William Zimmerman (C25)
Richmond Artillery, Purcell Artillery, Captain Joseph
McGraw

Cavalry
Stuart's Division
Major General J. E. B. Stuart

Hampton's Brigade, Brigadier General Wade Hampton
1st North Carolina, Colonel Lawrence Baker
1st South Carolina, Colonel John Black
2nd South Carolina, Colonel Matthew C. Butler
Phillip's Legion, Lieutenant Colonel W. W. Rich
Cobb's Legion, Colonel Elijah Young
Jeff Davis Legion, Lieutenant Colonel J. F. Waring

Robertson's and Jones' Brigades
Brigadier General Beverly Robertson
4th North Carolina, Colonel D. D. Ferebee
5th North Carolina
6th Virginia, Major C.E. Flourney
7th Virginia, Lieutenant Colonel Thomas Marshall
11th Virginia, Colonel L. L. Lomax

Fitzhugh Lee's Brigade, Colonel Thomas Munford
1st Virginia, Colonel James H. Drake
2nd Virginia, Colonel T. T. Munford
3rd Virginia, Colonel Thomas H. Owen
4th Virginia, Colonel Williams C. Wickham
5th Virginia, Colonel T. L. Rosser

Jenkins' Brigade, Brigadier General A. G. Jenkins
14th Virginia, Major Benjamin Eakle
16th Virginia, Colonel Milton Ferguson
17th Virginia
34th Virginia Battalion, Lieutenant Colonel V.A. Witcher
36th Virginia Battalion.
Jackson's Battery, Captain Thomas E. Jackson

W. H. F. Lee's Brigade, Colonel J. R. Chambliss
2nd North Carolina
9th Virginia, Colonel Richard L. T. Beale
10th Virginia, Colonel J. Lucius Davis
13th Virginia, Lieutenant Colonel Phillips

Stuart Horse Artillery, Major R. F. Beckham
Breathed's Battery, Captain James Breathed
Chew's Battery, Captain R. F. Chew
Griffin's Battery, Captain W. H. Griffin
McGregor's Battery, Captain W. M. McGregor
Moorman's Battery, Captain M. N. Moorman
Hart's Battery, Captain J. F. Hart

Sources:

Alexander, E. P. *Fighting For The Confederacy.* Chapel Hill: University of North Carolina Press, 1989.

Coddington, Edwin. *The Gettysburg Campaign.* New York: Charles Scribner's Sons, 1968.

Martin, David G. *Confederate Monuments At Gettysburg.* Hightstown, N.J.: Longstreet House, 1986.

OR, 1, 27, 2, 282-291.

Army of the Potomac
Major General George Gordon Meade

First Army Corps, Major General John Newton
Third Division, Major General Abner Doubleday
Third Brigade, Brigadier General George Stannard
13th Vermont, Colonel Francis Randall
14th Vermont, Colonel William Nichols
16th Vermont, Colonel Wheelock Veazey

Artillery Brigade, Colonel Charles Wainwright
1st Pennsylvania Light, Battery B, Captain James Cooper

4th U. S., Battery B, Lieutenant James Stewart (F28)*
1st New York, Battery L, Lieutenant George Breck (F31)*
5th Maine Light, Lieutenant Edward Whittier (F32)*

Second Army Corps
Major General Winfield Scott Hancock
Second Division, Brigadier General John Gibbon
First Brigade, Brigadier General William Harrow
19th Maine, Colonel Francis Heath
15th Massachusetts, Colonel George Ward
1st Minnesota, Captain Nathan Messick
82nd New York (2d Militia), Lt. Colonel James Huston

Second Brigade, Brigadier General Alexander Webb
69th Pennsylvania, Colonel Dennis O'Keefe
71st Pennsylvania, Colonel Richard Penn Smith
72nd Pennsylvania, Colonel De Witt Baxter
106th Pennsylvania, Lieutenant Colonel William Curry
(2 Companies)

Third Brigade, Colonel Norman Hall
19th Massachusetts, Colonel Arthur Devereux
20th Massachusetts, Captain Henry Abbott
7th Michigan, Major Sylvanus Curtis
42nd New York, Colonel James Mallon
59th New York (Four Companies), Capt. William
McFadden

Unattached: 1st Company, Massachusetts Sharpshooters, Captain William Plumer

Third Division, Brigadier General Alexander Hays
First Brigade, Colonel Samuel Carroll
8th Ohio, Colonel Franklin Sawyer

Second Brigade, Colonel Thomas Smyth
14th Connecticut, Major Theodore Ellis
1st Delaware, Captain Thomas Hizar
12th New Jersey, Major John Hill
108th New York, Lieutenant Colonel Francis Pierce

Third Brigade, Colonel Eliakim Sherrill
39th New York, Major Hugo Hildebrandt (Four Cos.)
111th New York, Colonel Clinton MacDougall
125th New York, Lieutenant Colonel Levin Crandell
126th New York, Colonel Eliakim Sherrill

Artillery Brigade, Captain John Hazard
1st New York Light Battery B, Captain James Rorty (F14)
1st Rhode Island Light, Battery A, Capt. William Arnold
(F17)
1st Rhode Island Light, Battery B, Lieutenant Fred
Brown, Lieutenant William Perrin (F15)
1st United States, Battery I, Lieut. George A. Woodruff,
Lieutenant Tully Mcrea (F20)
4th United States, Battery A, Lieutenant Alonzo Cushing,
Sergeant Frederick Fuger (F16)

Fifth Army Corps
Artillery Brigade, Captain Augustus P. Martin
1st Ohio Light, Battery I, Captain Frank Gibbs (F4)
5th U. S., Battery D, Lieut. Benjamin Rittenhouse (F3)
3rd Mass. Light, Battery C, Lt. Aaron Wolcott (F2)*
1st New York, Battery C, Captain Almont Barnes (F1)*

Sixth Army Corps
Artillery Brigade, Colonel Charles Tompkins
Massachusetts Light, 1st Battery A, Capt. William
McCartney
New York Light, 1st Battery, Captain Andrew Cowan
2nd U. S., Battery G, Lieutenant John Butler
5th U. S., Battery F, Lieutenant Leonard Martin

Eleventh Army Corps
Artillery Brigade, Major Thomas Osborn
13th New York Light, Lieutenant William Wheeler
1st Ohio Light, Battery I, Captain Hubert Dilger (F27)
1st Ohio Light, Battery K, Captain Lewis Heckman
4th U. S., Battery G, Lieutenant Eugene Bancroft (F25)
1st New York, Battery I, Captain Michael Wiedrich (F29)*

Twelfth Army Corps
Artillery Brigade, Lieutenant Edward Muhlenberg
4th U. S., Battery F, Lieutenant Sylvanus Rugg (F33)*
5th U. S., Battery K, Lieutenant David Kinzie (F34)*
1st New York, Battery M, Lieut. Charles Winegar (F35)*
Pennsylvania Independent Light, Battery E, Lieutenant
Charles Atwell (F36)*

Artillery Reserve, Brigadier General Robert O. Tyler
1st Regular Brigade, Captain Dunbar Ransom
1st U. S., Battery H, Lieutenant Chandler P. Eakin (F24)

3rd U. S., Batteries F and K, Lieut. John Turnbull (F18)
4th U. S., Battery C, Lieutenant Evan Thomas (F12)
5th U. S., Battery C, Lieutenant Gulian Weir

1st Volunteer Brigade, Lt. Colonel Freeman McGilvery
Massachusetts Light, 5th Battery, with 10th New York
       Battery attached, Captain Charles Phillips (F10)
Massachusetts Light(Bigelow's), Lt. Richard Milton (F19)
New York Light, 15th Battery, Captain Patrick Hart (F9)
Pennsylvania Light, Batteries C and F, Captain James
                    Thompson (F11)

2nd Volunteer Brigade, Captain Elijah Taft
5th New York Independent Battery, Capt. Elijah Taft (F26)
2nd Conn. Independent Battery, Capt. John Sterling (F7)

3rd Volunteer Brigade, Captain James Huntington
1st New Hampshire, Battery A, Capt. Fred Edgell (F22)
1st Ohio Battery H, Lieutenant George Norton (F21)
1st Pennsylvania, Batteries F and G, Captain Robert
                    Ricketts (F30)
1st West Virginia, Battery C, Captain Wallace Hill (F23)

4th Volunteer Brigade, Captain Robert Fitzhugh
6th Maine, Battery F, Lieutenant Edwin Dow (F6)
1st New Jersey, Battery A, Lieutenant Augustus Parsons
1st New York, Battery G, Captain Nelson Ames (F5)
1st New York, Battery K, Captain Robert Fitzhugh
1st Maryland Light, Battery A, Captain James Rigby (F37)*

Cavalry Corps Artillery Reserve
3rd Pennsylvania Heavy Artillery, Capt. William Rank (F8)
9th Michigan Battery, Captain Jabez Daniels (F13)

Sources:

Busey, John W., and Martin, David G. *Regimental Strengths and Losses at Gettysburg.* Hightstown, N.J.:   Longstreet House, 1986.

Coddington, Edwin. *The Gettysburg Campaign.*

Crumb, Herb Ed. *The Eleventh Corps Artillery at Gettysburg: The Papers of Major Thomas Osborn.* Hamilton, N.Y.: Edmonston Publishing, 1991.

Hunt, Henry J. *Three Days At Gettysburg.* Edited by William

R. Jones Golden, Colorado: Outbooks, 1981.

Longacre, Edward G. *The Man Behind The Guns: A Biography of Henry J. Hunt.* Cranburg, N.J.: A. S. Barnes & Co., 1977.

Naisawald, N. Van Loan. *Grape and Canister.* New York: Oxford University, 1960.

OR, 1, 27, 1, 155-167.

Raus, Edmund, Jr. *A Generation on the March—The Union Army at Gettysburg.* Lynchburg, Va.: H. E. Howard, 1987.

Map Information

The fold-out map accompanying this book seeks to portray, as accurately as possible, the positions of all Federal and Confederate units near the Angle at the crest of the charge. The reverse of the map seeks to portray the positions, as accurately as possible, of the individuals in the book and a few selected additional men. All positions are based on primary documents. The Federal units are placed at their location at the height of the charge; the Confederates are portrayed as coming up the slope just before the crest. Virtually all accounts agree that the Confederates were in a mass, not in perfect lines of battle, after they crossed Emmitsburg Road, and thus their lines are drawn with dotted lines to indicate flexibility. The Federal troops of Harrow's and Hall's brigades arrived at the copse of trees out of formation, so they too are represented by broken lines. All positions are as accurate as information allows them to be, and are subject to revision. Finally, since the timing of the assault is somewhat in question, all times on this map are approximate, and are calculated with the assumption that the charge began at 3:00 p. m.

Map I: Units.
Federal Artillery

1. 1st U. S. Battery I. Captain George Woodruff. Lieutenant Tully Mcrea. Four 12 pdr. Napoleons.

1A. Lieutenant John Egan's section, Two 12 pdr. Napoleons.

2. 9th Massachusetts Light. Lieutenant Richard Milton. Two 12 pdr. Napoleons.

3. 3rd U. S. Batteries F & K. Lieutenant John Turnbull. Two 12 pdr. Napoleons.

4. 5th U. S. Battery C. Lieutenant Gulian Weir. Six 12 pdr. Napoleons.

5. 1st Rhode Island Battery A. Captain William Arnold. Six 3" Ordnance rifles.

6. 4th U. S. Battery A. Lieutenant Alonzo Cushing. Two 3" Ordnance rifles.

7. 11th New York Independent. Lieutenant Havelock's section. Two 3" Ordnance rifles. Attached to 1st New York Battery K, Captain Robert Fitzhugh commanding.

7A. 1st New York Battery K. Captain Fitzhugh. Two 3" Ordnance rifles.

8. 1st New York Independent. Captain Andrew Cowan. Six 3" Ordnance rifles.

9. 1st New York Battery B. Lieutenant Robert Rogers. Two 10 pdr. Parrotts.

10. 1st New Jersey battery A. Lieutenant Augustus Parsons. Six 3" Ordnance rifles.

11. 1st New York Battery K. Captain Robert Fitzhugh. Two 3" Ordnance rifles.

12. 13th New York Independent. Lieutenant William Wheeler. Four 3" Ordnance rifles.

Map 2: Individuals.
Federals

1. Private Francis Galway, 8th Ohio.

2. Private T. S. Potter, 8th Ohio.

3. Lieutenant E. Bicknall, 1st Massachusetts Sharpshooters.

4. Lieutenant Tully McCrea, 1st U. S. Battery I.

5. Private Levi Baker, 9th Massachusetts Light Artillery.

6. Major Thomas Osborn, 11th Corps Artillery.

7. Captain F. Edgell, 1st New Hampshire Artillery.

8. Captain George Bowen, 12th New Jersey.

9. Chaplain Ezra Simons, 125 New York.

10. Brigadier Alexander Hays, 3rd Division, 2nd Crops.

11. Lieutenant Gulian Weir, 5th U. S. Battery C.

12. Brigadier General John Gibbon, 2nd. Division, 2nd Corps.

13. Lieutenant Henry Russell, 72nd Pennsylvania.

14. Assistant Surgeon Francis Wafer, 108th New York.

15. Sergeant W. Stockton, 71st Pennsylvania.

16. Colonel J. Mallon, 42nd New York.

17. Captain John Hazard, 2nd Corps Artillery.

18. Lieutenant Frank Haskell, Aide to Gibbon.

19. Captain Robert McBride, 71st Pennsylvania.

20. Brigadier Alexander Webb, 2nd Brigade, 2nd Division, 2 Corps.

21. Private Marshall Sherman, 1st Minnesota.

22. Lieutenant Alonzo Cushing, 4th U. S. Artillery, Battery K.

23. Lieutenant Colonel W. Van Rensselaer, 80th New York.

24. Private Daniel Bond, 1st Minnesota.

26. Brigadier Henry Hunt, Artillery Commander, Army of the Potomac.

27. Corporal R. Whittock, 69th Pennsylvania.

28. Private Alexander Mc Dermott, 69th Pennsylvania.

29. Private W. Good, 72nd Pennsylvania.

30. Sergeant John Plummer.

31. Colonel Norman Hall, 7th Michigan. 3rd Brigade, 2nd Division, 2nd Corps.
32. Colonel Arthur Devereux, 19th Massachusetts.
33. Colonel Theodore Gates, 80th New York(20th NYSM).
34. Captain Henry Abbott, 20th Massachusetts.
35. Lieutenant Richard Rogers, 1st New York Battery B.
36. Lieutenant Augustus Parsons, 1st New York Battery A.
37. Lieutenant William Wheeler, 13th New York Artillery.
38. Major General Winfield Scott Hancock, 2nd Corps.
39. Brigadier George Stannard, 3rd Brigade, 3rd Division, 1st Corps.
40. Colonel Wheelock Veazey, 16th Vermont.
41. Private Ralph Sturtevant, 16th Vermont.
42. Private William Lochran, 1st Minnesota.
43. Sergeant Frederick Fuger, 4th U. S. Battery A.
44. Lieutenant Colonel Freeman McGilvery, Reserve Artillery.
45. Captain Patrick Hart, 15th New York Artillery.
46. Lieutenant E. Dow, 6th Maine Battery B.
47. Major Edmund Rice, 19th Massachusetts.
48. Corporal John Rhodes, 1st Rhode Island Battery.
49. Ziegler's Grove.
50. 13th & 16th Vermont, flanking position.
51. 13th & 16th Vermont, first position.
52. Lieutenant George Woodruff, 1st U. S. Battery I.

Confederates

1. Lieutenant R. McDowell, 11th Mississippi.
2. Lieutenant A. J. Baker, 11th Mississippi.
3. Private J. Howell, 11th Mississippi.
4. F. Howell, 11th Mississippi.
5. Lieutenant William Peel, 11th Mississippi.
6. Colonel Birkett D. Fry, Archer's Brigade.
7. Brigadier Isaac Trimble, Pender's Division.
8. Captain James Harris, 7th North Carolina.
9. Brigadier General James Lane, Lane's Brigade.
10. Captain A. S. Haynes, 11th North Carolina.
11. Lieutenant Colonel S. Shepard, 7th Tennessee.
12. 26th North Carolina.
13. Lieutenant Henry Moore, 38th North Carolina.
14. Captain J. Turney, 1st Tennessee.
15. 7th Tennessee, 13th Alabama, 5th Alabama Battalion cross wall.
16. Captain June Kimble, 14th Tennessee.

17. Captain Henry Owen, 18th Virginia.

18. Corporal A. Williams, 56th Virginia.

19. Brigadier General Lewis Armistead, Armistead's Brigade.

20. Colonel W. Stuart, 28th Virginia.

21. Lieutenant J. Lee, 28th Virginia.

22. Corporal L. Williams, 56th Virginia.

23. Lieutenant G. W. Finley, 56th Virginia.

24. Private R. Taylor, 53rd Virginia.

25. Lieutenant Colonel Rawley Martin, 53rd Virginia.

26. Captain Michael Spessard, 28th Virginia.

27. Brigadier General Richard Garnett, Garnett's Brigade.

28. Colonel J. B. Magruder, 57th Virginia.

29. Lieutenant J. Lewis, 11th Virginia.

30. Lieutenant Wyatt Whitman, 53rd Virginia.

31. Sergeant D. B. Easley, 14th Virginia.

32. Corporal J. Carter, 53rd Virginia.

33. Private E. Williams, 14th Virginia.

34. Colonel J. Hodges, 14th Virginia.

35. Lieutenant W. Wood, 19th Virginia.

36. Private John Dooley, 1st Virginia.

37. Sergeant Randolph Shotwell, 8th Virginia.

38. Captain J. Smith, 11th Virginia.

39. Colonel W. Patton, 7th Virginia.

40. Lieutenant Colonel Carrington, 18th Virginia.

41. Private J. R. Polak, 1st Virginia.

42. Major M. Turner, 7th North Carolina.

43. Private E. Williams, 14th Virginia.

44. Major Englehard, Aide to Trimble.

45. Brigadier General James Kemper, Kemper's Brigade

46. Brigadier General Johnston Pettigrew

47. 1st New York Battery B, temporarily captured.

48. Captain T. Holland, 28th Virginia.

49. Colonel R. Mayo, 3rd Virginia.

50. Colonel W. S. Christian, 55th Virginia.

51. Major Louis Young, Aide to Pettigrew

52. Private J. R. McPherson, 28th Virginia.

53. Major Charles Peyton, 19th Virginia.

54. Brigadier General Cadmus Wilcox, Wilcox's Brigade.

55. Major General George Pickett, Pickett's Division.

56. 3rd, 11th & 24th Virginia cross wall.

57. Angle.

58. Copse of Trees.

59. 11th & 24th Virginia refuse line to stop Stannard's flank attack.

Artillery Engaged Between 1:00 and 3:00 P.M.
Map on page 136

Federal

1. 1st New York, Battery C. Capt. Almont Barnes. Four 3" Ordnance rifles.
2. 3rd Massachusetts Light, Battery C. Wolcott. Six 12 pdr. Napoleons.
3. 5th United States, Battery D. Lt. Benjamin Rittenhouse. Six 10 pdr. Parrotts.
4. 1st Ohio Battery L. Gibbs. Six 12 pdr. Napoleons.
5. 1st New York Battery G. Capt. Nelson Ames. Left of McGilvery's line. Four 12 pdr. Napoleons.
6. 6th Maine Light. Lt. Edwin Dow. Six 12 pdr. Napoleons.
7. 2nd Connecticut Light. Capt. John Sterling. Four James rifles, Two 12 pdr Howitzers.
8. 1st Pennsylvania Battery H. Capt. Wm. Rank. Two 3" rifles.
9. 15th New York. Capt. Patrick Hart. Four 12 pdr. Napoleons.
10. 5th Massachusetts (10th New York attached). Captain Charles Phillips. Six 3" rifles.
11. Pennsylvania Artillery, Batteries C and F. Thompson. Five 3" rifles.
12. 4th U. S. Battery C. Lt. Evan Thomas. Six 12 pdr. Napoleons.
13. 9th Michigan. Capt. Jabez Daniels. Six 3" rifles.
14. 1st New York Battery B. Capt. James Rorty. Four 10 pdr. Parrotts.
15. 1st Rhode Island Battery B. Perrin. Six 12 pdr. Napoleons.
16. 4th U. S. Battery A. Lt. Alonzo Cushing. Six 3" rifles.
17. 1st Rhode Island Battery A. Capt. William Arnold. Six 3" rifles.
18. 3rd U. S. Batteries F and K. Lt. John Turnbull. Two 12 pdr. Napoleons.
19. 9th Massachusetts Light. Lt. Richard Milton. Two 12 pdr. Napoleons.
20. 1st U. S. Battery I. Lt. George Woodruff. Six 12 pdr. Napoleons.
21. 1st Ohio Light Battery H. Lt. George Norton. Six 3"

rifles.

22.   1st New Hampshire Battery   Capt. Frederick Edgell. Six 3" rifles.

23.   1st West Virginia Battery C. Capt. Wallace Hill. Four 10 pdr. Parrotts.

24.   1st U. S. Battery H. Capt. Eakin. Six 12 pdr. Napoleons.

25.   4th U. S. Battery G. Lt. Eugene Bancroft. Six 12 pdr. Napoleons.

26.   5th New York Battery. Capt. Elijah Taft. Five 20 pdr Parrotts.

27.   1st Ohio Battery I. Capt. Hubert Dilger. Six 12 pdr Napoleons.

28.   4th U. S. Battery B. Lt. James Stewart. Two 10 pdr Napoleons.

29.   1st New York Battery I. Capt. Michael Weidrich.   Six 3" rifles.

30.   1st Pennsylvania Batteries F and G.   Capt. Bruce Ricketts. Six 3' rifles.

31.   1st New York Battery L. Breck. Five 3' rifles.

32.   5th Maine Light Battery E. Whittier. Six 12 pdr Napoleons.

33.   4th U. S. Battery F. Lt. Sylvanus Rugg. Six 12 pdr. Napoleons.

34.   5th U. S. Battery K. Lt. David Kinzie. Four 12 pdr Napoleons.

35.   1st New York Battery M. Winegar. Four 10 pdr Parrotts (only two engaged.)

36.   Pennsylvania Light Battery E. Atwell. Six 10 pdr. Parrotts.

37.   Maryland Light Battery A. Rigby. Six 3' rifles.

38.   Artillery trains and second position of combined artillery reserve.

39.   Reserve Artillery. Cooper, Weir, Wheeler, Fitzhugh, Parsons, Cowan, Williston, Butler, Martin, Harn, McCartney.

40.   Reserve Artillery. Heckman, Heaton.

Sources

Busey, John W., and Martin, David G. *Regimental Strengths and Losses at Gettysburg.* Hightstown, N.J.: Longstreet House, 1986.

Coddington, Edwin *The Gettysburg Campaign.*

Crumb, Herb Ed., *The Eleventh Corps Artillery at Gettysburg: The Papers of Major Thomas Osborn* Hamilton. New York: Edmonston Publishing, 1991.

Hunt, Henry J. *Three Days at Gettysburg.* Edited by William

R. Jones. Golden, Colorado: Outbooks, 1981.

Longacre, Edward G. *The Man Behind The Guns: A Biography of Henry J. Hunt.* Cranbury, N.J.: A. S. Barnes & Co, 1977.

OR, 1, 27, 1.

Raus, Edmund Jr. *A Generation on the March.* Lynchburg, Va.: H. E. Howard, 1987.

Confederate

1. Palmetto Light Artillery. Captain Hugh Garden. Two 12 pdr Napoleons and Two 10 pdr. Parrotts.

2. Branch Artillery (13th North Carolina Battalion). Captain A. C. Latham. One 6 pdr. gun, one 12 pdr. Howitzer, three 12 pdr. Napoleons.

3. Madison Artillery. Captain George Moody. Four 24 pdr. Howitzers.

4. Charleston Light Artillery. Captain William Bachman. Four 12 pdr Napoleons.

5. Richmond Battery. Captain W. W. Parker. Three 3" Ordnance rifles and one 10 pdr. Parrot.

6. Bedford Artillery. Captain T. C. Jordan. Four 3" Ordnance rifles.

7. Bath Virginia Artillery. Capt. O. B. Taylor. Four 12 pdr. Napoleons.

8. Washington Artillery, 3rd Company. Captain M. Miller. Three 12 pdr. Napoleons.

9. Washington Artillery, 4th Company. Captain Joseph Norcom. Two 12 pdr. Napoleons, one 12 pdr. Howitzer.

10. 1st North Carolina Artillery, Battery A. Captain B. C. Manly. Two 12 pdr. Napoleons., two 3" Ordnance rifles.

11. Washington Artillery, 2nd Company. Captain J. B. Richardson. Two 12 pdr. Napoleons, one 12 pdr. Howitzer.

12. Fauquier Artillery. Captain R. M. Stribling. Four 12 pdr. Napoleons., two 20 pdr. Parrotts.

13. Richmond "Fayette" Artillery. Macon. Two 12 pdr. Napoleons., two 10 pdr. Parrotts.

14. Richmond "Hampton" Artillery. Caskie. Two 12 pdr. Napoleons., one 3" Ordnance rifle, one 10 pdr. Parrott.

15. Lynchburg Artillery. Blount. Four 12 pdr. Napoleons.

16. Sumter Artillery, Battery B. Patterson. Four 12 pdr. Howitzers, two 12 pdr. Napoleons.

17. Troup County Light Artillery. Captain H. H. Carlton, Lieutenant C. W. Motes. Two 12 pdr. Howitzers, two 10 pdr. Parrotts.

18. Ashland Artillery. Lieutenant James Woolfolk. Two 12 pdr. Napoleons., two 20 pdr. Parrotts.

19. Madison Light Artillery. Captain George Ward. One 12 pdr. Howitzer, three 12 pdr. Napoleons.

20. Albemarle "Everett" Artillery. Captain James Wyatt. One 12 pdr. Howitzer, two 3" Ordnance rifles, one 10 pdr. Parrott.

21. Sumter Artillery, Battery C. Captain John Wingfield. Three 3" Ordnance rifles, two 10 pdr. Parrotts.

22. Sumter Artillery, Battery A. Captain Hugh Ross. One 12 pdr. Howitzer, one 12 pdr. Napoleons., one 3" Navy rifle, three 10 pdr. Parrotts.

23. Fredericksburg Artillery. Captain E. A. Marye. Four 3" Ordnance rifles.

24. Richmond Artillery, "Crenshaw's Battery." Captain Johnston. Two 12 pdr. Howitzers, two 12 pdr. Napoleons.

25. Pee Dee Artillery. Lieutenant William Zimmerman. Four 3" Ordnance rifles.

26. Richmond Artillery, "Purcell's Battery." Captain John McGraw. Four 12 pdr. Napoleons.

27. Richmond Artillery, "Letcher Battery." Captain T. A. Brander. Two 12 pdr. Napoleons., two 10 pdr. Parrotts.

28. Richmond Howitzers. Captain David Watson. Four 10 pdr. Parrotts.

29. 1st Rockbridge Artillery. Captain A. Graham. Four 20 pdr. Parrotts.

30. Richmond Howitzers, 3rd Battery. Captain B. H. Smith. Four 3" Ordnance rifles.

31. Danville Artillery. Captain R. S. Rice. Four 12 pdr. Napoleons.

32. 2nd Rockbridge Artillery. Lieutenant Samuel Wallace. Two 12 pdr. Napoleons., two 3" Ordnance rifles.

33. Virginia Battery, aka Richmond Artillery, "Johnson's Battery." Captain M. Johnson. Four 3" Ordnance rifles.

34. Powhatan Artillery. Lieutenant John Cunningham. Four 3" Ordnance rifles.

35. King William Artillery. Captain W. Carter. Two 12 pdr. Napoleons., two 10 pdr. Parrotts.

36. Jeff Davis Artillery. Captain W. J. Reese. Four 3" Ordnance rifles.

37. Richmond Artillery, "Orange Battery." Captain W. Fry. Two 3" Ordnance rifles, two 10 pdr. Parrotts.

38. Hardaway Artillery. Captain W. B. Hurt. Two Whitworth rifles.

39. Artillery Reserve and ammunition trains.

40. Richmond Artillery, "Courtney Battery." Captain W. A. Tanner. Four 3" Ordnance rifles.

41. Louisiana Guard Artillery. Captain C. A. Green. Two 3" Ordnance rifles. Two 10 pdr. Parrotts.

42. Charlottesville Artillery. Captain James Carrington. Four 12 pdr. Napoleons.

43. Staunton Artillery. Captain A. W. Garber. Four 12 pdr. Napoleons.

44. Fluvanna Artillery. Captain J. L. Massie. Three 12 pdr. Napoleons., one 3" Ordnance rifle.

45. Amherst Artillery. Captain T. J. Kirkpatrick. Three 12 pdr. Napoleons.

46. 1st Georgia Regular Artillery. Captain John Milledge. Two 3" Ordnance rifles, one 10 pdr. Parrott.

Sources

Alexander, Edwin Porter. *Fighting For The Confederacy.*
Coddington, Edwin. *The Gettysburg Campaign.*
Martin, David G. *Confederate Monuments At Gettysburg.*
OR, 1,27, 2.
Wise, Jennings C. *The Long Arm of Lee: The History of the Artillery of the Army of Northern Virginia.* 2 Vols. Lincoln: Universitys of Nebraska Press, 1991.

INDEX

"God! it was magnificent."

of 4750 only 1,000 make it back